CHEROKEE INTRUDER CASES
DOCKETS OF HEARINGS
1901–1909
VOLUME I

TRANSCRIBED BY

JEFF BOWEN

NATIVE STUDY
Gallipolis, Ohio
USA

Copyright © 2014
by Jeff Bowen

ALL RIGHTS RESERVED
No part of this publication may be reproduced
or used in any form or manner whatsoever
without previous written permission from the
copyright holder or publisher.

Originally published:
Baltimore, Maryland
2014

Reprinted by:

Native Study LLC
Gallipolis, OH
www.nativestudy.com

Library of Congress Control Number: 2020914991

ISBN: 978-1-64968-024-2

Made in the United States of America.

Other Books and Series by Jeff Bowen

1901-1907 Native American Census Seneca, Eastern Shawnee, Miami, Modoc, Ottawa, Peoria, Quapaw, and Wyandotte Indians (Under Seneca School, Indian Territory)

1932 Census of The Standing Rock Sioux Reservation with Births And Deaths 1924-1932

Census of The Blackfeet, Montana, 1897- 1901 Expanded Edition

Eastern Cherokee by Blood, 1906-1910, Volumes I thru XIII

Choctaw of Mississippi Indian Census 1929-1932 with Births and Deaths 1924-1931 Volume I

Choctaw of Mississippi Indian Census 1933, 1934 & 1937, Supplemental Rolls to 1934 & 1935 with Births and Deaths 1932-1938, and Marriages 1936-1938 Volume II

Eastern Cherokee Census Cherokee, North Carolina 1930-1939 Census 1930-1931 with Births And Deaths 1924-1931 Taken By Agent L. W. Page Volume I

Eastern Cherokee Census Cherokee, North Carolina 1930-1939 Census 1932-1933 with Births And Deaths 1930-1932 Taken By Agent R. L. Spalsbury Volume II

Eastern Cherokee Census Cherokee, North Carolina 1930-1939 Census 1934-1937 with Births and Deaths 1925-1938 and Marriages 1936 & 1938 Taken by Agents R. L. Spalsbury And Harold W. Foght Volume III

Seminole of Florida Indian Census, 1930-1940 with Birth and Death Records, 1930-1938

Texas Cherokees 1820-1839 A Document For Litigation 1921

Choctaw By Blood Enrollment Cards 1898-1914 Volumes I thru XVII

Starr Roll 1894 (Cherokee Payment Rolls) Districts: Canadian, Cooweescoowee, and Delaware Volume One

Starr Roll 1894 (Cherokee Payment Rolls) Districts: Flint, Going Snake, and Illinois Volume Two

Starr Roll 1894 (Cherokee Payment Rolls) Districts: Saline, Sequoyah, and Tahlequah; Including Orphan Roll Volume Three

Visit our website at **www.nativestudy.com** to learn more about these and other books and series by Jeff Bowen

This series is dedicated to my big brother,
Jerry Bowen
who taught me how to persevere.

INTRODUCTION

The records in this volume have been transcribed from the National Archival film rolls 7RA53 2-3 Cherokee Hearings on Intruder Cases, Dockets of Hearings on Intruder Cases 1901-1909. For definition purposes there are two parties involved with each case within these pages. One is the "Intruder" and the other is the "Allottee". The term "Intruder" refers to an illegal resident in the Cherokee Nation who is living on land that does not belong to him/her. The term "Allottee" refers to a legal resident of the Cherokee Nation who has been allotted, or given, a parcel of tribal land in the Cherokee Nation through the Dawes Act of 1898-1914.

"In November, 1906 the Senate Select Committee visited Vinita in the Cherokee Nation as part of its tour of Indian Territory to investigate the tribes' situation under the Five Tribes Bill. There it heard testimony from Chester Howe, who claimed to represent 'about one hundred families who were really Indians' but had been rejected by the tribe. One of Howe's clients was William Stevens, whose case became the basis for the Supreme Court's ruling that the 1896 act was constitutional. Howe argued that the Dawes Commission had spent 'less than eight minutes for each application' under that act and that his client therefore had not had a fair hearing. Stevens, who was present, had been born in Ohio and moved into the Cherokee Nation in 1869; he claimed to be one-quarter Cherokee. He had built improvements which were appraised by the three member commission established in 1893, but he refused to accept the $1,117 offered by the tribe because the receipt for the payment contained a waiver of his claim to citizenship. Like many of the people designated as intruders by the tribe, he had stayed on the land and used the 'protection papers' issued by the Indian agent to avoid being removed."

"James Davenport, the attorney who had represented the tribe in this affair, pointed out that Stevens had originally claimed to be a member of another tribe, that his case had twice been appealed unsuccessfully to Congress and the Supreme Court, and that he had refused to comply with an order of the Federal Court at Muskogee to vacate the land even though it had been upheld by the U. S. Court of Appeals for the Eighth Circuit. Howe countered that his client had been 'stripped of his property' and that Congress had refused to grant relief when it was considering the Cherokee Agreement of 1902 because it 'was very loath to open any rolls on account of the contention that there would flow into this country a river of applicants.' The Cherokees denied they had stripped Stevens of anything, but they had sold his property at public auction in 1902 in accordance with a provision in the Curtis act. Howe concluded his plea to the senators by saying that Stevens's 'children have been beggard[sic], his property confiscated' and that he had 'lost the work of a lifetime for the insignificant sum of $382.' Howe filed a written memorial with the committee, but Stevens never was enrolled."[1]

Interestingly, the Stevens' decision before the Supreme Court is referenced five times in Felix S. Cohen's *Handbook of Federal Indian Law, 1982 Edition*. The case actually makes references under the subject of I.R.S. taxation rulings and Indian

---

[1] *The Dawes Commission* by Kent Carter p 121-122, para 3 and 4.

land under trust. "Whether the exemption extends to individual trust property held by an Indian other than an original allottee or her/his heirs was considered in *Stevens v. Commissioner*. In interpreting *Squire v. Capoeman*, the I.R.S. had ruled that trust transfers by gift, devise or inheritance, intrafamily purchases, and purchases by 'needy Indians' out of restricted funds would maintain the income tax exemption. But in *Stevens* the Indian plaintiff had used unrestricted funds to purchase three parcels of trust land, which were placed in trust for him under Section 5 of the Indian Reorganization Act, and the I.R.S. sought to tax the income from these parcels. The court held that the income was exempt under the congressional policy the Supreme Court relied upon in *Capoeman*, particularly because Interior Department policy had consistently treated the different categories of allotted lands alike for tax purposes. The I.R.S. has acquiesed[sic] in *Stevens*, so it is settled that allotted lands acquired by purchase are within the tax exempt status held in *Capoeman*; and there is no restriction on the amount, origin, or intended uses of exempt lands owned by an individual Indian."[2]

The intruders' cases found in these pages are intriguing on a number of counts. There cases refer to hundreds of people because of the assortment of individuals referenced on behalf of both plaintiffs and defendants: allottees, intruders, as well as lawyers. In some cases researchers may have to make their own determination as to whether an intruder qualified as a Cherokee citizen. While an ancient family legend may assert that one's ancestors were *Indians*, the determinations in the Stevens' case leaves much up in the air. On the one hand, the intruder is considered to be a land owner, according to the Supreme Court's reference to how he funded his purchase as an "individual Indian". On the other hand, the intruder does not appear on a roll even though his land is protected under papers issued by the Indian Agent. His land ends up being auctioned off by the Cherokee Nation and in the decision within this series (Case #45, Volume I, page 12-13) his outcome is listed under the heading "Action, No return of service, no answer filed"; under "Remarks, contest pending, Case dismissed for want of prosecution, dismissed." His case as an Indian was important enough to reach the highest court in the land, but he is declared forever null and void--his claim as a Cherokee forgotten except perhaps by his descendants.

There are over 1,300 cases within these two volumes. The last 170 cases were mostly illegible due to poor microfilm quality. This transcriber was able to determine almost every single Allottee's and Intruder's name except in approximately six cases. To give as much information as possible, I have transcribed every entry to the best of my ability even though each Allottee's and Intruder's name of record is the most important part of these documents for genealogical purposes.

Jeff Bowen
Gallipolis, Ohio
NativeStudy.com

---

[2] Felix S. Cohen's *Handbook of Federal Indian Law* p 394-395 para 2

This document titled *Public Auction Indian Land Sale* is likely similar to the auction postings from the Cherokee Intruder cases during 1901 - 1909.

Blank 668—6-16-14-20M

PUBLIC AUCTION INDIAN LAND SALE
UNDER GOVERNMENT SUPERVISION.

The following allotted Indian land will be offered for sale at Public Auction at the office of

E. C. BACKENSTOCE, FIELD CLERK,

MADILL, OKLAHOMA,

AT TWO O'CLOCK, P. M.,

THURSDAY, NOVEMBER 12, '14.

Case No. 10959½—Ethel Tonubbee, nee Jack, Miss-Choc. Roll #759. 150 acres. SW4 of SE4 of SE4; SE4 of SW4 of SE4 of Section 13. NE4 of NE4 of NE4; S2 of NE4 of NE4; NW4 of NE4; E2 of SW4 of NE4; SE4 of NE4 of Section 24, Township 5 south, range 3 east in Marshall County. 100 acres tillable, 50 acres in cultivation; 50 acres hilly and gravelly; 60 acres timber land; sandy loam and light gravelly soil; 320 rods wire fencing; 6 miles from Simpson, Oklahoma. Appraisement $1950. Terms: CASH.

Title to be taken in its present condition.

Ten per cent. of the highest bid must be deposited in the hands of the Field Clerk on the day of the sale in the form of a bank draft payable to W. M. Baker, Cashier and Special Disbursing Agent, Union Agency, the remainder of the purchase price to be paid within ten days of call therefor.

Written bids, accompanied by ten per cent. of the amount thereof, if received by the Field Clerk prior to the hour of sale given above, will be opened and considered at the time of sale the same as if the bidder made such offer orally. Such written bids may be presented to the Field Clerk or mailed to him at the above address.

No bids for less than the appraised value will be considered.

The right is reserved to reject any and all bids.

Muskogee, Oklahoma,   DANA H. KELSEY,
Union Agency.   United States Indian Superintendent.

October 12, 1914.

Below is found the Guion Miller application #35320 (pages v-ix) concerning William Stephens/Stevens, which was rejected.

Immediately following the application is an affidavit (8 pages) that Stephens/Stevens used for his Intruder case (Case #45, Volume I, pages 12-13), as well as in his Guion Miller case. This affidavit gives the whole story behind his situation as well as naming the Indian Agent, Jno. B. Jones, who issued Mr. Stevens protection papers during that time and states in his findings that Stevens was in fact a Cherokee. The document also has his name as Stevens but has his signature spelled as "Stephens" as on his Miller application. There are also four letters of correspondence to the commission from his lawyer Philip H. Cass.

No. 35320

EASTERN CHEROKEES

APPLICATION OF

William Stephens,

For share of money appropriated for the Eastern Cherokee Indians by the Act of Congress approved June 30, 1906, in accordance with the decrees of the Court of Claims of May 18, 1905, and May 28, 1906.

COURT OF CLAIMS
EASTERN CHEROKEES
Rec. AUG 21 1907

Special Commissioner of the Court of Claims,
601 Ouray Building, Washington, D. C.

Sir:

I hereby make application for such share as may be due me of the fund appropriated by the Act of Congress, approved June 30, 1906, in accordance with the decrees of the Court of Claims of May 18, 1905, and May 28, 1906, in favor of the Eastern Cherokees. The evidence of identity is herewith subjoined.

Note: Answers to all questions should be short, but complete. If you can not answer, so state.

1. State full name—
    English name: William Stephens.
    Indian name: ShoeBoots.
2. Residence and post office: Coffeyville, Kansas.
3. County:
4. State:
5. How old are you? 79   Born December 9, 1827.
6. Where were you born? Ohio
7. Are you married? Yes
8. Name and age of wife or husband: Anna Eliza Stephens, age 64.
9. To what tribe of Indians does he or she belong? None, White
10. Name all your children who were living on May 28, 1906, giving their ages:

	Name.	Age.	Born.
(1)	Samantha J. Ayres	52	1855
(2)			
(3)			
(4)			
(5)			
(6)			

11. Give names of your father and mother, and your mother's name before marriage:

    Father—English name: Robert Stephens
            Indian name: White man
    Mother—English name: Sarah Jane Ellington Shoe Boots
            Indian name:
            Maiden name:
12. Where were they born?
    Father: Ohio.
    Mother: Georgia, Hightower river.

13. Where did they reside in 1851, if living at that time?
    Father: not living.
    Mother: Ohio
14. Date of death of your father and mother:
    Father: 1850 or 1851 on Illinois river bet. St. Louis + Alton
    Mother: 1874 near Chetopa, Kans., in Ind. Ter.
15. Were they ever enrolled for money, annuities, land or other benefits? If so, state when and where, and with what tribe of Indians: Do not think was ever enroled
16. Name all your brothers and sisters, giving ages, and residence if possible:

NAME	BORN	DIED
(1) Clarinda Jas		dead
(2) Jacob		dead
(3) Mary		dead
(4) John		dead
(5) Shelby Charles		dead dead
(6) Sarina Sarah Jane		dead dead.

17. State English and Indian names of your grandparents on both father's and mother's side, if possible:
    Mother's ~~FATHER'S~~ SIDE.
    Captain Shoe Boots
    Teaskiyarga full blood Cherokee chieftan
    Clarinda Ellington
    MOTHER'S SIDE.

18. Where were they born? Georgia and Fort Morgan, Ky, respy
19. Where did they reside in 1851, if living at that time? Dead. Died 1827.
20. Give names of all their children, and residence, if possible:
    (1) William Ellington   not living
    (2) John Ellington   not living
    (3)
    (4)
    (5)
    (6)

21. Have you ever been enrolled for money, annuities, land or other benefits? If so, state when and where, and with what tribe of Indians: _No._

22. To assist in identification, claimant should give the full English and Indian names, if possible, of their parents and grandparents back to 1835: _Given in previous answers so far as is known._

REMARKS.
(Under this head the applicant may give any additional facts which will assist in proving his claim.)

I solemnly swear that the foregoing statements made by me are true to the best of my knowledge and belief.

(Signature) _William Stephens_

Subscribed and sworn to before me this _15th_ day of _August_ 1907.

Philip H. Cass
Notary Public.

My commission expires _Feby. 17, 1908._

AFFIDAVIT.
(The following affidavit must be sworn to by two or more witnesses who are well acquainted with the applicant.)

Personally appeared before me _Pete Ayer_ and _W. R. Stubblefield_, who, being duly sworn, on oath depose and say that they are well acquainted with _William Stephens_ who makes the foregoing application and statements, and have known _him_ for _10_ years and _25_ years, respectively, and know _him_ to be the identical person _he_ represents _himself_ to be, and that the statements made by _him_ are true, to the best of their knowledge and belief, and they have no interest whatever in _his_ claim.

Witnesses to mark.

Signatures of Witnesses
Pete Ayer
W. R. Stubblefield

Subscribed and sworn to before me this _15_ day of _August_ 1907.

My commission expires _Feby. 17, 1908._

Philip H. Cass
Notary Public.

NOTE.—Affidavits should be made, whenever practicable, before a notary public, or clerk of the court, if sworn to before an Indian agent or disbursing agent of the Indian service, it need not be executed before a notary, etc.

TO THE HONORABLE SELECT COMMITTEE
of the
SENATE COMMITTEE ON INDIAN AFFAIRS.

   The undersigned Cherokee Indians by blood respectfully
represent that they are a duly selected committee represent-
ing certain claimants who deem themselves greatly wronged
by the legislation heretofore enacted with regard to the enrollment of the Cherokee people, and, feeling that they have
grievances which can only be remedied by congressional action,
respectfully ask permission to lay before your honorable committee, and, through it, the Committee on Indian Affairs of the
Senate, the following facts:
   That, through inadvertence, there has been excluded from
the rolls of the Cherokee Nation a number of persons who are
Indians in law and in fact, and who have been for from twenty-
five to forty years residents in good faith of the Cherokee Nation, with undisputed Indian blood and rights therein, the sole
objection to the enjoyment of which has been the fact that they
were not enrolled upon any of the tribal rolls, and that thereby
a great injustice has been done. This difficulty arose from the
following facts:
   The Cherokees acquired their title to their home unde the
treaty of New Echota of December 29, 1835, and this treaty,
while it contemplated the establishment of a Cherok e National
Goevernment, also contemplated the enjoyment of equal rights
by all Cherokees. After th emigration, repeated invitations
were sent to their brethren in the ea t to join them in the
west, and the term "brethren in th east" did not apply to
those who remained, and are now known as the Eastern Cherokees
alone, but to those who were scattered through the country for-
merly occupied by the nation. In 1841, the Cherokee council
extended an invitation by resolution. The Treaty of 1846,
section 8, made provision for transportation for those who would
consent to join their people in the west, and Chief Downing
issued a general invitation to all of the Cherokee people to
come and join with the Nation.
   It is true that immediately following the war in 1866
white men who were not Cherokees began to intrude upon the
Cherokee lands, and the legislation directed against these
people was just and reasonable, but it was so worded that in
the end a great advantage was taken over innocent persons who
were bona fide Indians and residents. A number of families
having Cherokee blood came to the Cherokee Nation from 1866 to
1896. They met no opposition in the occupation of unappropri-

(2)

ated, and unimproved lands.

The Cherokee National government, at various times, appointed commissions to pass upon citizenship, in some cases approving, in others denying, but these claimants whose ancestors were clearly Cherokees were permitted to go before the United States Indian Agent, in early days at Talequah, and subsequently at Muskogee, and there make proof of their Cherokee blood, and were given what is known as "protection papers" i. e., a finding by the Agent to the effect that they had furnished satsifactory proof of their being Cherokees in fact, and that they should not be disturbed until they had an opportunity in some way to secure a trial upon the questions of fact.

Relying upon these protection papers, these men opened up farms, erected houses, built schools and churches, and were the real and actual persons who made the name of Cherokee synonomous with that of the advanced and civilized Indians.

During this time, other persons with no rightful claim to Cherokee blood had also intruded upon the lands of the Nation, and, against such intrusion, the Cherokees rightfully protested. Their protests took form in the ratification of the agreement for the sale of the Cherokee outlet under the act of March 3, 1893, 27th Stats. 641, and therein a great injustice was done in this, that it gave to the Cherokee National authorities a right to say without trial whether or not a man was an intruder. It is true that there were at this time many properly termed "intruders," but a list was immediately prepared containing the names of 2,858 heads of families, and including the names of about 100 heads of families who were fully entitled under every law, treaty, and properly construed enactment.

These men saw that their homes were threatened, that their children were about to be disinherited, and, finding no immediate remedy possible, they sought protection in further legislation, which was secured by a provision contained in the act of March 21, 1895, 28 Stats. 903, directing a suspension of the proceedings until improvements made prior to August 11, 1886, could be appraised, it being believed that those who had migrated to that country prior to that time were entitled to some consideration at the hands of the government and the officials of the Cherokee Nation.

Thereupon, a board of appraisers was appointed, who reported upon a total number of 315 cases, and allowed awards

in 117 cases, of a total amount of $74,180.56. This was
subsequently modified by deducting certain freedmen claims,
leaving a total award in 89 cases of $68°645.36.

The appraisers had no authority to determine the merits
of any cases--merely the value of the improvements, afterde-
ducting the value of the land rental of the land. It was in
no sense an adjudication of the rights of the parties.

The authorities of the Cherokee Nation then tendered to
each of the parties the amount of the award, accompanying such
tender by a receipt, in which they waived their claims to
Cherokee citizenship, and all claims of every nature whatever
against the Cherokee Nation. In the majority of cases, the
parties refused to accept the award if obliged to sign such
a receipt, there having been no adjudication of their rights
and the tender was not kept good by deposit or otherwise. In
1902, the Cherokee Nation then proceeded at public auction,
held at different points, to sell the improvements appraised,
and the bidders being confined to Cherokee citizens, it being
known that the sale would be contested, trifling sums were
bid for valuable homes.

The matter stood in this condition when the Dawes Commission reported to Congress in 1894 and 1895 that the National
government was rotten; that citizenship rights therein had been
made the subject of barter and sale. That this National government was not competent to make a roll of its citizens, and thereupon Congress authorized the Dawes Commission, under act of June
10, 1896, to prepare a roll of the Five Tribes. Applications
to be filed within ninety days from June 10, 1896, and to be
passed upon within three months from that time, allowing an
appeal from such action to the district court of the proper district.

Under the rights so granted, about 30,000 applications were
made. Men with no shadow of right other than that they desired
to obtain something of value, made application, but among them
a small number of rightful claimants. The result was practically
a general denial. No other course was possible, considering the
time allowed, while the commission was presentt in the Territory, as, allowing full work by every member for the twenty-four
hours of the day, there were about eight minutes to be given
each application, and it is fair to say that no decision upon
the merits was rendered in any of the disputed cases represented by your petitioners.

Thereupon, appeals were prosecuted to the district court.
These appeals were less than 200 in number, and constituted
the more meritorious class.

These people had by this time become poor. They knew they were Indians by blood; they knew that they had been residents for many years in that country; that their children had been born to the allegiance of the nation; that they had exercised every privilege except that of voting, and that they had been included in what is known as the "intruder roll." In some cases they were striken from the roll after having been enrolled. They sought justice in the court. The judge referred the cases to two masters in chancery to take evidence and render findings of fact. This was done at the expense of the applicants who were appellants, and, in some cases the last cow was sold to pay expenses.

After the master's report had been rendered, finding them to be Indians and residents, the demurrer filed by the Nation was, by the district court, sustained, on the sole ground that they were not upon the approved roll. They knew that in the beginning. The judge of the western district and the Commission to the Five Civilized Tribes were aware of that fact, their sole object being to be placed upon that roll, and we find this condition in the district courts at that time.

Judge Hosea Townsend held in the southern district that the test of citizenship was blood. That the right came from birth, and, where a peal was prosecuted, admitted the applicant.

Judge Clayton, in the Central district held that Indian blood must be accompanied by bona xide residence, and, where both these requirements were shown, admitted the parties.

Judge William M. Springer held that, no matter whether the parties were Indians by blood and bona fide residents of the country or not, they must show that they had been enrolled by the National authorities prior to June 10, 1896. In other words, the Dawes Commission had no power to add to the rolls of the Cherokee people.

It is believed by your petitioners and applicants that the purpose in creating the Dawes Commission and granting them this power to make rolls was to give them the right to add to the roll where the arty was entitled. Among none other of the nations has it been held to the contrary.

Your petitioners then sought an appeal to the Supreme Court of the United States, and the same was granted, but the act was so worded that the Supreme Court took jurisdiction only for the purpose of passing upon the constitutionality of the act of June 10, 1896, and, while the facsf were proven and admitted, no remedy was granted.

(5)

WE ALLEGE THAT WE REPRESENT THE WHEAT WINNOWED FROM THE CHAFF; that the few hundred persons for whom we speak are BONA FIDE CHEROKEE CITIZENS whose wrongs have not been equalled in the western hemisphere, unless it is by the expulsion of the French from Arcadia. We desire before the closing of the affairs of the Five Civilized Tribes to be allowed a fair presentation, and in proof thereof, we refer to one record as being a complete one, and being a court record, substantiating the facts set forth.

This case ¥ the case of William Stevens (Stephens?). The history of this man is as follows:

Captain Shoe Boots, Teaskiyarga, a full-blood Cherokee Indian chief of a band of Cherokees, captured a white girl named Clarinda Ellington, in Kentucky, and carried her to Georgia, where she became his wife, and there was born to them three children as the issue of this marriage; two sons and a daughter, one of the sons being William Ellington Shoe Boots, and the other John Shoe Boots. William Ellington Shoe Boots' name appears upon the roll of 1851. (He afterwards adopted his mother's name of Ellington.) After the borth of these children, the fireinds of the wife traced her to her home and induced her to return to her relatives and th home of her childhood. She went with her children, and never returned. The daughter, Sarah, married Robert Stevens, a white man in the southern portion of the State of Ohio, and there was born to them William Stevens, a one-fourth blood Cherokee. William Stevens, in eesponse to Chief Downing's invitation, came to the Cherokee country in 1869, and removed there permanently in 1870. There he reared his family, clearedout farms, built houses, and erected improvements, which, in 1893, amounted to many thousands of dollars, a portion of which only had been made prior to August 11, 1866.

Soon after establishing residence, he made application for his mother and himself for re-admission and enrollment as citizens of the Nation. The Commission which h ard the case was convinced of the genuineness of his claim of Cherokee blood, and so re ported to the Chief, but rejected his application pon a technical ground. Upon this report Chief Mayes, in a message to the general council, stated his confidence in the honesty and genuineness of the claim, and advised the passage of an act recognizing the applic mt as a full citizen, but, for some unknown reason, this was never done.

On the 6th day of December, 1873, he went before the United States Indian Agent at the agency then located at Talequah, in conformity with the practice approved by the Secretary of the Interior, and offered proof showing that he was in fact and law a Cherokee Indian, and was entitled to improve the lands then occupied by himself, and, upon such proof, the following paper was issued to him:

United States Agent for the Cherokees, Talequah, C. N., Dec. 6, 1873.

This is to certify that Sarah Dictus and William Stevens have brought proof to show that they have filed their claims for citizenship before Cherokee council through proper channel, but that no action was reached in their case.

I have also information that there is good evidence to show that these parties are Cherokees by blood. They will, therefore, not be interfered with until further notice from this office.

Jno. B. Jones,
U. S. Agent for Cherokees.

That at no time, and in no place, have the facts submitted to John B. Jones, Indian Agent, as to the blood of William Stevens ever been controverted by the Cherokee Nation, but, after the passage of the act of March 3, 1893, William Stevens ascertained that his name had been put upon the list of intruders "socalled," or upon the intruders' roll, and that at that time he had improvements of the value of $10,000.PP upon lands which he owned under the title under which Cherokee lands were held and owned by Cherokee citizens.

That later the appraiser appointed by the Honorable Secretary of the Interior appraised said improvements, but refused to appraise any except such as were made prior to August 11, 1886, and did not include any purchased by him or made after that time; that said appraisement was to be found on 234 of the list (See House doc. 54 Congress first session, No. 116) and the value as then found for such improvements was $1,177.50, that the representatives of the Cherokee Nation tendered this amount to him accompanied by a receipt in which he waived his citizenship and claims thereto, and that he replied to the same to the effect that he had never had a trial, nor a hearing upon the merits of his case; that he was a Cherokee in law and fact, and refused to accept such an amount and sign such a receipt.

Thereupon, on October 25, 1902, one John Coody, a representative of the National authorities, collected together a small body of men in the town of Lenepah, and as an officier, of the Cherokee Nation, held a public auction or sale, and sold all the improvements of the said William Stevens for the sum of $382.00.

That, upon the passage of the act of June 10, 1896, William Stevens made proof of the facts above set forth before the Commission to the Five Civilized Tribes, and upon a denial by them of his claim as a citizen, appealed to the district court. That the case was referred by the judge of the western district to R. P. DeGraffenreid as special master for findings of fact. That said master found each and every allegation of the said William Stevens to be true, and so reported to the court. That after said finding, without any exceptions thereto being filed, the judge of said court sustained a demurrer upon the ground that, not being enrolled by the National authorities, William Stevens was entitled to no relief.

That, thereupon, under the authority granted, this case was appealed to the Supreme Court of the United States, and is reported in 174 U. S. p. 445.

That the court, in passing upon this matter, held that the only proposition before it was the constitutionality of the act of June 10, 1896, said court, however, holding on page 488:

"We repeat that in view of the paramount authority of Congress over the Indian tribes, and of the duties imposed on the Government by their condition of dependency, we cannot say that Congress could not empower the Dawes Commission to determine, in the manner provided, who were entitled to citizenship in each of the tribes and make out correct rolls of such citizens, an essential preliminary to effective action in promotion of the best interests of the tribes. It may be remarked that the legislation seems to recognize, especially the act of June 28, 1898, a distinction between admission to citizenship merely and the distribution of property to be subsequently made, as if there might be circumstances under which the right to share in the latter would not necessarily follow from the concession of the former."

That, under these decisions and this law, William Stevens has lost the work of a lifetime for the insignificant sum of $382.00, and that this tender has not been kept and made good; but on the contary, has been since expended in some other way.

That his children have been beggared, his property confiscated, in violation of the fundamental law of the land, but without right of recovery by him in view of his dependent condition, due to the wardship of the applicant in the past, and the guardianship of the Government both in the past and present.

(8)

RELIEF PRAYED.

Your committee represent that they can furnish records of at least eight or ten cases similar to the case above cited, for the inspection of the members of the Select Committee, if desired. They file herewith the record in the Supreme Court showing the facts set forth, the appraisement record, a plat of ground, and offer nothing which is not capable of direct and positive proof. They ask for no relief which will delay the final closing of the affairs of this Nation. They are only seeking to make effective and just the laws which have heretofore been passed, and ask nothing which a court of equity would not grant were it not for the special plenary authority which Congress possesses over the Indian people.

They do request that the Secretary of the Interior be authorized to add to the roll such persons as are found by the court records to be Indians by blood, residents of the Nation in good faith at the date of the passage of the act of June 10, 1896, and who, under any reasonable construction of the law, were actually entitled to enrollment at that time. This will reopen no case; delay no proceedure; but simply grant the right to those who are entitled. The records are completely made; the number is small. The justice of the application cannot be denied. The masters' reports in every case show the exact status of the people. Only those who are Indians are asking for relief.

Your committee respectfully represent that in closing the affairs of this Nation, their prayer may receive consideration.

They further represent that they each of them have been and are law abiding citizens. That they have never been accused of any crime, nor charged with any violation of law; that they have stood by and seen their homes taken from them, and their children beggared, relying upon the final justice of the great Government of the United States; that the time has now come for final action. They realize that because there were many who had no rights, the few who did have were deprived of that which was theirs, but this condition no longer exists. This can be speedily, easily, and inexpensively granted, and they especially pray for an opportunity to present in a simple and plain manner the facts herein set forth t the full committee of the Senate, and for such further relief as may be deemed proper by your committee.

Respectfully submitted,

State of Kansas,
County of Montgomery, ss.

Personally appeared before me, a Notary Public, within and for the county and State aforesaid, William Stephens, of lawful age, who being duly sworn according to law; deposes and says:

That the name of affiant's maternal grandmother was Clarinda Allen; that she was a resident of Kentucky, near Mount Sterling, that State; that about the year 1800 she was stolen and carried off by the Cherokee Indians; that she was white, and about seventeen years of age; that the band of Cherokees who stole her carried her off to Georgia with them, and their Chief Shoeboots took her as his wife; that they had three children, John, William, and Sarah Allen, the mother of affiant; that the relatives of his grandmother thought she was killed, and did not know of her whereabouts until long after her abduction; that a Kentucky trader who lived near Mount Sterling, Ky., learned, while trading with the Indians of the history of their chief's wife, and recognizing the name and circumstances of her abduction, reported the facts back to her relatives; that thereupon they invited the chief and his family to come and visit them; that this he refused to do, but sent his wife, and children on a visit to Kentucky, with the request that they should return in a certain number of moons; that fearing that some harm might come to them, if they returned, they remained in Kentucky and never went back to Georgia; that affiant's mother married a white man named Stephens and moved to Clark County, Ohio; that affiant does not know the date of such removal; that affiant was born in Clark County, Ohio, December 9, 1837; that affiant resided there until nineteen years old, and then went to Illinois; that affiant lived in Illinois until the Civil War, served in the army, and returned there after his discharge, and continued to reside in Illinois until the Dawning Commission invited all Cherokees to return to the Nation; that affiant went to the Cherokee Nation in 1896; that for the reasons stated, affiant was not enrolled on the roll of 1881; that affiant's mother was with affiant, and died in the Cherokee Nation, about the year 1871; that affiant's mother was never enrolled at any time with the Cherokees; that affiant went to the Agent Jones, when he came to the Cherokee Nation and secured a certificate directing the Cherokees not to molest affiant, as he was a Cherokee Indian; that affiant voted for Chief about 1898 or 1899, and was thereafter and otherwise recognized as a member of the Cherokee tribe until until the Dawes Commission rejected his claim to citizenship; that affiant bought farms and sold them the same as any other Cherokee; that affiant was never sold or owned by any person, white or Indian, as a slave; that affiant moved to the west in 1879, as stated, from Fulton County, Illinois; that the facts to which he testifies are within his personal knowledge for the most part, and where hearsay, are well-authenticated family tradition by persons having knowledge of them, and further affiant saith not.

William Stephens

Subscribed and sworn to before me, this 10th day of June, A. D., 1909.

Philip H. Cass
Notary Public.

My commission expires, Febr. 17, 1912.

No. 35320.

May 20, 1908.

William Stephens,
    Coffeeville, Kans.

Sir:-

    Kindly advise this office why you were not enrolled with the Eastern Cherokees in 1851.

    Why were your parents never enrolled with the Eastern Cherokees?

    Did you ever live with the Cherokees as a recognized member of their tribe?

    Were you held as a slave? If so, were you owned by White people or Indians?

    When did you move to the West?

                  Respectfully,

                              Special Commissioner.

HWK/AIL

PHILIP H. CASS
ATTORNEY AT LAW
COFFEYVILLE, KANS.

July 31, 1909.

Hon. Guion Miller,
    Washington, D. C.
Dear Sir:

I am requested by William Stephens, applicant No. 35320 for participation in Eastern Cherokee money, to inclose you to a copy of a report made to Select Committee of the Senate Committee on Indian Affairs several years ago, giving a history of himself and family, and to inform you that he is endeavoring to get the testimony of a full-blood over in the east portion of Oklahoma who had a personal acquaintance with his ancestors.

The applicant is a very old and feeble man, destitute on account of the wrongs complained of in the report, and disabled now by an injury received in an accident for which a railway company is responsible.

He has no means with which to get testimony in this case, or properly prosecute it, and my services in this connection are gratis. If there is any way by which he could have the benefit of the evidence referred to in this report in behalf of this application, you would be doing a poor helpless old Indian a good turn which he would appreciate at its full worth, as he is an honest man.

The copy may have some typographical errors, but is in the main a correct one, and sets out the facts in regard to his history, and which it would seem to one not fully informed, to entitle him to the money asked for.

    Very respectfully,

    Philip H. Cass

App. No.35320.

August 4, 1909.

Phillip H. Cass, Atty.,
    Coffeyville,
        Kansas.

Sir:

    I am in receipt of your letter of July 31, 1909, relative to the application of William Stephens, No.35320, for participation in the Eastern Cherokee fund.

    In reply you are advised that from the statements contained in the affidavit made by the said William Stephens it is plain that he and his mother were not members of the Eastern Cherokee tribe in 1835, at the time the rights accrued under this judgment.

    In addition to that you are advised that William Stephens when notified to appear before one of my assistants for examination failed to appear. It does not therefore seem necessary in this case to make any further examination into the facts.

    Very respectfully,

        Special Commissioner.

GM:MLC.

Cherokee Intruder Cases 1901 - 1909

Date Received	No.	Allottee	Intruder
April 29, 1903	1	Claude S, Mary J. and Johnnie B. Shelton	J.S. and Nancy Hargrove

Action	Remarks
Service was had on May 16, 1903. July 21, 03 Sent to Policeman Chamberlain instructing him to place the Allottee in possession. July 27. Policeman referrs[sic] matters to this office for correct description. Aug. 8. descriptions corrected and Policeman Chamberlain instructed to place the Allottee in possession. Aug 25, 1903 Allottee Service had on April 30-13. Report of Dawes Commission being contested & no certificates issued.	Case being held for report of Dawes Commission. *(Line illegible)* On July 27 Policeman Chamberlain reports Allottee cannot accompy[sic] him on account of sickness in his family. Settled Closed. placed in possession.

Date Received	No.	Allottee	Intruder
April 8, 1903	2	Delila L. Morrison	Jefferson Measels

Action	Remarks
Service had on April 30-13. Report of Dawes Commission being contested & no certificates issued.	Contest pending. Dismissed.

Date Received	No.	Allottee	Intruder
(No date given.)	3	Walter G Fields Guardian Joseph A Fields	Monroe Burris and J.P. Bell

Action	Remarks
No complaint yet filed.	Settled.

Date Received	No.	Allottee	Intruder
April 11, 1903	4	Osceola Allen	W.F. Moritzky

Action	Remarks
No complaint yet filed.	Notice sent parties to vacate Aug. 8, 1903. Sept 17-1903. F.C. Lawrence accompanied by Allottee drove to place found defendant had gone to Missouri. Plaintiff thought he could make satisfactory settlement on the return of defendant Party notified to vacate Jan. 16-04

Cherokee Intruder Cases 1901 - 1909

	Settled see papers on file by order of plaintiff 3/20/04

Date Received	No.	Allottee	Intruder
April 16 1903	5	Lizzie H Sloan	Richard & Mary Shankling
Action		**Remarks**	
Report of Dawes Commission shows contest pending.		Contest pending. Dismissed	

Date Received	No.	Allottee	Intruder
April 25, 03	6	Geo. W. Rogers	David W. Vann Citizen
Action		**Remarks**	
Service was had on May 4, 1903. Sept 17 - 1903 Plaintiff made settlement previous to investigation failed to make report to this office.		Notice sent to alleged Intruder to vacate Aug. 7-1903. (Settled)	

Date Received	No.	Allottee	Intruder
May 4, 1903	7	Margaret E.A. Roberts	W. H. Lassiter
Action		**Remarks**	
Service was had on May 7, 1903. Report of Dawes Commission shows contest pending.		Contest pending. Dismissed.	

Date Received	No.	Allottee	Intruder
June 4, 1903	8	James J. Miller for himself & minor children, Louis, Charles & Jackson Miller	J. R. Hurst
Action		**Remarks**	
Service was had on June 15, 1903. Given to Policeman Chamberlain Aug 20/03 - to place the Allottees in possession Allottee placed in possession Aug. 26-1903 by Policeman Chamberlain.		Intruder notified to vacate Aug 14, 1903. Settled.	

Cherokee Intruder Cases 1901 - 1909

Date Received	No.	Allottee	Intruder
June 6, 1903	9	Mary L. McFarland	D.W. Vann
Action			**Remarks**
Service was had on June 17, 1903. Sept 17-1903 Allottee placed in possession.			Intruder ordered to vacate Aug. 7, 1903. Settled.

Date Received	No.	Allottee	Intruder
May 28, 1903	10	William L. Trott	Mrs. Elizabeth Howell W^m. Roark & James Ellis
Action			**Remarks**
Service was had July 6, 1903. Answer filed July 9, 1903-Plaintiff notified to appear at Vinita if he has his certificate of allotment			Intruders notified to vacate Aug. 10, 1903. Dismissed.

Date Received	No.	Allottee	Intruder
May 26, 1903	11	J.C. Cowels for minor Lucian B. Cowels	Wm Buskuk & Charley Coleman
Action			**Remarks**
Notice of service not returned.			Sept 17-1903 Wm Buskuk had a one year lean[sic] from one Chas Shawnee-a citizen who has filed a contest on said land. Dismissed

Date Received	No.	Allottee	Intruder
June 11, 1903	12	David I. Brown guardian for Bessie B. Shaw	Victoria M. Keys
Action			**Remarks**
Service was had June 20, 1903.			Party notified to vacate Aug 7, 1903, replies that he is a citizen & that this land was improved by him & he intends to file contest. Notified that contest entered 8/15/03 by V.M. Keys-see letter from Commission in file Dismissed.

Cherokee Intruder Cases 1901 - 1909

Date Received	No.	Allottee	Intruder
June 13, 1903	13	Eunice A Bankhead	Jessie Lareny & Henry Harrison
Action			**Remarks**
Notice of service had June 22, 1903. No answer filed. Answer filed Aug. 16, 1903-Plaintiff notified to appear at Vinita May 24-28-if she has her certificate of allotment.			Parties notified to vacate Aug. 7, 1903. Dismissed

Date Received	No.	Allottee	Intruder
June 17, 1903	14	J.B. Burgess & Elizabeth Burgess	John Pilgran & wife
Action			**Remarks**
Service was had on June 29, 1903. Report of Dawes Commission no certificate issued citizenship pending.			Citizenship Pending. Dismissed.

Date Received	No.	Allottee	Intruder
June 19-1903	15	Jennie Rose	Tom Stonebarger
Action			**Remarks**
Service was had June 27 1903 Communication from Plaintiff Jennie Rose on July 23, 1903 stateing[sic] she had made a contract with Defendant Stonebarger and case is settled.			Settled.

Date Received	No.	Allottee	Intruder
June 22, 03	16	Mary Blayburn	Silas Green
Action			**Remarks**
Service was had on July 1, 1903. Report of Dawes Commission states land has not been filed on by any one.			Parties notified of report of Dawes Commission Aug. 8, 1903. Dismissed.

Cherokee Intruder Cases 1901 - 1909

Date Received	No.	Allottee	Intruder
June 23, 03	17	John E, Victoria, Willie E & Grace Barks	John Richardson, Mary Summers & others
Action		**Remarks**	
No return of service, report of Dawes Commission shows contest pending.		Contest pending. Dismissed.	

Date Received	No.	Allottee	Intruder
Jan[sic]. 20-03	18	George Whitmire	John Landrum
Action		**Remarks**	
Service had June 29, 1903. Report of Dawes Commission shows contest pending.		Contest Pending. Dismissed.	

Date Received	No.	Allottee	Intruder
June 30, 1903	19	William R. Dawson for minor child John Hubert Dawson	Dan Walker
Action		**Remarks**	
Service had on July 11, 1903, report of Dawes Commission shows contest pending.		Contest Pending. Dismissed.	

Date Received	No.	Allottee	Intruder
July 13-03	20	Lillie O. Higgins for herself & minor children, Robt. J. & Nettie M. Higgins	J. N. Graham
Action		**Remarks**	
Service was had on July 15, 1903. Aug 10-03 Allottee placed in possession by Policeman Edmonds.		Defendant called at this office July 20, 1903 & agreed to vacate within 10 days from date which time was granted him by the agent. Settled.	

Cherokee Intruder Cases 1901 - 1909

Date Received	No.	Allottee	Intruder
July 15, 1903	21	Oliver W. Raley for himself & Martha Raley, Guardian for Minor children Oscar C, Jos. M & Geo W. Raley	Ben F. Lowery

Action	Remarks
Service had on July 17, 1903 Letter dated Sept 1, 03, instructing that parties have vacated & she has possession of her allotment.	Notice sent Defendant to vacate Aug 7-1903 Allottee in possession of her allotment Sept 1/03. Settled.

Date Received	No.	Allottee	Intruder
July 27, 1903	22	Rebecca Flying for minor children John, Jessie J. & Linda A Flying	Walter Foulks Walter Foulks *(re-written)*

Action	Remarks
Service had on Aug. 12, 1903 Answer filed Aug. 11- 1903	July 21,03 Defendant has vacated and said crops to one J.W. Gregg conzisting[sic] of (70) acres of corn and (30) acres broom corn consideration $450^{00}. Could not find plaintiff Dismissed

Date Received	No.	Allottee	Intruder
June 27, 1903	23	Wesley Walker for his minor son Walter H. Walker	Ed. Vann Citizen

Action	Remarks
Date of Service Aug 28-03 The Allottee placed in possession Sep 11-03 case is settled	(Settled)

Date Received	No.	Allottee	Intruder
Aug 25, 1903	24	Ella Sullivan for Wm J. Sullivan, Florence & Jefferson D Sullivan	Geo W. Swift

Action	Remarks
Case settled by Mr. Lawrance parties entered into a new contract	(Settled)

Cherokee Intruder Cases 1901 - 1909

Date Received	No.	Allottee	Intruder
Aug 20, 1903	25	J. R. Rogers	James Tivis
Action		**Remarks**	
Placed in the hands of Policeman Edmonds and Allottee placed in possession Aug 26, 1903		Settled.	

Date Received	No.	Allottee	Intruder
Sep 3-1903	26	W.P. McCullugh for minors Lillian M, Netton M & W^m M McCullugh	C.G. & Cynthia Brought
Action		**Remarks**	
Date of Service Sep. 7-03. Answer filed Sep. 10-1903 Given to Policeman Sunday Oct 9-1904. Plaintiff notified that guardian must be appointed May 9-1904. Set hearing at Vinita on May 24, 1904- May 26 - Summoned by James Davenport Atty for Plaintiff		Certificate issued by report of commission Settled. Settled	

Date Received	No.	Allottee	Intruder
Sep 4- 03	27	Russell R. Howard	Joseph James - Joseph Foster
Action		**Remarks**	
Date of Service had Sep. 8/03. Answer filed Nov. 4, 1903.		Plaintiff agrees to allow defendant to remain on allotment until he gathers his crops. Certificate issued by report of Commission Dismissed	

Date Received	No.	Allottee	Intruder
Sept 12, 1903	28	Thos. Lowe, Guardian of Fannie, Hallie & Arthur Johnson, heirs of Isreal Johnson, deceased	Olie Lewis, John Crockett and W. M. Sunday
Action		**Remarks**	
Notice sent 9/14/03		Contest pending. 5/20/05 Dismissed. See N° 498	

Cherokee Intruder Cases 1901 - 1909

Date Received	No.	Allottee	Intruder
Sept 12, 1903	29	Wm Henry Foreman, for minor children, Frank, Johnson, Alice & Mary F. Foreman	L. G. Gable
Action		Remarks	
Notice sent 9/15/03. Return of service Sept. 21-1903		Settled see papers on file Oct. 2-1903 Dismissed	

Date Received	No.	Allottee	Intruder
Sept 12, 1903	30	S.B. McGhee, for Belle McGhee, Bertie O & Buena Vista McGhee	R. B. Martin
Action		Remarks	
Notice sent 9/15/03- Ret. of service Sept 18-1903		Contest pending. Dismissed	

Date Received	No.	Allottee	Intruder
Complaint was verbal	31	Wm Steers	Sarah Mizer
Action		Remarks	
On verbal complaint of Allottee Wm Steers he was placed in possession of his allotment by Policeman Edmonds, Sept 24, 1903 Policeman Edmonds reports he has placed Sarah Mizer in possession of the allotment now under contest		Contest pending Dismissed	

Date Received	No.	Allottee	Intruder
Sept 23-1903	32	Lila Goodal for Wm Drowningbear	R W Farley
Action		Remarks	
Notice sent Sept. 23, 1903 Return of service Sept 28 Answer filed Dec. 21-03		Settled, see papers on file. Dismissed	

Cherokee Intruder Cases 1901 - 1909

Date Received	No.	Allottee	Intruder
Sept 24-1903	33	R M Walker	Jno Springer
Action		**Remarks**	
Notice sent Sept 24-1903 Return of service Sept 28-1903		Contest pending Dismissed	

Date Received	No.	Allottee	Intruder
Sept 30, 1903	34	Margaret Bibles	Marcus L Jorden
Action		**Remarks**	
Notice sent Oct. 1-1903 Return of service Oct 6-1903 Answer filed Oct. 7-1903 Plaintiff notified ~~that she must~~ to appear at Vinita May 22-5-28 if she has certificate of allotment Set for hearing at Vinita 8-9-04 Case heard evidence taken, all parties in interest being present & it is the decision of this office that the Allottee is entitled to possession Ready for Police. Sent to policeman Chamberlain Aug 17-04 See report of Policeman Chamberlain		No contest Cert in file Settled 9/16/04	

Date Received	No.	Allottee	Intruder
(No date given.)	35	Joseph D. Burgess for minor child Flora E Burgess	Sidney Sparks, Harve Norfork
Action		**Remarks**	
Notice sent Oct. 9-1903 No return of service No answer filed. Plaintiff notified that guardian must be appointed May 9, 1904. Given to Mr Hoyt May 12/04 for investigation & report. May 21, 04 Investigated by W R Hoyt & found that no guardian had been appointed Set for hearing at Vinita Dec 20-04		Certificate issued by report of Commission Settled. See letter from Plaintiff 12/12/04	

Cherokee Intruder Cases 1901 - 1909

Date Received	No.	Allottee	Intruder
Sept 26, 1903	36	Edward Lemaster	Nancy B Price
Action		**Remarks**	
Notice sent Oct. 12-1903 Return of service " 17-1903 Answer filed " 30-1903 Plaintiff notified to appear at Vinita if he has his certificate of allotment		No certificates Dismissed	

Date Received	No.	Allottee	Intruder
Oct 13, 1903	37	Mary M Ellis	Aaron Napper
Action		**Remarks**	
Notice sent Oct 18-1903 Return of service Nov 6 Answer filed Nov. 12-1903 Given to Wm R. Hoyt May 13, 1904 to investigate May 21, 1903-Allottee in possession See report of W.R. Hoyt in files		Certificate of allotment issued by report of Commission Settled.	

Date Received	No.	Allottee	Intruder
Oct 18-1903	38	Susie D Coates	James Wilkerson
Action		**Remarks**	
Notice sent Oct 18-1903 Return of service " 17-1903 No answer filed. Given to Wm R. Hoyt May 13/04 to investigate. Plaintiff in possession-See report of W.R. Hoyt May 21/04		Certificate of allotment issued by report of Commission. Settled	

Date Received	No.	Allottee	Intruder
Oct 18-1903	39	Joseph Fox McGehee	Geo Kozer and Blue Thompson
Action		**Remarks**	
Notice sent Oct. 12-1903 Return of Service Oct 15-1903 Answer filed Oct 31-1903		Certificate of allotment issued by report of Commission June 4 Commission *(Illegible)*	

Cherokee Intruder Cases 1901 - 1909

Set for hearing at Vinita May 24/04
Letters of guardianship on file May 16-1904

May 26-04 Plaintiff appeared evidence taken certificates exibited[sic]
& letters of guardianship

Ready for Police   Contest pending
Sent to Policeman Chamberlain
May 28-1904   (Illegible)   Dismissed

Date Received	No.	Allottee	Intruder
Oct 14-1903	40	Jno S Woodward	Isaac Eades
Action		**Remarks**	
Notice sent Oct 14-1903		No certificates	
Return of service Oct 26, '03			
Answer filed Oct 27-1903		Case dismissed for want of prosecution	
Notified to appear at Vinita Nov 24 to 28 if she has certificate of allotment		Dismissed	

Date Received	No.	Allottee	Intruder
Oct 12-1903	41	Nellie David	Isaac Eades
Action		**Remarks**	
Notice sent Oct 14-1903			
Return of service Oct 26, 1903		Case dismissed for want of prosecution	
No answer filed.			
Plaintiff notified to appear at Vinita May 24-28 if she has certificate of allotment		Dismissed	

Date Received	No.	Allottee	Intruder
Oct. 14-1903	42	Jno J Caldwell, for Jno C, Joella, and Benjamin Caldwell minors	F.N. Witt and J. Carroll
Action		**Remarks**	
Notice sent Oct. 14-1903		certificate of allotment issued by report of Commission	
Return of service Oct 21-1903			
Answer filed Oct 22-1903		May 26-Certificates exibited[sic]	
Plaintiff notified Mch 15/04 that guardian must be appointed		Contest filed see report of Commission in file therefore Dismissed	
Set for hearing at Vinita, I.T. on May 24, 1904		July 17, 1906 Letters of Guardianship returned to John J Caldwell in person	

Cherokee Intruder Cases 1901 - 1909

May 26-04 Case heard
No *(Illegible)*-being filed and certificates having been exibited[sic] was decided states *(illegible...)*
Letters of guardianship in file Mar 28-04
Sent to Policeman Chamberlain 5/28-04

Date Received	No.	Allottee	Intruder
Oct 14-03	43	W.L. Houdeshell for Grace, Mary & Jas. T. Houdeshell	J. L. Barker et al.

Action	Remarks
Return of service Oct 20, 1903 Answer filed " 26-03 Plaintiff notified that guardian must be appointed May 9-1904 Set for hearing at Vinita IT on May 25, 1904 May 26-04 Dismissed by W.W. *(Illegible)* for Plaintiff he being his Father-n-law	Certificate of allotment issued by report of Commission Settled

Date Received	No.	Allottee	Intruder
Oct 14-1903	44	Milo J Wiley for Addie Willey[sic]	Reed Vann

Action	Remarks
Notice sent Oct 15-1903 Ret. of service " 17-1903 No answer filed Plaintiff notified that a guardian must be appointed May 9, 1904 Given to Mr. Hoyt May 12/04 to investigate & make report May 24,04 Plaintiff in possession-See report of W.R. Hoyt May 29/04	Certificate of allotment issued by report of Commission Settled

Date Received	No.	Allottee	Intruder
Oct 1- 1903	45	Margaret A Suagee for Dennis, Thomas, Stan Jr., Bessie May & Ray L. Suagee	William Stevens

Cherokee Intruder Cases 1901 - 1909

Action	Remarks
No return of service No answer filed	Contest Pending Case dismissed for want of prosecution Dismissed

Date Received	No.	Allottee	Intruder
Sept 30-1903	46	Wm Buster for son Charles Buster	Harrison Bear et al

Action	Remarks
Notice sent Oct 21-1903 Return of service Oct 21-1903 No answer filed Plaintiff notified that guardian must be appointed May 9 -1904 Given to Mr Hoyt to investigate & make report May 12/04 May 16/04 W.R. Hoyt reports he found plaintiff in possession of his allotment	Certificate of allotment issued by report of Commission Settled

Date Received	No.	Allottee	Intruder
Set[sic]. 30-03	47	W. E. Rousey for son Paul E. Rousey	W. B. Sims

Action	Remarks
Notice sent Oct 21-1903	Mrs Rowsey[sic] called at this office today in person and informed me this matter was satisfactory settled and ordered case dismissed Dismissed Nov 13-1903

Date Received	No.	Allottee	Intruder
Oct 5-1903	48	Henry B. Gore	H. A. Henley

Action	Remarks
Notice sent Oct 21-1903 Return of service " 26-1903 No answer filed Given to Wm R. Hoyt May 13/04 to investigate	Certificate of allotment issued by report of Commission Settled

Cherokee Intruder Cases 1901 - 1909

May 21, 04 Allottee in possession
See report of W R Hoyt in files

Date Received	No.	Allottee	Intruder
Sep. 30-1903	49	John Ross McGhee	James McNeill
Action			**Remarks**
No return of service			Certificate not issued
" answer filed			
Plaintiff notified to appear at Vinita May 24-28 if he has cert. of allotment			Case dismissed for want of prosecution
			Dismissed

Date Received	No.	Allottee	Intruder
Oct 27-1903	50	Nellie David for Stephen David dec'd.	Isaac Eads
Action			**Remarks**
Notice sent Oct 28-1903			No certificate issued
Return of service Nov 8			
No answer filed			Case dismissed for want of prosecution.
Plaintiff notified to appear at Vinita May 24-28 if she has certificate of allotment			
			Dismissed

Date Received	No.	Allottee	Intruder
Oct 22-1903	51	John B Phariss	W. L. McDaniel
Action Nov			**Remarks**
Notice sent ~~Oct~~ 4-1903			(Settled)
			See letters in file

Date Received	No.	Allottee	Intruder
Nov 6-1903	52	George A.M. Taylor	Starkweather and Vivers[sic]
Action			**Remarks**
Notice sent Nov 7-1903			Certificate of allotment issued by report of Commission
No return of service			
Answer filed Dec 18-03			
Set for hearing May 24/04 at Vinita, I.T.			Settled
May 24 C. H. Taylor Father of G.A.M. Taylor called at Vanita[sic] to day and notified me he had possession.			

Cherokee Intruder Cases 1901 - 1909

Date Received	No.	Allottee	Intruder
Oct 24-1903	53	Mrs Annie Thomas	Samuel Wonen

Action	Remarks
Notice sent Nov 7-1903 No return of service No answer filed Plaintiff notified to appear at Vinita on May 25, 04 for investigation May 27-04 Plaintiff called at this office and advised satisfactory arrangements had been maid[sic] and dismissed Action	Certificates issued See report of Commission <u>Settled</u>

Date Received	No.	Allottee	Intruder
Oct 29-1903	54	Margaret E A Rhodes	Barnet Brewer

Action	Remarks
Notice sent Nov. 7-1903 No return of service " answer filed	Contest Pending Case dismissed for want of prosecution Dismissed

Date Received	No.	Allottee	Intruder
Nov 7-1903	55	Mary E Payne for James M, Lena E, W^m B, Maggie D, Edith B Payne	A.L. Smith

Action	Remarks
Notice sent Nov 19-1903 No return of service " answer filed Plaintiff notified that a guardian must be appointed May 9, 1904 10/13-04 Case settled and certificate returned upon request of plaintiff	Certificate issued Certificate in file Settled Dismissed

Date Received	No.	Allottee	Intruder
Nov 3-1903	56	Nannie Watson Nee Miller for Ray Miller	E. B. Garner

Action	Remarks
Notice sent Nov 17-1903. Return of service Nov 21-03 Answer filed " 25-03	Certificate of allotment issued as shown by report of Commission

Cherokee Intruder Cases 1901 - 1909

Plaintiff notified that a guardian must be appointed May 9, 1904. Set for hearing at Vinita IT on May 25, 04. Plaintiff called up over phone & advised that she had been in possession of her son's allotment since December/03-when the case was dismissed.	Settled

Date Received	No.	Allottee	Intruder
Nov 25-1903	57	Lena M Stinson	Charles Williams
Action			**Remarks**
Notice sent Nov. 27-1903 Return of service 12/4-03 No answer filed. Answer filed Mch 18, 1904 Set for hearing at Vinita May 26/04			Certificate of allotment received May 6-1904. See same in file.
May 26-04 Case set for hearing to day at Vonita[sic] Plaintiff apeard[sic] Defendant did not Ready for Police later Defendant apeard and agreed to vacate within 10 days from date			
			Dismissed

Date Received	No.	Allottee	Intruder
Nov 25-03	58	Annie Hamilton for Nannie, Squirrel & Roswell Hamilton	S. W. Waldron
Action			**Remarks**
Notice sent Nov. 27-1903. Return of service Nov. 30-03 No answer filed. Allottee called at this office and stated she was in possession of her allotment.			Settled

Date Received	No.	Allottee	Intruder
Mar 30-03	59	John Watkins	John Hanby
Action			**Remarks**

Notice sent Dec. 2-1903
  Return of Service Dec 7th 03
  No answer filed.
			No cert of allotment issued.
			Case dismissed for want of prosecution
			Dismissed

Cherokee Intruder Cases 1901 - 1909

Date Received	No.	Allottee	Intruder
Nov 27-03	60	Sarah Dolan (Fair)	Nancy Stewart
Action		Remarks	
No return of service " answer filed.		Contest pending. Case dismissed for want of prosecution. Dismissed	

Date Received	No.	Allottee	Intruder
Nov 27-03	61	Wm A. Qualls	Jack Martin et al
Action		Remarks	
No return of service Case dismissed for want of prosecution		Contest pending Dismissed.	

Date Received	No.	Allottee	Intruder
Dec 5-1903	62	Elizabeth & Houston Doming[sic]	Geo Fields
Action		Remarks	
Notice sent Dec 17-1903 Return of service Dec 29-03 Answer filed Jan. 4-1904 Set for hearing at Vinita May 27/04		Certificate of allotment issued by report of Commission ~~Settled~~ ~~See paper~~ on file from plaintiffs May 19-04	

Date Received	No.	Allottee	Intruder
Dec 14-03	63	James T. Miller	Rob Rooks et al.
Action		Remarks	
Notice sent Dec 24-1903 Return of Service 12/29-03 No answer filed. Case dismissed for want of prosecution		Contest Pending Dismissed.	

Cherokee Intruder Cases 1901 - 1909

Date Received	No.	Allottee	Intruder
Dec 8-1903	64	Noh[sic] S. Holland, Millie, Noah Jr, & Chas B Holland	Alexander Faulkner & Gus McClain

Action	Remarks
Notice sent Dec. 28-1903 Return of service Jan 2-1904 Answer filed Jan 4-1904. Plaintiff notified that guardian must be appointed May 9-1904. Plaintiff notified to appear at Vinita May 24-28 if he has certificate of allotment	No certificate issued Case dismissed for want of prosecution Dismissed

Date Received	No.	Allottee	Intruder
Dec 12-1903	65	Algia Measles for Thos. B. Measles	William Evans

Action	Remarks
Notice sent Dec. 28-1903 Return of service Dec 31-1903. Answer filed Jan. 1-1904 Plaintiff notified that guardian must be appointed May 9-1904 Set for hearing at Vinita IT on May 26, 1904	Certificate of allotment issued as shown by report of Commission Settled By order of Plaintiff May 17-04 - see same in file

Date Received	No.	Allottee	Intruder
Dec 8-1903	66	Kate Hilderbrand for Maggie " & Richard Deerinwater	J. L. Haskins

Action	Remarks

Notice sent Dec. 28-1903
  No return of service
  " answer filed
Return of service Jan. 7-1904
Plaintiff notified that a guardian must be appointed 5/9/04
	No certificate of allotment issued
	
	Case dismissed for want of prosecution
	
	Dismissed.

Cherokee Intruder Cases 1901 - 1909

Date Received	No.	Allottee	Intruder
Dec. 18-1903	67	Joseph Lemaster for John Adair Lemaster Fairland, I.T.	James & Mary B Price

Action	Remarks
Notice sent Dec 30-1903	No certificate of allotment issued.
No return of service	Cert. on file Jan 14-05
" answer filed	12/26/03 Com report no contest
Return of service Feb 15-1904	2/14/05 Com requested to advise as to contest
Answer filed Feb 27-1904	
Plaintiff notified to appear at Vinita May 24-28 if he has cert of allotment	2/17/05 Com advises no contest
Letter of guardian on file Jan 14-05	
Set for Vinita IT 11 o'clock A.M.	
2/11/05 Case called, Joseph Lemaster appeared and his testimony.	
James Price was present but refused to be sworn.	
2/25/05 Placed in hands of A.F. Chamberlain for removal of intruder	
3/22/05 Allottee in possession	
	Settled

Date Received	No.	Allottee	Intruder
Dec 17-1903	68	J. A. Duncan et al	S. L. Chism

Action	Remarks
Return of service 3/7/04	Settled, see paper on file 3/8-04.

Date Received	No.	Allottee	Intruder
Dec 28-1903	69	M.A. & Jesse Johnson	Joe Wear[sic]

Action	Remarks
Notice sent Jan 6-1904	No certificate of allotment issued
Return of service Jan 9-1904	Case dismissed for want of prosecution
Answer filed Sept 6, 1903[sic]	Dismissed

Date Received	No.	Allottee	Intruder
Jan 8, 1904	70	Wm Henry Foreman	John W Howard

Action	Remarks
Notice sent Jan 8-1904	Contest Pending
Answer filed by Plaintiff Jan 14-1904	
Return of service Jan 13-04	Dismissed see #126
3/14/05 Instructions sent in case #126. see said case.	

Cherokee Intruder Cases 1901 - 1909

Date Received	No.	Allottee	Intruder
Jan 8-1904	71	Wm Henry Foreman for Frank Johnson, Alia & Mary F. Foreman	L. G. Gable
Action			Remarks

Notice sent Jan 8-1904
Return of service Jan 13-1904
Answer filed Jan 23rd/04
Plaintiff notified that guardian must be appointed May 9, 1904
   Case dismissed for want
     of prosecution
			~~Contest pending on Wm H. Foreman~~
			~~land only~~
			
			Dismissed

Date Received	No.	Allottee	Intruder
Jan 15, 1904	72	Trixie Davis	----- Scoville
Action			Remarks

Notice sent Jan. 16-1904
 Return of Service 2/4-04
Answer filed Feb 15, 04
   Case dismissed for want of
     prosecution
			Contest Pending
			
			Dismissed

Date Received	No.	Allottee	Intruder
Jan 16, 1904	73	David Chuwalooky	----- Scoville
Action			Remarks
Notice sent Jan. 16, 1904 No return of service No answer filed Plaintiff asked to advice[sic] office of the status of the case May 12-1904 Return of service 2/4-04 Sent to Policeman Chamberlain 5/28-04			Certificates issued & in files Settled see report of Policeman in file 7/2/04

Date Received	No.	Allottee	Intruder
Jan 16 -04	74	Henry Nicholson for Jessie, Nathaniel, Luy[sic], Drucilla & Bessie Watson	Rube Evans
Action			Remarks
Notice sent Jan. 16-1904. Return of service Jan. 26-1904.			Certificate of allotment issued Settled placed in possession by Stedham

20

Cherokee Intruder Cases 1901 - 1909

Guardianship papers filed- Answer filed. Set for hearing May 31/04 - Given Capt. John C. West-8-1904 to place Allottee in possession	June 20-04. Letters of guardianship return to guardian 7/16/04 -

Date Received	No.	Allottee	Intruder
Jan 7-1904	75	Mary F. Jones	Silas Collier
Action			**Remarks**
Notice sent Jan 20-1904 Return service Jan 28-04 Plaintiff notified to appear at Vinita May 24 to 28 if she has cert of allotment No answer filed. Case dismissed for want of prosecution			No certificate of allotment issued Dismissed

Date Received	No.	Allottee	Intruder
Jan 6-1904	76	Henry Thomas & Hannah Thomas for Grace Thomas	R. B. Hutchinson
Action			**Remarks**

Notice sent Jan 20-1904
 	
Plaintiff notified that a guardian must be
appointed 5/9/04
No return of service
" Answer filed
   Set for hearing Jan 3/05
   Dismissed   See mem in file
			Commission reports Certificates issued.
			
			Dismissed

Date Received	No.	Allottee	Intruder
Dec 30-1903	77	Marion Evans for herself -Mattie Evans -	Lucian King
Action			**Remarks**
Notice sent Jan 20-1904 Return of service Jan 27-04 Answer filed Plaintiff notified that guardian must be appointed May 9-1904 Letters of guardianship filed May 16, 1904			No certificate of allotment issued Dismissed

Cherokee Intruder Cases 1901 - 1909

Case dismissed for want of prosecution	

Date Received	No.	Allottee	Intruder
Jan 13-1904	78	Jane James F. Boyd *(Illegible)* W. H. Norwood	Rube Hawkins
	Oct 30 1906	Allottment[sic] Certificate 41238 Homestead certificate 3498 delivered to J.M. Boyd in person	

Action	Remarks
Notice sent Jan 23, 1904 Return of Service 2/5-04 Answer filed Fe. 12, 1904 Set for hearing at Vinita IT on May 26/04 May 27 Case heard and held for Briefs 20 days Jan 3[sic] Case submitted to department for decision 5/25/05 Parties informed that in compliance with decision of the ~~Department of the Interior~~ attorney general approved May 12 1905 that she had a right to make contract under the law and in consequence defendant will not be disturbed and case	Certificates of allotment issued

Date Received	No.	Allottee	Intruder
Jan 20, 1904	79	John D. West for Bert West	John Payton

Action	Remarks
Notice sent Feb. 1, 1904 Plaintiff notified that a guardian must be appointed May 9, 1904 Plaintiff notified to appear at Vinita May 24-28 if he has cert. of allotment No answer filed Case dismissed for want of prosecution.	No certificate of allotment issued. Dismissed.

Cherokee Intruder Cases 1901 - 1909

Date Received	No.	Allottee	Intruder
Jan. 20, 1904	80	Wiley Mulkey	Dick Steen

Action	Remarks

Notice sent Feb. 1, 1904
Service had Feby 6-04
<s>Sent for</s> Given to W^m R Hoyt May 13, 04
to investigate
No answer filed
    Set for hearing Jan 3 05
    See letter from plaintiff
	Certificate of allotment issued
	
	Dismissed.
	Upon request of Plaintiff <s>Jan</s> Dec 28/04

Date Received	No.	Allottee	Intruder
Jan 12, 1904	81	Benj F Bice for himself & Lela Bice	John G Douglas

Action	Remarks

Notice sent Feb 4-1904
Return of service Feb 8-1904
Answer filed Feb 10, 1904
Guardianship papers on file
Plaintiff notified that if he has cert of
allotment to appear at Vinita May 24-28
    Letters of Guardianship returned to
    Benj F Brue[sic] 6/14/05
	No certificate of allotment issued
	
	Case dismissed for want of prosecution.
	
	Dismissed.

Date Received	No.	Allottee	Intruder
Jan. 28-1904	82	Morris F. Isbell	Wm Thompson

Action	Remarks
Notice sent Feb 5-1904 Return of Service 2/8-04 Answer filed Feb 13, 1904 Set for hearing at Vinita May 25/04 May 25-04 Case heard and decided Allottee was entitled to possession Given to Policeman Chamberlain May 28/04 to place Allottee in possession See Chamberlain's report 6/17/04 - Allottee in possession-	Certificate of allotment issued Settled

Cherokee Intruder Cases 1901 - 1909

Date Received	No.	Allottee	Intruder
Jan 30-1904	83	James P Riley for Edward E Riley	George Garrett

Action	Remarks
Notice sent 2/13/04 Return of service Feb 23-04 Plaintiff notified that a guardian must be appointed May 9, 1904 - Given to W^m R Hoyt to make investigation & to make report-5/12/04	Commission reports certf[sic] issued - Settled See file

Date Received	No.	Allottee	Intruder
Feb 6, 1904	84	Chas W Riddle for Thos. B. Childers	Jean Mullen

Action	Remarks
Notice sent Feb-13-04 Return of service Feb 24-1904 Plaintiff notified that the matter will be investigate if they call at Vinita, I.T. from May 24-28 *(Illegible)* May 12/04- No answer filed Set for hearing at Vinita 8-9-04 Aug. 9-04 No appearance by either party	Certificate in file Given S A Mills 8/29/04 Settled by order of plaintiff.

Date Received	No.	Allottee	Intruder
Feb 4-1904	85	Leonidas Dobson for Harry Lee Dobson	J W. Hays

Action	Remarks
Notice sent Feb 16-1904 Plaintiff notified that a guardian must be appointed May 9, 1904 No answer filed " return of service Case dismissed for want of prosecution.	~~Commission reports certificates issued~~ No certificates of allotment issued Dismissed

Cherokee Intruder Cases 1901 - 1909

Date Received	No.	Allottee	Intruder
Feb 1-1904	86	Nellie & Wm Highland	P. Shanahan

Action	Remarks
Notice sent Feb 16-1904 Return of service Feb 26-04 Plaintiff notified to appear at Vinita from May 24th to 28 incl. when the matter will be investigated May 17/04 May 26 Alottee[sic] called and exibited[sic] certificate no answer filed by *(Illegible)* for Police Notices sent May 12-04 No answer filed Set for hearing at Vinita 8-10-04 Aug 10-04, No appearance by either party. Set for hearing at Vinita Feb 7-05 2/7/05 Case called. No appearance by either party	Commission reports certificate issued 2/27/05 Report of A.F. Chamberlain filed states that matter has been settled satisfactorily Case Dismissed Dismissed

Date Received	No.	Allottee	Intruder
Feb 2-1904	87	John L Rogers	John Sousley

Action	Remarks
Notice sent Feb 16-1904	Settled See papers in file

Date Received	No.	Allottee	Intruder
Feb 3-1904	88	John F Ward	F.M. Lucker

Action	Remarks
Notice sent Feb 16-1904 Return of service Feb 21-1904 Answer filed Mch 27, 1904 ~~Plaintiff~~ Set for hearing at Vinita May 27/04 Defendant apeard[sic] Plaintiff did not	Commission reports certificates issued Case dismissed for want of prosecution

Defendant said he was grazing the land and was satisfied could and hold said land, he would give possession unless he made arangements[sic]
May 27-04 Plaintiff asked that case be again set for hearing as it was impossible for him to appear on May 27-04

Set for hearing at Vinita 8-9-04	Dismissed

Cherokee Intruder Cases 1901 - 1909

Date Received	No.	Allottee	Intruder
Feb 16-1904	89	John Housebug for Bettie, Johnson, Robert Hermie Housebug	E. N. Ratcliff

Action	Remarks
Notice sent Mar. 2-1904 Return of service 3/12/04 Answer filed Mch 12, 1904 Plaintiff notified Mar 12 that guardian to be appointed Set for hearing at Vinita IT on May 27, 04 Set for hearing at Muskogee, I.T. Feby 20, 1905 2/15/05 Letter dated 2/13/05 received from Plaintiff stating *(Illegible)* had been settled and requests that can be dismissed. Case dismissed as requested, 3/23 Rental contract returned to E.N. Ratcliff	Commission reports certificates issued 3/22 1906 Returned to John Housebug in person one Bill of Sale and copy of rental contract

Date Received	No.	Allottee	Intruder
Feb 11-1904	90	John W Holland for Robert & Maggie Holland	Wallace Shaw

Action	Remarks
Notice sent Mar. 2-1904 Return of service 3/19/04 *(Illegible)* Plaintiff on Mch 23$\underline{rd}$ -04, that it will be necessary for guardian to be appointed before Action can be taken. Answer filed Nov. 5, 1904 Case dismissed for want of prosecution	No certificates of allotment issued Dismissed

Date Received	No.	Allottee	Intruder
Jan 19-1904	91	Charles Walters for W$\underline{m}$, Annie & Jimie Walters	W.C.P. Edwards et al

Action	Remarks
Notice sent Mar 2-04 Return of service 3-7-04 Answer filed Mch 14, 1904 Plaintiff notified that a guardian must be appointed before Action can be taken 5/9/04	No certificate of allotment issued Case dismissed for want of prosecution Dismissed

Cherokee Intruder Cases 1901 - 1909

Date Received	No.	Allottee	Intruder
Feb 12-1904	92	D.M. Marrs for David M Marrs Jr.	Jack Sanders

Action	Remarks
Notice sent Mar 2-1904 Return of service 3/11/04 Guardianship papers on file Answer filed Mch. 12, 1904 Set for hearing at Vinita IT on May 26/04 Submitted to department June 18/04 for instructions Department instructs to take No Action until contest is settled Dismissed	Commission report certificate issued Case dismissed for want of prosecution

Date Received	No.	Allottee	Intruder
Feb 8-1904	93	George Blevins	Jane Devaney et al

Action	Remarks
Notice sent Mar 2-1904 Answer filed Mch 12, 1904 Plaintiff notified to appear at Vinita May 24-28 if he has certificate of allotment Case dismissed for want of prosecution	Certificate of allotment issued Dismissed

Date Received	No.	Allottee	Intruder
Feb 8-1904	94	Joseph Blevins	----- Bart et al

Action	Remarks

Notice sent Mar 2-1904
Return of service 3/9/04
Set for hearing at Vinita Feb 1-05
   2/7/05 Answer filed by Wilson & Davis Vinita Attys for defendant No appearance by plaintiff. Write Com requesting report as to contest on land in question Letter written 2/14/05
                              2/7/05 Com reports land in contest
Case dismissed for want of prosecution
	Contest Pending
	
	Dismissed

Cherokee Intruder Cases 1901 - 1909

Date Received	No.	Allottee	Intruder
March 5, 1904	95	Mary E Comer for herself and R. Lee Comer, guardian for W^{m}. J. Comer	E.C. Perriman

Action	Remarks
Notice sent Guardianship papers March 21, 1904 issued	Certificate issued and on file
Return of service Answer filed Mch 28/04- Mch 26, 1904 Set for hearing at Vinita on May 24/04	Cert returned to R. Lee Comer in person 7/19/04
May 24 Plaintiff by his Atty Wm B. Thompson of Vinita	Allottee in possession see Chamberlain report
No apearance[sic] by Defendant -for Police May 28/04 Letter to Policeman Chamberlain to place Allottee in possession	
Dismissed	

Date Received	No.	Allottee	Intruder
Mar. 3 1904	96	Sarah Tindels nee Ragsdale	I. W. Wilson

Action	Remarks
Notice sent Answer filed Apr 14,'04 Mar 30-1904 Set for hearing at Muskogee Return of service Aug. 2-04 Apr 16-1904 Aug-2-04 Defendant appeared Plaintiff did not Case dismissed for want of prosecution	No certificate Cert of allotment reissued 6/28/04

Dismissed |

Date Received	No.	Allottee	Intruder
March 4th, 1904	97	Kate Russell	John Marlin

Notice Sent	Action	Remarks
April 4th 1904 Return of service April 6th, '04	Answer filed April 14, 1904 Set for hearing at Vinita, I.T. on May 28/04	Certificate issued by report of Commission 5/25-04 Dismissed See Memorandum in file

Cherokee Intruder Cases 1901 - 1909

Date Received	No.	Allottee	Intruder
Mar 29" 04	98	Francis M. Dixon (nee Moole)	George W. Dixon
Notice Sent	**Action**		**Remarks**
Mar 30" 1904 Return of service April 2nd, 1904	Answer filed April 7, 1904 Set for hearing at Vinita, I.T. May 25, 04 May 25 Dismissed by Plaintiff See *(Illegible)* in file		Commission reports certificate issued Settled

Date Received	No.	Allottee	Intruder
April 7" 1904	99	Mary Buffington	Joseph Lynch
Notice Sent	**Action**		**Remarks**
April 12th 1904 Return of Service April 18th 1904	Answer filed April 21, 1904 Set for hearing at Vinita May 27th -1904		Commission reports certificate issued Certificate of allotment in case
May 27 Case heard to day and *(Illegible)* alottee[sic] is entitled to possession May 28/04 Letters to Policeman Chamberlain to place alottee[sic] in possession July/6/04 Policeman notified to take no Action			June 22nd 04 Commission advises contest pending Dismissed

Date Received	No.	Allottee	Intruder
March 23rd [sic]	100	George West Vann	Jason Carson
Notice Sent	**Action**		**Remarks**
April 22nd 1904 Return of service 5/3/04	Plaintiff notified to appear at Vinita May 24-28 if he has cert of allotment Answer filed May 14-1904 Case dismissed for want of prosecution		No certificate of allotment issued Dismissed

Date Received	No.	Allottee	Intruder
March 28th 1904	101	Wm J. Shoemaker for his three minor children. Dora Ann, Franklin C. and David W. Shoemaker	A. O. Lackey
Notice Sent	**Action**		**Remarks**
April 22, 1904	Plaintiff notified that guardian must be appointed May 9-1904 No answer filed " return of service Case dismissed for want of prosecution		No certificate of allotment issued Dismissed

Cherokee Intruder Cases 1901 - 1909

Date Received	No.	Allottee	Intruder
April 27-04	102	Lemuel A. Marks guardian for Mary J, James O, W$^{\underline{m}}$ A Burgess	John Hatcher & Robert Martin
Notice Sent		**Action**	**Remarks**
Notice sent May 3-1904 Return of service 5/16/04		Guardianship papers on file Case dismissed for want of prosecution Set for hearing at Vinita May 27-1904 No answer filed	Certificate issued & in file
May 27 Continued by agreement of both parties			Dismissed

Date Received	No.	Allottee	Intruder
Apr 19-1904	103	Mary J. Moore	I.P. Shanahan
Notice Sent		**Action**	**Remarks**
May 12-04 Return of service		No answer filed May 9-1904 Case dismissed for want of prosecution	No certificate of allotment issued- Dismissed

Date Received	No.	Allottee	Intruder
April 16-1904	104	John Todd	Harley Burkhart
Notice Sent		**Action**	**Remarks**
May 5-1904 Return of service 5/13/04		No answer filed Case dismissed for want of prosecution	No certificate of allotment issued Dismissed

Date Received	No.	Allottee	Intruder
May 7, 1904	105	John T. Bankhead for minor son, John H. Bankhead	A. D. Reeves
Notice Sent		**Action**	**Remarks**
May 9, 1904 Return of service May 16-04		Plaintiff notified May 9, 1904 that guardian must be appointed Set for hearing at Vinita May 27-1904 Answer filed May 18-04	Certificate of allotment received and in file- Settled by Plaintiff but returned to Allottee Dismissed

30

Cherokee Intruder Cases 1901 - 1909

Date Received	No.	Allottee	Intruder
May 11, 1904	106	George Smith and his wife, Betsey Smith	Charlie Young

Notice Sent	Action	Remarks
May 16, 1904	Return of service 5/17/04 Set for hearing at Vinita May 27-1904 Answer filed May 17-1904	Certificates in files - Dismissed Cert. returned to Allottee by request 6/29/04
	Defendant appeared; plaintiff did not appear at Vinita but appeared at Muskogee on May 27th as he misunderstood place of hearing - Set for hearing Muskogee June 29-04 Case settled on request of plaintiff & certfs returned to plaintiff-	Dismissed

Date Received	No.	Allottee	Intruder
May 2-1904	107	Eugene Cook Smith	Dave Eller

Notice Sent	Action	Remarks
May 17-1904 Return of service May 20, 1904	Set for hearing at Vinita May 27-1904 No answer filed Case dismissed for want of prosecution	Certificate issued by report of Commission Dismissed

Date Received	No.	Allottee	Intruder
April 12-1904	108	S. R. Lewis adm of Jennie & Johnson Cornsilk	James Wooley & Chas Vanflett[sic]

Notice Sent	Action	Remarks
May 17-1904	Guardianship papers on file Return of service 5/19/04	Certificates issued by report of Commission
	Ans filed May 17/04 Set for hearing at Vinita 8-10-04 Aug. 10-04, No appearence[sic] by either party	Contest filed against Johnson Corsilk[sic]	Ettie Braner[sic] June 2-see report of Com in Cherokee case 42.

	Set for hearing at Vinita Feb 7-05
	  Cancelled no appearance by plaintiff
	  2/7/05 J.T. Davenport appeared for defendant who reports that parties defense do not claim any land except that in contest
	    3/6/05 Plaintiff advises he has possession of all lands except contested
		Dismissed

Cherokee Intruder Cases 1901 - 1909

Date Received	No.	Allottee	Intruder
May 4, 1904	109	Spencer L & Lula L. Alberty	Tam May
Notice Sent		**Action**	**Remarks**
May 31-1904			Settled
			Case settled see communication from plaintiff 6/7/04
			Dismissed

Date Received	No.	Allottee	Intruder
May 28-1904	110	Iddo G Cass	Mike Shuham
Notice Sent		**Action**	**Remarks**
May 31-04		Return of service June 6-04 No answer filed Set for hearing at Vinita 8/10/04 Dismissed by agreement of parties concerned - See mem. in file	Cert in file - Settled

Date Received	No.	Allottee	Intruder
May 28-04	111	Alice Carpenter	R. L. Murphy
Notice Sent		**Action**	**Remarks**
May 31-04		Return of service 6/7/04 Certificates returned to Allottee Allottee acknowledges receipt of certificate 7/5/05 Case dismissed for want of prosecution	Cert in file Commission reports 6/29 contest filed Dismissed

Date Received	No.	Allottee	Intruder
June 3-1904	112	David Taylor	John Crocket
Action			**Remarks**
June 6-05 Return of service 6/10/04 6/24-Commission advises that appeal has been taken in Contest Case from Com to Com of Ind. Affairs-See letter in file			Cert in file Contest Pending. Dismissed

Cherokee Intruder Cases 1901 - 1909

Date Received	No.	Allottee	Intruder
June 13-1904	113	Ollie Thompson	J. H. Arter
Notice Sent		**Action**	**Remarks**
June 14-1904 Return of service July 29-04		No return of service No answer filed Set for hearing at Vinita 8-10-04 Aug 10-04 No appearance by either party Ans. filed Aug. 8-04	Cert in file Given SA Mills 8/29/04 Settled by order of plaintiff Certificate returned to Allottee 6/26-05

Date Received	No.	Allottee	Intruder
May 13-1904	114	James B West	Nicy Vann
Notice Sent		**Action**	**Remarks**
June 14-04		Answer filed 7/12/04 Return of service 7/21/04 7/25/04 Instruction issued to Policeman Chamberlain to place Allottee in possession	Cert issued by report of Commission Contest pending 11/26-Letter asking Com. if contest is settled- Com. reports contest pending Nov 29-04
		Sept 21, 1904. Report of Arthur F Chamberlain filed showing that he went to allotment to place Allottee in possession and found him absent, at which he was shown notice from Dawes Com that defendant had been allowed to contest. Dismissed	

Date Received	No.	Allottee	Intruder
May 18-04	115	Elsie Harper	Jack Goss
Notice Sent		**Action**	**Remarks**
June 14-1904 Service had 6/18/04		Answer filed 6/21/04 Case dismissed for want of prosecution	No certificate of allotment issued Dismissed

Cherokee Intruder Cases 1901 - 1909

Date Received	No.	Allottee	Intruder
May 27-04	116	William B Wyly	L.A. Parker
Notice Sent		**Action**	**Remarks**
June 16-04 Return of service 6/24/04		Answer filed 7/5/04 Set for hearing 10/12/04 Continued until Oct 19-by consent of both parties 10/19-04 see memorandum in file 11/8/04-Attys for plaintiff & defendant file agreement in which it is agreed that defendant is to remain on the premises until Jan 1-05.	No certificate of allotment issued Certf. in file Certificate return to Allottee 6/26/05 Dismissed

Date Received	No.	Allottee	Intruder
June 20, 1904	117	Clara Foreman for herself & guardian for Daniel Tyner, a minor	Charley Mayhue
Notice Sent		**Action**	**Remarks**
June 23, 1904 No return of service		Wrote plaintiff to file Guardianship papers 6/23/04 No answer filed Set for hearing at Vinita 8-11-04 Aug -12-04 Dismissed at request of plaintiff	Certificate in file Settled

Date Received	No.	Allottee	Intruder
June 20, 1904	118	Peter Soldier for himself & for Whitaker & Julia Soldier	F. M. Crowell
Notice Sent		**Action**	**Remarks**
June 23/04 No return of service Return of service Aug 2-04 Aug. 11-04 2/15/05		Wrote plaintiff June 23/04 to file Letters of Guardianship No answer filed Set for hearing at Vinita 8-11-04 Ans. filed Aug 6-04 No appearance by either party Certificates returned to Peter Soldier Eucha, I.T. incompliance with his request of 2/12/05	Certificates in file Given Mills 8/29/04 Settled by order of plaintiff Cetificate[sic] returned 2/15/05.

Cherokee Intruder Cases 1901 - 1909

Date Received	No.	Allottee	Intruder
June 21, 1904	119	Elizabeth M Robinson	F. M. Goatly, Lawrence, & Henry Smith
Notice Sent		**Action**	**Remarks**
June 23-04 Notice serviced 6/27/04		Answer filed July 1-04	Cert in file Settled Plaintiff in possession 7/20/04 Certificates returned 11/9/04

Date Received	No.	Allottee	Intruder
June 28-1904	120	Joseph T. McDaniel & Kate E. McDaniel	Andy Council defendants claim to be Cherokee freedmen
Notice Sent		**Action**	**Remarks**
6/29/04		Return of service July 6, 1904 No answer filed Set for hearing 9/13/04 No apperance[sic] by either party Set for hearing at Muskogee on Feb 2nd 1905 2/2/05 No appearance by defendant. Plaintiff appeared in person, his evidence taken and case given to Lee L Wyley Ind Police Tahlequah, I.T. See report of R. Lee Wyly Mch 31 1905 Instructions not executed and additional instructions sent him 4/1/05 above instructions withdrawn	Cert in file Given S.A. Mills 8/26/04 Cert. returned Allottee in person 9/20/04 Dismissed

Date Received	No.	Allottee	Intruder
June 29-04	121	Thos. S. Brown Collinsville, I.T.	John H. French
Notice Sent		**Action**	**Remarks**
July 1/04		Return of service 7/19-04 Ans. filed Aug 2-04 Case dismissed for want of prosecution	Certificates issued by report of Commission Contest pending See report of Com 9/12/04 Dismissed

35

Cherokee Intruder Cases 1901 - 1909

Date Received	No.	Allottee	Intruder
July 5-1904	122	Perry Rowe	Joseph T. Johnson
Notice Sent		**Action**	**Remarks**
July 6-04 Aug 13-04		Return of service 7/13/04 Answer filed 7/19/04 Set for hearing at Vinita 8-11-04 Plaintiff appeared, defendant did not Dismissed by order of Allottee 9/2/04	Cert in file Certificate delivered to Allottee 9/2/04

Date Received	No.	Allottee	Intruder
July 12- 04	123	Margurate E. McAdoo & Sue Eiffert, by J. T. McAdoo Atty in Fact	Mrs. Georgia Scott
Notice Sent		**Action**	**Remarks**
July 12-04		(No information given.)	Cert in file Settled Same in file Cert return Dr. F McAdoo 7/20/04 Dismissed

Date Received	No.	Allottee	Intruder
July 13-04	124	Sarah C. Alston	Fred & Wm Hockett
Notice Sent		**Action**	**Remarks**
July 15-04		Return of service 7/18/04 Answer file 7/20/04 Given to Cap. West to place Allottee in possession Aug 14-04- Allottee placed in possession by John C. West Aug 15-04	Cert in file. Settled Certificate returned 9/29/04 Dismissed

Date Received	No.	Allottee	Intruder
July 20-1904	125	James M Wade	Lige Kelly
Notice Sent		**Action**	**Remarks**
July 20-04		Return of service 7/20-04 No answer filed Case set to be heard Jan 3/05 Case dismissed for want of prosecution	Cert in file 6/26/05 Certificate returned to Allottee Dismissed

Cherokee Intruder Cases 1901 - 1909

Date Received	No.	Allottee	Intruder
July 20-04	126	W<u>m</u> H. Foreman	John W. Howard
Notice Sent		**Action**	**Remarks**
July 21-04 Return of service 7/27-04		See case # 70. Ans filed 8-2-04 3/13/05 Instructions given Theo E Stidham to place Allottee in possession and report Action to this office. 3/23/05 Report of Theodore Stidham of placing Allottee in possession filed 4/3/05 Report of Theodore Stidham of Mch 22, 1905 that he placed Allottee in possession Mch 22, 1905 Dismissed	Certificates issued by report of Commission

Date Received	No.	Allottee	Intruder
July 25, 1904	127	Thomas R. Gourd	*(No name given)*
Notice Sent		**Action**	**Remarks**
July 25, 1904		Set for hearing at Vinita 8-12-04 Aug 12-04 No appearance by either party <s>Cert ret'd by request of plff see letter in file</s> Dismissed	Cert of allotment in file Given SA Mills 8/29/04 See report of Mills Sept 16-04 9/20/04 Certificate ret'd to Allottee

Date Received	No.	Allottee	Intruder
July 25, 1904	128	Sarah R. Gourd	*(No name given)*
Notice Sent		**Action**	**Remarks**
July 25, 1904		Set for hearing at Vinita 8-13-04 Aug. 12-04 No appearance[sic] by either party Dismissed	Certificates in file Given S.A. Mills 8/29/04 See report of Mills 9/16/04. 9/21/04 Certificate ret'd.

Date Received	No.	Allottee	Intruder
July 25, 1904	129	Mariah R. Gourd	*(No name given)*
Notice Sent		**Action**	**Remarks**
July 25, 1904		Set for hearing at Vinita 8/12/04 Aug 12-04 No appearance[sic] by either party	Certificates in file Given SA Mills 8/29/04 See report of Mills 9/16/04

Cherokee Intruder Cases 1901 - 1909

	9/4/04 Certificate ret'd to Allottee Dismissed

Date Received	No.	Allottee	Intruder
July 25, 1904	130	Eliza R. Gourd	*(No name given)*
Notice Sent	**Action**		**Remarks**
July 25, 1904	Set for hearing at Vinita 8-12-04 Aug 12-04 No appearence[sic] by either party		Certificates in file Given Mills 8/29/04 See report of Mills 9/16/04 9/21/04 Certificate ret'd to Allottee Dismissed

Date Received	No.	Allottee	Intruder
July 26, 04	131	Victoria Arnold	Joe Parkenson
Notice Sent	**Action**		**Remarks**
July 28, 04 Return of service July 30-04	Set for hearing at Vinita 9-12-04 Ans. filed 8-5-04 Settled by agreement of parties concerned Aug 12-04		Cert of allotment in file Settled. 6/26/05 Certificate returned to Allottee Dismissed

Date Received	No.	Allottee	Intruder
July 25, 04	132	S. M. Abbott, for Rosie R. Abbot deceased	M.A. Gibson, D.W. Butts & H. Lenant
Notice Sent	**Action**		**Remarks**
July 28, 04 Return of Service Aug 3-04	Set for hearing at Vinita 8-12-04 Case heard, evidence taken & it is the decision of this office that the Allottee is intitled to possession. Defendant given thirty days to remove his improvements See mem. in file		Cert of allotment in file. Dismissed

Cherokee Intruder Cases 1901 - 1909

Date Received	No.	Allottee	Intruder
July 29-04	133	W<u>m</u> H & Nannie H Durham	Geo W. Eaton, Jim York, & J. D. Sellors[sic]
Notice Sent		**Action**	**Remarks**
July 30-04 Return of Service Aug 4-04		Set for hearing at Vinita 8-12-04 Case heard evidence taken No Action can be taken until ~~evidence~~ Guardian is appointed See mem. in file	Cert. issued by report of Com. Dismissed

Date Received	No.	Allottee	Intruder
July 28-04	134	Minnie V. Souther	Daniel Walker & H.A. Jester
Notice Sent		**Action**	**Remarks**
Aug. 2-04		Ans. filed Aug. 17-04 Return of service Aug. 15-04 Given Policeman *(Illegible)* on 10/6/04	Certificate in file Given SA Mills 8/26/04 See report of Mills Sept 14-1904 Dismissed. 7/14/05 Certificates were turned over to the restriction department

Date Received	No.	Allottee	Intruder
Aug. 4-04	135	Amanda P. Morgan	J.T. Hairston
Notice Sent		**Action**	**Remarks**
Aug. 5-04		Return of service Aug. 12-04 Ans. filed Aug. 15-04 Dismissed by order of Allottee 9/30/04	Certificates in file Certificates given to husband of Allottee in person Jan 13 - 05

Date Received	No.	Allottee	Intruder
Aug. 6-04	136	Ruth B. Evans	Lusian[sic] King
Notice Sent		**Action**	**Remarks**
Aug 6-04		Return of service Aug. 13-04 Ans. filed Aug. 19-04 Case dismissed for want of prosecution	Certificates in file In contest see report Commission dated Aug. 27-04 Nov 9 - Certificates returned

Cherokee Intruder Cases 1901 - 1909

	to A.L. Querry Dismissed

Date Received	No.	Allottee	Intruder
Aug. 5th 1904	137	O.C. Hardin, legal guardian of Altie E. Ross	Rufus Burton
Notice Sent		**Action**	**Remarks**
Notice sent Aug 8/04 Return of service 8-11-04		Ans. filed Aug. 16-04 Case dismissed for want of prosecution	Certf & Letters of guardianship in file- Contest pending 6/26/05 Certificate returned to legal guardian Dismissed

Date Received	No.	Allottee	Intruder
Aug. 10-04	138	Laura Kerr nee Greenfeather	Mrs. S. E. Armstrong
Notice Sent		**Action**	**Remarks**
Aug. 13-04		Return of Service Aug. 24" 1904 ~~3/13/05~~ Certs 8215, 5982 returned to O W Kerr Vinita, I.T. 3/17/05	Cert in file Withdrawn by Laura Kerr by letter dated 8/23/04. Dismissed by order of S.A. Mills *(Illegible)* be enclosed in report

Date Received	No.	Allottee	Intruder
Aug. 4-04	139	Lenora Heapae for minors	Chas. Tritthart
Notice Sent		**Action**	**Remarks**
Aug. 19-04		Return of service 8/29/04 Answer filed 9/3/04 9/25/04 Defendants agree to surrender possession in 20 days next which was granted see communication in file	Certificates in file- Letters of guardianship on file Given S.A. Mills 8/22/04 6/26/05 Certificates returned to legal guardian Dismissed

Cherokee Intruder Cases 1901 - 1909

Date Received	No.	Allottee	Intruder
Aug. 17-04	140	C.E. Holderman for minors	Mrs. Jacob Ross, & others
Notice Sent		**Action**	**Remarks**
Aug. 17-04		Return of service 9/1-04 9/17 Defendants notified to vacate	Certificates in file Given S.A. Mills 8/29/04 10/1/04 Asked Commission to advise whether this land is in contest Contest pending Certificates returned to Guardian 1-27-05 Dismissed

Date Received	No.	Allottee	Intruder
Aug. 17-04	141	C.E. Holderman for minors	David Ross et al
Notice Sent		**Action**	**Remarks**
Aug-17-04		Return of service 8/27/04	Certificates in file Given SA Mills 8/29/04 9/25/04 Defendants notified to vacate 10/1/04 Asked Commission to advise whether this land is in contest Certificates returned to Guardian on 1-27-05 See No 140 Dismissed

Date Received	No.	Allottee	Intruder
Aug. 17-04	142	C.E. Holderman for minors	David Ross et al
Notice Sent		**Action**	**Remarks**
Aug. 17-04		Return of service 8/26/04	Certificates in file Given S.A. Mills 8/29/04 Defendants notified of vacate 10/1/04 Asked Commission to advise whether this land in in contest Certificates returned to Guardian on 1-27-04[sic] See No 140 Dismissed

Cherokee Intruder Cases 1901 - 1909

Date Received	No.	Allottee	Intruder
Aug. 17-04	143	C.E. Holderman for minors	David Ross et al
Notice Sent		**Action**	**Remarks**
Aug. 17-04		Case dismissed for want of prosecution	Certificates in file Given SA Mills 8/29/04 Defendants notified to vacate 10/1/04 Asked Commission whether this land is in contest Certificates returned to Guardian on 1-27-05 See # 140 Dismissed

Date Received	No.	Allottee	Intruder
Aug. 17-04	144	C.E. Holderman for minors	David Ross et al
Notice Sent		**Action**	**Remarks**
Aug. 17-04		Case dismissed for want of prosecution	Certificates in file Given SA Mills 8/29/04 Defendants notified to vacate 10/1/04 Asked Commission whether this land is in contest Certificates returned to Guardian on 1-27-05 See # 140 Dismissed

Date Received	No.	Allottee	Intruder
Aug. 17-04	145	Sarah Wickett	David Williams
Notice Sent		**Action**	**Remarks**
Aug. 17-04		Return of Service Aug. 28" 1904 9/15/04 Defendants given till Oct 15 - 1904 to vacate	Cert issued by report of Com Report requested from Mills 9/2/04 Dismissed

Cherokee Intruder Cases 1901 - 1909

Date Received	No.	Allottee	Intruder
Aug. 17-04	146	Ross Boland	Jake Newport
Notice Sent		**Action**	**Remarks**
Aug. 17-04		Service returned 8/26/04	Cert issued by report of Com
			Given SA Mills 9/3/04
		No service see original notice	10/3/04 See report of SA
		returned from Dead Letter of	Mills
		file Jan 7, 1905	Dismissed

Date Received	No.	Allottee	Intruder
Aug. 17-04	147	Lamech Smith heir & father of Jesse Smith	J. H. Arter
Notice Sent		**Action**	**Remarks**
Aug. 17-04		Return of Service Aug. 29" 1904	Certificates in file
		Set for hearing Sep. 29-04	
		Reset for hearing at Muskogee Feby in 1905	
		2/20/05 Both parties appeared. It was agreed on part of defendant that he would pay the rent as agreed and comply with his contract which was accepted by plaintiff	
			Cert 7954, 9728
		4/11/05 Dismissed	

Date Received	No.	Allottee	Intruder
Aug. 16-04	148	Laura Parris for minors	Joseph Rollings
Notice Sent		**Action**	**Remarks**
Aug. 17-04		(No information given)	Cert issued by report of Com
			Given SA Mills 9/3/04
			Settled by S.A. Mills
			9/26/04

Date Received	No.	Allottee	Intruder
Aug 22" 04	149	J W Foster Guardian of Jessie L Hendricks	W L Lowery, P L Rumsey and Harrison Bears
Notice Sent		**Action**	**Remarks**
Aug. 27" 1904		Return of Service 9/1/04	Certificates in file
		Sent Policeman Chamberlain 9/15/04	Letters of Guardianship filed
		Cert returned to Allottee Dec 7-04	Given SA Mills 9/3/04
		2/18/06 Letters of guardianship returned to	Settled by S.A. Mills
		J.W. Foster, in person -	9/26/04

Cherokee Intruder Cases 1901 - 1909

Date Received	No.	Allottee	Intruder
Aug 24" 1904	150	William H Durham Guardian of Wincie M Durham	James D Sellers Geo. W. Eaton Jim York & Mrs York
Notice Sent		**Action**	**Remarks**
Aug. 27" 04		Return of Service 8/31/04 Answer filed 9/6/07 Set for hearing at Muskogee Oct 7, 1904 at 1:30 PM 10/13-Given to Policeman Chamberlain- Sent Sunday 10/22/04 - See report of Sunday 10/24/04 Dismissed	Certificates in file Letters of Guardianship filed Settled Nov 14 - 1904 Letters of Guardianship and Certificates of Allotment returned.

Date Received	No.	Allottee	Intruder
Aug. 25" 1904	151	Arch E Nelms	J. K. Browning
Notice Sent		**Action**	**Remarks**
Aug 27" 1904		Return of service 9/5/04 Answer filed 9/20/04	Certificates in file Given SA Mills 9/3/04 Settled by report of Mills 9/27/04 Cert returned to Allottee Dec 29/04

Date Received	No.	Allottee	Intruder
Aug. 25" 1904	152	A G Robinson Guar. of Fannie E Robinson	Henry & Lawrence Smith
Notice Sent		**Action**	**Remarks**
Aug 27" 1904		Answer filed 9/12/04 Return of service 8/31/04	Certificates in file Letters of Guardianship issued Given SA Mills 9/4/04 Settled upon application of plaintiff. Certificates returned Nov. 9, 1904

Cherokee Intruder Cases 1901 - 1909

Date Received	No.	Allottee	Intruder
Aug 25" 1904	153	A.G. Robinson Guar-Leander Willis	Henry & Lawrence Smith
Notice Sent		**Action**	**Remarks**
Aug. 27" 1904		Return of service 8/31/04	Certificates in file Letters of Guardianship issued (in file) Given SA Mills 9/3/04 Settled upon application of plaintiff Certificates returned to Allottee

Date Received	No.	Allottee	Intruder
Aug 25" 1904	154	A.G. Robinson Guar-Charles Robinson	F.M. Goatly
Notice Sent		**Action**	**Remarks**
Aug 27" 1904		Answer filed 9/12/04 Return of service 8/31/04	Certificates in file Letters of Guardianship issued (in file) Given SA Mills 9/3/04 Settled upon application of plaintiff Certificates returned to Allottee

Date Received	No.	Allottee	Intruder
Aug 31" 04	155	Nelson Moore	A.G. Wilkerson
Notice Sent		**Action**	**Remarks**
Sept 2" 1904		Return of service 9/10/04 Ans. filed Sept 19, 04 Dismissed upon request of plaintiff See Mills report Cert ret^d to Allottee 6/9/05	Certfs allotment in file Given SA Mills 9/3/04 Settled

Cherokee Intruder Cases 1901 - 1909

Date Received	No.	Allottee	Intruder
Sept 1" 04	156	Annie McNeer (Spybuck)	A W Lord
Notice Sent		**Action**	**Remarks**
Sept 2" 1904		Return of service 9/13/04 3/27/05 Certificate returned to Henny Spybuck who states that land held by defendant is in contest. Dismissed	Given Mills 9/3/04 ~~Certfs issued~~ Certificates in file 10/27/04 Letter asking Commission to advise if any part of said land is in contest November 9, 1904 Nov. 12-Lands all involved in contest by report of Commission

Date Received	No.	Allottee	Intruder
Sept 1" 1904	157	T.J. Daugherty Guar. of Thos Marcus Pheasant	Anderson Rogers
Notice Sent		**Action**	**Remarks**
Sept. 2" 1904		Return of service 9/6/04 See report of S.A. Mills & letter of Guardian 9/3/04	Certfs in file Letters of Guardianship on file Given SA Mills 9/3/04 Settled 6/26/05 - Certificate and letter of guardianship *(Illegible)* & legal guardian

Date Received	No.	Allottee	Intruder
Sept. 3" 1904	158	Julia Brownson	Nan McClarney et al
Notice Sent		**Action**	**Remarks**
Sept. 3" 1904		Return of service 9/10/04 Ans. filed Sept. 19, 04 See report of Mills, A.A. 9/3/04	Certfs. in file Given Mills 9/3/04 Dismissed upon application of Allottee 1-4/05

Cherokee Intruder Cases 1901 - 1909

Date Received	No.	Allottee	Intruder
Sept. 2" 1904	159	Rufus Cochran Guar. of Minor children	Jno. Baldridge et al
Notice Sent		**Action**	**Remarks**
Sept. 3" 1904 Return of Service Sept. 19, 04		Letter of guardianship in file	Certfs in file Given S-A-Mills 9/16/04 9/24/04-Have asked Commission if Contest is pending. Portion in contest see report of Commission Dismissed for want of prosecution

Date Received	No.	Allottee	Intruder
Sep-6-04	160	William Phillips	Henry McClure
Notice Sent		**Action**	**Remarks**
Sept 6-04 Ret of service 9/16/04		Answer filed 9/19/04 Claim contest pending have asked to be advised if contest if pending 10/3/04 In Contest	Letters of Guardianship Cert in file Given S.A. Mills 9/16/04 11/25/04 Certificates returned to Allottee Dismissed for want of prosecution

Date Received	No.	Allottee	Intruder
Aug 25-1904	161	Sallie Manuel	Tailor Eldridge
Notice Sent		**Action**	**Remarks**
Sept. 7-04		Return of service 9/12/04 Answer filed Sept 13, 1904 Case set to be heard Jan. 3rd-05 Continued until Jan 10-05 See memo in file - Certificates ret'd to Sallie Manuel Jan 10-05	Certs in file Letter asking Commission to advise of any part of said land is in contest Nov. 9, 1904 Commission advises that in contests are pending Nov 12, 1904 Dismissed

Cherokee Intruder Cases 1901 - 1909

Date Received	No.	Allottee	Intruder
Set[sic]-6-04	162	C.W. Poole guardian of Walton C & Carlisle Poole	Geo H Wetzel

Notice Sent	Action	Remarks
Sept 8-04 Return of Service Sept. 19, 04	(No information given)	Cert in file Letters of Guardianship on file Given S-A-Mills 9/16/04 Dismissed. see report of Mills 6/26/05 letters of guardianship ret'd

Date Received	No.	Allottee	Intruder
Sep 7-1904	163	Lacie & Sallie Raincrow	W$^{\underline{m}}$ Carpenter

Notice Sent	Action	Remarks
Sep-9-04 Return of Service 9/17/04	Answer filed 9/19/04 4/4/05 Certs N$^{\underline{o}}$ 10382, 12848, 10383, 12850 returned to P E *(Illegible)* Spavinaw, I.T. See letter filed therein	Cert in file Given S-A-Mills 9/16/04 Defendant surrendered possession to Allottee 9/20/04 by report of Mills Dismissed

Date Received	No.	Allottee	Intruder
Sept 9-04	164	Laura E Payne	J.W. Trindle

Notice Sent	Action	Remarks
Sep 12-04	Allottee in possession See report of Mills in file	Cert issued Given S.A. Mills 9/16/04 Settled

Date Received	No.	Allottee	Intruder
Aug 21-1904	165	Maggie Locust	Rev Gilbert Thompson & J.W. Reed

Notice Sent	Action	Remarks
Sep. 14-04 Return of Service 9/20/04	Answer filed 9/29/04 10/14-04 No appearance by plaintiff Dr Fite called and stated that a contest would be filed in this case at once See memorandum in file	Cert issued by report of Commission Set for hearing Oct. 14-1904 Contest Pending Dismissed for want of prosecution

Cherokee Intruder Cases 1901 - 1909

Date Received	No.	Allottee	Intruder
Sep. 12-1904	166	James Sunday for Thomas Sunday	John Johnson et al
Notice Sent		**Action**	**Remarks**
Sep. 17-1904 Return of service 9/20/04		10/17-04 Policeman Roach ordered to place Allottee in possession	Cert in file Given S.A. Mills 9/16/04 Report of S.A. Mills received 10/11-04 Settled Placed in possession by Policeman Roach 10/10/04

Date Received	No.	Allottee	Intruder
Sep 3-1904	167	Mrs Ida Chrismon	James Cooper
Notice Sent		**Action**	**Remarks**
Sep 19-04 Return of service 9/19/04		Answer filed 9/29/04	Cert issued by report of Com Given SA Mills 9/16/04 Oct 10-04 Case dismissed upon recommendation of S.A. Mills who found that defendant was not holding any of the lands of plaintiff and plaintiff so understands

Date Received	No.	Allottee	Intruder
Sept. 14, 1904	168	Zelena Campbell	Emily Walker
Notice Sent		**Action**	**Remarks**
Sept 21, 1904		Return of Service 10/18-04 Answer filed Oct 28th Set for hearing at Vinita Dec 20-04 Set for hearing at Vinita 2/7/05	Certfs in file Letter asking Commission if any part of said land is in contest Nov 9, 1904 Nov. 12 Commission advises no part of lands involved in contests

    2/7/05 Case called. Allottee being present, no appearance on part of defendant
        Plaintiff sworn and testimony taken. Lines are to be correctly located and plat of same furnished Agent.
    2/11/05 Plat filed showing lines and location of buildings
        Case sent to police.

Cherokee Intruder Cases 1901 - 1909

6/1/05 Case settled as shown by letter from plaintiff dated May 27 1905 and certificate # 16034 & 12598 returned to her Timber Hill, I.T.
6/19/05 Allottee acknowledges receipt of certificates
Dismissed

Date Received	No.	Allottee	Intruder
Sept 17, 1904	169	Geo. W. Bushyhead	W. G. Ash
Notice Sent		**Action**	**Remarks**
Sept 21, 1904		Set for hearing at Vinita Dec 20-04 Answer filed 12/13/04 Certs returned to Allottee on the 15 June 1905	Certf in file Letter to Commission asking to advise if lands or any portion thereof be in contest Com reports Nov 17-04 that no portion of land is in contest Settled by order of plaintiff 12/12/04

Date Received	No.	Allottee	Intruder
Sept 19, 1904	170	Tillman Wright and wife, Melinda D. Wright, nee Walkingstick	George Brown
Notice Sent		**Action**	**Remarks**
Sept 27, 1904		Return of service 10/2/04 Case to be heard Jan 3-05 Jan. 4-05 Given Policeman Chamberlain with instructions to place Allottee in possession 2/27/05 Report of Chamberlain filed but returned to Allottee 6/1/05	Certf in file Letter to Commission asking to advise if said lands or any portion thereof be in contest Nov 10, 1904 Com reports Nov 17, no part of land in contest Dismissed

Date Received	No.	Allottee	Intruder
Sept 19, 1904	171	Malissa Ross	Bud McKinley & Green Hamilton
Notice Sent		**Action**	**Remarks**
Sept 21, 1904		Return of service 9/26/04 Set for hearing at Vinita Feb. 7-05 3/6/05 Returned certificate to Allottee in person this day	Certf in file Commission report part in contest Case dismissed for want of prosecution

Cherokee Intruder Cases 1901 - 1909

Date Received	No.	Allottee	Intruder
Sept 19, 1904	172	Amanda Young	J.H. Harwood
Notice Sent	**Action**		**Remarks**
Sept 23, 1904	Return of service 9/26/04 Answer filed 9/30/04 Set for hearing at Vinita Dec 20-21		Certf in file Letter asking Commission if any part of said lands be in contest 11/9/04 Nov 12-Commission advises no part of land in contest Dismissed by plaintiff Atty

2/2/05 Certificate returned upon request to Amanda Young Nowata Ind. Ter.

Date Received	No.	Allottee	Intruder
Sept 20, 1904	173	Frances F Pitts	Jim Sellers
Notice Sent	**Action**		**Remarks**
Sept 23, 1904	Return of service 10/1/04 10/7/04 Defendant called at this office & stated he was not living on the land, nor no one was & Allottee could take possession; She was so advised Certs returned to Allottee 6/1/05 Recpt[sic] ack. of Cert 6/6/05		Certf in file Dismissed 6/1/05

Date Received	No.	Allottee	Intruder
Sept 14, 1904	174	Skillie Vann	Sam R. Saunders
Notice Sent	**Action**		**Remarks**
Sept 23, 1904	Service returned 10/1/04 Ans filed 10/1/04 Case dismissed for want of prosecution		Certf in file Letter asking Commission if any part of said lands are in contest Nov. 9, 1904 Nov 12-Commission advises all the lands in contest Contest Dismissed 6/26/05 Certificate returned to Allottee

Cherokee Intruder Cases 1901 - 1909

Date Received	No.	Allottee	Intruder
Sep 20-04	175	Alex Clapp for Francis & James Clapp	Alex Philpot Henry Eiffert & Bill Fredrick
Notice Sent		**Action**	**Remarks**
Sep 23-04		Oct 13-04 Case settled and dismissed by request of plaintiff	Cert in file Letter asking Commission if any part of said lands be in contest Nov. 9, 1904 Nov. 12 Commission advises no contest 6/26/05 Certificate returned Allottee Dismissed

Date Received	No.	Allottee	Intruder
Sep 9-1904	176	~~Delphia Humatubby~~	~~Mr Carter~~
Notice Sent		**Action**	**Remarks**
Sep 23-04		Case dismissed for want of prosecution	~~Cert issued by report of Com~~ Dismissed

Date Received	No.	Allottee	Intruder
Sep 15-04	177	D W Leerskov gdn. of Mary N. Andrea & Melina N Leerskov	J. T. Barnes
Notice Sent		**Action**	**Remarks**
Sep 23-04		10/3/04 Return of service Dismissed by request of Plaintiff See mem in file	Cert in file No contest by report of Commission Certificates returned by grdn on 3/8/05

Cherokee Intruder Cases 1901 - 1909

Date Received	No.	Allottee	Intruder
Sep 16-04	178	W^m A Cooper gdn of Pegeon[sic] & Joe Sanders	Jacob M Fadden Babe N Reynolds & Sim Whitm*(Illegible)*
Notice Sent		**Action**	**Remarks**
Sep 23-04		10/3/04 Return of Service 10/20/04 Sent Policeman Chamberlain to place guardian in possession	Cert issued by report of Com Contest pending Letter asking Commission to advise if any contest are pending on said lands Nov 9, 1904 Nov 9 All lands in contests Dismissed

Date Received	No.	Allottee	Intruder
Sep 21, 1904	179	Alice M Vandergriff nee Remson	W^m H Doherty & Frank Adams
Notice Sent		**Action**	**Remarks**
9/24/04		10/3/04 Return of Service Answer filed 10/1/04 10/6/04 Asked the Cherokee Land Office to advise if land is contested 10/12-04 Commission advises that a part of said land is involved in contest proceedings Set for hearing at Vinita Feb 7-05	Cert in file

2/7/05 Case called. Husband appeared as agent of plaintiff who admits that only 20 acres involved in complaint which is yet in contest before Commission. Certificates returned this day to Lee Vandergriff in person, and case dismissed
                                                                                     Dismissed

Date Received	No.	Allottee	Intruder
Sep 21-04	180	Wattie Greece	Ed & Mary Suagerty
Notice Sent		**Action**	**Remarks**
9/24/04		return of service 9/28/04	Cert in file Cert returned Allottee 10/1/04 Settled Defendants have vacated

Cherokee Intruder Cases 1901 - 1909

Date Received	No.	Allottee	Intruder
Sep 13-1904	181	Walter H Hawkins	Ella Bryant

Notice Sent	Action	Remarks
Sep 26-04	Set for hearing at Vinita Dec. 20-04	Cert issued by report of Com no contest 9/20/04
	Return of service Dec 21-04	
	Dec 21-04 Case heard. Plaintiff appeared Defendant did not. Plaintiffs	
2/27/05 Partial report of Chamberlain filed -further to follow	evidence taken decided that Allottee is intitled to possession Ready for Police Sent Chamberlain Jan 10/05	
	2/18/05 Case dismissed and report of Com as to allotment returned to Sam Hawkins in person	

Date Received	No.	Allottee	Intruder
Sep 23-04	182	Eldrigde[sic] Newton gdn. of (Illegible) C Newton	John Ragsdale

Notice Sent	Action	Remarks
Sep 17-04	Letters of Guardianship on file	Cert in file
Return of service	Ans. filed Oct 10/04	Oct 27 Nov 17 Commission
Oct 5-04	10/20 Asked Com. to advise if contest is pending	advises no part of land in Contest
	Case set to be heard Jan 4-05	
	Jan 4 - 05 Case heard: decided that Allottee is intitled to possession	
	Jan 4 - 05 Given to policeman Thompson with instructions to place Allottee in possession	
	2/14/05 Letter requesting return of papers Dismissed and Certificate & guardianship papers returned	

Date Received	No.	Allottee	Intruder
Sep 28-04	183	Andy Cordry, guardian of Beula Pettet[sic]	Bill Choate & O Jackson

Notice Sent	Action	Remarks
Sep 28-04	Letters of guardianship on file	Cert in file
	10/3/04 Return of Service	Contest
	10/7/04 Asked Commission to advise if land is in contest	
4/28/05	Plaintiff appeared in person and stated contest had been decided in

Cherokee Intruder Cases 1901 - 1909

his favor and that he was in possession of land, and certificates N⁰ 14530, 18966 and guardianship papers were returned to him.
Dismissed

Date Received	No.	Allottee	Intruder
Sep 21-04	184	Georgie K Pope, gdn of Clem W. Roberst[sic] S & Madalyn Pope	W. A. Lesley
Notice Sent		**Action**	**Remarks**
9/29/04		Letters of guardianship on file 10/3/04 Return of Service Answer filed Oct 6/04 Case set to be heard Jan 4-05 Jan 4 - 05 Case heard: decided that Allottee is intitled to possession Jan 4 - 05 Given Policeman Thompson with instructions to place Allottee in possession of her land	Cert in file Letter asking Commission if any part of said land is in contest Nov 9 -1904 Nov 12 Commission advises no contest 2/27/05 Ex policeman Thompson reports that he placed Allottee in possession and made report to this office
	3/1/05	Letter received from Plaintiff requesting return of certificates & guardianship paper. Sent certificates N⁰ˢ 8026, 5832, 5831, 8025, 8024, 5830, and grdship pa[sic] to Georgia K Pope Tahlequah, I.T.	

Date Received	No.	Allottee	Intruder
Sept. 30" 1904	185	Jerry Vann	Mary ~~Nancy~~ Calwell
Notice Sent		**Action**	**Remarks**
10/3/04		Return of service 10/7/04 Answer filed 10/8/04 Case dismissed for want of prosecution	Certfs in file 10/14-04 Commission asked to advise if contest proceeding involving any portion of said allotment Oct 20-Commission advises part of land contested by Mary Calwell 6/26/05 Certificate retnd to Allottee Dismissed

Cherokee Intruder Cases 1901 - 1909

Date Received	No.	Allottee	Intruder
Sept. 30" 1904	186	Mary Lowery	D.C. Kenyon
Notice Sent		**Action**	**Remarks**
10/3/04		Return of service 10/17-04 Answer filed 10/18/04 Set for hearing at Vinita 2/7/05 2/7/05 Case called. No appearance by either party 2/10/05 Com. reports that plaintiff has relinquished all her right to the land embraced in complaint and case is therefore dismissed	Certfs. in file Oct. 24-Commission advises part of land in contest

Date Received	No.	Allottee	Intruder
Sept. 30" 1904	187	W<u>m</u> H Miller c/o Geo. E. M<u>c</u>Culloch	Ben Jarbo et al
Notice Sent		**Action**	**Remarks**
10/3/04		Return of service Oct 20, 1904 10/24-Asked Com to advise if contest is pending Answer filed Oct 17 Case set for hearing Nov 25-04 Case heard & it was decided that Allottee is intitled to possession (See mem. in file) Defendant given until Dec. 5<u>th</u> to remove his possession	Certfs. in file Oct 27-Commission advises no part of land in contest 4/6/05 Certificates N<u>os</u> 18529, 14238 returned to W<u>m</u> H Miller in person

Date Received	No.	Allottee	Intruder
Sept. 30, 1904	188	Andrew Tyson legal guardian of Lillie B Tyson	----- Craig et al
Notice Sent		**Action**	**Remarks**
Oct 3, 1904		Return of Service 10/12-04 Answer filed 10/12-04 10/24-Asked Com. to advise if contest is pending 4/13/05 Letters of guardianship returned to plaintiff also certificates of allotment N<u>os</u> 10608, 8636	Letter of Guardianship- Certfs of allotment in file Oct. 27 Commission advises all lands in contest Contest Dismissed as all of lands in in contest <u>Dismissed</u>

Cherokee Intruder Cases 1901 - 1909

Date Received	No.	Allottee	Intruder
Aug 10, 1904	189	C.V. McGaw legal guardian of Rinty and Minnie Catcher	Thos McGarty and Robert Bearden

Notice Sent	Action	Remarks
Oct. 3, 1904 Return of service Oct 12, 1904	Dismissed: See mem. in file	Letters of Guardianship and Certfs of al[sic] Returned in file

Date Received	No.	Allottee	Intruder
Oct 6, 1904	190	John G Butler for Mary U. E. Butler	John McDougal

Notice Sent	Action	Remarks
Oct 8/04	Return of Service 10/18-04 Answer filed Oct 20, 1904 Set for hearing at Vinita Dec 20-04 Dec. 20-04 Case heard: evidence taken No Action taken Allotee instructed to have a blue *(Illegible)* made and he would be placed in possession at once Defendant agreed to vacate within ten days from date Certificates returned to Allottee 6/27/05	Certfs & Letters of Guardianship in file 10/18-04 Commission asked to advise if any portion of said land was involved in contest proceedings Oct 22-Commission advises no part of land in any contest Dismissed

Date Received	No.	Allottee	Intruder
Oct 3, 1904	191	Sallie Manuel for Bessie McCullough	Taylor Eldridge

Notice Sent	Action	Remarks
Oct 8, 1904 Return of service 10/20/04	Answer filed Oct. 20 Case set to be heard Jan 3-05 Dismissed See mem in file	Certf in file Answer filed Oct. 20 Letter asking Commission to advise if any portion of said land is in contest 11/9/04 Nov. 12-Commission advises no part of land in contest Certificates ret'd to Sallie Manuel Jan 11-05

Cherokee Intruder Cases 1901 - 1909

Date Received	No.	Allottee	Intruder
Oct 6, 1904	192	Louisa Bean for Murphy Bean	John Foge[sic] & Jack Mchale

Notice Sent	Action	Remarks
Oct 10, 1904	Answer filed 10/19-04 Return of service October 18th 1904 Case dismissed for want of prosecution	Certfs in file Oct. 24-Commission advises part of land in contest 6/26/05 Certificates retnd to Allottee Dismissed

Date Received	No.	Allottee	Intruder
Oct 6, 1904	193	F. O. McCaffree for Anna L Byrd	Joseph Faulk

4/28/05 - Com requested to advise as to contest ~~and~~
5/18/05   Instructions issued to Elijah Henderson to place Allottee in possession and report his Action to this office
5/24/05   Report of Henderson filed

Notice Sent	Action	Remarks
Oct 10, 1904 Return of service Oct 24/04 Dec 21-04	Answer filed Nov. 4-04 Set for hearing at Vinita Dec 20-04 Plaintiff appeared Defendant did not Plaintiffs evidence taken Defendants Atty was present and was told to have his client at Muskogee on Tuesday Dec 27-04 so his evidence could be taken Dismissed Dec report of Chamberlain filed in N° 212 Certificate returned 4/4/05 N° 9892, 12146	Certf & Letters of Curatorship[sic] in file Letter asking Commission to advise of any part of said land is being contested Nov 9, 1904 Nov. 12-Commission advises no part of land in contest See 212- Jan 10/05-Asked Com if land is in contest Report of Commission advises contests filed Jan 14

Date Received	No.	Allottee	Intruder
Sep 3-1904	194	Robert Allen gdn of Marcellus & Isom M. Allen	Henry Kerr & Geo Maynard

Notice Sent	Action	Remarks
Oct 10 -04	Letters of guardianship on file Return of service 10/17-04 Answer filed 10/18/04	Cert in file Oct. 21st Commission

Cherokee Intruder Cases 1901 - 1909

Dec 5 -04	Case: Set for hearing Dec 5-04 Case heard: Defendant Kerr agreed to surrender possession other defendant did not appear nor anyone on his behalf. It is the dicision[sic] of this office that the Guar. is intitled to possession Given Capt. West with instructions to place Allottee in possession Dec. 6-04 Allottee placed in possession by Thos E Stidham Jan 20-	advised no part of land in Contest Dismissed 6/26/05 Certificates returned

Date Received	No.	Allottee	Intruder
Oct 8-04	195	Lewis W. Lyman	Wm Osborne
Notice Sent		**Action**	**Remarks**
Oct 10-04		Return of service Dec 8-04 Set for hearing at Vinita Dec. 20-04	Cert in file
	Dec 20-04	Plaintiff appeared Defendant did not. Plaintiffs evidence taken decided that Allottee is intitled to possession Ready for Police Sent to Policeman Chamberlain Jan 10/05 6/26/05 Certificates returned to Allottee	Dismissed

Date Received	No.	Allottee	Intruder
Oct 8-04	196	Thomas Davis legal heir of Chancey Davis	Blake & Ann Johnson

Apr. 15-07 Dfndt advised no action can be taken by this office

May 31 - 06 Plaintiff requests that the names of W^m and Napoleon Davis and Bud Slaughter and Martha Stout be added to the Dfdts in this case JS Davenport Atty Vinita IT
May 24/06 Order of Court filed by Plaintiff
  "   29 "   Com^r reports that Dfdts have been finally rejected
June 7/ "   Defendants directed to vacate at once otherwise an order will be issued to remove then
June 14/ "   Plaintiff reports that Dfdts will not vacate
June 16/ "   Instructions issued to Policeman W^m M Sunday to place ptf in possession
  Nov 9, 1906 Policeman Sunday requested to report
  Nov 13, 1906 Policeman Sunday reports placing plntf in possession June 29, 1906
  Nov 15, 1906 Case dismissed for want of prosecution. See report in Cherokee $^\#$762

Cherokee Intruder Cases 1901 - 1909

Notice Sent	Action	Remarks
Oct 10-04	Return of service Oct. 20, 1904 Answer filed Oct. 22 Set for hearing at Vinita Dec 21-04	Asked Commission if contest on land Oct 24-Commission advises no part of land in contest
Dec 21-04	Case heard: all parties in[sic] interested being present & No Action taken	Continued one day Commission reports no contest Jan 15, 1905
	4/26/05 Case held up pending instruction from the Department Action withheld, defendants being a Cherokee freedman	
May 5th 06	In accordance with instruction from The Department of the Interior of April 19th 1906 Com^r to the Five Civ Tribes requested to advise this office as to the status of allotment of Chancey Davis	
May 24	Decree of US Court determining heirship filed by Plaintiff	

Date Received	No.	Allottee	Intruder
Oct 13-04	197	Dave L Guyette, legal guardian of Edith B, William B, Maggie D and Lena Payne, and as Attorney for James M. Payne, adult.	Jack Mills, by William Mills

Notice Sent	Action	Remarks
Oct 13-04	Return of Service	Certificate in file Letter of guardianship in file Letter asking Commission if any part of said land is in Contest, Nov. 9, 1904 Nov. 12 Commission advises no contests Dismissed

Date Received	No.	Allottee	Intruder
Oct 14-04	198	Mack Collier	Sam Roberts

Notice Sent	Action	Remarks
Oct. 14-04	Return of service Oct. 17, 1904 Answer filed Oct 20-04 Set for hearing at Vinita Dec 21-04 Dec. 22. Plaintiff reports he has possession	Certificate in file 10/14-04 Commission asked to advise if said land or any portion thereof was being contested Oct. 20th Commission advises no part of land

Cherokee Intruder Cases 1901 - 1909

	involved in contest
	Dismissed
	Certificates returned
	Jan 14, 1905, to Allottee

Date Received	No.	Allottee	Intruder
Oct 14, 1904	199	John Timpson	John Gillstrap
Notice Sent	**Action**		**Remarks**
Oct. 25, 1904	Return of Service 11/12/04		Certificates on file 10/25/04
	Case set to be heard Jan 4-05		Ask Commission if land is in
	Dismissed See mem in file		contest proceedings 10/27/04
			11/3-04 Commission advises no contest pending

Date Received	No.	Allottee	Intruder
Oct 12, 1904	200	Lillie A Rhodes	C. H. Franks
Notice Sent	**Action**		**Remarks**
Oct 25, 1904	Return of service Nov 13-04		
	Set for hearing at Vinita Dec. 21-04		
Dec 21-04	Defendant appeared Plaintiff did not		
	Defendant states that he is not in possession		
	Set for hearing at Vinita Feb 7-05		
2/7/05	Case called. No appearance by either party		
2/9/05	Letter received from defendant stating he is not in possession. A letter relative to the matter in reply to be written from Gen Office		
	See memo in file		
	Dismissed		

Date Received	No.	Allottee	Intruder
Oct. 21, 1904	201	Rider Rattler for Lillie Rattler	T. P. Fortenberry, et al
Notice Sent	**Action**		**Remarks**
Oct. 25, 1904	Return of Service 10/31		Certificates on file 10/26/04
	Given policeman Stedham with instructions to place Allottee in possession		No contest pending
			Dismissed
			No report of policeman Stedham

Cherokee Intruder Cases 1901 - 1909

Date Received	No.	Allottee	Intruder
Oct 17 '04	202	Sarah Crutchfield for self & Mary "	George Moorehead
Notice Sent		**Action**	**Remarks**

Oct 21, '04		Return of Service Nov. 7, '04
		Answer filed Nov 11, '04
			Certificates on file
			Letter to Commission asking if any cases are pending
			    Oct. 27, 1904
			10/31/04 Commission advises that all of Sarah Crutchfield's land in contest & part of Mary's
			6/26/05 Certificate returned to Allottee
			    Dismissed

Date Received	No.	Allottee	Intruder
Oct. 19, 1904	203	Walter Smith for Rachel, Amanda A. and Mary E. do	James McCulloch
Notice Sent		**Action**	**Remarks**

Oct. 27, 1904
 	
Dec 21-04
		Return of Service 11/9/04
		Set for hearing at Vinita Dec 21-04
		Settled by agreement of parties concerned
		See mem in file
			Certificates in file
			Asked Commission if any contest are pending
			Oct. 27 1904
			11/2/04-No part of land in contest
			Cert returned to Allottee
			    Dec 21-04
			    Settled

Date Received	No.	Allottee	Intruder
Oct 19, 1904	204	Walter Smith for minor son Datus Smith	Daniel Freeman
Notice Sent		**Action**	**Remarks**
Oct 27, 1904 Dec 21-04		Return of Service Nov 1, 1904 Set for hearing at Vinita Dec 21-04 Plaintiff states that he is in possession	Certificates on file Asks Commission if any contests are pending Oct. 27, 1904 10/31/04-Commission advises no contest pending

Cherokee Intruder Cases 1901 - 1909

	Certs returned in person to Walter Smith 5/8/05 Settled

Date Received	No.	Allottee	Intruder
Oct 19, 1904	205	Walter Smith for Isaac and Call cay al Smith minors	W. W. Breedlove
Notice Sent	**Action**		**Remarks**
Oct. 27, 04 Dec 21-04	Return of Service 11/17-04 Set for hearing at Vinita Dec 21-04 Dismissed by request of Plaintiff		Certificates on file Asks Commission if there are any contests pending Oct. 27, 1904 10/31/04 Commission advises no contests pending Cert returned to Allottee Dec 21-04 Settled

Date Received	No.	Allottee	Intruder
Oct 19, 1904	206	Millard F. Hicks	John Partain
Notice Sent	**Action**		**Remarks**
Oct. 27, 1904 Dec 22-04	Return of Service 11/7/04 Set for hearing at Vinita Dec 21-04 Case heard: evidence taken Decided that Allottee is intitled to possession		Certificates on file Asks Commission if there are contests pending Oct. 27, 1904 11/2/04-No part of land included in complaint is in contest Cert returned to Allottee Dec 22-04 Dismissed

Date Received	No.	Allottee	Intruder
Oct 19, 1904	207	Martha L Hyatt nee Walker	Tennessee Trammell
Notice Sent	**Action**		**Remarks**
Oct 27, 1904	Case set to be heard Jan 4-04[sic] Allottee in possession by report of Defendant received Dec 22, 1904		Certificate on file Asks Commission if any contests are pending

Cherokee Intruder Cases 1901 - 1909

	Plaintiff advised he has possession, on Dec 30	Oct. 27, 1904 10/31/04 -Com advises no contest pending 6/26/05 Certificates returned to Allottee[sic] Settled !

Date Received	No.	Allottee	Intruder
Oct 1, 1904	208	Henry D. Nave	Benj. Bryan
Notice Sent		**Action**	**Remarks**
Oct. 27, '04 12/19		Return of Service Nov. 7, 1904 Answer filed Nov. 10, 1904 Set for hearing Dec 24-04 Dismissed on aplication[sic] of Plaintiff and Certificates returned	Certificates on file Asks Commission if any contests are pending Oct 27, 1904 11/2/04-Com advises no contest pending Agreed by Plaintiff that defendant shall remain in possession until Jan 1-1905 See memorandum attached to answer Dismissed

Date Received	No.	Allottee	Intruder
Oct 18, 1904	209	William B. Cline by father Ezekial Cline	Frederick Nemise
Notice Sent		**Action**	**Remarks**
Oct 27, 1904		Nov 9th-Letter from father of Allottee asking that case be dismissed Certificates returned 9/11/04[sic] Return of Service Jan	Certificates on file Asks Commission if any cases are pending Oct 27, 1904 Oct. 31-No contests pending Dismissed!

Date Received	No.	Allottee	Intruder
Oct 18, 1904	210	Charles Clark	Jake Haymon
Notice Sent		**Action**	**Remarks**
Oct 27, 1904		Return of Service 11/5/04 Case set to be heard Jan 4-05	Certificates on file. Asks Commission if any contests are pending

Cherokee Intruder Cases 1901 - 1909

		Plaintiff advises he has possession of land Jan 18	Certificates returned to Allottee Jan 25, 1905 Dismissed!

Date Received	No.	Allottee	Intruder
Oct. 17, 1904	211	Daniel Frazier	Oscar Hayes
Notice Sent		**Action**	**Remarks**
Oct. 27, '04		Case set to be heard Jan 5-'05 Settled see memo in file	Certificates on file Asks Commission if any contests are pending Oct. 27, 1904 10/31/04-Commission advise no contest is pending Cert returned to Allottee Dec 4-04

Date Received	No.	Allottee	Intruder
Oct. 15, 1904	212	Georgia C. McCaffree	Joseph Faulk
Notice Sent		**Action**	**Remarks**
Oct. 27, '04		Notice served, 11/9/04 Answer filed Nov. 18-1904 Set for hearing at Vinita Dec 21-04	Certificates on file Asks Commission if any contests are pending Oct. 27 '04
	2-27-05	Instructions sent to A.F. Chamberlain to place Allottee in possession and report Action to this office 3/28/05 Report of Chamberlain filed stating that Allottee was in possession & case dismissed and certificates returned in this and Case 193 4/4/05 Certs N° 12144, 9890.	No part of land in the complaint is in contest See #193 Jan 10/05 Letter to Com asking if land is in contest Commission reports on Jan. 14 that there are no contests pending See report in [sic] Dismissed

Date Received	No.	Allottee	Intruder
Oct 27, 1904	213	Susie Fox, for Lucinda Fox	A. W. Erwing
Notice Sent		**Action**	**Remarks**
Oct. 31, 1904		~~Notice sent 11/5/04~~ Return of service Dec 2-04	Certificates of allotment on file

Cherokee Intruder Cases 1901 - 1909

Set for hearing Jan 5-05	Asks Commission if any portion of said lands are in contest 11/9/04
	Nov. 12 Commission advises no part of land in contest
	<u>Dismissed</u>
	For disposition of Certificates see Case #214

Date Received	No.	Allottee	Intruder
Oct. 27, 1904	214	Susie Fox	J. N. Erwing
Notice Sent		**Action**	**Remarks**
Oct. 31, 1904		~~Notice sent 11/5/04~~	Certificates on file
		Return of service Dec. 2-04	Letter asking Commission to
		Ans filed Dec. 6-04	advise of any part of said
		Set for hearing Dec. 24-04	lands be in contest
	Dec. 21-04	Case heard decided that Allottee is intitled to possession	Nov 9, 1904 Commission advises no part of land in contest
			Nov 12/04
			~~See #193~~
			Jan 12/05 - ~~Asked Com if land is in contest~~
		Dismissed upon statement of her sister Eliza Fox to whom Certifs N° 6705, 5525 were reclaimed in person this 13<u>th</u> day of March 1905 to whom also was delivered copy of contract	

Date Received	No.	Allottee	Intruder
Oct 21, 1904	215	C. C. Roberts for Edna & Amy Roberts	Sam Williams
Notice Sent		**Action**	**Remarks**
Oct 31/04		Set for hearing at Vinita Dec. 21-04	Certificates of allotment and
	Dec 21-04	Settled by agreement	letters of guardianship on file
	May 4<u>th</u>	Lease contract which was filed in this case is transferred to Case #1158	Letter asking Commission to advise if said lands are in
	5-7-08	Copy of testimony mailed to W<u>m</u> H. Hall at Claremore, Okla	contest Nov 9, 1904 Nov 12-Commission advises no part of land in contest

Cherokee Intruder Cases 1901 - 1909

			Cert returned to Allottee Dec. 21-04

Date Received	No.	Allottee	Intruder
Oct. 28, 1904	216	Betsey Axton nee Captain	P.D. Kirk and A. M. Gott Glass & Weaver Attys for plaintiff
Notice Sent		**Action**	**Remarks**
Oct. 31, 1904		Return of Service Nov. 4 Set for hearing at Vinita Dec. 21-04 Set for hearing at Vinita 2/7/05	Certificate of allotment on file Letter asks Commission to advise if any part of said lands be in contest Nov 9, 1904
	2/7/05	Case Called. No appearance by either party. Set for hearing at Claremore, I.T. April 18, 1905 at 9 A.M. 4/18/05 Case called. Upon written statement filed stating that all differences had been settled by new lease and agreement and case was	Nov 12-Commission advises no part of land in contest

Dismissed |
| | | Certificate No 14324 returned to counsel for plntiff[sic]. | |

Date Received	No.	Allottee	Intruder
Oct. 29, 1904	217	Julia Hall	William Lynch
	Jan. 30 06	Letter in depson[sic] dept sustaining agents decision	
Notice Sent		**Action**	**Remarks**
Oct. 31, 1904		Return of Service 11/5/04 Answer filed 11/12/04 Set for hearing at Vinita Dec. 21-04	Certificate of allotment on file Asks Commission to advise
	Dec 17-04	Case heard evidence taken all parties in interest being present Decided that Allottee is intitled to possession Ready for Police	if any portion of said lands are in contest Nov 9, 1904 Commission advises no part of land in contest Nov 12, 1904
	Dec. 23-04	Protest filed by Defendant Jan 11-05 Papers transmitted to Dept. for instructions Sent Chamberlain Jan 10/05	3-29-05 Report of Arthur F Chamberlain filed stating that Allottee was in full possession of allotment and he requests that certificates of allotment be returned. 3/30/05 N°s 14178, 11328

Cherokee Intruder Cases 1901 - 1909

				retnd to Allottee
				Case dismissed

Date Received	No.	Allottee	Intruder
Oct. 25, 1904	218	Eliza & Ella Ratcliff	James Colbert
			defendant claims to be Cherokee freedman

Notice Sent	Action	Remarks
Oct. 31, 1904	Return of Service 11/7/04	Certificates of allotment on file
	Answer filed 11/16/04	
	Set for hearing at Vinita Dec 23-04	Letter asking Commission if any portion of said lands is in contest Nov 9, 1904
Dec 23-04	Case heard-All parties in interest being present ~~Defendant was~~	
See #436	See mem in file	Nov. 12-Commission advises no contest pending
	Held under Departmental instructions of Mch 7, 1905	
	Cherokee freedman case	Certs N° 22074, 22073, 16398, 16397 returned to Jeff Evans husband not father of children
June 12	Case dismissed for want of prosecution	
	See #436	4/24/05 & case dismissed

Date Received	No.	Allottee	Intruder
Oct. 24, 1904	219	Ann Eliza Gray	T. A. Wood

Notice Sent	Action	Remarks
Oct. 31, 1904	Answer filed 11/10/14	Certificate of allotment on file
	Return of service Nov. 28-04	
	Set for hearing at Vinita Dec 23-04	Letter asking Commission if any portion of said land is in contest Nov. 9, 1904
Dec. 23-04	Dismissed by request of Plaintiff's Atty	
		Nov. 12-Commission advises no part of land in contest
		6/26/05 Certificate returned to Allottee
		Dismissed

Cherokee Intruder Cases 1901 - 1909

Date Received	No.	Allottee	Intruder
Oct. 24, 1904	220	Nellie Larey	John Trueman and John R Young
Notice Sent		**Action**	**Remarks**
Oct 31, 1904 Dec 23-04		Return of service Nov 28-04 Ans. filed Nov. 29-04 Set for hearing at Vinita Dec 23-04 Dismissed by request of Plaintiff's Atty	Certificate of allotment on file Letter asking Commission to advise if any portion of said land is in contest Nov 9 1904 No. 12-Commission advises no lands in contest 6.26.05 Certificates returned to Allottee

Date Received	No.	Allottee	Intruder
Nov 1-04	221	Andrew A Brown for James B., Lilly M., Wm M. & Myrtle Brown	W^{m} J & George Bright
Notice Sent		**Action**	**Remarks**
Nov 1-04		Return of service Nov 2nd/04 Defendants called in person & presented a lease Set for hearing 1/5/05 Dec 25, Plaintiff asks case to be dismissed	Certificates in file Letter asking Commission if any portion of said lands be in contest Nov. 9, 1904 Nov. 12-Commission advises no contests in said lands pending 1/6/05 Dismissed see memorandum in file Cert returned to Allottee Jan. 5, '05

Date Received	No.	Allottee	Intruder
Oct. 29, 1904	222	Switch Foreman for Effer E, Mary E, & Nettie E	J.F. & C.M. McClellan
Notice Sent		**Action**	**Remarks**
Nov. 2, '04 Dec. 23-04		Nov. 9-Return of Service Answer filed 11/10 Set for hearing at Vinita Dec. 23-04 Dismissed by personal request of Plaintiff	Certificates of allotment in file Letters of guardianship in file Letter asking Commission if there are any portions of said land in contest 11/9/04

Cherokee Intruder Cases 1901 - 1909

	Nov. 12-Commission advises no part of land in contest Cert returned to Allottee Dec. 23-04

Date Received	No.	Allottee	Intruder
Nov. 2, 1904	223	Riley Keys, for Riley V. Keys	Arthur Hodges
Notice Sent		**Action**	**Remarks**
Nov. 4, 1904		Return of Service 11/9/04 Set for hearing 1/5/05 Dismissed see mem. in file	Certificates of allotment in file Letter asking Commission if any portion of said lands be in contest 11/9/04 Commission advises no part of land in contest Cert. returned to Allottee Dec. 28-04 Dismissed Dec. 14, '04 Certificates returned

Date Received	No.	Allottee	Intruder
Nov. 2, 1904	224	Jane Byrd by Edward Byrd	Rosa Blackwell and tenants
Notice Sent		**Action**	**Remarks**
Nov. 4, 1904		Return of service 11/12/04 Set for hearing at Vinita Dec 23-04	Certificate exhibited Letter asking Commission if any portion of said lands be in contest 11/9/04 Nov. 12-Commission advises no contests pending 12/13-04-N^2 of N^2 of NW^4 of Sec 32-24-17 Designated by R.C. Adams as surplus holdings- Dismissed.

70

Cherokee Intruder Cases 1901 - 1909

Date Received	No.	Allottee	Intruder
Nov. 2nd, 1904	225	David L. Carey	Samuel G. Victor
Notice Sent		**Action**	**Remarks**
Nov. 7, 1904		Ans. filed Nov. 23-04 Return of service No. 19/04 Set for hearing at Vinita Dec. 23-04 Dec. 23-04 Dismissed by request of Plaintiff	Certificates of allotment on file Asks Commission if any part of land is in contest Com reports Nov. 14-04, No portion of land in contest Cert returned to Allottee Dec. 23-04

Date Received	No.	Allottee	Intruder
Nov. 2nd, '04	226	John T. Fletcher for Nora Fletcher	Emmette Blevins
Notice Sent		**Action**	**Remarks**
Nov. 7, 1904		Set for hearing 1/5/05 Given to Chamberlain on Jan. 6, 1905 Jan. 13 - Instructions to policeman withdrawn Plaintiff notified by wire that defendant has moved	Certificates of allotment on file Asks Commission if any part of land is in contest Com reports Nov. 14-04 No portion of land in contest 6/26/05 - Certificates returned to Allottee Dismissed!

Date Received	No.	Allottee	Intruder
Nov. 7-1904	227	Ada G. Eaton	John and Walter Simpson
Notice Sent		**Action**	**Remarks**
Nov. 16-1904		Return of service Nov. 25-04 Ans. filed Nov. 28-04 Set for hearing 1/6/05 Jan 5th Attorney for plaintiff requests case dismissed as defendants have moved 5/20/05. Certs returned to Ada G Smith Moody, I.T. N°s 15738, 15737, 20895	Certificates in file Commission asked if contest pending as to any portion of said land 11/16-04 Com. reports that no portion of land is in contest Dismissed!

Cherokee Intruder Cases 1901 - 1909

Date Received	No.	Allottee	Intruder
Nov 7-04	228	Elizabeth Sturdivant	Dee Brown
Notice Sent		**Action**	**Remarks**
Nov. 16-1904		Case: Settled by request of plaintiff Nov. 23-04 Jan. 5th p[sic] 4/4/05 Certs 12855 returned to Allottee Cherokee City Ark.	Certificates in file 11/16-04 Commission asked if contest pending as to any portion of said land Com. reports no portion of land in contest Nov. 22-04 Settled

Date Received	No.	Allottee	Intruder
Nov. 7-04	229	Wattie Polecat for Isaac Polecat	W.R. and Thomas Flood
Notice Sent		**Action**	**Remarks**
Nov. 16-1904		Return of service Nov. 28-04 Set for hearing 1/6/04[sic] Answer filed Dec. 22-1904 Reset for hearing at Muskogee, I.T. Feby 20, 1905. June 26 ~~Aug 30-05~~ Case dismissed by Allottee is *(Illegible)* and has as gdn. Allottee acknowledges receipt of her certificate 7/5/05	Certificates in file 11/16-04. Commission asked if any contest now pending as to any portion of said land. Com. reports no portion of land in contest Nov. 22-04 6/26/05- Certificates returned to Allottee Dismissed

Date Received	No.	Allottee	Intruder
Nov. 8-1904	230	Sarah Tyner for Della and Daniel Tyner	J. B. Perry
Notice Sent		**Action**	**Remarks**
Nov. 16-1904		Return of service Nov. 22-04 Set for hearing at Vinita Dec 23-04 Set for hearing at Vinita 2/8/05 2/8/05 Commission advises by wire that all lands embraced in complaint are in contest, and case is dismissed.	Certificates in file 11/16-04 Commission asked if contest pending as to any portion of said land Com. reports a portion of land is in contest Nov. 22-04 Dismissed

Cherokee Intruder Cases 1901 - 1909

Date Received	No.	Allottee	Intruder
Nov. 9-1904	231	Jennie Buford for Walter and Johnson Buford	Thomas D. Sexton and Son
Notice Sent		**Action**	**Remarks**
Nov. 16-1904		Return of service Nov. 22-04 Ans. filed Nov. 22-04 Set for hearing at Vinita Dec 23-04 Dec 23-04 Dismissed: Plaintiff states that he is in possession	Certificates issued by report of Commission, see letter to Commission in case #282

Date Received	No.	Allottee	Intruder
Oct. 27-1904	232	Samuel F Edmonds for himself and Bessie, Beulah A, Hazel D. and Emma B. Edmonds	George N. Gaberile
Notice Sent		**Action**	**Remarks**
Nov. 16- 1904		Return of service Nov. 29-04 Set for hearing at Vinita Dec. 23-04 Dec 23-04 Case heard Decided that Allottee is intitled to possession 2/23/05 Case dismissed for want of prosecution upon personal application of plaintiff.	10/31-04, Commission requested to advise if certificates have been issued and if any portion of said land was being contested. 11/9-04 Commission reports certificates issued and no contest was pending as to said land

Date Received	No.	Allottee	Intruder
Nov 10-1904	233	William M. Gillespie	F. I. Hill
Notice Sent		**Action**	**Remarks**
Nov 16-1904		Return of service Nov 22-04 Ans. filed Nov 29-04 Set for hearing at Vinita Dec 23-04 Dec 23-04 Case heard: Defendant did not appear. Decided that Allottee is intitled to possession Ready for Police Sent Chamberlain Jan 10-05 to place Allottee in poss 2/17/05 Chamberlain reports allottee is in possession by means of a *(illegible)* satisfactory to her.	Certificates in file 11/16-04 Commission asked if any portion of said land was being contested Com reports no portion of land in contest Nov. 22-04 3/17/05 Certs #16471, 2210 retnd by request Dismissed

Cherokee Intruder Cases 1901 - 1909

Date Received	No.	Allottee	Intruder
Nov 10-1904	234	James Davis, for himself and for Laura and Alley Davis	Kane Bros and tenants
Notice Sent		**Action**	**Remarks**
Nov 16-1904		Set for hearing at Vinita Dec 22-04 Answer filed 10/12/04	Certificates in file 11/16-04 Commission asked to advise if any contest proceeding now pending as to any portion of said land Com. reports no portion of land in contest Nov. 22-04 Dismissed by request of plaintiff allotment cert returned to Allottee

Date Received	No.	Allottee	Intruder
Nov 14-1904	235	Maggie S. Hill	Dr Geo. Glaze and tenant
Notice Sent		**Action**	**Remarks**
Nov 16-1904		Return of service Nov. 23-04 Ans filed Nov. 28-04 Set for hearing at V[sic] Dec 24-04 Dismissed by request of plaintiff Dec 21-04 See mem in file	Certificates in file 11/16-04 Commission asked to advise if contest proceedings have been instituted on any portion of said land Com reports no portion of land in contest

Date Received	No.	Allottee	Intruder
Nov 14-1904	236	John Timson for his minor children, John and Maude Timson	C.R. and George Applegate and John Gilstrap
Notice Sent		**Action**	**Remarks**
Nov 16-1904		Ans filed Nov 16-04 Return of service Nov 25-04 Set for hearing 1/6/04[sic] Dismissed See mem in file	Certificates in file 11/16-04 Commission asked to advise if any portion of said land is in contest Com reports Nov. 15-04 No portion of land in Contest Nov. 22-04 Com. reports that a portion of land is in contest
	5/15/05	Plaintiff comes and states that Applegate vacated as agreed Jan 1, 1905	

Cherokee Intruder Cases 1901 - 1909

Date Received	No.	Allottee	Intruder
Nov 12-1904	237	Jennetta Griffin	Rev Lee Clyde
Notice Sent		**Action**	**Remarks**
Nov 16-1904		Return of service Nov 23-04 Ans. filed Nov. 28-04 Set for hearing 1/6/05 Case heard; defendant has no contract & agreed to surrender possession See memo in file	Certificate in file 11/16-04 Commission asked to advise if any portion of said land is in contest Com. reports that no portion of land is in contest Nov 22 04 Dismissed

Date Received	No.	Allottee	Intruder
Nov 16-1904	238	Albert V. McGhee, for himself and Nellie J, Rosa M, Clavattie[sic] and Bluford McGhee	A. A. Morgan
Notice Sent		**Action**	**Remarks**
Nov 17-1904 Nov 29-04		Return of service Nov. 22-04 Dismissed by request of plaintiff. See mem. in file Allottee acknowledges receipt of his certificates 7/5/05	Certificates in file 11/17-04 Commission asked to advise if any portion of land is involved in contest Com reports that no portion of land is in contest Nov. 22-04 6/26/05 Certificate returned to Allottee Dismissed

Date Received	No.	Allottee	Intruder
Nov 16-1904	239	Lydia Partain Spavinaw I.T.	Dan Boney and Wife
Notice Sent		**Action**	**Remarks**
Nov 17-1904		Return of service Nov. 25-04 Set for hearing 1/6/05 Case continued until Jan 20/05 on acct of sickness of defendant See certificate of physician Set for hearing at Vinita Feb 8/05 A.M.	Certificate in file 11/17-04 Commission asked to advise if any portion of said [sic] is involved in contest Com. reports no portion of land in contest Nov. 22-04

75

Cherokee Intruder Cases 1901 - 1909

2/7/05 Case called. Husband of Allottee appeared for her and his testimony taken. No appearance made by defendant. Case placed in hands of Chamberlain to investigate.
4/2/05 See Chamberlain's report. Defendant is full blood and improvements are property of family who will file a contest & case dismissed.

<u>Dismissed</u>

Date Received	No.	Allottee	Intruder
Nov 15-1904	240	W. P. Thorne for Walter and Jacob H. Thorne	Emanuel Ward Defendant claims to be a Cherokee Freedman
Aug 8- 1906		Case set for hearing at Vanita[sic] I.Ty. Aug 21- 1906 All parties notified	Col Blue Atty for Defendant
Aug 16, 1906		See letter in file from Starr and Patton Attys at Vinita I Ty. Also departmental letters.	
Aug 21- 1906		Proof of Service ret'd dated Aug 20-1906.	
" 21 1906		Case called at Vinita ITy & Pltf present. No appearance by defndt. Testimony of pltf taken.	
Sept. 26- 1906		Com^r requested to report if any contest pending _motion to review citizenship_	
Oct 2 1906		Com^r reports no motion to review citizenship of Dfndt	
Oct 26, 1906		Judgement[sic] rendered for plntf	
Oct 27- 1906		Instructions issued to U.S. I.P. Barbee of Afton I Ty	
Jany 26, 1907		Policeman Barbee requested to report	
Feby 4, 1907		In view of Policeman Barbee's report. Plntf requested to advise	
June 15, 1907		in order that he *(Illegible)* be placed in possession Certs returned to plff and he was requested to advise in re. possession	

Notice Sent	Action	Remarks
Nov 17- 1904	Set for hearing 1/7/05	Certificates in file
June 25-1907 *Letter from plff.* *June 29/7 - Case Dismissed*	Return of service Dec. 16-04 Service not sufficient. Duplicate mailed again. Set for hearing at Vinita Feb 8-05	11/17-04-Commission asked to advise if any portion of said land was involved in contest proceedings Com. reports no portion of land in contest Nov. 22-04
	2/8/05 Case called, plaintiff appeared by guardian stating service will be had and same forwarded to Muskogee, I.T.	
May 8 1906	In compliance with Departmental instructions of April 19th 1906 Com^r is requested to furnish this office with the status of Allotment of Plf and of the citizenship of the Dfd	

Cherokee Intruder Cases 1901 - 1909

June 18 1906	Com^r reports no motion for review of citizenship case of Dfdt pending

Date Received	No.	Allottee	Intruder
Nov. 16- 1904	241	Rufus Miller for Mary and Ida Miller	C. E. Holderman & O. E. Lonchbaugh
Notice Sent		**Action**	**Remarks**
Nov. 17-1904 ~~Dec 22-04~~ Duplicate Notice that 1/7-05 2/14/05		Set for hearing 1/7/05 ~~Case heard evidence taken decided that Allottee is intitled to possession~~ *(illegible...)* Return of Service, Jan 26, '05 Answer filed 2/2/05 Parties appeared, parties settled in open court and agreement was written out and filed in case, and certificates returned to Allottee this day.	Certificates in file 11/17-04 Commission asked to advise if any portion of said land is involved in contest proceeding Com. reports no portion of land in contest Nov. 23-04 Dismissed

Date Received	No.	Allottee	Intruder
Nov. 21- 1904	242	Sarah Corkrum nee Davis	Geo. Davis
Notice Sent		**Action**	**Remarks**
Nov. 21- 1904		Return of service Dec. 8-04 Set for hearing 1/7/05 Case dismissed for want of prosecution on 1/7/05 defendant agreeing to vacate within 15 days. (see mem. in file). 3/13/05 Policeman Smith reports placing Allottee in possession	Cert in file 11/21/04 Commission asked to advise if any portion of said land is in contest Com. reports no portion of land in contest Nov. 29-04 Dismissed

Date Received	No.	Allottee	Intruder
Nov. 17- 04	243	Marion Y. Wood	John Wooden et al
Notice Sent		**Action**	**Remarks**
Nov. 22		Return of Service Dec. 2-04 Set for hearing at Vinita Dec. 23-04 Set for hearing at Vinita 2/8/05 2/8/05 Case called. No appearance by	Allotment Cert. in file Com. reports no portion of land in contest Nov. 29-04 Commission reports portion

Cherokee Intruder Cases 1901 - 1909

either party. 2/28/05 Certificate N° 20146 returned to Marion F. Wood Zena, I.T. in compliance with his written request.	of land in contest Jan. 20, '05 Dismissed

Date Received	No.	Allottee	Intruder
Nov 21-04	244	Ida L. Hinds	Boney Shewmaker[sic]
Notice Sent		**Action**	**Remarks**
Nov. 22 7/8/05		Return of service Nov. 29-04 Ans. filed Dec. 2-04 Set for hearing 1/7/05 Allottee acknowledges receipt of his certificates	Certificates On file Com. reports no portion of land in contest Nov. 29-04 Contest pending. See plat in file. 6/26/05 Certificate returned to Allottee Dismissed

Date Received	No.	Allottee	Intruder
Nov 22-04	245	Beaver Chuwalooky	S. C. Hill
Notice Sent		**Action**	**Remarks**
Nov. 29-04 Dec. 22-04		Set for hearing at Vinita Dec 22/04 Return of service Dec. 9-04 Ans. filed Dec. 9-04 Case heard: evidence taken all parties in interest being present. No Action taken Sent to Chamberlain Jan 10-05 1/19/05 Restraining order applied for 1/28/05 Restraining order denied by U.S. Court 2/20/05 Matter submitted to Department for instructions and defendant by his Attorney Kornegay & Turner threatens to bring Action for damages against the Agent.	Cert in file Dec. 6-04 Com reports no portion of land in contest 3/19 Certificates returned Dismissed By order W. W. B.
7/27 P. L. Lofer Dist Atty informs *(Illegible)* that matter has been referd[sic] to him for *(Illegible)* in Court by Deft			

Cherokee Intruder Cases 1901 - 1909

Date Received	No.	Allottee	Intruder
Dec. 5-04	246	Mack Downing	A.G. Thomas et al
Notice Sent		**Action**	**Remarks**
Dec. 6-04		Set for hearing 1/7/05 Return of Service 12/9/04 Heard at Muskogee ~~and sent to policeman to place party in possession.~~ Reset for hearing Jan. 21, '05. Instructions to Stidham & withheld on acct. of re-hearing. Reset for hearing Feby 4,'05.	Cert. in file Com. reports no portion of land in contest Certs 16072 12620 ret'd
	2/28/05	Case dismissed for want of prosecution upon written application of plaintiff dated 2/21/05 and certificates returned to him at Hoaley[sic], I.T.	
			Dismissed

Date Received	No.	Allottee	Intruder
Nov. 27-04	247	V. E. Morris for minors	C.E. Holderman
Notice Sent		**Action**	**Remarks**
Dec. 8-04		Set for hearing at Vinita Dec. 22-04 Return of service 12/10/04 Ans. filed Dec. 16-04	Cert in file com. reports no portion in contest
	Dec. 22-04	Case heard: evidence taken all parties in interest being present Decided that Allottee is intitled to possession Holderman agreed to give possession at once 3/16/05 Instructions issued to R. Lee Wyley to place Allottee in possession and report Action to this office 3/31/05 Report of R. Lee Wyley filed herein: Allottee placed in possession	Certificates returned to Allottee 6/27/05 6/26/05 Certificates returned
			Dismissed

Cherokee Intruder Cases 1901 - 1909

Date Received	No.	Allottee	Intruder
Nov. 30-04	248	Elizabeth Williams	Thomas Ward
Notice Sent		**Action**	**Remarks**
Dec. 8-04		Set for hearing at Vinita Dec. 22-04 Return of service 12/12/04 Answer filed 12/10/04	Cert in file Contest Pending Com. reports no portion of land in contest Dec. 22 Commission reports land in contest. 6/26/05 Certificates returned to Allottee Dismissed

Date Received	No.	Allottee	Intruder
Nov. 30-04	249	Elizabeth Williams for minors	B. H. Young
Notice Sent		**Action**	**Remarks**
Dec 8-04		Set for hearing at Vinita Dec. 22-04 Return of service 12/12/04 Set for hearing at Vinita Feb. 8-05	Cert in file Com. reports no portion of land in contest 2/8/05 Agent wires that Com advises contest has been filed on lands in *(Illegible)*
	2/8/05	Case Called. No appearance by either party. Subsequent to calling case telegram was received from Agent, which is noted in margin above	
	5/17/05	Certs N° 24908, 18151, 24909, 18152, 24914, 18155, 24912, 18154, 24911 & 18153 returned in compliance with request of Allottee.	
			Coweta, I.T.

Date Received	No.	Allottee	Intruder
Nov. 30-04	250	Mayes C. Y. for minors	W. Q. Hancock
Notice Sent		**Action**	**Remarks**
Dec 8-04		Set for hearing at Vinita Dec. 22-04 Return of service Dec. 16-04 Ans. filed Dec. 16-04 Set for hearing at Vinita 2/8/05	Cert in file Com. reports no portion of land in contest
	2/8/05	Case called. No appearance by either party.	

Cherokee Intruder Cases 1901 - 1909

2/23/05	Letter dated 2/13/05 stating that the matter has been settled and requests return of certificate. Case dismissed for want of prosecution and certificates returned.

Date Received	No.	Allottee	Intruder
Dec 3-04	251	Edward T. Goodman for minors	Walter Cauley
Notice Sent		**Action**	**Remarks**
Dec 8-04		Set for hearing at Vinita Dec. 22-04	Cert in file
		Return of service 12/12/04	Com reports no portion of land in contest
Dec. 23-04		Dismissed by personal request of Plaintiff	6/26/05 Certificates returned to Allottee

Date Received	No.	Allottee	Intruder
Dec. 3-04	252	Nora E. Keefer nee Rice	Curt and Bell Yate
Notice Sent		**Action**	**Remarks**
De. 8-04		Set for hearing at Vinita Dec. 22-04	Cert in file
		Set for hearing at Vinita 2/8/05	Com. reports no portion of land in contest
		2/2/05 Letter received from Allottee that case has been satisfactorily settled and requests that certificate be returned to her and case dismissed. Case dismissed for want of prosecution & certificates returned to Nora E. Keefer nee Rice Bartlesville I.T.	

Date Received	No.	Allottee	Intruder
Dec. 3-04	253	Roxie D. Berry	George Hendricks
Notice Sent		**Action**	**Remarks**
Dec 8-04		Set for hearing at Vinita Dec 22-04	Cert in file
		Answer filed 12/13-04	Com reports no portion of land in contest
Dec. 22-04		Case heard: evidence taken all parties in interest being present	
			Certs N$^{\underline{o}}$ 6891, 6746
		Sent to Chamberlain Jan 10-05.	
3/1/05		A. F. Chamberlain reports Allottee in possession and requests that certificate be returned to Roxie D. Berry Stilwell, I.T.	

Cherokee Intruder Cases 1901 - 1909

Date Received	No.	Allottee	Intruder
Dec. 3-04	254	Laura Wilson nee Fields	Charles Noushee
Notice Sent		**Action**	**Remarks**
Dec. 8-04		Set for hearing at Vinita Dec. 22-04 Return of service 12/13/04 Dismissed by request of Plaintiff	Cert in file Cert returned Dec. 22-04 Com. reports no portion of land in contest

Date Received	No.	Allottee	Intruder
Dec. 3-04	255	Moses O. Fields	Dr. Summer Burton
Notice Sent		**Action**	**Remarks**
Dec 8-04		Set for hearing at Vinita Dec. 22-04 Return of service Dec. 16-04 Ans. filed Dec. 22-04	Cert in file Com. reports no portion of land in contest
	Dec. 22-04	Case heard: evidence taken all parties in interest being present <u>Dismissed</u>	<u>Dismissed</u> 6/26/05 Certificate returned to Allottee

Date Received	No.	Allottee	Intruder
Dec. 3-04	256	John Scott for minors	Henry Rider
Notice Sent		**Action**	**Remarks**
Dec. 8-04		Set for hearing at Vinita Dec. 22-04 Answer filed 12/10/04 Return of service Dec. 19-04	Cert in file All land in contest by report of Com. Dec. 16-04 Dismissed 6/26/05 Certificate returned to Allottee

Date Received	No.	Allottee	Intruder
Dec. 12, 1904	257	Ada Vann for herself & Nannie Ruth Vann	Tom & Horne Howell, Julius Reeder &
Set for hearing at	1^{30} PM	Jan 18/05	____ Hutchinson
Notice Sent		**Action**	**Remarks**
Dec 13-04		Return of Service 12/17/04 Answer filed Dec. 19, 1904 Set for hearing Jan. 18, 1905 at	Cert on file 12/13/04 Asked Commission if any contest

Cherokee Intruder Cases 1901 - 1909

	Muskogee, I.T.	on land
		Com. reports no portion of
	Defendant Mr. Comstock appeared	land in contest
	et al-plaintiff did not received notice	~~Answer filed Dec. 19/05~~
	in time	
	Set for 2/25/05 at Muskogee, I.T.	
2/25/05	Cancelled. Plaintiff appears and desires to dismiss case as to all parties defendant hereto except Julius Reeder, and her certificates returned to her in person Dismissed!	

Date Received	No.	Allottee	Intruder
Dec. 1-04	258	Eli Tadpole for Annie, Okla, Lilian, Emma & Wm H. Tadpole	Samuel Wheeler

Notice Sent	Action	Remarks
Dec. 13-04	Return of Service 12/17/04	Cert on file
	Answer filed 12/21/04	12/13/04 asked Commission
	Set for hearing at Vinita 2/8/05	if any contest on land
		Com. reports no portion of land in contest

2/8/05 Case called. Parties appeared in Court and after a full discussion of the case, the matter between Tadpole and Wheeler was satisfactorily arranged and new contract was entered into and case dismissed.
Certificates returned to Eli Tadpole in person.

Date Received	No.	Allottee	Intruder
Nov. 23, 1904	259	Leonidas R. Johnson	George Bell
			Curtis and Watts Attys
			Sallisaw IT
	Jan 30th 1906	This office is informed that Dfdt Bell has again taken possession	
		and instructions have today been issued to Tandy W.	
	Feb 16th 1906	Adair to Remove him	
		Policeman Tandy W. Adair reports that he has place Ptf	
	May 10 1906	Johnson in possession of his homestead	
		Certified copies of certain letters mailed to Curtis and Watts.	
		(See carbon in file)	
			Dismissed

Cherokee Intruder Cases 1901 - 1909

Notice Sent	Action	Remarks
Dec. 13- 1904	Return of service Dec. 29-04	Cert on file
		12/13/04 Asked Com if any
	Set for hearing at Muskogee, I.T.	contest on land
	Feby 20, 1905	Com. reports no portion of
	2/20/05 No appearance by either party.	land in contest
	3/3/05 Instructions sent to R Lee Wyley to place Allottee in possession and report the matter to this office.	
	3/27/05 Report of R Lee Wyly that he place Allottee in possession March 23, 1905, filed & case was Dismissed	
	Allottee ack. receipt of certificates 6/26/05	
	7/18/05 Certificates returned to Allottee	
	2/30 1906 Instructions sent Tandy W Adair to place Allottee in possession	

Date Received	No.	Allottee	Intruder
Dec. 5-1904	260	Pasy Fox	I. W. Ewning

Notice Sent	Action	Remarks
Dec. 13- 04	Return of service Dec 19, 1904	Cert on file
	Set for hearing at Muskogee, I.T.	12/13/04 asked Com if any
	Feby 20, 1905	contest on lands
	2/20/05 Case called, complaint to be amended and C.W. Turner made defendant and ret for 2/27/05 at Muskogee, I.T. at 1 ^{30} P.M.	Com. reports no portion of land in contest
	Notice served on both parties.	
	2/27/05 Case called, all parties present. Defendant agrees to put land in cultivation and to pay twenty dollars at once. Case then dismissed. Certificates and papers returned to Allottee in person.	

Date Received	No.	Allottee	Intruder
Dec. 10-04	261	Samuel S. Starr	Joe Harron

Notice Sent	Action	Remarks
Dec. 13-1904	Return of Service 12/16/04	Cert in file
	Answer filed Feby 20 1905	12/13-04 asked Com if any
	Set for hearing at Muskogee, I.T.	contest on lands
	Feby 20, 1905	Com. reports no portion of
	2/20/05 Case called: Defendant to pay Allottee exactly in term with contract, and allowed two weeks to	land in contest R.P. DeGraffenreid Atty for defndt.

Cherokee Intruder Cases 1901 - 1909

pay certain notes, or fully satisfy the Allottee, if not settled in two weeks defendant to be removed Plaintiff advises case settled & wants certificates		Dismissed

Date Received	No.	Allottee	Intruder
Dec 6-1904	262	I. J. Howard guardian Geo Samuel Howard	Bill & Mary Hunter
Notice Sent		Action	Remarks
Dec 13-04		Return of service dec[sic] 24-04 Set for hearing at Vinita 2/8/05	Cert in file 12/13/04 asked Com if any contest on lands
	2/8/05	Case called: No appearance by plaintiff. Defendant appears in person and agrees that he makes no claim to land of any improvements thereon except some board in a house on premises, not nailed, and further that he will vacate in a few days or as soon as weather permits him to cover his house Plaintiff appeared subsequent to entry as above and agreed to same 3/21/05-Plaintiff states he is in possession Cert. returned to Allottee 6/1/05 Receipt of Allotment certs Ack. 6/9/05	Com. reports no portion of land in contest Dismissed

Date Received	No.	Allottee	Intruder
Dec 10-1904	263	Bird Dubblehead for Filey E. Dubblehead	A. P. Bolden
Notice Sent		Action	Remarks
Dec 13-1904		Return of Service 12/20/04 Answer filed Set for hearing at Muskogee, I.T. 2/21/05 7/28/05 Allottee Ack. receipt of certificates	Cert in file 12/13/04 asked Com if any contest is pending Com. reports no portion of land in contest 6/26/05 Certificates returned to Allottee Dismissed

Cherokee Intruder Cases 1901 - 1909

Date Received	No.	Allottee	Intruder
Nov. 11-04	264	Fannie E. Chandler	Alexander Walker
Notice Sent	**Action**		**Remarks**
Dec 13-1904	Set for hearing at Vinita 2/8/05		Commission reports no contest & cert issued
	2/8/05 Case called, no appearance by either party		
	2/9/05 Letter dated 2/8/05 that she is too sick to appear, also stating that defendant is sick and not likely to appear		~~Dismissed~~
	Set for hearing at Claremore, I.T. April 28, 1905 at 9:30 A M		
	6/12/05 Case dismissed upon receipt of a letter from plaintiff that defendant had vacated her lands		Dismissed

Date Received	No.	Allottee	Intruder
Dec 10-1904	265	Mattie J Bell for Sallie F Newman	Jeff Ethridge
Notice Sent	**Action**		**Remarks**
Dec 13-04	Return of service Dec 19-04		Cert in file 12/13-
	Set for hearing at Vinita 2/9/05		asked Commission if any contest on lands
			Com. reports no portion of land in contest
	2/2/05 Letter received stating that fences have been removed and that no further Action is needed and case returned Jany 10/05 Mattie J Bell		Cert. returned to Allottee Jan. 10-05 dismissed and certificates Owasso Ind Ter

Date Received	No.	Allottee	Intruder
Dec 2-1904	266	Phenia Bean	Walter D. Simpson
Notice Sent	**Action**		**Remarks**
Dec 13-1904	Case withdrawn by plaintiff Dec. 13 '04		Cert in file
			12/13-04 asked Com if any contest on lands
			Com. reports no contest
			Certificates returned
			Jan 6, 1905
			Dismissed

Cherokee Intruder Cases 1901 - 1909

Date Received	No.	Allottee	Intruder
Dec 3-1904	267	Joseph L. Manus Peggs, I.T.	John Monyer[sic] John W Moyers

Notice Sent	Action	Remarks
Dec 13-04	Return of service Dec. 22-04 Answer filed Dec. 24 '04 Set for hearing at Vinita 2/9/05	Cert in file 12/13 asked Com if any contest on lands
	2/9/05 Case called / witnesses were sworn as follows: Joseph L. Manus is plaintiff and John W Moyers, J.J. Musgrave & W.H. Hatfield for defense.*(Illegible)* Dean also sworn for defense.	Com reports no portion of land in contest Chas B Rogers, Atty at Law Vinita, I.T.

3/14/05 Instructions sent to R Lee Wyley to place Allottee in possession and report to this office Action in the matter.
3/22/05 Policeman Wyly reports placing Allottee in possession   Settled.
6/26/05 Certificates returned to Allottee

Date Received	No.	Allottee	Intruder
Nov. 30-1904	268	John A Keys for himself & Stuart Keys	V. Lamb

Notice Sent	Action	Remarks
Dec 13-1904	Return of service 12/16/04 Answer filed Dec. 24, '04 Set for hearing at Muskogee, I.T. Feby 21, 1905 10 A.M.	Cert in file 12/13-04 asked Com if any contest on lands Com. reports no portion of land in contest

2/21/05 W. T. Hunt appeared as attorney for defendant, no ~~plaintiff~~ appearance by plaintiff and no Action taken.
                                                                 2/16 Certificates returned
7/10/05 Plaintiff requested to advise this office if he has possession of his land or if he has made satisfactory arrangements
2/16 Dismissed upon request of of[sic] Ptf.   2/16 Dismissed

Cherokee Intruder Cases 1901 - 1909

Date Received	No.	Allottee	Intruder
Dec 3-1904	269	Thos. J. Conand for Thos W. & John N. Conand	J. W. Stream

Notice Sent	Action	Remarks
Dec 13-04	Return of Service 12/19/04	Cert in file
		12/13-asked Com if any contest on lands
		Com. reports no portion of land in contest
		Settled
	4/8/05 Certificates 5910, 8123, 2121, 1817 returned by request to Thomas J Coward Fawn, I.T.	
		Dismissed

Date Received	No.	Allottee	Intruder
Dec 3-1904	270	Naomi A. & Theo L. Litten	H. A. Gay

Notice Sent	Action	Remarks
Dec. 13-04	Return of Service Feby 20, 1905	Cert. in file
		12/13-04 asked Com if any contest on lands
		Com. reports no portion of land in contest
		Cert. returned to Allottee Jan 10-05
		Dismissed upon application of plaintiffs.

Date Received	No.	Allottee	Intruder
Nov. 29-1904	271	James W. Vann for himself & Florence Vann	Lee Kallam

Notice Sent	Action	Remarks
Dec 13-04	Return of Service 12/26/04	Cert on file
		12-13-asked Com if any contest on land
		Com. reports Contest pending
		Settled by request of Allottee
		Cert returned to Allottee Jan 12-05

Cherokee Intruder Cases 1901 - 1909

Date Received	No.	Allottee	Intruder
Nov. 30-04	272	James D. Wilson for himself & Letitia M. Wilson	Wheeler DeMorse
Notice Sent		**Action**	**Remarks**
Dec 13-04　　　　　　2/10/05		Return of Service 12/19/04 Given Policeman Chamberlain with instructions to place All in possession Jan 6th - And Jan 10th A.F. Chamberlain reports that peaceable possession will be given with 3 days.	Cert in file 12/13 asked Com if any contest on lands Com reports no portion of land in contest

Settled. |

Date Received	No.	Allottee	Intruder
Nov. 26-1904	273	Jeff D. McCoy for Grover & Laura McCoy	B. Milligan et al
Notice Sent		**Action**	**Remarks**
Dec 13-04		Return of service Dec. 27-04 Answer filed Jan. 17 1905 (also that defendants will contest) Answer filed	Cert on file 12-13- asked Com if any contest Com. reports no portion of land in contest Certificates returned to Allottee by request Jan 25 (?)/5/05 Com advises Norman T Drake that lands are in contest

Dismissed |

Date Received	No.	Allottee	Intruder
Nov 18-04	274	Daniel Hornett for himself & Jennie, Sarah, Charley & Lucinda Hornett	Eliza Mills
Notice Sent		**Action**	**Remarks**
Dec 13-04		Return of Service Dec 30 Answer filed & brief by attorney ~~Jan~~ Dec 30 Set for hearing at Muskogee, I.T. Feby 21, 1905	Commission reports cert. issued & no contest

Geo E McCulloch Atty for Dfndnt Vinita, I.T. |

Cherokee Intruder Cases 1901 - 1909

2/21/05 Case called: Agreement was made by Daniel Hornett and Attorney for defendant and papers signed by each, relinquishing, and of the acceptance of premises in question, and same filed this day and case dismissed.

2/24/05 Lease returned this day to Geo E McCulloch in person

Dismissed

Date Received	No.	Allottee	Intruder
Dec 13-1904	275	Raw Lee, guardian of Jesse Thompson & John H. Tyner	Niles & Mrs. McTush
Notice Sent		**Action**	**Remarks**
Dec 13-1904		Return of Service 12/19/04	Cert on file
			12/13-asked Com if any
	2/11/05	Plaintiff appears and states that land is in contest and case dismissed. Cert returned to Plaintiff in person 6/1/05	contest on lands Com. reports land not in contest Jan 5- Part of land in contest. See mem. in file.

Date Received	No.	Allottee	Intruder
Dec 14-04	276	William Duncan for minor	Jane Couts
Notice Sent		**Action**	**Remarks**
Dec 23-04		Return of service Jan. 3-05	Cert in file
		Set for hearing at Vinita 2/9/05	
	2/9/05	Case called/ Plaintiff appeared by his father William Duncan, no appearance by the defndt. Judgment by default. Case given to A.F. Chamberlain with instructions to see that fence is placed on land, and put Allottee on his land	1/31/05 Com reports in contest
	3/3/05	Report of A.F. Chamberlain that matter had been satisfactorily settled.	
			Dismissed
		Certificates returned to Allottee 6.27.05	

Cherokee Intruder Cases 1901 - 1909

Date Received	No.	Allottee	Intruder
Dec 20-04	277	James S. Fuller for minor	Mack Ringale

April 12 Report of Eldon Lowe filed and case dismissed
upon request of Plaintiff. Certificates returned.
                                                                Dismissed

Notice Sent	Action	Remarks
Dec 23-04	Return of services Dec. 27-04	Cert in file
	" " " Jany 31, 1905	
	Set for hearing at Muskogee, I.T.	
2/21/05	Plaintiff appears and advises that the defendant would probably not appear as he had agreed to vacate premises	1/3/05 Com reports in contest
2/18/05	Answer filed	
7/10/05	Plaintiff requested to advise this office if he has possession of his land or if he had made satisfactory arrangements	
	Mch 18 Referred to Eldon Lowe for investigation	

Date Received	No.	Allottee	Intruder
Dec. 20-04	278	Anderson Silk for minors	Geo. Mages et al

Notice Sent	Action	Remarks
Dec 23-04	Return of Service 12/23/04	Cert in file
	Answer filed Jan. 3rd	Letter to Commission
	Set for hearing at Muskogee, I.T. Feby 21, 1905	asking if there be any contest on said land
	Answer of Blue and Bulger 2/21/05 requesting that no Action be taken as lands are contested.	1/31/05 Com reports lands in contest
Aug 10 - 1906	Com^r requested to advise this office if there is any contest pending on Allotment concerned in this case	
Aug 20, 1906	Com^r reports contest & motion for rehearing pending in case of Luella & Kitt Snoden.	
Aug 31, 1906	Pltf notified of contest & that case is dismissed in this office.	
	Case dismissed in view of contest	
	Allotment Cert No. 8055, 9841, 9842, & 8050 ret'd this day	Dismissed,

Cherokee Intruder Cases 1901 - 1909

Date Received	No.	Allottee	Intruder
Dec. 20-04	279	Henry Thompson for minor	Geo. Mages et al
Notice Sent		**Action**	**Remarks**
Dec 23-04		Return of Service 1/2/05	Cert. in file
			1/31/05 Com reports land contest, yet undetermined
5/3/05		Lucinda Thompson appeared in person as mother of minor named in this case and states that they had decided to endeavor to get land elsewhere and they desired to withdraw the case and same was dismissed and certificate N⁰ 8014, 9799, returned to Lucinda Thompson in person	
			Dismissed

Date Received	No.	Allottee	Intruder
Dec. 16-04	280	Melvin J. Zinn	R. W. Zinn
Notice Sent		**Action**	**Remarks**
Dec 23-04		Return of services Dec 31-04	Cert in file
		Set for hearing at Vinita 2/9/05	
		1/31/05 Upon receipt of written request signed by Allottee case was dismissed and certificate returned to her at Zena Ind Ter.	
			1/31/05 Com reports no contest
			Dismissed

Date Received	No.	Allottee	Intruder
Dec 16-04	281	Walter G Fields for minor	John Bohanan et al
Notice Sent		**Action**	**Remarks**
Dec 23-04		Return of service Dec 26/04	Cert in file
		Set for hearing at Muskogee, I.T. Feby 21, 1905	

1/31/05 Commission reports no contest
Dismissed 6/6/05 as claimant reports he is in possession - Ctfs No: 2029 and 2382 ret^d to W. G. Fields in person same date.

Cherokee Intruder Cases 1901 - 1909

Date Received	No.	Allottee	Intruder
Dec 13-04	282	Jack Jones	Wiley Williams
Notice Sent		**Action**	**Remarks**
Dec. 23-04		Return of Service Dec 30 '04 Cert returned to Allottee 6/8/05 Dismissed	Cert in file 1/25/05 Com reports that a part of lands are on contest 1/31/05 Com reports land is also claimed by Wattie L. Mayfield ~~2/26/05~~

Date Received	No.	Allottee	Intruder
Dec 20-04	283	Lewis R Mulkey for minor	Mr Echols
Notice Sent		**Action**	**Remarks**
Dec. 23-04			Cert in file

Set for hearing at Muskogee 3/28/05 1/31/05 Com reports no
3/28/05 Case called. Plaintiff   contest
appeared in person and it appears that the Muskogee Development
Co should have been made defendant and case was continued to be
heard April 20, 1905
Dismissed upon written application of plaintiff of April 19, 05
                    6/26/05 Certificates returned to Allottee

Date Received	No.	Allottee	Intruder
Dec 20-04	284	Mary J Luke for self et al	John Yargin et al
Notice Sent		**Action**	**Remarks**
Dec 23-04		Return of Service Dec 28 Answer filed Jan 3 '05 Set for hearing at Muskogee IT Feby 23, 1905	Cert in file 1/31/05 Com reports no contest

2/21/05 Letter received from W R Allen enclosing affidavit of
plaintiff that agreeable arrangements have been made and
requesting that case be dismissed, which is accordingly done.
                                      Dismissed
                6/26/05 Certificate returned to Allottee

Cherokee Intruder Cases 1901 - 1909

Date Received	No.	Allottee	Intruder
Dec 21-04	285	Nathaniel D Willis for minors	Alex S. Lewis

Notice Sent	Action	Remarks
Dec 21-04	Return of service Jan 3-04[sic] Set for hearing at Muskogee, I.T. Feby 23, 1905	Cert in file 1/31/05 Com reports land in contest & not determined
	2/23/05 Complaint withdrawn by plaintiff and certificate returned to him in person at Muskogee, I.T. this day and case dismissed.	
	3/3/05 See answer of defendant filed Feby 28, 1905	
	Dismissed	

Date Received	No.	Allottee	Intruder
Dec 28-04	286	Dennis B. Hereford	O. L. Hayes

Notice Sent	Action	Remarks
Dec. 28-04	Return of Service, 1/7/05	Cert in file
2/10/05	Answer by Hayes Mercantile Co filed dated 2/6/05 Set for hearing at Muskogee, I.T. Feby 23, 1905	1/31/05 Com reports no contest
2/23/05	Case called. Defendant appear by self and Atty Thos H Owen and case held open.	
3/16/05	Case called. No appearance by plaintiff. Defendants appeared in person and by Attorney and it being third time case had been set and no appearance by plaintiff case was dismissed	
3/16/05	Certs 8738 & 10749 returned this day by WWB.	

Date Received	No.	Allottee	Intruder
Dec 9-04	287	Dick Hill et al	Jim Walker

4/5/05 Defendant appears and his testimony taken
5/28/05 Judgment rendered in favor of defendant.
Dismissed

Notice Sent	Action	Remarks
Dec 28-04	Return of service Jan 3-05 Answer filed Jan 6 '05 Set for hearing at Muskogee, I.T. Feby 24, 1905	Cert issued by report of Com

Cherokee Intruder Cases 1901 - 1909

2/25/05   Case called. Plaintiff appeared. Letter received from the defendant dated 2/22/05 requesting on account of illness in his family that case be postponed, which was consented to by plaintiff, and case was postponed to March 1, 1905
3/1/05   No appearance by either party.
3/2/05   Letter from plaintiff requesting postponement of case on account of illness, and case set for hearing at this office Mch 13, 1905,1.[30] P.M. and notice of sent both parties
3/13/05 ~~No appearance by either party~~ plaintiff appeared and evidence taken and same is in file. No appearance by defendant

Date Received	No.	Allottee	Intruder
Dec 7-04	288	Richard Pann	John Farlow
Notice Sent		Action	Remarks
Dec 28-04		Set for hearing at Muskogee, I.T. Feby 23, 1905 2/23/05 Case called. No appearance	Cert issued by report of Com. Dismissed

Date Received	No.	Allottee	Intruder
Dec 17-04	289	Mrs. Cinthy A. Welch	H. W. Talbort[sic]
Notice Sent		Action	Remarks
Dec 28-04		Return of service Dec. 31-04 Answer filed Dec. 31.1904 Set for hearing at Vinita 2/9/05 2/9/05 Case called, no appearance by either party 7/26/05 Case dismissed by request of plaintiff See same in file Case set for hearing at Claremore on Aug. 1st-05	Cert issued by report of Com

95

Cherokee Intruder Cases 1901 - 1909

Date Received	No.	Allottee	Intruder
Dec 17-04	290	James H. Thompson	W$^{\underline{m}}$ H. Hough
Notice Sent		**Action**	**Remarks**
Dec 28-04		Return of Service Jan 3 1905 Answer filed Jan. 4, '05 Set for hearing at Vinita 2/9/05	Cert issued by report of Com
	2/9/05	Case called. No appearance by either party.	
	2/13/05	Letter of 2/7/05 received from plaintiff stating that parties have vacated premises. Case dismissed.	
	2/15/05	Dismissed upon [sic] Dismissed	

Date Received	No.	Allottee	Intruder
Dec 30-04	291	Thomas J. Hendricks	Robt Woodall
Notice Sent		**Action**	**Remarks**
Dec 31-04		Return of Service 1-17-05	Cert in file
		Set for hearing at Muskogee, I.T. Feby 23, 1905.	1/31/05 Com reports no contest
	2/23/05	Parties all present. It haveing[sic] been ascertained what the difficulty was, and agreed to by defendant that he would pay $25 to Allottee and otherwise comply with contract, the case upon motion of Allottee was dismissed and certificates returned to Hendricks in person.	
	5/4/05	See instructions to Chamberlain sent this day for removal of defendant	
			Dismissed

Date Received	No.	Allottee	Intruder
Dec 23-04	292	Sallie Downing	John Vann et al
Notice Sent		**Action**	**Remarks**
Dec 31-04		Return of Service Jan. 9, 1905 Answer filed Jan 10, 1905 Set for hearing at Muskogee, I.T. Feby 24, 1905	Cert in file 4/31/05 Com advises that land described is in contest and not yet determined
			Dismissed

Cherokee Intruder Cases 1901 - 1909

Date Received	No.	Allottee	Intruder
Dec 23-04	293	George Mefford for minor Ramona, I.T.	Frank Lowe

Notice Sent	Action	Remarks
Dec 23-04	Return of Service 1/4/05 Ans filed Jan 7/05 Set for hearing at Vinita 2/9/05 2/9/05 Case called. George Mefford appeared for plaintiff, no appearance by defendant Case held for report of Com as to contest 7 17/05 Case dismissed as there is contest pending *Dismissed*	Cert in file 2/31/05 Com advises no contest 7/13/05 Com. reports land in contest

Date Received	No.	Allottee	Intruder
Dec 28-04	294	Zeke Whitmire for minors Parsons Ks	Henry McAnnerm et al Claim freedom rights Starr and Patton Attys
May 29/06		Com^r reports that Dfdts have been denied citizenship as freedmen	Blue and Bulger Atty Vinita IT

June 7/06 Case set for hearing at Claremore, I.T. 6/19/6
" 14/06 Answer filed by Starr and Patton Attys
" 19/06 Case called at Claremore Mr Starr appered[sic] for Dfdt, no appearance by Ptf
J.C. Starr states that Dfdts did not claim to be in possession by virtue of Contract of any nature, that their only claim to possession is that they are claimants for ~~applicants~~ for citizenship and that a motion for review is now on file with the Com^r if said motion is denied that Dfdts are to vacate at once otherwise they will be removed
6/19/05 Dfdts appeared no evidence taken   June 26 Com^r requested to report
July 17th 1906 Com^r reports a motion to reopen citizenship case of ~~Ptfs~~ Defendant is now pending case is therefore Dismissed

Cherokee Intruder Cases 1901 - 1909

Date Received	No.	Allottee	Intruder
Dec 28-04	294	Zeke Whitmire for minors	
Notice Sent		Action	Remarks
Dec 31-04			Cert in file
	2/9/05	Case called and case continued to Feby 18, 1905 to be heard at Muskogee, I.T. No appearance by plaintiff, Col Blue for defendt. 2/18/05 Case called, No appearance by plntiff. Col Blue appeared for defndts.	1/31/05 Com reports no contest Blue & Bulger Vinita, I.T. Attys for defense.
	3/2/05	Letter received from plaintiff 2/28/05 and on account of sickness in his family Case set for hearing at some future date and 3/29/05 Certificates returned by W.W.B.	
	7 1906	In compliance with instructions contained in Departmental Letter of April 19th, 1906 Com[r] has today been requested to furnish this office with that status of the Allotments of Sequoyah Moses and Edward Whitmire	

(The above case, #294, given again with the Allottee and Intruder information covered by what appears as a blank sheet of paper and the Action and Remarks areas filled in.)

Date Received	No.	Allottee	Intruder
Dec 27-04	295	Victoria Welch for minor	Dr S. R. Bate et al
Notice Sent		Action	Remarks
Dec 31-04		Return of Service Jan 7, 1904[sic] Answer filed Jany 11, 1905 Set for hearing at Muskogee, I.T. Feby 24, 1905	Cert in file 1/31/05 Com advises portion of land in contest

98

Cherokee Intruder Cases 1901 - 1909

> 2/28/04[sic] Letter received from plaintiff dated 2/27/05, sworn to, requesting that this case and N° 297 be dismissed and request was complied with and case dismissed. Letter filed herein.
> 6/26/05 Certificates returned to Allottee
> Dismissed

Date Received	No.	Allottee	Intruder
Dec 29-04	296	Emma E. Heath	Mr. Morgan et al
Notice Sent		**Action**	**Remarks**
Dec 31-04		Return of Service 1-3-05 Answer filed 2/4/05	Cert in file
			Commission reports selection of allotment and no contests pending Dec 3/04
		Given Theodore E Stidham U.S. Indian police Jan. 20, 1904[sic] with instructions to place Allottee in possession. withheld order to Stidham and case set for hearing at Muskogee, I.T. 2/23/05 at 1.$\underline{30}$ P.M.	1/31/05 Com reports no contest
	2/20/05	Plaintiff informs Agent that she is in possession of her land and requesting return of certificates. Certificates returned in person to husband of Emma E Heath 2/23/05 and case dismissed	

Date Received	No.	Allottee	Intruder
Dec 27-04	297	Victoria Welch nee Seabolt	Dr. Turnham
Notice Sent		**Action**	**Remarks**
Dec 31-04		Return of Service 12/31/04 Answer filed Jan 9, '05 also Jany 16, 1905 Set for hearing at Muskogee, I.T. Feby 23, 1905	Cert in file Com advises that land is in contest 1/31/05
	2/25/05	Letter from plaintiff dated 2/22/05 under oath, requesting that this case, and N° 295 be dismissed and request was complied with and case dismissed. Letter filed in Case #295	6/26/05 Certificates returned to Allottee Dismissed

Cherokee Intruder Cases 1901 - 1909

Date Received	No.	Allottee	Intruder
Dec 24-04	298	Sam Hawkins for minor	Sherman Bryant
	June 5 1906	Allottment[sic] certificates No 12040 & 15183 ret.	
	Sept 7 1906	~~Recpt~~ S.H. Hawkins Ack. receipt of Allottment	
	Sept 11	certificates	
		Pltf advised that this office will take no Action until citizenship of Dfdts is determined.	

Notice Sent	Action	Remarks
Dec 31-04	Set for hearing at Vinita 2/9/05	Certs in file
2/9/05	Case called. Case continued for ten days	
	and to be heard at Muskogee, I.T. Feby 18, 1905, and made special. Return of service 2/4/05	1/31/05 Com reports no contest
	2/18/05 Case called at 1.30 P.M. Evidence of witnesses taken and Attorney of defendant to file certain papers	
	3/15/05 Defendant claims rights as freedman and under Departmental instructions of March 7, 1905 case held in abeyance, subject to order from Department	
	May 8 1906 In compliance with Departmental instructions of April 19th 1906 Com[r] is requested to furnish this office with Status of Allotment Ptfs' and citizenship of the Dfdt	
	June 5 1906 Case dismissed as motion for review of citizenship case of Ptf is pending before Commissioner	Dismissed

Date Received	No.	Allottee	Intruder
Dec 24-04	299	Cynthia Tucker	T. J. Butter

Notice Sent	Action	Remarks
Dec 31-04	Return of service Jan 3-05	Cert in file
1/19 - 05	Complaint withdrawn by Attys for Plaintiff filed against rong[sic] *(Illegible)*	1/19-05 Certificates withdrawn by Attys
	Dismissed withdrawn by plaintiff's attorneys	1/31/05 - Com reports no contest

Cherokee Intruder Cases 1901 - 1909

Date Received	No.	Allottee	Intruder
Dec 29-04	300	Andy Irons	Willie Harris
Notice Sent		**Action**	**Remarks**
Dec 31-04		Set for hearing at Muskogee, I.T. Feby 24, 1905	Cert issued by report of Com 6/26/05 Dismissed

Date Received	No.	Allottee	Intruder
Dec 29-04	301	Lizzie James	W. E. Dye
Notice Sent		**Action**	**Remarks**
Dec 31-04		Set for hearing at Vinita 2/9/05 Return of Service, Jan. 9 Answer filed Jan. 17, 1905	Cert issued by report of Com
	2/9/05	By agreement Attys of both parties sent by phone to Bennett, the case was continued. Refers to cases #302 & 303. Attys to notify office of date of trial agreed upon.	
	3/17/05	Upon calling case, attorneys for both parties request case dismissed which was done.	Dismissed

Date Received	No.	Allottee	Intruder
Dec 29-04	302	Charles H. James for minor	W. E. Dye
Notice Sent		**Action**	**Remarks**
Dec 31-04		Set for hearing at Vinita 2/10/05 Return of Service Jan 9	Cert issued by report of Com
	2/9/05	See note in case No 301 applying to this case	
	3/17/05	Upon appearance of attorneys for both parties case was upon motion Dismissed	

Date Received	No.	Allottee	Intruder
Dec 29-04	303	Charles James for minor	W. E. Dye
Notice Sent		**Action**	**Remarks**
Dec 31-04		Set for hearing at Vinita 2/10/05 Return of Service Jan 9, '05	Cert issued by report of Com
	2/9/05	See note relative to case N° 301, which refers to this case	
	3/17/05	Case called. Agreed by attorneys for each party that case be dismissed	

Cherokee Intruder Cases 1901 - 1909

Date Received	No.	Allottee	Intruder
Dec 30-04	304	John Vickery	Mrs Georgia Scott et al.
Notice Sent		**Action**	**Remarks**
Dec 31-04		Return of Service Jan 3rd '05 Answer filed Jan 17, '05	Cert in file 1/31/05 Com reports land in contest, not determined 3/20/05 Cert returned to John W. Vickery Dismissed

Date Received	No.	Allottee	Intruder
Dec 31-04	305	Ned Downing Peggs I.T.	Mrs. Susan Vansickle
		4/27/05 Certificate N°s 6430, 5288 returned to plaintiff at Peggs I.T. upon his request	
Notice Sent		**Action**	**Remarks**
Dec 31-04		Return of service Jan 4 Answer filed Jan 9, 1905 Set for hearing at Vinita 2/10/05	Cert in file 1/31/05 Com advises No contest.
	2/10/05	Case called plaintiff appeared in person, no appearance by defendant Judgment by default for plaintiff and matter placed in hands of A. F. Chamberlain for removal of defendant	
	3/2/05	Instructions sent this day to R. Lee Wiley to place Allottee in possession and report to this office 3/23/05 Policeman Wyly reports placing Allottee in possession on Mar 20/05	Settled

Date Received	No.	Allottee	Intruder
Jan 3-04[sic]	306	Mary Adams ~~et al~~. and minor, Andrew Meyers	Bartles et al.
Notice Sent		**Action**	**Remarks**
Dec 31-04		Return of Service 1-5-05 Set for hearing at Muskogee, I.T. Feby 24, 1905	Cert in file

Cherokee Intruder Cases 1901 - 1909

3/30/05. Plaintiffs husband appeared and stated that trespasser had removed his cattle from allotment in complaint and case was dismissed and certificates N°s 19974, 28083, 19973 & 28082 returned in person to Wm H. Adams.	Commission reports no contests, Jan 10, 1905 on allotment of minor Commission reports on Jan 16, 1905, no contests
	Dismissed

Date Received	No.	Allottee	Intruder
Dec 31-04	307	Hattie Smith for other	Blackburn and Hutchinson
Notice Sent		**Action**	**Remarks**
Jan 3-05		Return of service Jany 26, 1905	Cert in file
	1/28/05	Set for hearing at Muskogee, I.T. Feby 24, 1905	
	2/3/05	Answer - duplicate filed	
	2/24/05	Case called. ~~Testimony~~ All parties appeared in person or by attorneys. Testimony of Hattie Smith developed that while she was in possession of power of attorney from her husband that she was but 17 years of age, and Atty for defendant demurred on the ground that she was not by age qualified to act and case was dismissed and certificates power of attorney returned in person to Hattie Smith. See mem in case.	

Date Received	No.	Allottee	Intruder
Dec 30-04	308	Susan Hendricks nee McClain	Robert L. Woodall
Notice Sent		**Action**	**Remarks**
Jan 3-04		Answer filed Jan 4, 1905	Cert in file
		Set for hearing at hearing[sic] at Muskogee I.T. 2/20/05	Commission reports no contests Jan 10, 1905
	2/13/05 Qualification refiled Sept 2-05	All parties appeared. It being ascertained where the trouble was, and agreed on part of defendant to pay $25 to Allottee and otherwise comply with his contract, upon motion of plaintiffs husband case was dismissed and certificates returned to him in person. See mem in case.	
	5/4/05	See instructions sent this day to Chamberlain	
			Dismissed

Cherokee Intruder Cases 1901 - 1909

Date Received	No.	Allottee	Intruder
Dec 22-04	309	Sarah Tyner	Curtis Flippin et al
Notice Sent	**Action**		**Remarks**
Jan 3-04	Return of service Jan 2-04		Cert issued by report of Com
	Set for hearing at Vinita 2/10/05		
2/8/05	Case called Testimony of plaintiff taken and case held open.		
	Instructions issued to policeman Saml Edmonds to place Allottee		
3/15/05	in possession and report Action in the matter to this office		
	3/23/05 Report of Sam Edmonds filed, showing that Allottee had		
	been placed in possession and case		Dismissed

Date Received	No.	Allottee	Intruder
Dec 29-04	310	George McLaughlin	Laura E. Gray
Notice Sent	**Action**		**Remarks**
Jan 4-05	Return of Service Jan 7, 1905		Cert issued by report of Com
	Answer filed Jan 12/05		
	Set for hearing at Vinita Feb-10-05		1/24/05 Com reports no contest
2/10/05	Case called. Letter from Com exhibited by Frank L Young		
	under date 1/25/05 that land is contested. Case dismissed.		
			Dismissed

Date Received	No.	Allottee	Intruder
Jan 6, 1905	311	James M. Graham	A. J. Fortune
Notice Sent	**Action**		**Remarks**
Jan 7, 1905	Return of Service Jan 11		Certificate in file
	Set for hearing at Vinita 2/10/05		Letter to Commission asking
	Request for hearing at Muskogee,		if there be any contests
	I.T. Feby 25, 1905		pending Jan 7, 1905
	2/17/05 Dismissed upon request of plaintiff and certificates		
	returned to Allottee.		

Date Received	No.	Allottee	Intruder
Jan 11, 1905	312	Levi Fulsom	James Marrs
Notice Sent	**Action**		**Remarks**
Jan 19, 1905	Return of service 2/11/05		Commission reports
			certificates issued and in
	from Levi Fulsom		contests. Jan 10, '05
	3/13/05 Letter ^ dated Mar 11, 1905, stating that the		
	land has been given to him, and the case Dismissed		

Cherokee Intruder Cases 1901 - 1909

Date Received	No.	Allottee	Intruder
Jan 9, 1905	313	Alex Ross	O. C. Hardin
		7/1/05 Plaintiff Alex Ross Ack. receipt of certificates	|//
Notice Sent		**Action**	**Remarks**
Jan 19, 1905		Return of Service Jan 21	Certificates in file
		Answer filed Jan. 21, 1905	Letter to Commission asking if there be any contests on
		Case set for hearing at Muskogee I.T. Feby 25, 1905	land 1/19/05 Commission advises no contests pending Jan. 24
	2/25/05	Case called. Plaintiff and his attorney appeared and his testimony taken. O.C. Hardin then sworn and testimony taken, and it appearing that the only contract existing was a verbal one made prior to Allottee filing on premises. It was therefore decided that Allottee should be placed in possession	
	3/16/05	Instructions sent to Monnie McIntosh to place Allottee in possession and report Action in the matter to this office	
		Settled	
		3/22/05 Policeman McIntosh reports placing Allottee in possession	
		6/26/05 Certificates returned to Allottee	

Date Received	No.	Allottee	Intruder
Jan 5, 1905	314	W. T. Partin[sic], guardian of Everett T. Partin Ramona, I.T.	Clarence and Wm Gorham
Notice Sent		**Action**	**Remarks**
Jan 19, 1905		Set for hearing at Vinita 2/10/05	Commission reports
		Return of service Jany 27, 1905	Certificates have been issued and no contests are pending, Jan. 10, '05
	2/10/05	Case called. Wm T. Partain appeared for plaintiff, no appearance by defendant, judgment by default entered for plaintiff	2/11/05 Certificates filed N°s 7259, 7632, 7258, 7631 Original letters of guardianship filed.
	2/25/05	Instructions to A.F. Chamberlain to place Allottee in possession and report to this office.	
		3/28/05 Report of Chamberlain filed stating plaintiff was in possession and wants certificates returned.	
		Certificates as numbered in margin above returned 4/4/05 and case Dismissed	

Cherokee Intruder Cases 1901 - 1909

Date Received	No.	Allottee	Intruder
Dec 22, 1904	315	Ole Olson, for Andrew B. Olson	Robert McDonald
Notice Sent		**Action**	**Remarks**
Jan 19, 1905		Set for hearing at Vinita 2/10/05 Return of Service Jan 24	Commission reports Certificates have been issued and that there are no contests pending Jan 10/05
	2/10/05	Case called. No appearance by either party	
	2/10/05	Letter received from plaintiff that defendant had vacated land and plaintiff is in peaceable possession. Case therefore dismissed	

Date Received	No.	Allottee	Intruder
Dec 23, 1904	316	Lincoln Buffalo	Alex Rector and wife
Notice Sent		**Action**	**Remarks**
Jan 19, 1905		Set for hearing at Vinita 2/10/05 Return of Service Jany 28 1905	Commission reports see [#]315 Certificate issued and no contests pending Jan 10 1905
	2/10/05	Case called. All parties appear in person. Defendant agrees to give possession of land involved and Allottee agrees to pay forty dollars for improvements Case Dismissed and certificates returned to Allottee in person	
	2/25/05	Instructions issued to A.F. Chamberlain to remove defendant and place Allottee in possession.	
	4/3/05	Report of A. F. Chamberlain filed showing that Allottee was placed in possession of allotment.	
			Dismissed

Date Received	No.	Allottee	Intruder
December 27, '04	317	William Crittenden	A.D. Morton
Notice Sent	**Action**		**Remarks**
Jan 19, 1905	Return of Service Jan 23rd Answer filed Jan. 25, '05		Commission reports no contests and that Certificates have been issued Jan 10 1905 See [#]315 Dismissed

Cherokee Intruder Cases 1901 - 1909

Date Received	No.	Allottee	Intruder
Jan 7, 1905	318	Stand W. Davis	Gilbert W. Nicholson
Notice Sent		**Action**	**Remarks**
Jan 19, 1905		Set for Muskogee, I.T. 3/15/05 3/17/05 Upon written application of plaintiff case was <u>dismissed</u> Certificates returned to Allottee 6/22/05	Certificates in file. Letter to Commission asking if there be any contests pending Jan. 19. Commission reports no contests Jan 24.

Date Received	No.	Allottee	Intruder
Jan 14, 1905	319	Herman Weaver	John Kettle
Notice Sent		**Action**	**Remarks**
Jan 19, 05		Return of Service Jan 25, '05 Set for Muskogee IT 3/14/05 3/14/05 Case called. Plaintiff appeared in person and upon his application the case was dismissed	Certificates in file. Letter to Commission asking if there be any contests pending Jan 19. Commission reports no contests Jan 24. 6/26/05 Certificates returned to Allottee Dismissed.

Date Received	No.	Allottee	Intruder
Jan 19, 1905	320	Frank Phillips: for self and minors, Spencer D, Ewell, Ula Maud Phillips Sperry I.T.	Ed. Bell
Notice Sent		**Action**	**Remarks**
Jan 19, 1905		Set for hearing at Vinita 2/10/05 2/10/05 Case called. Frank Phillips appeared personally, no appearance by defendants Judgment by default entered in favor of plaintiff and case given to police.	Certificates in file. Letter to Commission if there be contests pending, Jan 19, 1905. Commission reports no contests Jan 24, 1905 6/26/05 Certificates returned to Allottee

Cherokee Intruder Cases 1901 - 1909

3/15/05	Instructions issued to Policeman W^m M Sunday to place Allottee in possession and report Action in matter to this office	
4/3/05	Report of Sunday that he placed Allottee in possession March 21, 1905 and case	Dismissed
7/18/05	Allottee Ack. receipt of his certificates	

Date Received	No.	Allottee	Intruder
Jan 12, 1905	321	Abraham Heistand for Adam Heistand Thomas and Foreman Muskogee Attys for Plaintiff	R. J. Boyd
Notice Sent		**Action**	**Remarks**
Jan 19, 1905		7/10/05 Plaintiff requested to serve motion sent to him and make return to this office	Certificates in file. Letter to Commission asking if there be any contests Jan. 19, 1905
		3/14/05 Set for hearing at Muskogee IT 3/14/05 No appearance by either party Case set for hearing at Muskogee on July 26-05	Commission reports no contests Jan. 24
		7/26/05 No appearance by either party	
		7/27/05 Case dismissed by personal request of plaintiff and certificates ret'd	

Date Received	No.	Allottee	Intruder
Jan 10, 1905	322	Eliza Baker, for Freddie E. and Etta M. Baker M.T. Baker is the legal gdn of Freddie E. and Etta M. Baker	Willis G. Ash
Notice Sent		**Action**	**Remarks**
Jan 19, 1905		Set for hearing at Vinita 2/10/05	Certificates on file Letter to Commission asking if there be any contests filed Jan 19 Commission reports no contests Jan. 24, '05

Cherokee Intruder Cases 1901 - 1909

2/2/05	Letter received from Eliza Baker that satisfactory arrangements had been made and requesting that case be dismissed, and certificates returned to Mrs. Eliza Baker. ~~Collinsville~~ Owasso, Ind Ter
	Dismissed

Date Received	No.	Allottee	Intruder
Jan 7, 1905	323	Jennie Martin	Lee P. Moore
Notice Sent		**Action**	**Remarks**
Jan 19, 1905		Return of Service Jan 23 Answer filed Jan 26, '05 (Defendant says he will move soon as possible, see file)	Certificates on file Letter to Commission asking if there be any contests Jan 19, 1905 Commission reports no contests Jan 24
	2/23/05	Instructions sent policeman McIntosh to place Allottee in possession and report to this office.	
	3/1/05	Report of McIntosh that Allottee was placed in possession Feby 27, 1905 filed and case Dismissed	
		6/26/05 Certificates returned to Allottee	

Date Received	No.	Allottee	Intruder
Jan 7, 1905	324	Samuel and Amanda Perry Ramona, I.T.	Rheuben Swan
Notice Sent		**Action**	**Remarks**
Jan 20, 1905		Set for hearing at Vinita 2/10/05 Return of Service Jan 24, 1905	Certificates in file Letter to Commission asking if there be any contests filed Jan 20 Commission advises no contests Jan 24, '05
	2/10/05	Answer filed Jan 25, '05 Case called. Samuel Perry, testimony taken, parties then settled the matter amicably and case dismissed and certificates returned to Allottees in person	
			Dismissed

Date Received	No.	Allottee	Intruder
Jan 18, 1905	325	Mrs. Maria Lynch, nee Smith, for herself and Cicero L. Lynch, Jr.	~~Mr~~. and Mrs Scott

Cherokee Intruder Cases 1901 - 1909

Notice Sent	Action	Remarks
Jan 20, 1905	Return of Service Jan 24, '05	Certificates in file
	Set for Muskogee IT 3/15/05	Letter to Commission asking if there be any contests filed Jan 20
		Commission advises no contests Jan 24
	3/15/05 Case called. Plaintiff appeared in person and states she is in possession of the lands. It further appears from her statement that the contention between parties is for the improvements and rents, and she was advised that such matters were not within the jurisdiction of the agent.	
	Case dismissed and Certificates N° 17574, 23948, 26603 returned to Allottee in person.	Dismissed

Date Received	No.	Allottee	Intruder
Jan 18, 1905	326	Mrs. Georgia A. Stokes, gdn of Gretta E. Stokes	Harry Stead and ----- Lamb

Notice Sent	Action	Remarks
Jan 20, 1905	Return of Service Jan 24, '05	Certificates in file
	1/30/05 Answer filed	Letters of Guardianship in file.
	Set for hearing 2/10/05	
2/11/05	Case called. No appearance by either party	Letter to Commission asking if there be any contests pending Jan 20
	Case set for hearing at Claremore Aug 1st-05	Commission advises no contests Jan 24, 1905
	3/19/06 Referred to Eldon Lowe for investigation	
Mch 30	Report of Eldon Lowe filed and case dismissed upon request of Ptf	
	Certificate returned	Dismissed

Date Received	No.	Allottee	Intruder
Jan 16, 1905	327	Jennie Blackbird	Jim Berley and Joe Dartson

Notice Sent	Action	Remarks
Jan 20, 1905	Answer filed Jany 31, 1905	Certificates in file
	Return of service Jany 28, 1905	Letters to Commission asking if there be any contests pending, Jan 20
	Set for 2/25/05 at Muskogee, I.T.	
2/14/05	Case called, compromise effected	

Cherokee Intruder Cases 1901 - 1909

| | and upon motion of plaintiff case dismissed and Certificates returned to her in person | Commission advising no contests on Jan 24, '05 Dismissed |

Date Received	No.	Allottee	Intruder
Jan 18, 1905	328	William C. Hampton for self & Ritchie L., and Floratta M. Hampton Whiteoak I.T.	Bud ~~Miller~~ Miles et al
Notice Sent		**Action**	**Remarks**
Jan 20, 1905		Set for hearing at Vinita 2/10/05 Answer filed Jan 19, 1905 Return of Service, Jan 27, '05 amended answer filed 2/3/05	Certificates in file Letter to Commission asking if there be any contests Jan 20 Commission reports no contests Jan 24

2/10/05 Case called. By agreement case continued to 2/11/05
2/11/05 Case called at 2.30 P.M. William C Hampton appeared for self and children and testimony taken. Fred L. Kelley sworn for defense
Defendants want time to introduce Mr. Kornegay to testify as to contract.
4/1/05. Plaintiff requests that case be dismissed and copy of contract and certificates 1013, 891, 890, 1012, 10815, 13454, 1010, 888, returned to W. H. Kornegay Atty at Law Vinita, I.T.
Dismissed

Date Received	No.	Allottee	Intruder
Jan 21, 1905	329	Lelia R Richards for self, and Joe R., and also for minors-Beatrice, Carrollton M and Earl Richards Contract returned to Allottee 7/12/05	Mrs. Elizabeth Osborn
Notice Sent		**Action**	**Remarks**
Jan 25, 1905		Return of service 2/1/05 Brief filed 6/9/05 Set for hearing Feb. 11, 1905 at Vinita, I.T.	Certificates in file Letter to Commission asking if there be any contest pending Jan 25, 1905

111

Cherokee Intruder Cases 1901 - 1909

> 1/31/05 Com. reports no contest
> Certs # 11641, 14640, 14641, 11625, 14639, 11623, 14638, 11622
> Certs ret'd 6/7/05

2/19/05 Continued by stipulation for allotment of plaintiff and defendant indefinitely.

4/11/05 Set for Claremore, I.T. April 21 1905

11/17/05 Case called, All parties appeared in person. Testimony taken and it was agreed that attorneys should file briefs, the attorney for defendant allowed fifteen days after receipt of brief of attorney for plaintiff.
Judgement[sic] rendered in favor of defendant as to Lelia R. Richards and Dismissed as to the answers for the want of a Legal Guar.

Dismissed

6/10/05 Certificates returned to plaintiff

Date Received	No.	Allottee	Intruder
Jan 19, 1905	330	Charles J. Shawnee for William Shawnee	Joshua Vineyard
Notice Sent		**Action**	**Remarks**
Jan 25, 1905		Return of service Jany 28, 1905 filed 1/30/05 Set for hearing at Vinita on Feb 11, 1905.	Certificates in file. Letter to Commission asking if there be any contests filed, Jan. 25, 1905 1/31/05 Com reports no contest
	5/11/05	Case called no appearance by either party	
	2/21/05	Instructions sent to A. F. Chamberlain to place Allottee in possession and report to this office.	
	2/28/05	Case dismissed upon receipt of letter from Allottee that he is in possession	
		3/28/05 Report of Chamberlain filed.	Dismissed
		6/26/05 Certificate returned to Allottee	

Cherokee Intruder Cases 1901 - 1909

Date Received	No.	Allottee	Intruder
Jan 23, 1905	331	John N. and Dovie Cox	George M. Ward

Notice Sent	Action	Remarks
Jan 25, 1905	Return of service dated Jany 28 1905 filed 1/30/05 Answer filed Jany 31, 1905 Set for hearing at Vinita on ~~Jan~~ Feb 11, 1905	Certificates in file Letter to Commission asking if there be any contests filed Jan. 25 '05 1/31/05 Com reports land in contest, not determined
	2/11/05 Case called. Both parties appeared in Court. All land embraced in complaint in contest except twenty acres which Ward is to give up and remove his fences to line. Certificates returned to Allottee in person.	
		Dismissed.

Date Received	No.	Allottee	Intruder
Jan 10, 1905	332	John Johnson	Mary Caldwell

Notice Sent	Action	Remarks
Jan 25, 1905	Return of service Jany 30, 1905	Certificates in file Letter to Commission asking if there be any contests Jan 26, 1905
	Set for Muskogee, I.T. 3/15/05 3/15/05 It appearing from a letter from Dawes Com, to Allottee, that land is under contest, therefore case was dismissed and Certificate N° 23113 delivered to plaintiff in person	1/30/05 Com reports no contest 3/15/05 Dismissed

Date Received	No.	Allottee	Intruder
Jan 23, 1905	333	Thomas Weaver c/o R.H. Couch, Atty	E.B. Willis

Notice Sent	Action	Remarks
Jan 25, 1905	Return of service Jany 20, 1905 Answer filed 2/2/05	Certificates in file Letter to Commission asking if there be any contests filed, Jan 26, 1905.
	3/3/05 Instructions sent to policeman R. Lee Wiley to place Allottee in possession and report Action to this office 3/15/05 Policeman Wyly reports he placed plaintiff in possession	1/31/05 Com reports no contest 6/9-05 Certificates 18373 *(Illegible)* given Couch in person Dismissed

Cherokee Intruder Cases 1901 - 1909

Date Received	No.	Allottee	Intruder
Jan 21, 1905	334	Virgil C. Holland	Ben Roger[sic]

Notice Sent	Action	Remarks
Jan 25, 1905	Return of service Jany 28, 1905 Feb 25/05 Instructions sent Policeman Chamberlain to place Allottee in possession 3/22/05 Allottee reports he is in possession See Chamberlain's report also 4/24/05 Certificate N°s 16578 & 22338 returned to Virgil C Holland Manard I.T. per request of Allottee	Certificates in file Letter to Commission asking if there be any contests pending Jan 26, '05 1/30/05 Com reports no contest Settled Dismissed

Date Received	No.	Allottee	Intruder
Jan 23, 1905	335	Thomas J. White	Willy Johns

Notice Sent	Action	Remarks
Jan 25, 1905	Return of service Jany 25, 1905 2/17/05 Plaintiff notified that land is in contest and not determined and case dismissed in accordance therewith. 7/1/05 Plaintiff Thomas J. White acknowledges receipt of certificates	Certificates in file Letter to Commission asking if there be any contests pending Jan 26 1/30/05 Com reports that land is in contest & not determined Dismissed 6/26/05 Certificates returned to Allottee

Date Received	No.	Allottee	Intruder
Jan 23, 1905	336	Cynthia Tucker	Luis Elias Sanders R. E. Butler

Notice Sent	Action	Remarks
Jan 25, 1905 " 27- 1905	Return of service Jany 30, 190$5^{1/3}$1/05 " " " Jany 25, 190$5^{3}$/31/05 2/15/05 Answer by Butler filed 3/6/05 Papers filed by Butler 3/9/05 Attys for plaintiff advises case dismissed	Certificates have been in file but returned to plaintiffs attorneys see case #299 Letter to Commission asking if there be any contest Jan 26 1/22/04[sic] Com reports no contest Dismissed !

Cherokee Intruder Cases 1901 - 1909

Date Received	No.	Allottee	Intruder
Jan 23, 1905	337	George Ewers, Jr for Tams Bixby and Charles Ewers	John Wilkins and Mrs Pair Wilkins Wife
		5/27/05 Case set for hearing at Muskogee, I.T. June 9 1905 at 2 P.M.	

Notice Sent	Action	Remarks
Jan 25, 1905	Return of service 2/4/05	Certificates in file
		Letter to Commission asking
	Set for hearing at Vinita on Feb. 11, 1905	if there be any contest pending Jan 26, 1905
		1/30/05 Com reports no contest
2/12/05	Case called. George Ewers appeared for plaintiff and testimony taken. No appearance by defendants and judgment by default rendered.	
2/16/05	Letter received from defendant dated 2/15/05 enclosing affidavits that no notice was ~~sent~~ received by them until 2 o'clock of the day case was set for hearing at Vinita, filed in case.	
2/24/05	In consequence of above notation and claim, instructions to police were withheld and case reopened and set for hearing at Muskogee I.T,	
3/3/05	Mch 3, 1905, 2 PM Case called. Defendant appeared, no appearance by plaintiff and case to be set for hearing and notice sent parties	
Dismissed	Certs ret^{d} 6/9/05 to plaintiff in person	

2/23/05 Instructions sent to Chamberlain.

Date Received	No.	Allottee	Intruder
Jan 23, 1905	338	Mrs. Ollie Robin	----------------

Notice Sent	Action	Remarks
Jan 25, 1905	Return of service 2/10/05	Certificates in file.
	Set for Muskogee, I.T. 3/16/05	Letter to Commission on Jan. 26, asking if there be any contests pending
		1/30/05 Com reports no contest
3/16/05	Case called. All parties present, held Allottee was to be placed in possession and instructions issued to policeman Certificates N$^{\underline{o}}$ 9235, 11370, delivered to Eli Robin - husband of plaintiff in person	
3/16/05	Instructions given policeman Tom Roach to place Allottee in	

Cherokee Intruder Cases 1901 - 1909

	possession and report Action in matter to this office.
4/11/05	Information having reached this office that land had been vacated and Allottee was in possession and case was Dismissed

Date Received	No.	Allottee	Intruder
Jan 23, '05	339	Mary Jackson for self & Lula Jackson	-----------------

Notice Sent	Action	Remarks
Jan 25, 1905	2/1/05 Return of service	Certificates in file.
		Letter to Commission asking
	Set for hearing Muskogee IT 3/16/05	if there be any contests pending-Jan 26, 1905
	5/15/05 Upon written application of Allottee Certificates N°s 21210, 29779, 29777 and 21209 were returned to her at Porum and case Dismissed	

Date Received	No.	Allottee	Intruder
Jan 19, 1905	340	William H. Brown for self and Birt M. Brown	Jim Hunt

Notice Sent	Action	Remarks
Jan 25, 1905	Return of service Jany 28, 1905	Certificates in file.
		Letter to Commission asking if there be any contests pending Jan. 26, '05
		1/15/05 Com reports no contest
	3/2/05 Instructions sent to policeman Monnie McIntosh to place Allottee in possession and report Action in this office	
	Answer and letter filed Mch 3, 1905.	
	3/22/05 Policeman McIntosh reports that he placed Allottee in possession	Settled
	4/6/05 Certificates N° 27090, 19472, 27092, 19493 returned to Allottee in person	

Cherokee Intruder Cases 1901 - 1909

Date Received	No.	Allottee	Intruder
Jan 23, 1905	341	Margaret E. Wilkie Sharp	Joseph P. Scott

Notice Sent	Action	Remarks
Jan 25, 1905	Return of service Feby 18 1905	Commission reports
	" " " 21/1905	certificates issued and no contests Jan. 20, 1905
		3/23/05 ~~Com reports that~~
2/23/05	See letter of Allottee dated 2/20/05 asking that case be withheld until further notice from her is received	
	Answer of defendant filed	
	3/19, 1906 Referred to Eldon Lowe for investigation	
April 20	Report of Eldon Lowe filed and case dismissed upon request of Plaintiff	
		Dismissed

Date Received	No.	Allottee	Intruder
Jan 23, 1905	342	Charles W. Downing	Lenord[sic] Gatly

Notice Sent	Action	Remarks
Jan 25, 1905	Return of service 2/2/05	Commission reports
		Certificates issued and no
	Set for Muskogee, I.T. 3/16/05	contests Jan 20, 1905
3/16/05	Case called. Dfdnt appears in person and advises he is not in possession of land claim'd by plntiff[sic], nor does he claim any right thereto	
	He also informs me that Chas W Downing is a minor being about 4 years old. No appearance in behalf of plntiff named	
	3/28/05 Com advises that land in complaint is in contest	
		Dismissed

Date Received	No.	Allottee	Intruder
Jan 20, 1905	343	Charles Bell c/o George & Julian Attys	W. E. Dye
			JA Tillotson Atty for Defendant
			Nowata, I.T.

3/19th 1906 Referred to Eldon Lowe for investigation
3/23 Report of Eldon Lowe filed and case dismissed upon request of Ptf.

5/25/05 Instructions sent to Elijah Henderson to place Allottee in possession
6/30/05 Policeman Henderson reports unable to execute order at

Cherokee Intruder Cases 1901 - 1909

this time c/o tribal tax occupying his time, see report filed #450
July 31st - 05   Report of policeman Henderson filed

Notice Sent	Action	Remarks
Jan 26, 1905	Return of service Feby 10, 1905	Commission reports no contests and Certificate issued
	Set for hearing at Vinita on Feb 11 1905	Jan 10 1905 see #312
	2/11/05 Case called. No appearance by either party	
	3/17/05 Plaintiffs' attorney requests that case be postponed until further notice is received from him, and agreed to by defendants attorney Set for Claremore, I.T. April 21, 1905, no hour	Certs 17396, 23717 not filed, exhibitia[sic] 4/21/05
	4/21/05 Case called, all parties present & by counsel. Testimony taken. Agreed to give parties chance to settle. Attorney for plaintiff to advise if settlement is made	

Dismissed

Date Received	No.	Allottee	Intruder
Jan 26, '05	344	Mary Patterson	John Shoemaker and T. J. Jordan

Notice Sent	Action	Remarks
Jan 26, 1905	Return of service Feby 2/05 Answer filed Feby 11, 1905	Certificates in file Letter to Commission asking if there be any contests pending Jan 26 1/30/05 Com reports no contest
	2/11/05 Case called. Mary Patterson appeared in person and her testimony taken. No appearance by Defendants.	
	2/27/05 Instructions sent to A.F. Chamberlain to place Allottee in possession and report to this office. 3/29/05 Report of Arthur F Chamberlain filed herein	
	7/5/05 Plaintiff Ack. receipt of certf. Dismissed 6/26/05 Certificate returned to Allottee	

Date Received	No.	Allottee	Intruder
Jan 24, 1905	345	Jack Rose Mulkey	J. W. Echols

Notice Sent	Action	Remarks
Jan 26, 1905	Return of service Jany 30, 1905	Certificates in file. Letter to Commission asking

Cherokee Intruder Cases 1901 - 1909

2/14/05	Plaintiff appeared in person and admitted that he was a minor and case was dis-missed and papers transferred to Nº 283.	if there be any contests pending, Jan. 26, '05 Dismissed

Date Received	No.	Allottee	Intruder
Jan 25, 1905	346	Joe Hildebrand guardian of Jessie and Louis Bibles.	Walter Ross
Notice Sent		**Action**	**Remarks**
Jan 27, 1905		Return of service Jany 31, 1905 Set for hearing at Vinita on Feb. 11, 1905.	Certificates in file Letter to Commission asking if there be any contests Jan 27, 1905 1/30/05 Com reports no contest
	2/11/05	Case called. Joe Hildebrand appeared and testimony taken. Guardian filed on lands and then made lease of lands without approval of Court. Case dismissed. Certificates returned <s>Certificates ret'd to pltf</s> <s>Dism</s>	Dismissed

Date Received	No.	Allottee	Intruder
Jany 31, 1905	347	Warseat Lucy for self and Levi & Ella Warseat c/o J.A. Tillotson Atty, Nowata, I.T.	George W. Case Nowata, I.T.
Docketed		**Action**	**Remarks**
2/1/05		1/31/05 Notices sent Return of Service Feby 6, 1905 Answer by Geo H[sic] Case filed 2/15/05	1/31/05 Com requested to advise if there was any contest on lands or part thereof 1/31/05 Certificates filed. 2/6/05 Com reports lands <u>not</u> in contest.
	3/2/05	Instructions issued to defendant that he must vacate premise at earliest convenience	
	5/5/05	Instructions issued to Saml Edmonds to place Allottee in possession reporting Action to this office	
	5/15/05	Dismissed upon written application of Allottee and Certificate returned to her Certfs ret'd to pltf. Dec 13-05	Dismissed

Cherokee Intruder Cases 1901 - 1909

Date Received	No.	Allottee	Intruder
Jany 28, 1905	348	Nash, F. H. for Hilda Nash Ft Gibson, I.T.	Tom Walker & wife
Docketed		**Action**	**Remarks**
2/3/05		2/2/05 Notice sent for service Return of service 2/5/05	Certificate file Cherokee # 4596, 5579
		2/23/05 Instructions issued to policeman Theodore E Stidham to place Allottee in possession and report Action to this office	2/3/05 Com requested to advise to contest 2/7/05 Com advises no contest
	2/28/05	Report of Theo E Stidham that he had placed Allottee in possession filed herein and <u>case dismissed</u>	
			Dismissed
		6/26/05 Certificate returned to Allottee	

Date Received	No.	Allottee	Intruder
Jany 31, 1905	349	Keys W.R.W.C. for G.A.L. Keys 5 Muldrow IT vs	J. M. Nichols Muldrow IT
Docketed		**Action**	**Remarks**
2/3/05		2/2/05 Notices sent for service	Certificate file N⁰ 4413 2/3/05 Com requested to
		Set for hearing at Muskogee, I.T. 3/16/05	advise as to contest 2/7/05 Com advises no
	3/16/05	No appearance	contest
	5/17/05	Certf returned to plaintiff by request filed herein	

Date Received	No.	Allottee	Intruder
Jany 31, 1905	350	Brown, William & Mary Dewey, I.T. vs	Dan Ware Dewey I.T.
Docketed		**Action**	**Remarks**
2/3/05		2/2/05 Notices sent for service. Set for hearing at Claremore, I.T. April 18, 1905 at 10 A.M.	Certificates filed #11360, 11361, 14221, 14222
	4/13/05	Upon receipt of letter from plaintiff dated April 10 1905 in which it is stated defendant has	2/3/05 Com requested to advise as to contest 2/7/05 Com advises <u>No contest</u>

Cherokee Intruder Cases 1901 - 1909

vacated land and plaintiff is now in possession, the case was dismissed	
Certs 11360, 11361, 14221, 14222 returned to plaintiff in person 5/23/05	Dismissed

Date Received	No.	Allottee	Intruder
Jany 31, 1905	351	Elliott, William Harlan by vs Anna Elliott Vian, I.T.	Mary T. Cauley
Notice Sent		**Action**	**Remarks**
2/2/05		Return of Service Feb 7, 1905	Certificates filed
		Answer of Mary McCauley filed	#24128, 24129, 17681
Docketed		7/15/05	2/3/05 Com requested to
2/3/05		Case set for hearing at Claremore on	advise as to contest
		Aug. 1st/05	2/7/05 Com reports land is in
	Aug 1st	Case called and it appears that the land in controversy is contended by the defendant the plaintiff having possession of the rest of her land consequently the case was	contest
			Dismissed
		and certificate were[sic] returned to Allottee in person	
	3/16	Certificate N° 24128 withdrawn by plaintiff to be used in contest pending before Com. delivered William Elliott	

Date Received	No.	Allottee	Intruder
Jany 31, 1905	352	Elliott Annie for vs Pennie K *(or R)* Elliott Vian, I.T.	Tom Glass Defendant Glass is a full blood and a portion of the land filed on is his own home
Notice Sent		**Action**	**Remarks**
2/2/05		Return of Service Feb 7, 1905	Certificates filed
Docketed	2/15/05	Answer by Tom Glass filed, saying	#24127, 24126, 17680
2/3/05		that as soon as lines are established he will put his fence on line	2/5/05 Com requested to advise as to contest
			2/7/05 Com advises land
		Case set for hearing at Claremore on Aug 1st-05	contested and not determined
			2/7/05 Com advises no contest
	Aug 1st 05	Case called all parties being present and it appears that there is no guar. consequently case was	

Cherokee Intruder Cases 1901 - 1909

	and certificate returned	Dismissed

Date Received	No.	Allottee	Intruder
Jany 31, 1905	353	Elliott Annie vs Vian, I.T. Docket 2/3/05	James Tatum

Notice Sent	Action	Remarks
	2/2/05 Return of Service, Feb 7, 1905	Certificates filed #17679, 24125, 24124
		2/3/05 Com requested to
	Set for hearing at Muskogee, I.T.	advise as to contest
	3/16/05	2/7/05 Com advises no contests pending
	3/17/05 Instructions issued to Monnie McIntosh to place Allottee in possession and report Action to this office	
	4/18/05 Report of Monnie McIntosh that the defendant has given Allottee possession and case was Dismissed Certificates returned to Allottee 7/7/05	
	7/25/05 Allottee Ack. receipt of certificates	
June 19 1906[sic]		

Date Received	No.	Allottee	Intruder
Jany 30, 1905	354	Provence Maggie E vs nee Cummings Adair, I.T. Docketed 2/3/05	N.E. Little and Harve Martin Adair, I.T. Martin is applicant as Cher Freedman Starr and Patterson Attys Vinita
	May 29/06 Com[r] reports that Dfdts have been denied citizenship 6/9 Case set for hearing at Claremore IT June 19/06		
	June 19 Answer of Defendants filed Case called at Claremore Plaintiffs appeared and Mr Starr appeared for Dfdt, no evidence was taken as Atty for Dfdt stated that no contract existed between the Ptf and Dfdt. But that a motion to review the citizenship case of the Dfdt is now pending before Com[r]. If no case is pending before Com[r] Dfdts will be removed June 26 Com[r] requested to report as to citizenship of Harve Martin		

Cherokee Intruder Cases 1901 - 1909

Notice Sent	Action	Remarks
July 17 1906	Com^r reports a motion pending ~~for~~ to reopen citizenship case of Harve Martin is now pending therefore case is Dismissed	Dismissed

Date Received	No.	Allottee	Intruder
Jany 3			

(partial/obscured text visible:)
.T.
as
tys
Case
r
t stated
at a
pending

If no case is pending before Com^r Dfdts will be removed June 26 Com^r requested to report as to citizenship of Harve Martin

Notice Sent	Action	Remarks
2/2/05	Notices sent for service	Certificate filed #1172, 14775
2/4/05	Return of service	
2/13/05	Answer filed dated 2/11/05 Set for hearing at Muskogee, I.T. 3/17/05	2/5/05 Com requested to advise as to contest 2/7/05 Com reports no contests pending

3/17/05 Case called. Plaintiff appears and acknowledged that Martin is an applicant as a Cher Freed, therefore under Departmental instructions of Mch 7 1905 the case is withheld.
Later. Defendant Harve Martin appeared and his testimony was taken when it was developed that said Martin is a claimant as a Cherokee freedman as stated above.
(Illegible) 1906
In compliance with Departmental instructions of April 19th 1906 Com^r is requested to furnish this office with status of allotment of Ptf and of citizenship of Dfdt.

Cherokee Intruder Cases 1901 - 1909

Date Received	No.	Allottee	Intruder
Feby 1, 1905	355	Thompson Henry & Lucinda Braggs, I.T.	vs Elizabeth Duncan Coffeyville, Ks
		Docketed 2/3/05	Claimant for citizenship as Cher Freedman
July 20 1906			and Jewell C. Duncan
1906 Aug 10,		Plntf notified of dismissed because of advise[sic] from Com^r that motion is pending in his office for rehearing of citizenship case of Jewel C Duncan	
			Dismissed

Notice Sent	Action	Remarks
2/2/05	Sent for service Return of service Feby 20 1905 Certificate returned to Allottee Sept 19	Certificates filed Fdm 8993, 8992 2/3/05 Com requested to advise as to contest 2/7/05 Com reports land is in contest
May 8 1906	In compliance with Departmental instructions of April 19th 1906 Com^r is requested to furnish this office with status of allotment of pltf and of citizenship of Dfdt	
June 11/06	Com^r again requested to report as it appears that report filed by him under date of May 29 is in *(Illegible)*	
June 19 1906	Com^r reports no motion to reopen or review pending	
July 18 "	Com^r requested to advise if a motion to review was filed prior to June 26 1906	

Date Received	No.	Allottee	Intruder
Feby 1 1905	356	Lee, Rau for Amelia Alice Ft Gibson, I.T. Docketed 2-3-05 Plaintiff asked today if that[sic] defendant is a freedman *(illegible...)*	vs Elizabeth Dunken[sic] Coffeyville, Kans

Notice Sent	Action	Remarks
2/3/05	Notices sent for service Return of service Feby 20 1905 Certificates returned to plaintiff July 7-05	Certificate filed fdm $^{\#}$ 7437 2/3/05 Com requested to advise as to contest 2/7/05 Com reports that land

Cherokee Intruder Cases 1901 - 1909

	is in contest
May 8 1906	In compliance with Departmental instructions of of[sic] April 19<u>th</u> 1906 Com^r is requested to furnish this office with status of Amelia A Lee and of citizenship of Elizabeth Duncan
May 29 "	Com^r reports that citizenship has been denied Dfdt
June 8 "	Case set for hearing at Claremore IT 6/19/06
" 9 "	Case called at Claremore IT Plaintiff appears and requested that case be dismissed as he states he is now in possession
	Dismissed

Date Received	No.	Allottee	Intruder
Feby 1 1905	357	Silk, Anderson & Annie Braggs, I.T. Docketed 2-3-05	vs Elizabeth Duncan Coffeyville, Ks J C Duncan
July 20 1906		Com^r reports a motion for review of citizenship case is pending of J C Duncan only	
Aug 16 1906		Com^r asked to advise this office if motion to reopen was filed prior to June 26 1906	
Aug 18 1906		Com^r advised no motion filed to reopen a review case of Elizabeth Duncan further that a motion for rehearing is pending, in the case of Elizabeth Duncan further that a motion for rehearing is pending, in the case of Robert C, Harry A, Jewell, Joel C. and Benjamin F Duncan as Cherokee Freedman filed June 23 1906	
Aug 20 1906		In view of above stated conditions case dismissed & parties notified	
			Dismissed

Notice Sent	Action	Remarks
2/2/05	Notices sent for service	Certificates filed 8738, 8739
	Certificates returned to plaintiff Sept 18/05	2/3/05 Com requested to advise as to contest
2/21/05	Case dismissed, land in contest	1/31/05 Com reports land in contest not yet determined
		2/7/05 Com report portion of land in contest.
	Defendant claims to be an applicant for citizenship *(illegible....)*	
May 8 1906	In compliance with Departmental instructions of April 19 1906 Com r is requested to report as to the status of allotment of Ptfs and of citizenship of Dfdt.	
" 27 "	Com^r report that Dfdt has been denied citizenship	

Cherokee Intruder Cases 1901 - 1909

June 8	"	Case set for hearing at Claremore IT June 19/06
" 19	"	Case called at Claremore Neither party appeared

Date Received	No.	Allottee	Intruder
Feby 1, 1905	358	Hall Josephne[sic] for self vs and Georgiana Jennie Hall & Joseph Coody Ft Gibson, I.T. Docketed 2-3-05	Mose Rose Coffeyville, KS Claims as Cher Freedman
Notice Sent		Action	Remarks
2/2/05		Notices sent for service Set for hearing at Muskogee, I.T. 3/17/05	Certificates filed Fdm #21524, 16063, 16062, 21525 16064, 21526

3/17/05 Case called. No appearance by plaintiff, Defendant appears in person, testimony taken and held under instructions of Department March 7 1905 relative to Cherokee Freedman   3/17/05 Com reports portion is now in contest
4/27/05 Certificates numbered in margin hereof were returned to Josephine Hall Braggs, I.T. in compliance with her written request.
May 8 1906 In compliance with Departmental instructions of April 19th 1906 Com^r is requested to furnish this office with status of the allotments of the Ptfs and of the citizenship of the Defendants
June 5 1906 Case dismissed as Com^r reports that citizenship cases of Dfdts is now pending before Dept.   Dismissed

Date Received	No.	Allottee	Intruder
Jany 31, 1905	359	Ballard, William for Carrie Ballard Braggs, I.T. Docketed 2/3/05	vs James Cummings Wann, I.T.
Notice Sent		Action	Remarks
	2/2/05	Return of Service, Feb. 9, 1905 " " " Feby 24, 1905 Answer and bill of sale filed 3/3/05 Set for hearing at Muskogee, I.T. 3/17/05	Certificates filed Fdm #27245, 19603 2/3/05 Com requested to advise as to contest 2/7/05 Com advises no contests pending

126

Cherokee Intruder Cases 1901 - 1909

3/17/05 Case called. Plaintiff appeared in person and his evidence was taken. it being claimed in the answer that land has been contested, the Com was requested to advise relative thereto, and decision witheld[sic] until such information is received.	
Case dismissed by request of plaintiff Aug 29-05	3/23/05 Com advises no contest 3/13/05 Com advises no contest
Certificates returned to plaintiff Aug 30,05	Dismissed

Date Received	No.	Allottee		Intruder
Jany 31, 1905	360	Peters, Cynthia for Luvinia & Henry Rider Porum, I.T. Docketed 2/3/05	vs	Thos. B. Matthews et al Porum, I.T.
Notice Sent		**Action**		**Remarks**
2/2/05 2/05[sic]		Notices sent for service Return of service 2/9/05 Answer filed Set for hearing at Muskogee, I.T. 3/17/05		Certificates filed Fdm #21799, 30639, 21798, 30637 2/3/05 Com requested to advise as to contest 2/7/05 Com advises no contests pending
3/28/05		Case called. Plaintiff appeared in person. It appears that no one except Allottee is in possession and case was dismissed and certificates returned to Allottee in person. Certs Nº 21799, 30639, 21798, 30737		
				Dismissed

Date Received	No.	Allottee		Intruder
Jany 27, 1905	361	Wofford, Taylor Tahlequah, I.T. Docketed 2/3/05	vs	Dick Hardrick
Notice Sent		**Action**		**Remarks**
2/2/05		Notices sent for service Return of service Feby 24/05		Certificates filed Fdm #19886, 27693 2/3/05 Com requested to advise as to contest

Cherokee Intruder Cases 1901 - 1909

3/16/05	Land being in contest as shown by report of Com, case was dismissed and Certificates returned to Taylor Wofford	2/7/05 Com advises no contest Error *(Illegible)* Tahlequah, I.T. 3/11/05 Com advises contest on lands and not determined Dismissed

Date Received	No.	Allottee	Intruder
Feby 3, 1905	362	Wolfe, Joe grdn for Jeneva Wofford Baron, I.T. Docketed 2/3/05 with status of allotment of Jeneva Wofford and status of citizenship of Frank and Pearl Smith	vs Pearl and Frank Smith Elliott I.T. Claims as freedman
	June 5/06	Case dismissed as Com^r reports that a motion to review citizenship case of Defendants is now pending Certificates returned to Plaintiff	
	Nov 4/07	Com^r requested to advise as to status of citizenship of defendant	Dismissed
	Nov 11/07	Com^r reports Pearl & Frank Smith app for enrollment denied. Nov 19, 07 Case reinstated and plaintiff advised status of case	Dismissed
Notice Sent		Action	Remarks
2/2/05		Notices sent for service Return of service Feby 11 1905. Answer of Atty R.C. Osborn filed Feby 24/05	Certificates filed Fdm $^{\#}$ 18185, 14045 2/3/05 Com requested to advise as to contest
2/25/05		Set for hearing at Muskogee, I.T. March 1-1905 at 1^{30} P.M.	2/7/05 Com advises no contests on allotment
3/1/05		Case called. Parties all present. See agreement as to evidence taken in this case shall apply to cases 363/365/366. Testimony of plaintiff taken and Atty for defendant allowed until 15$^{\underline{th}}$ inst to introduce further testimony etc.	
3/14/05		In consequence of an order from Sec of Int to take no further steps to evict freedmen whose rights were undetermined, or free colored persons, residents of Cherokee Nation, instructions were sent parties that it would not be necessary for appearance until further notice. This refers to Cases 563, 564, 565, 566.	
May 8 1906		In compliance with Departmental instructions of April 19$^{\underline{th}}$ 1906 Com^r is requested to furnish *(No more information given.)*	

Cherokee Intruder Cases 1901 - 1909

Date Received	No.	Allottee	Intruder
Feby 2, 1905	363	Wolfe, Joe gardn[sic] for Peggie Sanders Baron, I.T. Docketed 2/3/05	vs Frank Smith Elliott I.T. Claims as freedman
Notice Sent		**Action**	**Remarks**
2/2/05		Notices sent for service Return of service Feby 11, 1905 Answer filed 2/16/05	Certificates filed Fdm # 14066, 18187 2/3/05 Com requested to
2/25/05		Set for hearing at Muskogee, I.T. Mch 1/05 1 30 P.M. See Nº 362 See note under Nº 362	advise as to contest 2/7/05 Com advises no contests pending
May 8 1906		In compliance with Departmental instructions of April 19th 1906 Com^r is requested to furnish this office with status of allotment of Peggie Sanders and status of citizenship of Frank Smith	
June 5		Case dismissed as Com^r reports that a Motion to review Dfdts citizenship case is now pending certificates returned to Ptf. Dismissed	

Date Received	No.	Allottee	Intruder
Feby 2, 1905	364	Wolfe, Joe grdn for Ruthie Downing Baron, I.T. Docketed 2/3/05	vs C.C. Smith et al Claims as freedman
Notice Sent		**Action**	**Remarks**
2/2/05		Notices sent for service Return of service Feby 11, 1905	Certificates filed Fdm # 18189, 14047
2/16/05		Answer filed by CC Smith. Same answer applies to cases #365, 366	2/3/05 Com requested to advise as to contest
2/25/05		Set for hearing at Muskogee, I.T. 3/1/05 1^{30} P.M. See 362 See note under Nº 362	2/7/05 Com reports land is in contest.
May 8, 1906		In compliance with Departmental instructions of April 19th 1906 Com^r is [sic]	
June 5		requested as to the status of Allotment of Ruthie Downing also the status of citizenship of the Defendants in this case Case dismissed as a motion for review is now pending before Com^r Certificates returned to Plaintiff Dismissed	

Cherokee Intruder Cases 1901 - 1909

Date Received	No.	Allottee		Intruder
Feby 2, 1905	365	Wolfe, Joseph	vs	C. C. Smith et al
		Baron, I.T.		Claims as freedman
		Docketed 2/3/05		

Notice Sent	Action	Remarks
2/2/05	Notices sent for service	Certificates filed
	Return of service Feby 11, 1905	Fdm #16151
	Answer filed in case #364	2/3/05 Com requested to
	Answer by Atty R.C. Osborn filed	advise as to contest
	Feby 21/05	2/7/05 Com reports no
2/25/05	Set for hearing at Muskogee, I.T.	contests on allotments
	3/1/05 1$\underline{^{30}}$ P.M. See N$\underline{^{o}}$ 362	
	See note under N° 362	
May 8 1906	In compliance with Departmental instructions of April 19$\underline{^{th}}$ 1906 Com$\underline{^{r}}$ requested to report as to the status of allotment Joseph Wolf, also as to the status of citizenship of Defendant	
June 5	Case dismissed and certificates returned to Ptf. as Com$\underline{^{r}}$ reports a motion to review citizenship of Dfds is pending Dismissed	

Date Received	No.	Allottee		Intruder
Feb 2nd 05	366	Wolfe, Joe	vs	C. C. Smith et al
		for Elizabeth Tieoskie		
		Baron, I.T.		Claims as freedman
		Docketed 2/3/05		

Notice Sent	Action	Remarks
2/2/05	Notices sent for service	Certificate filed
	Return of service Feby 11, 1905	Fdm #18302
	Answer filed in Case #364	3/2/05 Com requested to
	Answer by Atty R.C. Osborn filed	advise as to contest
	Feby 21/05	2/7/05 Commission advises
2/25/05	Set for hearing at Muskogee, I.T.	no contests
	3/3/05 at 130 P.M. See N$\underline{^{o}}$ 362	
	See note under N° 362	
May 8 1906	In compliance with instruction from the Department of April 19$\underline{^{th}}$ 1906,	
June 5	Com$\underline{^{r}}$ is requested to furnish this office with the status of allotment of Elizabeth Tieoskie, also if the Defendants have been denied citizenship	
	Case dismissed as Com$\underline{^{r}}$ reports motion for review of citizenship case of Dfdt is now pending	
	Certificates returned and case **Dismissed**	

Cherokee Intruder Cases 1901 - 1909

Date Received	No.	Allottee	Intruder
Dec 27, 1904	367	Secondine, Katie vs c/o George & Julian Attys Bartlesville I.T. Docketed	N.E. Dye

Notice Sent	Action	Remarks
2/4/05	Notices sent for service Return of service Feby 16 1905 Set for hearing at Muskogee 3/17/05	No Certificates filed 12/30/04 Com requested to advise as to contest
3/17/05	Upon appearance of attorneys for both parties, motion was made and case Dismissed	1/31/05 Com advises no contest. See letter in this case, which also refers to #368 Dismissed

Date Received	No.	Allottee	Intruder
Dec 26, 1904	368	Hindselman, W.E. vs Vera I.T. Docketed 2/4/05	C. L. Fancher, Vera I.T.

Notice Sent	Action	Remarks
2/4/05	Notices sent for service	No Certificates 1/26/04 Letters of Guardianship filed.
2/15/05	Letter of 8th received from plaintiff advising that Fancher has vacated premises and requesting return of papers and dismissal of case. Case dismissed and guardianship papers returned to plaintiff this day	12/30/04 Com requests to advise as to contest 1/31/05 Com advises that land not contested. See letter in #367 Dismissed

Date Received	No.	Allottee	Intruder
Jany 2nd 1905	369	Guyette, Dave L grdn for vs Anderson Tatum, heir of Genie Tatum Tahlequah, I.T.	Wm Thomas

Notice Sent	Action	Remarks
2/4/05	Notices sent for service Guardianship papers filed	Certificates files Fdm # 24496, 17895
2/28/05	Case dismissed and allotment	

Cherokee Intruder Cases 1901 - 1909

2/25/05	certificates and guardianship papers returned to Dave Notices were not served as it appears that a contest has been filed against the land of the Allottee and same are in file having been ret'd by plaintiff. Plaintiff also states that if contest is decided against them that they will confess judgment	L. Guyette Tahlequah, I.T. 2/4/05 Com requested to advise as to contest 2/21/05 Com reports land all in contest Dismissed

Date Received	No.	Allottee	Intruder
Feb 2, '05	370	George W Weaver, for Nannie and Wm Floyd Weaver	John Logan
Notice Sent		**Action**	**Remarks**
Feb 7, '05		Return of service Feby 20, 1905 Answer filed Feby 28, 1905 Set for hearing at Muskogee, I.T. 3/17/05-2/30 P.M.	Commission reports certificates issued and no contest 1/31/05
3/17/05 5/25/05		Case called, All parties present. Testimony of witnesses taken. It was agreed to submit matter to an arbitration and report statement to this office within ten days, stipulation taken by Stenographer and filed herein. See ~~arbi~~ stipulation as to time. 　　　　　　　　　　　　　　Case	Dismissed

Date Received	No.	Allottee	Intruder
Feb 2, 05	371	J. N. Vickery	James Shamblin
Notice Sent		**Action**	**Remarks**
Feb 7, 1905		Case dismissed for want of prosecution.	Commission reports Certificates not yet issued & no contests Jan 31, '05 See # 370 Dismissed

Date Received	No.	Allottee	Intruder
Feb 2, '05	372	Benjamin Whitfield, for self and Luke Whitfield	(No name given.)
Notice Sent		**Action**	**Remarks**
Feb 7, 05		Return of service Feby 11, 1905 Set for hearing at Muskogee, I.T.	Certificates issued by report of Commission and no

Cherokee Intruder Cases 1901 - 1909

		3/17/05	contest Jan 31, 1905
3/16/05	Plaintiff advises matter adjusted		(see No 370)
			Settled

Date Received	No.	Allottee	Intruder
Jan 31, 1905	373	Luey Lydia Bigfeather for self, George and deceased husband Ben Bigfeather	W.S. McCullough, June[sic] Miller & Wife
Notice Sent		**Action**	**Remarks**
2-7-05		Return of service Feby 25, 1905 Answer filed Mar 6, 1905 Set for hearing at Muskogee, I.T. 3/18/05	Commission reports certificates issued and no contests 1/27/05 Settled
	3/17/05	Plaintiff advises matter adjusted	2/3,1 '06[sic] certificates returned

Date Received	No.	Allottee	Intruder
Jan 30, 1905	374	Samuel Perry	Rheben[sic] Swan
Notice Sent		**Action**	**Remarks**
2-7-05		Service acknowledged by defendant 4/17/05 Set for hearing at Claremore, I.T. April 18, 1905 at 11 o'clock A.M.	Commission reports certificates issued and no contests 1/27/05 See report in N° 370
	4/17/05	Case called, plaintiff says this is an error and is settled and reference to case 324	Dismissed

Date Received	No.	Allottee	Intruder
Jan 30, 1905	375	George Smith for Daniel Smith address G.G. Smith Tahlequah	R. J. Borens Peggs I.T. Owen & Bailey Attys for Defndts
Notice Sent		**Action**	**Remarks**
2/7/05		Return of service Feby 11, 1905 Answer filed 2/15/05	Commission reports certificates issued and no
	2/27/05	Case set for hearing at Muskogee IT 3/13/05	contests 1/27/05 See report in # 373
	3/13/07	Case called. Defendants appear by person and by attorney.	

Cherokee Intruder Cases 1901 - 1909

        Case dismissed 6/7/05 See mem in file
3/15/05 Set for Hearing at Muskogee, I.T. Mch 31, 1905 2 P.M.
        3/31/05 Case called, plaintiff appeared in person and defendant by counsel only. Testimony of plaintiff side and case held open to Attys for defense
        4/6/05 Defendant and attorney for defense appeared and testimony taken
        5/23/05 Case considered and decision witheld[sic] until advice is received from dept of Int relative to right of natural guardian to enter into lease for minor child land and if agent can place natural guardin[sic] in possession

Date Received	No.	Allottee	Intruder
Jan 30, 1905	376	Margaret Ann Stewart for self and John W. and James A. S.	Daisy Yaden
Notice Sent		**Action**	**Remarks**
2-7-05		Return of service Feby 11, 1905 Answer filed by Daisy D Yadan[sic] 2/16/05 Set for hearing at Muskogee, I.T. 3/18/05	Commission reports certificates issued and no contest 2/27/05 See report in Nº 373 Cert. in file 3/10/05 Settled by order of plaintiff 3/17/05

Date Received	No.	Allottee	Intruder
Feb 4, 1905	377	Willis E. Miles, for Annie E, Jessie E, and Eliza Miles	Ed. Storrey W.M. Sidell Atty for Defendant.
Notice Sent		**Action**	**Remarks**
2-7-05		Return of service Feby 10, 1905 Answer filed Feby 18 1905 Set for hearing at Muskogee, I.T. 3/18/05	

Cherokee Intruder Cases 1901 - 1909

Date Received	No.	Allottee	Intruder
Feby 17, 1905	378	Payne, Laura E vs Big Cabin I.T. c/o J.S. Davenport Vinita, I.T.	W.C. White Big Cabin I.T.
	7/24/05	Brief and agreement on appeal filed by Atty Jas S. Davenport to be submitted to the department Case submitted up to the department on July 28 05	J.S. Davenport Atty for plaintiff O. L. Rider Atty for defendant
	Nov 10 05	Letter rec'd from dept ~~in~~ ~~wich~~ ~~which~~ upholding the agentr[sic] division and case dismissed	

Notice Sent	Action	Remarks
2/27/05	Return of Service Mar 6, 1905 " " " Mar 6, 1905 Answer filed March 14, 1905 Set for Muskogee, I.T. April 4, 1905 10 A.M.	Certificates filed N°s 3988, 3396 2/10/05 Com reports a portion of land is in contest 3/6/05 Letter to Com asking if there are any contests pending
	4/4/05 No appearance. 4/13/05 Attorney for plaintiff appears and states it has been agreed by Attorney for defense to try case another day at convenience of attorneys at Claremore, I.T. during week from 18th to 22 ^{d} not inclusive. Davenport to notify parties 4/21/05 Case called, all parties present in person and by counsel. Testimony taken. See same. Agreed that Mr Davenport shall file original contract, and case held open for consideration. 5/3/05 Copy of contract filed by Davenport. Dismissed 6/6/05 Judgment rendered in favor of Defendant 6/6/05 Certs returned to J.S. Davenport Atty for Plaintiff	3/11/05 Com advise land is in contest viz SE^{4} of SW^{4} of SE^{4} 32 - 24N 19E

Date Received	No.	Allottee	Intruder
Feby 10, 1905	379	Rogers, H. L. for vs Beulah E Rogers Stilwell, I.T.	Wm Kirkland et al Kirkland I.T. W.M. Cravens Atty for Plntff

Cherokee Intruder Cases 1901 - 1909

Notice Sent	Action	Remarks
2/27/05	Return of service Mch 18, 1905 Set for Muskogee, I.T. 3/27/05 10 A.M. Answer filed Mch 21, 1905 Set for hearing Muskogee, I.T.	Certificates filed N°s 20266, 20197 3/6/05 Letter to Com asking if there be any contests filed 3/11/05 Com advises no contest
4/27/05	Instructions issued to Theo E. Stidham to place plaintiff in possession and report his Action in the matter to this office. Report of Capt John C West filed Certs 20266, 20197 returned to H.L. Rogers Ft Smith, Ark and case	Dismissed see report of Capt West in file

Date Received	No.	Allottee	Intruder
Feby 14, 1905	380	Sanders Robert for wife and children vs Vian, I.T. c/o J.G. McCombs Atty Salisaw, I.T.	Thos Mills Vian, I.T.

Notice Sent	Action	Remarks
2/27/05	Return of service Mar 2, 1905 Set at Muskogee 3-27-05 at 10^{30} am 3/27/05 Case called, no appearance by either party. Answer filed March 14-17- 1905 in Case #407. Case reset, Muskogee, I.T. April 8, 1905 at 10^{00} A.M.	Certs filed. 18346, 25231, 25230, 25225, 18343, 25214, 18340, 25221, 18341 3/6/05 Letter to Com requesting information as to contests 3/11/05 Com advises no contest Report in N° 387
4/8/05	Case called, plaintiff appeared in person and by counsel, no appearance by defendant Testimony taken and it appearing that defendant has no contract except one expiring Jany 1, 1905 and instructions issued to Theodore Stidham to remove Intruder and place Allottee in possession, reporting his Action in matter to this office.	
5/26/05	See 407 Instructions issued to Tandy W Adair.	Dismissed
6/27/05	Allottee placed in possession by Policeman Adair 6/1/05 Certificates returned to plaintiff	

Cherokee Intruder Cases 1901 - 1909

Date Received	No.	Allottee	Intruder
Feby 9, 1905	381	Cheater, Sarah Grove Ind Ter	vs Benjamin Stogsdill Grove, I.T.

Notice Sent	Action	Remarks
2/27/05	Return of Service Mch 4, 1905 Answer filed Feby 23, 1905 Set for hearing at Muskogee, I.T. 3/18/05 Case continued to 3/20/05 (See telegram)	Cert filed N° 17068, 23179 3/11/05 Com advises no contest Report in #387
4/11/05	Instructions sent to A.F. Chamberlain to place Allottee in possession and report Action in this matter to this office	Homestead Cert 17068 & Allt " 23179
5/20/05	See report of Henderson.	Dismissed

Date Received	No.	Allottee	Intruder
Feby 6, 1905	382	Guthrie, Loren P Cookson I.T.	vs John W Griggs Cookson I.T.

Notice Sent	Action	Remarks
2/27/05	Return of Service Mar 4, 1905 Set at Muskogee, I.T. March 27 1905 11 A.M. 3/30/05. Letter received dated 3/25/05 signed by plaintiff and defendant jointly, stating that all differences between hem had been agreably[sic] adjusted and the case was dismissed	Cert filed N° 21105 3/6/05 Letter to Com asking if there are any contests pending 3/11/05 Com advises no contest Report in #387 6/27/05 Certificates returned to Allottee

Date Received	No.	Allottee	Intruder
Jany 25, 1905	383	Burr, Geo W. for Calvin & Alexander Burr Vera I.T.	vs W.W. Hadley et al Vera I.T.

Notice Sent	Action	Remarks
2/27/05	Return of service March 2, 1905 Answer filed 3/7/05 Set for hearing at Claremore, I.T. at 1$^{\underline{00}}$ P.M. 4/18/05	1/31/05 Certificates issued by report of Com and part of land in contest Cert on file.
4/17/05	Case called, all parties appeared and	2/11/05 Com reports ten

Cherokee Intruder Cases 1901 - 1909

7/11/05	it was decided that defendant shall be allowed to remove his fences and improvements and certificates Nº 16905, 16906, 22906, 22907 returned to Burr in person and case is Plaintiff asked to advise this office of contest before Com is determined	acres in contest Dismissed

Date Received	No.	Allottee	Intruder
Feby 7 1905	384	Miller, Frank & Malissa vs Braggs, I.T.	Will Hall Braggs, I.T. Archie D Jones Atty for plain.
Notice Sent		**Action**	**Remarks**
2/27/05		Return of service 3/2/05 Set for hearing at Muskogee, I.T. 3/18/05 Re-set " " " 3/31/05	Certs filed #19374 19375 3/11/05 Com advises no contest Report in Nº 387
		3/31/05 Case called: parties appeared in person and ~~it appearing~~ counsel for plaintiff desires to withdraws Action and certificates as numbered in margin above returned to plaintiff and case dismissed	

Date Received	No.	Allottee	Intruder
Feby 13, 1905	385	Fluorney[sic], J. Edgar and vs Oscar Flourney Owasso I.T.	James Bradford and Frisco R.R. Co. Dawson I.T.
Notice Sent		**Action**	**Remarks**
2/27/05		Return of service Mar 4, 1905 Set for hearing at Claremore, I.T. April 18, 1905 at 1³⁰ P.M.	Certs filed Nºs 31191, 22186, 19168, 14655 3/6/05 Letter to Com asking if there are contests pending
	4/17/05	Case called. All parties appeared in person. P.L. Soper as counsel for RR Co. Contention was that the records of the Com show 125 feet north of track for station purposes, while it appears that 150 feet had been segregated and approved by the Sec. It was agreed that Soper should furnish a copy of plat and survey.	3/11/05 Com advises no contest Report in 387

Cherokee Intruder Cases 1901 - 1909

6/8/05	Certificates numbered in margin returned to Flourney & case Atty P.L. Soper filed plat and survey	Dismissed

Date Received	No.	Allottee	Intruder
Feby 14, 1905	386	Downing, Houston & Elizabeth vs Southwest City, Mo	Geo W. Fields Southwest City, Mo Johnson Duncan Miami, I.T.
		Mch 19, 1906 Referred to Eldon Lowe for investigation	
	April 28	Report of S A Mills Eldon Lowe filed and case dismissed upon request of Plaintiff Certificates returned to Plaintiff	Dismissed

Notice Sent	Action	Remarks
2/27/05	Return of service 3/11/05	Certs filed # 5451, 4500, 5452, 4501
	Answer filed 3/14/05 Set for hearing at Claremore, I.T. April 18, 1905 at 2$^{\underline{00}}$ P.M. No appearance by either party Case set for hearing at Claremore on Aug 1st-05 No appearance by either party to be reset	3/6/05 Letter to Commission asking if there are any contests file. 3/11/05 Com advises no contest on lands Report of John M. Bacon filed Oct 9-05
	Aug 10-05 Letter from plaintiff rec'd stating that owing to sickness that they were unable to appear at hearing of case on Aug 1st-05	See same in file Plaintiff notified to take possession of his land and so notify this office
	Sept 6-05 Case to be reset Sent to John M. Bacon for investigation	

Date Received	No.	Allottee	Intruder
(No date given.)	387	White, Peter & Emma vs By L. W. Marks Vinita, I.T.	John Tucker & mother Woodley, I.T.

Notice Sent	Action	Remarks
2/27/05	Return of service Mch 2/1905	Certs filed # 3525, 4156
	Copies of Judgments in contest by Com filed	Letter to Commission asking if there be any contests pending 3/6/05
	4/11/05 Copies of above judgments and	

Cherokee Intruder Cases 1901 - 1909

	certificates No 3525 and 4156 returned to L.W. Parks[sic] Vinita, IT. and case Dismissed	3/11/05 Com advises no contest Report in this case

Date Received	No.	Allottee		Intruder
Feby 13, 1905	388	Stover, Lizzie Tahlequah, I.T.	vs	Cal Matson Bartlesville I.T.
Notice Sent		**Action**		**Remarks**
2/27/05		Return of service Mch 2/05 Answer filed 3/11/05 Set for hearing at Muskogee, I.T. 3/18/05 All parties in interest appeared & Mrs Stover verbally withdrew her complaint		Certs filed # 6636, 5463 3/11/05 Com advises no contest Report in Nº 402 Dismissed
4/25/05		Certificates No 6636, 5463 returned to Lizzie Stover Tahlequah, I.T.		

Date Received	No.	Allottee		Intruder
Feby 13, 1905	389	Grayson, Samuel Locust Grove, I.T.	vs	Lewis W Ross Locust Grove, I.T. J.R. Price Tahlequah, I.T.
Notice Sent		**Action**		**Remarks**
2/27/05		Set for hearing at Claremore IT April 18, 1905 at 4 P.M.		Certs filed #4010 3/6/05 Letter to Commission asking if there by any contests pending
4/18/05		Written request of plaintiff filed, asking that case be dismissed in consequence of matter having been settled case was dismissed and cert #4010 returned to plaintiff Locust Grove, I.T.		3/11/05 Com advises no contest Report in #402 Dismissed

140

Cherokee Intruder Cases 1901 - 1909

Date Received	No.	Allottee	Intruder
	390	*Void*	

Notice Sent	Action	Remarks
	Void	

Date Received	No.	Allottee		Intruder
Feby 21, 1905	390	Bean, Nancy J and Calvin Walkingstick Baron, I.T.	vs	J.C. Gray & James West Vinita, I.T.

Notice Sent	Action	Remarks
2/27/05	Set at Muskogee, I.T. 3/27/05 1^{30} PM	Certs filed #12603, 16043, 13881, 11128
	No appearance by either party	3/6/05 Letter to Com asking if there be any contests pending
	3/19 1906 Referred to Eldon Lowe for investigation	3/11/05 Com advises no contest
		Report in #402
April '2'	Eldon Lowe reports that there is a valid case which was executed by Ptf. Nancy J Bean et al to Dft J.C. Gray subsequent to the filing of this complaint and that Dft Gray has paid the rents and otherwise complied with the terms of the lease. Dft James West has vacated. Case dismissed as it appears that satisfactory settlement has been made. Certificates returned to Ptf.	
	Dismissed	

Date Received	No.	Allottee		Intruder
Feby 13, 1905	391	Johnson, Peggie Hulbert I.T.	vs	Harry Parker et al Hulbert I.T.

Notice Sent	Action	Remarks
3/6/05		Certs filed #8674, 10596
	Answer filed Mar 6, 1905	3/6/05 Letter to Com asking
3/27/05	Case set for hearing this day and parties appearing and upon examination it was decided that Allottee was entitled to the land and	if there are any contests pending 3/11/05 Com advises no contest. Report in № 402

141

Cherokee Intruder Cases 1901 - 1909

defendant was so instructed and
that he must get off, to which he agreed
within ten days or notice would issue to police to remove him
4/10/05   Instructions issued to R. Lee Wiley to place Allottee in
possession and report Action to this office
4/29/05   Report of R Lee Wyly filed stating that he had placed Allottee
in possession and case   Dismissed
6/27/05   Certificates returned to Allottee

Date Received	No.	Allottee	Intruder
Feby 24, 1905	392	Buffington, Alexander C vs for Georgia L Buffington Maple I.T.	G.W. Mansfield et al Maple I.T.
Notice Sent		**Action**	**Remarks**
2/27/05		3/15/05 Plaintiff advises case settled Certificates returned 6/27/05 Set at Muskogee, I.T. 3/28/05 10 am No appearance by either party	Certs filed 22964, 32667 3/6/05 Letter to Com asking if there be contests 3/11/05 Com advises no contest Report in N° 402 Settled

Date Received	No.	Allottee	Intruder
Feby 27, 1905	393	Hathcoat, Josie A vs Valeda Ks	John Falter Valeda Ks Roy Osborne Atty for Defendant
Notice Sent		**Action**	**Remarks**
2/27/05		Return of service March 2, 1905 Answer filed Mar 6, 1905 Set for hearing at Claremore, I.T. April 19 1905 at 9 A.M. 4/15/05 Upon receipt of the letter from plaintiff dated 4/13/05 requesting that no Action be taken in the matter ~~and~~ the case was 4/25/05 Certificates returned to Allottee at Wimer, I.T. N°ˢ in margin of case 4/18/05 Written request for dismissal of case filed.	Certs filed 21952, 30890 Letter to Com asking if there are any contests pending 3/6/05 3/11/05 Com advises no contest Report in #402 Dismissed

Cherokee Intruder Cases 1901 - 1909

Date Received	No.	Allottee	Intruder
Feby 21, 1905	394	Fox, Jennie vs White Oak I.T.	J. H. Mounts Catale I.T.
Notice Sent		**Action**	**Remarks**
2/27/05		Return of service March 2, 1905 Answer filed March 6 1905 Set for Muskogee, I.T. 3/27/05 10^{30} A.M.	Certs filed 23546, 16075 3/6/05 Letter to Commission asking if there are any contests filed
	3/29/05	Letter received stating that Mounts is removing from her possessions. 4-4/05 Plaintiff reports that Mounts has entirely removed from her lands and that she is in possession thereof and case if therefore dismissed	3/11/05 Com reports no contests. See report in N° 402 6/27/05 Certificates returned to Allottee

Date Received	No.	Allottee	Intruder
Feby 24 1905	395	Welcome, Amanda by vs her husband Lenard Welcome Muldrow, I.T. of Thos J Watts Atty	Robert Barnes Muldrow, I.T. Cherokee Freedman
Notice Sent		**Action**	**Remarks**
2/27/05		Return of service March 6, 1905 Set at Muskogee IT 3/28/05 at 11 am 3/28/05 Case called. Plaintiff ~~All parties~~ appeared in person and by counsel. Evidence taken and he was instructed to supply plat of land not in contest when further Action would be taken Certs returned to Allottee 6/1/05 Receipt of Allotment certs Ack by Thos J. Watts, Atty	Certs filed #21521, 30237 3/6/05 Letter to Commission asking if there are any contests 3/11/05 Part of land in contest
	May 8, 1906	This office acting under instructions from The Dept. dated April 19th 1906, requested the Com^r to furnish ~~this office with the~~ status of the Allotment of Amanda Welcome	
	June 5 1906	Case dismissed Com^r reports citizenship case of Plaintiff is now pending before the Dept.	Dismissed

Cherokee Intruder Cases 1901 - 1909

Date Received	No.	Allottee	Intruder
Feby 27 1905	396	Quinton, Joseph by his father Mack Quinton ~~Brushy~~ I.T. Hanson I Ty	vs Geo Tucker Nowata, I.T.
Aug 21 1906		Case called at Nowata I. Ty and all parties present and testimony taken. Certificates of allottment[sic] 17412 & 13469 filed by pltf	
Sept 26 1906		Com^r requested to report if contest is pending	
Oct 25 1906		Judgement[sic] rendered for plntf. All parties notified.	
" 25 1906		Instructions issued to Policeman Sunday.	
Jany 14 1906[sic]		Certificates Nos$^{17413\ \&\ 13470}_{17412\ \&\ 13469}$ returned to Mack Quinton in person at Muskogee IT, Says is in possession	
Jany 15 1907		Policeman Sunday asked to report	
Jany 21 1907		Policeman Sunday reports placed plntf in possession Nov 6-1906	
Jany 24 1907		Case dismissed	

Notice Sent	Action	Remarks
2/27/05	Return of Service Mar 4-1905	Certs filed #17413, 13470
	Answer filed 3/13/05	Letter to Commission asking if there are any contests filed 3/6/05
	Action suspended under a motion *(remainder illegible...)*	3/11/05 Com reports no contests. Report filed in #402
	Cherokee Freedman	
May 9 1906	In compliance with Departmental instructions of April 19 1906 Com^r is requested to furnish this office with the status of allotment of Ptf and of the citizenship of Dfdt.	
June 12 "	Com^r reports no motion for review of citizenship case of Dfdt pending	
June 6 "	Com^r reports no contest pending	
Aug 8 - 1906	Case set for hearing at Vanita[sic] I.Ty. Aug 21-1906 All parties notified.	

Date Received	No.	Allottee	Intruder
Feby 21 1905	397	Johnston, Mrs E. E. for Edmond F. Johnston Tahlequah, I.T.	James D Sellars Sageeyah I.T.

Notice Sent	Action	Remarks
2/27/05		Certs filed #9862, 8073
	Set for Muskogee, I.T. 3/28/05 at 1^{30} P.M.	3/6/05 Letter to Com asking if there are any contests filed.

Cherokee Intruder Cases 1901 - 1909

	3/28/05 Case called. Plaintiff appeared in person, plaintiff advised she should forward letters of guardianship, together with copy of contract
	4/13/05 Letters of guardianship filed, April 12 1905
	5/25/05 Testimony considered and judgment was rendered for plaintiff and she was requested to advise when it would be convenient for her to accompany policeman to take possession. Note: judgment witheld[sic] to ascertain relative to service
	Mch 19th 1906 Referred to Eldon Lowe for investigation
April 18	Report of Eldon Lowe filed and case dismissed upon request of Plaintiff. Certificates returned

3/11/05 Com advises no contest
Report in #402

Dismissed

Date Received	No.	Allottee	Intruder
Feby 23 1905	398	Bailey, Ella enrolled as Emma Smith Ft Gibson, I.T. vs	*(Illegible)* Lee Ft Gibson, I.T.
Notice Sent		**Action**	**Remarks**
2/27/05			Certs filed #33898, 33896, 28[sic] 23815 33897
3/29/05		Set for Muskogee IT 3/28/05 at 2 PM Letter received from Allottee that she had possession of her land, and in compliance with her request Certificates returned to her. Dismissed.	3/6/05 Letter to Com asking if there are any contests filed 3/11/05 Com advises no contest Report in #402 Dismissed

Date Received	No.	Allottee	Intruder
Feby 17, 1905	399	Nelson, Jennie for self vs Lola M, Wm N & Cora F Nelson Lenapah I.T.	Joe Smith Lenapah I.T.
Notice Sent		**Action**	**Remarks**
			Certs filed 15593 15588 15592, 15589
3/28/05		Letters not dated from Allottee stating matter had been settled and requests that certificates be returned to her at Lenapah I.T.	3/6/05 Letter to Com asking if there are any contests filed 3/11/05 Com advises no contest.

Cherokee Intruder Cases 1901 - 1909

3/29/05	Certificates returned to Allottee per request	See report in #402
		Dismissed
	Dismissed	

Date Received	No.	Allottee	Intruder
Feby 2-1905	400	Lipe, Mary vs Hulbert I.T. Oct 11-05	Geo Shaffer Tahlequah, I.T. Com. reports that pltf is freedman
Notice Sent		**Action**	**Remarks**
2/27/05		Answer filed April 14 1905 Set for Muskogee, I.T. 3-29-05 9 am	2/4/05 Com requested to advise as to contest 2/10/05 Com advises no contest and certs have been issued
		3/24/05 Party representing plaintiff appeared and was informed that it would be necessary to serve notices which had been heretofore mailed Set for hearing at Muskogee, I.T. April 26, 1905 at 2.30 P.M.	
4/26/05		Case called. All parties present. It appeared from a warranty deed exhibited that defendant was occupying lands bought from plaintiff and shows he is not occupying the homestead and case was	
			Dismissed

Date Received	No.	Allottee	Intruder
Feby 7, 1905	401	Estes, Sarah vs Choteau I.T.	James Vann et al
Notice Sent		**Action**	**Remarks**
2/27/05		Return of service Mar 2, 1905	Certs filed #8909 3/6/05 Letter to Com asking if there are any contests filed 3/11/05 Com advises no contest
		Set for Muskogee, I.T. 3/29/05 at 10:00 AM	Report in #402
3/27/05		Letter dated 3/25/05 from plaintiff stating that party had vacated her premises and ~~case~~ she will not appear and case was therefore dismissed, and certificates N° 8905 returned to Sarah Estes Choteau I.T.	
			Dismissed

146

Cherokee Intruder Cases 1901 - 1909

Date Received	No.	Allottee	Intruder
Feby 18, 1905	402	Ketcher, Ellis ~~Proctor~~, I.T. Muldrow	vs John F Warren Adair, I.T. Defendant is an Intermarried citizen

Notice Sent	Action	Remarks
2/27/05	Return of Service Mar 6-05 Answer filed Mch 15, 1905 Set for Muskogee, I.T. April 4 1905 3^{00} P.M. 4/4/05 Case called: defendant appeared but no appearance was made by plaintiff. Letter received from plaintiff on account sickness he cannot come. Defendant was allowed time to ~~arrangement~~ arrange for new contract and procure an agreement to dismiss	Cert filed #11790, 9590 3/6/05 Letter to Com asking if there are any contests pending 3/11/05 Com advises no contest Report of Com 3/11/05 withdrawn and filed in #393
4/14/05	Upon written application of plaintiff case was dismissed and certificates N°s 11790 & 9590 returned to Ellis Ketcher Muldrow, I.T.	

Date Received	No.	Allottee	Intruder
Feby 1(?) 1905	403	Splitnose, Tom Starville I.T.	vs Wm Fortenberry et al Starville I.T.

Notice Sent	Action	Remarks
2/27/05	Return of service 3/20/05 Set for Muskogee, I.T. 3-29-05 at 2^{30} P.M. 3-29-05 Case called. Parties appeared in person. Case was settled by an agreement to pay twenty five dollars immediately and balance for first year Oct 1, 1905, and an agreement was added to the original contract signed by defendant agreeing to pay hereafter, annual rent Oct 1 of each year, and case dismissed	2/3/05 Com requested to advise as to contest 2/7/05 Com advises that certificates have been issued no contest pending.

Cherokee Intruder Cases 1901 - 1909

Date Received	No.	Allottee	Intruder
Feb 10, 1905	404	George Adair for self and Yula and Pearl Adair	A. R. Ringo et al
Notice Sent		**Action**	**Remarks**
3/8/05		Return of service March 14 1905 Answer filed Mch 23, 1905 Set for Muskogee, I.T. 3/29/05 at $3^{\underline{30}}$ P.M. 4/3/04[sic] Letter received from plaintiff stating that case had been compromised and case <u>Dismissed</u>	2/23/05 Com reports Cert issued and no contests

Date Received	No.	Allottee	Intruder
Feb 25 1905	405	George W. Baldridge for Delila E Baldridge	Paden Allen and wife, Tom *(Illegible)*
Notice Sent		**Action**	**Remarks**
3/8/05		Return of service Mch 13, 1905 Set for Muskogee, I.T. 3-30-05 at $9^{\underline{30}}$ A.M.	2/23/05 Commission reports Cert. issued and no contests
3/30/05		Case called. Plaintiff appeared in person and stated that all differences between himself and defendants and the case was therefore <u>dismissed</u>	

Date Received	No.	Allottee	Intruder
Feb 25 1905	406	Mary C Boudinot	W$^{\underline{m}}$ St. Ore
Notice Sent		**Action**	**Remarks**
3/8/05			2/23/05 Com reports certificates issued and no contests
		Set for Muskogee, I.T. 3/30/05 at $10^{\underline{30}}$ A.M. 3/30/05 No appearance Case to be reset for hearing	
7/4/05		Case dismissed as the plaintiff states that she has possession of her land	
			Dis<u>miss</u>ed

Cherokee Intruder Cases 1901 - 1909

Date Received	No.	Allottee	Intruder
Feb 25, 1905	407	Robert S. Sanders	Thomas Mills
Notice Sent		**Action**	**Remarks**
3/8/05		Return of service Mch 11, 1905 Answer filed Mar 16, 1905 Set for Muskogee IT 3/30/05 1$\underline{^{30}}$ PM 3/30/05 Case called. Plaintiff appeared in person and stated that he was now in possession of his allotment and case was dismissed See 380	2/23/05 Com reports certificates issued and no portion of land in contest

Date Received	No.	Allottee	Intruder
3/6/05 Feb 25, 1906	408	R. F. Boudinot, for Harriet G. Boudinot Braggs, I.T.	Thomas Bittick and George Davidson Braggs, I.T.
Notice Sent		**Action**	**Remarks**
3/8/05		Set for Muskogee, I.T. 3/30/05 at 2$\underline{^{30}}$ P.M. 3/30/05 Case called. Plaintiff appeared and stated that Bittick has removed and left the country and that he desires to make a new contract with Davidson who is not objectionable to plaintiff and case was dismissed June 11 1906 Com$^\underline{r}$ reports no contest See case No #639	2/23/05 Com reports certificates issued and no part of land involved in contest

Date Received	No.	Allottee	Intruder
Feb 25, 1905	409	Mary J. Green	W. A. Pickard
Notice Sent		**Action**	**Remarks**
3/8/05		Set for Muskogee, I.T. 3/30/05 at 3$\underline{^{30}}$ PM 3/30/05 No appearance Case to be reset for hearing 3/19 1906 Referred to Eldon Lowe for investigation May 31/06 Report of Eldon Lowe filed and case dismissed at plaintiff's request, copy of contract returned to plaintiff	2/23/05 Com reports no contests and certificates issued

Cherokee Intruder Cases 1901 - 1909

Date Received	No.	Allottee	Intruder
Mar 7 1905	410	Martha Duncan	Charles Gartuer
Notice Sent		**Action**	**Remarks**
3/8/05			Certificates in file
			3/8/05 Letter to Com
			asking if there are any
		Set for Muskogee IT 3/31/05 at 10^{30}	contests pending
		A.M.	3/14/05 Com reports
		3/31/05 no appearance	no contests
		Case to be reset for hearing	
		3/19/1906 Sent to Eldon Lowe for investigation	
	April 6	Case dismissed upon request of Ptf and certificates returned to her	
	April 16th	Report of Eldon Lowe filed	
			Dismissed

Date Received	No.	Allottee	Intruder
2/23/05	411	Lucy Davis, nee Gates	King David
Notice Sent		**Action**	**Remarks**
3/8/05		Return of service March 11, 1905	Certificate in file
		Answer filed 3/21/05	3/8/05 Letter to Com-
		Set for Muskogee, I.T. 3/31/05 at	asking if there are any
		11^{00} am	contests pending
	May 9 1906	3/31/05 no appearance	3/14/05 Com advises
		In compliance with Departmental	no contests
		instructions of April 19th 1906 Com^r	No Action taken under
		is requested to furnish this Office	instructions from dept
		with status of allotment of Ptf and of	3/7/05
		citizenship of Ddfds[sic]	
	June 12 "	Com^r reports motion for review is pending Case dismissed and	
		certificates returned to Plaintiff	

Date Received	No.	Allottee	Intruder
3/3/05	412	Mary A. Baker, for	Brit Turner
		Myrtle E & Malissa E Baker	
Notice Sent		**Action**	**Remarks**
3/8/05		Return of service March 11 1905	Certs in file
		3/22/05 Dismissed upon written	Letter to Com asking if there
		application of Allottee as she	be any contests pending
		reports defendant vacated	3/8/05
		premises March 20/05	3/14/05 Com reports
			no contests

Cherokee Intruder Cases 1901 - 1909

	Dismissed
6/27/05	
	Certificates returned to plaintiff

Date Received	No.	Allottee	Intruder
Mar. 6, '05	413	Agnes P. Pfannkuche	Ned Hoskins
Notice Sent		**Action**	**Remarks**
3/8/05		Return of Service Mch 11 1905	Certificates in file
			3/8/05 Letter to Com asking
		Set for Claremore, I.T. April 19,	if there are any contests
		1905 at 9^{30} A.M.	3/13/05 Com reports
			no contests
4/27/05		Letter of 4/16/05 requests that case be dismissed - received at the office during session of Court at Claremore, I.T. Certificates N° 10373 & 12840 returned to plaintiff at Vinita IT and case	
			Dismissed

Date Received	No.	Allottee	Intruder
Feb 27 1905	414	Polly Scott	Hill Jinkinses[sic]
		Rose I.T.	
Notice Sent		**Action**	**Remarks**
3/8/05		Return of service 3/21/05	Certificates in file
		Answer filed Mch 23, 1905	Letter to Com asking if there
		Set for Claremore, I.T. April 19,	are any contests pending
		1905 at 10^{00} A.M.	3/8/05
		No appearance by either party	
		Case to be reset for hearing	
		Case set for hearing at Claremore on Aug 1 - 05	
	Aug 1st	Case called, defendant appeared no appearance by the plaintiff defendants evidence taken and case and certificates returned to George W Laughlin	Dismissed

Cherokee Intruder Cases 1901 - 1909

Date Received	No.	Allottee	Intruder
2/28/05	415	Mary Choate	Will Box
Notice Sent		**Action**	**Remarks**
3/8/05		Return of service March 11, 1905	Certificates in file
			Letter to Com-
		Set for Muskogee, I.T. 3/31/05 at 1^{00}	asking if there are any
3/31/05		PM	contests 3/8/05
		No appearance by either party	3/14/05 Com reports
7/27/05		Case to be reset for hearing	no contests
		Plaintiff's husband called today and	
		stated that his wife now has	Dismissed
		possession	
		of her land and case was	
		and certificates ret'd	

Date Received	No.	Allottee	Intruder
2/24/05	416	Annie L Craig	John Briggs
Notice Sent		**Action**	**Remarks**
3/8/05		Return of service Mch 14, 1905	Certificates in file
		Answer filed Mch 23, 1905	3/8/05 Letter to Com-
		" " Mch 21, 1905	asking if there are any
		Set for Muskogee, I.T. 3/31/05	contests pending
		at 1^{30} PM	3/14/05 Com reports
1 P.M.		3/31/05 Case called all parties being	no contests
		present. It appearing that contract	Com reports no contest
		was illegal and defendant was	3/14/05
		informed that he must vacate lands	
		within ten days in which to remove	See memo in file.
		Certificates returned to Allottee	Case dismissed for want
		5/25/05	of prosecution
		June 23-05 [sic]	

Date Received	No.	Allottee	Intruder
Feb. 28, '05	417	William L. Humphrey minor child Cora L Hightower	John E Speer and family
			D Bailey Attys[sic] for plaintiff
			Z. T. Walrond[sic] Atty for defendant

Cherokee Intruder Cases 1901 - 1909

Notice Sent	Action	Remarks
3/8/05	Return of service Mch 11, 1905 Answer filed 3/18/05 " " 3/21/05 Set for Muskogee, I.T. 3/31/05 at $2^{\underline{30}}$ PM	Certificates in file 3/8/05 Letter to Com asking if there are any contests pending 3/14/05 Com advises no contests
2.30 PM	3/31/05 Case called, all persons interested present in person and by counsel. Testimony taken. Defendants attorney granted time to file copy of contract. 4/4/05 Copy of contract filed	
6/7/05	Case dismissed as no Guar has been appointed and Allottee is a minor Certs ret'd to Allottee 6/7/05	

Date Received	No.	Allottee	Intruder
3/27/05	418	Jemima Leach for John A and Peggie Leach	Jim and Sam Thompson Clayton & Brainerd Attys for guardian John Watkins Atty at Law Muskogee, I.T. for Defendant

Notice Sent	Action	Remarks
3/8/05	Return of service March 11, 1905 Answer filed 3/15/05 Set for hearing at Muskogee, I.T. Mch 28, 1905 $2^{\underline{30}}$ P.M.	Certificates in file 3/8/05 Letter to Com-asking information as to impending contests
3/28/05	Case called. Plaintiff and defendant appear in person, defendant represented by John Watkins Counsel. Evidence taken. Case taken under consideration	3/17/05 Com reports no contests
3/31/05	Mail copy of testimony to Attys for guardian	
5/25/05	Dismissed and plaintiff advised that guardian should be appointed and certs returned.	Case Dismissed

Cherokee Intruder Cases 1901 - 1909

Date Received	No.	Allottee	Intruder
3/2/05	419	Emeline Crain	D. A. Wilson
Notice Sent		**Action**	**Remarks**
3/8/05		Return of service March 11, 1905 Answer filed March 21, 1905 Set for Claremore, I.T. April 19, 1905 at 10^{30} A.M.	Certificates in file Letter to Commission asking if there are any contests 3/8/05 3/14/05 Com reports no contests
4/19/05		Case called. No appearance by plaintiff. Defendant an adopted citizen appeared in person. His testimony taken	
6/7/05		Dismissed see mem in file Cert ret'd to Allottee 6/7/05	Case dismissed for want of prosecution.

Date Received	No.	Allottee	Intruder
2/23/05	420	Celia ~~Albert~~ Lawhead for John On-the-hill Spavinaw I.T.	A. F. Dawns
	7/3/05	Allottee placed in possession and case <u>Dismissed</u> See report of Chamberlain in file	
Notice Sent		**Action**	**Remarks**
3/8/05		Return of service Mch 18, 1905 Answer filed March 31, 1905	Cert in file Letter to Com 3/8/05 asking if there are any contests 3/14/05 Com reports no contests
		Set for Muskogee, I.T. 4/1/05 at 4^{00} PM	
		4/1/05 Case called. Albert Lawhead appeared for mother of John-on-the-hill and his evidence taken Decided that Allottee should be placed in possession and instructions were given to Capt. John C West to put Allottee in possession and report to this office his Action in the matter 4/14/05 Instructions to West countermanded and matter placed in hands of Arthur F Chamberlain.	

Date Received	No.	Allottee	Intruder
3/4/05	421	Alexander D Davis Ramona, I.T.	Robert H. and Anna L. Brown

Cherokee Intruder Cases 1901 - 1909

Notice Sent	Action	Remarks
3/8/05	Return of service Mch 11, 1905 Answer filed Mch 22, 1905 Set for Claremore, I.T. April 19, 1905 at 10^{30} A.M.	Certificates in file Letter to Commission asking if there are any contests 3/8/05 3/14/05 Com advises no contest on land
4/13/05	Upon written application of plaintiff Case was 6/27/05 Certificates returned to Allottee	Dismissed

Date Received	No.	Allottee	Intruder
2/20/05	422	Josie Chandler	Mr Osborn

Notice Sent	Action	Remarks
3/8/05	Return of Service, Mar 14, 1904[sic] Set for Muskogee, I.T. 4/1/05 at 3^{00} PM 4/1/05 Case called. No appearance. 4/5/05 Upon receipt of written application of Allottee, case was	Certificates are in Removal of Restrictions Deft Letter of inquiry sent to Commission on Mar 8, 1905 3/14/04 Com advises no contests Dismissed

Date Received	No.	Allottee	Intruder
2/27/05	423	Lizzie B Gladney	Mr Moore and Oscar Goddard

Notice Sent	Action	Remarks
3/8/05	Return of service 3/18/05 Set for Muskogee, I.T. 4/1/05 at 2^{30} PM 7/14/05 Case to be reset for hearing Case dismissed as the plaintiff states that she has possession of her land See same in file	Certificates in file Letter to Commission asking if there are any contests Mar 8, 05 3/14/05 Com advises no contests Dismissed

Cherokee Intruder Cases 1901 - 1909

Date Received	No.	Allottee	Intruder
2/27/05	424	Sarah Downing Locust Grove IT	L. J. Smart

3/29 1906 Referred to Eldon Lowe for investigation
April 10 Eldon Lowe reports that there were no improvements whatever upon the allotment of the Plaintiff and that she could take possession at any time.
April 14, 1906 Plaintiff advised to take possession
Case dismissed and rental contract returned
                                                                Dismissed

Notice Sent	Action	Remarks
3/8/05	Return of service Sept 21-05	Certificates in file
		3/8/05 Letter to Com asking
	Set for Claremore, I.T. April 19,	if there are any contests
	1905 at 11 am	pending
	No appearance by either party	3/14/05 Com reports
	Case to be reset for hearing	no contests
	Continued by request of plaintiff	
	~~dated~~ filed July 29-05 and	
	certificates ret^{d} to Allottee	
	This entry is an error,	~~Dismissed~~
	case is not dismissed.	
	New notices sent on Aug 11th - 05	
Sept 6 - 05	Sent to John M Bacon for investigation	

Date Received	No.	Allottee	Intruder
2/25/05	425	J. W. Ellis for Richard and Blair Ellis	J. W. Davis

Notice Sent	Action	Remarks
3/8/05		Certificates in file
		Letter to Com asking if there
		are any contests 3/8/05
	Set for Muskogee, I.T. 4/1/05	3/14/05 Com advises
	at 1$^{\underline{30}}$ P.M.	no contests
	No appearance by either party	
Aug 1st-05	Case to be reset for hearing	
	Case dismissed and certificates returned to plaintiff	
	See carbon in file	

Cherokee Intruder Cases 1901 - 1909

Date Received	No.	Allottee	Intruder
3/7/05	426	Charles Miller, for Henry and Ida Miller	S. G. Victor
Notice Sent		**Action**	**Remarks**
3/10/05		Return of service 3/22/05	Certificates in file 3/10/05 Letter to Com in regard to contests 3/23/05 Com reports no contest
		Set for Muskogee, I.T. 4/1/05 at 10^{30} am	
		3/31/05 Plaintiff calls and said that he would appear by 11 A.M. 4/1/05 Case called. Plaintiff appeared in person and defendant also in person. It appears that Charles Miller has been duly appointed guardian by the U.S. Court, that he entered into a contract with defendant which was approved by Court and ~~therefore made~~ therefore this office is without jurisdiction and case was <u>dismissed</u> See mem in file Certificates returned to Charles Miller No. 546, 610, 611, 547.	

Date Received	No.	Allottee	Intruder
3/7/05	427	James Russell	John Lowe
Notice Sent		**Action**	**Remarks**
3/11/05-7/10/05		Plaintiff requested to serve notices that were sent to him and make return to this office	Certificates in file Letter to Com in regard to contests 3-10-05
		Set for Muskogee, I.T. 4/1/05 at 9^{30} A.M. No appearance by either party Case to be reset for hearing Case set for hearing at Muskogee on July 26 - 05	
7/26/05		No appearance by either party 3/19 1906 Sent to Eldon Lowe for investigation	
April 24		Report of Eldon Lowe filed and case dismissed upon request of Plaintiff Certificates returned to Plaintiff	
			Dismissed

Date Received	No.	Allottee	Intruder
2/27/05	428	Jerome Martin Chelsea, I.T.	Frank Cunningham Chelsea IT

Cherokee Intruder Cases 1901 - 1909

Notice Sent		Action	Remarks
3/13/05	7/10/05	Plaintiff requested to serve notice that was sent to him and make return to this office Set for Claremore, I.T. April 19, 1905 at $2^{\underline{00}}$ P.M. No appearance by either party Case to be reset for hearing Case set for hearing at Claremore on Aug 1st - 05	Mch 7/05 Commission report Certificates issued & land not in contest
	7/28/05	Case dismissed by request of plaintiff See letter in file	Dismissed

Date Received	No.	Allottee	Intruder
2/14/04	429	Dora Ware (Zenora Ware) Muldrow, I.T.	James Streitter

Notice Sent	Action	Remarks
3/13/05	Return of service 3-16-05 Case in to be set for hearing	March 7-05 Commission reports Certificates issued and land not in contest
	Case set for hearing at Muskogee on July 26 - 05	
7/25/05	No appearance by either party	
	3/9/1906 Referred to Eldon Lowe for investigation	
April 27	Report of Eldon Lowe filed and case dismissed upon request of Plaintiff	
		Dismissed

Date Received	No.	Allottee	Intruder
2/27/05	430	Nancy J. Du Bois, nee Osage Dawson, I.T.	R. M. Smiley Dawson

Notice Sent	Action	Remarks
3/13/05	Return of service not dated except 1905 Answer filed Mch 20, 1905 Set for Claremore, I.T. April 19, 1905 at $3^{\underline{00}}$ P.M. No appearance by either party Case to be reset for hearing Case set for hearing at Claremore on Aug 1st 1905	Commission report under date of March 7/05 Certificates issued & land not in contest

Cherokee Intruder Cases 1901 - 1909

Sept 6 - 05 No appearance by either party Sept 18 - 05 Sent to John M. Bacon for investigation Case dismissed by request of plaintiff See report of Bacon in file	Dismissed

Date Received	No.	Allottee	Intruder
2/27/05	431	Susan Martin, Chelsea, I.T.	Frank Cunningham Chelsea
Notice Sent		**Action**	**Remarks**
3/13/05		Allottee is a minor and case is dismissed Set for Claremore, I.T. April 19, 1905 at 3^{30} P.M. No appearance by either party Case to be reset for hearing Mch 19 1906 Referred to Eldon Lowe for investigation April 7 Eldon Lowe reports that complainant is a minor and complaint was filed for her by John Martin as natural Gdn. A lease contract was executed by John Martin as natural Gdn and was advised that he would have to become legal Gdn of this minor before this office could entertain a complaint Case Dismissed	Mch 7/05 Commission reports Certificates issued & land not in contest

Date Received	No.	Allottee	Intruder
2/27/05	432	Frank Martin Chelsea, I.T.	Frank Cunningham Chelsea, I.T.
Notice Sent		**Action**	**Remarks**
3/13/05		Sept 6-05 Sent to John M Bacon for investigation Set for Claremore, I.T. April 19- 1905 at 4^{00} P.M. No appearance by either party Case to reset for hearing Sept 9-05 Case dismissed by report of John M. Bacon in which he states that the plaintiff has possession of his land	Mch 7/05 Com reports Certificates issued and land not in contest Dismissed

Cherokee Intruder Cases 1901 - 1909

Date Received	No.	Allottee	Intruder
2/27/05	433	John Martin Chelsea, I.T.	Frank Cunningham Chelsea
Notice Sent		**Action**	**Remarks**
3/13/05		Plaintiff requested to send notices that were sent to him and make return to this office Case to be reset for hearing Case set for hearing at Claremore on Aug 1st/05 No appearance by either party	Mch 7/05 Commission reports Certificates issued and land not in contest
Sept 6 - 05		Sent to John M Bacon for investigation	
Sept 9 - 05		Case dismissed as the report of John M Bacon, with which was enclosed a letter from the plaintiff states that the Allottee has possession of his land	Dismissed

Date Received	No.	Allottee	Intruder
3/10/05	434	James M. Fields, for Clyde and Bertha G Fields Fairland,, I.T.	W. N. Hobbs Fairland,, I.T.
Notice Sent		**Action**	**Remarks**
3/13/05		Return of service, Mar 19, 1905 Answer filed Mch 25, 1905 Set for Claremore, I.T. April 20 1905 at 9 A.M.	Mch 7/05 Commission reports Certificates issued and land not in contest
4/20/05		Case called. No appearance by plaintiff. Defendant appeared in person. Defendant and policeman notifies that Action had been commenced in US Court for unlawful *(Illegible)* & *(Illegible)* Case held open Contract delivered to Defendant Case set for hearing at Claremore on Aug 1st - 05 Case dismissed by request of plaintiff filed July 29 - 05	

Cherokee Intruder Cases 1901 - 1909

Date Received	No.	Allottee	Intruder
2/27/05	435	Jesse B Burgess, Claremore, I.T.	Geo. S. Swift Owasso, I.T.

Notice Sent	Action	Remarks
3/13/05	Return of service March 27, 1905 Answer filed March 30, 1905	Mch 7/05 Com reports certificates issued and land not in contest
	Set for Claremore, I.T. April 20, 1905 10 A.M.	
	4/20/05 Case called. All parties present in person and by counsel. Testimony taken. See memorandum in case.	
	Decision rendered for defendant and case	Dismissed
	Note: Parties were once placed in possession - See #14	
	Contract delivered to Allottee	

Date Received	No.	Allottee	Intruder
2/20/05	436	Eliza and Ella Ratliff, c/o Mrs. Annie Evans (Guardian) Kansas, I.T.	James Colbert See #218
Aug 15 1906		Communication from Annie Evans again asking Action by this deptmt	
Aug 18 1906		Mrs Annie Evans notified that ~~form~~ motion is still pending & that this office can take no Action	
Mch 26, 1907		Com^r asked as to status of citizenship of Jas Colbert	
Apr 6, 1907		" reports Jas Colbert denied Mch 11, 1907. No motion for review	

Notice Sent	Action	Remarks
3/13/05	Return of Service 3-17-05 Answer filed Mch 30, 1905 Case held under Departmental instructions of Mch 7, 1905	Mch 7/05 Com reports certificates issued & land not in contest
May 7	In accordance with directions from the Department under dates of April 19' 06, Com^r is requested to furnish this office with the status of the allotment of Eliza and Ella Ratliff	
June 12 1906	Com^r reports motion for review is pending Case dismissed	

Cherokee Intruder Cases 1901 - 1909

Date Received	No.	Allottee	Intruder
2/25/05	437	Rufus Tadpole, for minors, Grover and Elmer Tadpole Hulbert, I.T.	H. A. Hills Hulbert I.T.
Notice Sent		**Action**	**Remarks**
3/13/05		Return of service 3-17-05 Case to be reset for hearing Case set for hearing at Claremore on Aug 1st - 05 No appearance by either party	Mch 7/05 Com reports certificates issued & land not in contest
Sept 6 - 05		Sent to John M Bacon for	
" " "		investigation	
Mch 19 '06		Instructions withheld	
April 19		Referred to Eldon Lowe for investigation	Case dismissed
		Report of Eldon Lowe filed and upon request of Plaintiff	Dismissed
		~~Aug 15 1906 Communication from~~	

Date Received	No.	Allottee	Intruder
2/18/05	438	Lizzie and Ursey A Henderson c/o W. F. Henderson Ochelata, I.T.	Nate West Oglesby, I.T.
Notice Sent		**Action**	**Remarks**
3/13/05		Set for hearing at Claremore, I.T. April 20, 1905, 10^{30} am	Mch 7/05 Com reports certificates issued and land not in contest
4/27/05		Upon receipt of letter from Lizzie Henderson stating case had been settled and case	Dismissed

Date Received	No.	Allottee	Intruder
2/27/05	439	Mrs Emma Renfrow for Felix G. Cowan, Afton, I.T.	Henry S. Hill Bluejacket, I.T.
Notice Sent		**Action**	**Remarks**
3/13/05		Return of service 3/16/05 Set for Claremore, I.T. April 20,	Certificates in file 3/13/05 Letter to Com asking if land is in contest

Cherokee Intruder Cases 1901 - 1909

	1905 at 11 A.M.	3/18/05 Commission reports
4/20/05	Case called. Plaintiff appears in person but no appearance by defendant. Testimony of plaintiff taken and she was informed that unless a new contract was entered into between herself and Hill, that upon her notice to the Agent that no such contract had been entered Hill would be removed from the land	no contest
4/28/05	Plaintiff appears and states that she in possession and certificates N° 18223, 14062 delivered to her in person & case Dismissed	

Date Received	No.	Allottee	Intruder
2/25/05	440	J. C. Dannenberg Atty in fact for Daniel E. Dannenberg Tahlequah, I.T.	L. H. and Elizabeth Harrington & John & Cynthia Morgan Coffeyville, Kans

Aug 8 - 1906 Case set for hearing at Vanita[sic] I.Ty Aug 21 - 1906
All parties notified
Aug 18 1906 See letter in file from Starr & Patten Attys Col Blue Atty for Defnds Vanita[sic] I. Ty. also departmental letter which advises that this office take no further Action until instructed by department
Aug 21 1906 Case called at Vanita[sic] I Ty. No appearance by either party
Aug 21 1906 Physician's certificate as to health of Jno Morgan in file.
Same Ack. 8/23/06

Notice Sent	Action	Remarks
	Sept 20 1906 Jno C Danenberg[sic] advised that this office can take no further Action until advised by the Department to do so and case dismissed	

Date Received	No.	Allottee	Intruder
2/25/05	440	J. C. Dannenberg	L. H. and Elizabeth

Cherokee Intruder Cases 1901 - 1909

	Aug 21 1906	Physician's certificate as to health of Jno Morgan in file. Same Ack.
8/23/06		
Notice Sent	**Action**	**Remarks**
3/13/05	Return of service April 15, 1905	Certificates in files 3/13/05
	Affidavit of defendant John Morgan as to his application for enrollment as Cherokee freedman filed	Letter to Com asking if land is in contest 3/18/05 Com reports no contest
April 24	Plaintiff asks for possession as he states he understands Dfds have been rejected as Cherokee Freedman	
	5/5 *(Illegible)* advised that further Action ~~would~~ will be taken as soon as status of allotment of D.E. Dannengberg[sic] is obtained from Com^r	
May 9 1906	Com^r requested to report	
June 12 "	Com reports no motion for review in in[sic] the citizenship case of Dfdt pending	

Date Received	No.	Allottee	Intruder
3/13/05	441	John and Lucinda Starr Grove, I.T.	James McCoy Bartlesville I.T.
	Dec 9-05	Report of Backenstoce filed today states that defdt does not claim possession of pltfs land and case dismissed and pltf notified to take possession	Dismissed
Notice Sent		**Action**	**Remarks**
3/14/05		Return of service Mar 18 1905	Certificate *(Illegible)* no files
Sept 6 - 05		Sent to John M Bacon for investigation	3/14/05 Letter to Com asking if land is in contest 3/20/05 Com advises
		Set for hearing at Claremore, I.T. April 20 1905 at 1^{00} PM	no contest
		Answer filed April 21, 1905. It will be seen, above answer was received at this office during session at Claremore, I.T. hence same was not on file at that time. It does not seem that any appearance was made by either party in response to above call of case.	
		Case set for hearing at Claremore on Aug 1st 05	
		No appearance by either party	

Date Received	No.	Allottee	Intruder
3/13/05	442	I. N. Journeycake for Buster B Journeycake Nowata, I.T.	Williams, Ann now ~~Ann Turk~~ Ann Vann Nowata Joe M Loftay[sic] Atty Claims as Cherokee freedman

(Note: continuation from the end of this case)

citizenship as a Cherokee Freedman and that said application is now before the Comr under the name of Ann Vann
June 22 Case called at Claremore both parties present evidence taken Allotment Cert
No 18360 filed by Ptf motion for continuance filed by Dfdt... corrected. Dfdt claims to be enrolled by Comr as Ann Williams, July 2 Comr requested to report as to citizenship of Ann Williams
July 16 1906 Comr reports motion pending before the Department but that he has recommed[sic] that motion be dismissed
July 20th 1906 Plaintiff advised as to status of case
July 23 Comr requested to furnish this office with further information, when he has been advised as to Action of the Dept.
7/30/06 Comr states that he will advise when citizenship of Ann Williams has been finally disposed of
Dec 19-06 Comr reports dfndt denied citizenship
Dec 27, 1906 Judgement[sic] found for plntf. Dfndt requested to vacate within ten days
Jany 12, 1907 Policeman J. L. Walker of Dewey I Ty "Instructed."
Jany 28, 1907 Policeman Walker reports he placed plntf in possession
Feby 2, 1907 Case dismissed

Notice Sent	Action	Remarks
3/14/05	Return of Service Mar 14-1905 Answer filed Mch 24, 1905	Certificate #18360 filed 3/14/05 Letter asking if land is in contest 3/20/05 Com advises no contest
3/29/05	Witheld[sic] under instructions from Department of March 7, 1905	
4/17/05	Certificate numbered in margin returned to I.N. Journeycake Nowata, I.T.	
May 9, 1906	In compliance with Department instructions of April 19 1906; Comr is requested to furnish this office with status of allotment of Ptf and of	
May 18, "	citizenship of Defendant in this case	
22	Case set for hearing at Claremore, I.T. June 22/06 Additional answer filed in which Dfdt has claims that she is an applicant for	

(Note: continued at the beginning of this case)

Cherokee Intruder Cases 1901 - 1909

Date Received	No.	Allottee	Intruder
3/13/05	443	Dorcas Wilson Maysville, Ark.	John Cochran and Joseph Earp Maysville, Ark.
Notice Sent		**Action**	**Remarks**
3/14/05		Return of service April 9, 1905 Answer filed April 12 1903[sic] Case to be set for hearing Case set for hearing at ~~Cal~~ Claremore on ~~the~~ Aug 2nd No appearance by either party Letter from defendant Earp filed July 31st - 05	Certificate #20853 filed and Letter to Com 3/14/asking if land is in contest 3/20/05 Com advises no contest
Sept 6 - 05		Sent to John M. Bacon for investigation	
Oct 2 - 05		Case dismissed by request of pltf See report of Bacon in file Certificates returned to pltf Oct. 17 - 05	Dismissed

Date Received	No.	Allottee	Intruder
3/13/05	444	George W. Waters, Jr Briartown I.T.	Jesse J Perry and Henry Star[sic]
Notice Sent		**Action**	**Remarks**
3/14/05		Return of Service March 18, 1905 Case to be set for hearing Case set for hearing at Muskogee on July 26-05 No appearance by either party	Certificates Nos 24630 & 35122 in file 3/14/05 Letter to Com asking if land is in contest 3/20/05 Com advises
Feb 6 - 06		Case dismissed by personal request of pltf and cert ret'd to him	no contest <u>Dismissed</u>

Date Received	No.	Allottee	Intruder
3/13/05	445	Altha Humphrey Foreman I.T.	Montgomery Gist Foreman J. G. McCombs Atty for Defdt
	5/26/05	Case called. All parties present. Testimony taken and judgment rendered for plaintiff and defendant given [sic] days to vacate unless an agreement to continue was mad between him and the plaintiff	

Cherokee Intruder Cases 1901 - 1909

Notice Sent	Action	Remarks
3/14/05	Return of service March 22, 1905 Answer filed Mch 27, 1905	Certificates in file- 3/14/05 Letter to Com asking
4/6/05	Upon written application of Allottee stating that defendant had removed from her land and in compliance with her request Certificate No 28308 was returned to her and case was	if land is in contest Cert #28308 filed 3/20/05 Com advises no contest Dismissed
New Notices sent May 10, 1905		
Case reinstated	New return of service May 13, 1905 Answer filed May 16, 1905 Set for hearing at Muskogee, I.T. May 26, 1905 at 3^{30} P.M.	
5/26/05	Bill of sale filed by Atty for defendant	
6/12/05	Certs retrd to A. E. Patterson Atty for Plaintiff	

Date Received	No.	Allottee	Intruder
3/13/05	446	Iola M Sult, nee Dawson Lenapah I.T.	Aggie Little Lenapah I.T. Claims as Cherokee freedman

Notice Sent	Action	Remarks
3/16/05	Return if service, Mar 18, 1905 Answer filed Mar 22, 1905 Case witheld[sic] under Departmental instructions of March 7, 1905	Certificates in file 3/16/05 Letter to Com asking if land is in contest Nos of Certfs 23482 & 33373
6/27/05	Upon the written request made by plaintiff case was Dismissed -	3/23/05 Com reports no contest 6/27/05 Certificates returned to Allottee

Date Received	No.	Allottee	Intruder
3/14/05	447	Mattie Timms Hereford, I.T. Set for hearing at Muskogee on Jan 31 - 06	Albert A Taylor Tahlequah, I.T. J.W. Orr of Vinita is also one of the defdts
	Jan 31 - 06	Case called, all parties present, evidence taken Defdt to file affidavits. 3/7 Judgement[sic] rendered in favor of Dft both parties	Huckleberry, of Muskogee, Atty for defdt.

Cherokee Intruder Cases 1901 - 1909

| | notified and copy of Judgement sent to each. Case dismissed *Dismissed* | |

Notice Sent	Action	Remarks
3/16/05	Return of service Mar 23, 1905	Nos 17072 & 23190 Certificates in file
	Return of service 6/30/05	3/16/05 Letter to Com asking
5/4/05	Duplicate notices sent	if land is in contest
	Case to be set for hearing on July 26-05	
7/26/05	Case called and testimony of Plaintiff taken (L.B.) Defendant failed to appear Ans filed Aug 18 - 05	
Oct. 14 - 05	Defendant notified to appear at this office on Oct 21st 05	
Oct 23 - 05	Defendant appeared today and states that he will again appear on the 30th with contract and other papers	
Oct 30 - 05	Defdt appeared today and case continued until Nov. 21 - 05 when both parties will be requested to appear See letter to pltf in file	
Nov 21/05	No appearance by either party	

Date Received	No.	Allottee	Intruder
3/13/05	448	Richard Ketcher Baron, I.T.	J. R. Walker Nowata P.O. in Dewey
Mch 19, '06		Case set for hearing at Claremore for Mch 30th 1906	
Mch 30		Case comes at Claremore neither party appeared	S.A. Tillotson Atty for Defdt
3/30		Dft Dfs states he can not appear on account of sickness (Mch)	
April 3rd		Referred to John Viets for investigation	
May 22		John Viets reports that contract is not being complied with	
" 24		Dfs request to advise this office as to whether he is using the land for agricultural or grazing purposes May 29 ans by Dfdt	

Cherokee Intruder Cases 1901 - 1909

Notice Sent	Action	Remarks
(Illegible)/05	Return of service 3/22/05 Answer filed April 8, 1905 " " by Atty 5/15/05 Case to be set for hearing Case set for hearing at Claremore on Aug 2nd plaintiff Case called ~~all parties~~ being present and represented by Atty plaintiff's evidence taken See evidence in file (?)-23-05 Defendant appeared today and case is to be reset as he stated that he was sick and unable to appear at last hearing June 8/06 Defendant requested to appear before Mr Bennett at Claremore I t June 19/06 June 19 Claremore IT Defendant did not appear as requested Aug 8-1906 Case set for hearing at Vanita[sic] IT Aug 21-1906 ~~All parties~~ notified Dft only. Aug 21-1906 Case called at Vanita I.Ty. neither party appeared Jany 22, 1907 Case <u>dismissed</u> & certificates <u>returned</u>	Certificates of Allotment in file #17324 & 2360 3/16/05 Letter to Com asking if land is in contest

Date Received	No.	Allottee	Intruder
3/13/05	449	John Foreman c/o J. Howard Langley Atty Pryor Creek IT	W. B. Hodson Greenbrier I.T.

Notice Sent	Action	Remarks
3/16/05 4/20/05 5/17/05	 Answer filed Mch 21, 1905 Claims that land is in contest Set for Claremore, I.T. April 20, 1905 at 11⁰⁰ A.M. Notice of contest and summons filed with letter of J.C. Starr Case dismissed and certificates returned to Allottee	Certificates Nos 11253 & 14075 in file 3/16/05 Letter to Com asking if land is in contest 5/13/05 Com reports that all of the land in controversy is involved in contest Dismissed

Cherokee Intruder Cases 1901 - 1909

Date Received	No.	Allottee	Intruder
3/17/05	450	Rob Rogers Oolayah I.T.	L. J. Snarr Certificates returned to plaintiff in person
		7/12/05 Sent to Capt John C West with instructions to place Allottee in possession and make report to this office Contracts returned to Clem Rogers Claremore Ind Ter on Aug 14th - 05 Case set for hearing at Claremore on Aug 19th - 05	Contract returned to Attyr Lahay and Shaw Oct 20-05 June 22 - 06 Instructions sent to policeman Hargrove to place the pltf in possession See carbon in file

Notice Sent	Action	Remarks
3/20/05	Return of service March 31, 1905 Answer filed April 7, 1905	Certificates in file 3/20/05 Letter to Com in regard to contest
	Set for Claremore IT April 20, 1905 2^{00} PM	3/27/05 Com advises no contest
Jan 26-06 Case dismissed by request of pltff		
	4/20/05 Case called. Both parties appeared in person. Testimony taken and defendant was advised that is he desired to remain on the land he must arrange with him and make payments to him or orders would issue to police to remove him. Notice to be sent to Agent. Sent Policeman Henderson with instructions to place Allottee in possession 6/3/05	
Dismissed	6/30/05 Policeman Henderson reports that he is unable to execute the order at this time as he is occupied in the matter to Tribal tax. see report filed this day	

Date Received	No.	Allottee	Intruder
3/16/05	451	Dennis Beans for self & Johnson & Debbie N Beamer Roland I.T.	Wiley Williams and Durham

Notice Sent	Action	Remarks
3/20/05	Return of service March 24, 1905 Answer filed Mch 28, 1905 " " of Wyley Williams 3/31/05	Certificates in file 3/20/05 Letter to Com in regard to contests 3/29/05 Com reports no contest

Cherokee Intruder Cases 1901 - 1909

4/1/05 Defendant claims he is not on lands described in complaint, and case appearing to be a question of lines, plaintiff was advised to furnish correct survey of same before Action could be taken
Case set for hearing at Muskogee on July 26 - 05   Certs N° 23177 22558
7/26/05 No appearance by either party   22557 returned to plaintiff at Roland I.T.
4/15/05

See letter from plaintiff in file   letter from defendant filed July 26 - 05
Mch 19 '06 Referred to Eldon Lowe for investigation
April 26 Report of Eldon Lowe filed and   case dismissed
upon request of Plaintiff

Date Received	No.	Allottee	Intruder
3/28/05	452	George Ketcher Baptist, I.T.	Johnson Sixkiller Baptist I.T.

Notice Sent	Action	Remarks
3/20/05	Return of service Mch 25, 1905 Answer filed April 3, 1905 Case to be set for hearing Case set for hearing at Claremore on July Aug 2nd	Certificates in file 3/20/05 Letter to Com in regard to contests 3/27/05 Com reports no contest
	Aug 2nd Case called, plaintiff appeared no appearance by defendant plaintiff evidence taken judgement[sic] for plaintiff ready for police	Certificates returned to pltf Nov 3 - 05 Dec 20th Pltf placed in possession by Capt West and case <u>Dismissed</u> See report in file
	Nov 3 - 05 Instructions issued to Capt West to investigate this matter and if need be, place the pltf in possession.	

Date Received	No.	Allottee	Intruder
3/17/05	453	Miss Georgia Benge Adair, I.T.	William Todd & wife Claims as Cherokee freedman
Aug 16 1906		Letter from this office to Muskogee advising her as to status of case also telling her that if complaint is filed at this office same shall had ree prompt attention.	
Mch 28 1907		Plntf asks thru Com^r as to status of case	

Cherokee Intruder Cases 1901 - 1909

Apr 1, 1907	Com[r] asked as to citizenship of dfndts
Apr 8, 1907	Com[r] reports Rachel Todd refused citizenship Nov 22 1904 application of W[m] Todd refused Dec 5 - 1903
Apr 11, 1907	Notices sent plntf to serve on dfndt
Mch 18, 1907	Proof of service returned dated Apr 16th 1907
May 28, 1907	Case set for hearing at Muskogee, I.T. June 11 1907 - All parties notified -
June 11 '07	Case called ~~no appearance~~ both parties present testimony taken. Cert 12784 filed by plff covering surplus allotment

Notice Sent	Action	Remarks
3/20/05	Return of service March 24, 1905 Answer filed March 27, 1905 Set for Claremore IT April 20 1905 11am	Certificates in file 3/20/05 Letter to Com in regard to contests 3/27/05 Com reports no contest
4/14/04 *July 18-07 Judgement [sic] given in favor of ptf and defdt vacate turned 10 days in which to*	Upon request of plaintiff, case was withdrawn from Claremore calender[sic], and reset for hearing at Muskogee IT April 26, 1905 at 2P.M. No appearance by either party *Dismissed* Case to be reset for hearing	Aug 23-07 Capt West reports Allottee in possession See report in file Case dismissed
May 9 1906 *Mch 27-08 Allotment certificates ret'd to Plf*	In compliance with departmental instructions of April 19th 1906 Com[r] is requested to furnish this office with status of Allotment of Plaintiff and of Citizenship of Dfdt in this case	
June 19	Com[r] reports motion for review pending Case dismissed and certificates returned to Ptf	
" "	Com[r] reports no motion to reopen citizenship case of W[m] Todd	

Date Received	No.	Allottee	Intruder
3/11/05	454	John Deerinwater for son Charles c/o Thos T Watts, Atty Muldrow, I.T.	Thos. Bell or Smith et al Roland, I.T.

Notice Sent	Action	Remarks
3/30/05	Return of service March 24, 1905 Answer filed Mch 31, 1905 Set for Muskogee, I.T. April 15, 1905 at 1^{30} P.M. Answer filed April 15, 1905	Certificates in file 3/20/05 Letter to Com in regard to contests 3/27/05 Com reports no contest

4/15/05 Case called. No appearance.
May 9 1906 In compliance with Departmental instructions of April 19th 1906

Cherokee Intruder Cases 1901 - 1909

June 12 1906	Comʳ is requested to furnish this office with status of Allotment of Ptf and of citizenship of Defendants in this case. Comʳ reports motion for review pending Case dismissed and certificates returned 　　　　　　　　　　　　　　　　　Dismissed

Date Received	No.	Allottee	Intruder
3/20/05	455	Thomas Hickey, for Nellie M, Rachel, William, John, Richard & Mary Lou Hickey　　Nowata, I.T.	C. L. Harkins
7/12/05		Sent to Capt. John C. West with instructions to place the Allottee in possession and report to this office 　　　　Ctfs. 24711 - 24347 to Nellie M. Hickey & 13594 - 17-602 " Rachel C.E. Hickey retᵈ in person to Nellie M. Hickey 11/27/05	3/19 Dismissed by Order W.W.B.

Notice Sent	Action	Remarks
3/22/05	Return of service April 17, 1905 Answer filed Mch 27, 1905 Set for Claremore, I.T. April 20 1905 　　　　3³⁰ P.M. 4/20/05 Case called. Both plaintiff and defendant appeared in person. Case continued to Saturday April 29, 1905 at Muskogee, I.T. by consent of parties. 5/1/05 Case called, all parties present in person. Testimony taken from which it appears that two of the children were of age and defendant was not entitled to hold their lands. That as to the lands held by other children, the matter was held in abeyance until instructions were received in cases of a similar kind from the Department	Certificates in file 3/22/05 Letter to Com in regard to contests 3/29/05 Com reports <u>no contest</u>
	6/10/05 Dismissed as to minor complaints only	
	6/10/05 Decided that Nellie M. and Rachael Hickey are entitled to possession	
	6/10/05 Defendant notified to vacate at once	

Date Received	No.	Allottee	Intruder
3/20/05	456	Robt F Morrison, guardian of Delila L. Morrison Ochelata, I.T.	John Palmer and Albert Okerson

Cherokee Intruder Cases 1901 - 1909

Notice Sent	Action	Remarks
3/23/05	Return of service March 28, 1905 Answer filed March 31, 1905 Set for Claremore, I.T. April 21, 1905 no hour specified	Certificates in file Letters of Gdnship " " 3/23/Letter to Com in regard to contests
4/21/05	Case called. Both parties present. Contention was apparently one of line. It running through a very small portion of a log-house an defendant was given ten days to remove house, and certificates were returned to Morrison and case	3/29/05 Com reports no contest Certs 13238, 252 Dismissed

Date Received	No.	Allottee	Intruder
3/23/05	457	Walter Smith for Isaac & Callcayah Smith Fairland, I.T.	W.W. Breedlove and F. M. Conner Fairland,

Notice Sent	Action	Remarks
3/25/05	Return of service April 1, 1905 Set for Claremore, I.T. April 21, 1905 at 9 A.M.	Certificates in file 3/25/05 Letter to Com relative to contests 3/30/05 Com reports
	4/21/05 Case called. All parties appeared in person. Testimony taken and it was decided that ~~plaintiff~~ defendant was entitled to possession and certificates returned to plaintiff and case was	No contest Certs No 4276, 3627, 3628 4277 Dismissed

Date Received	No.	Allottee	Intruder
3/23/05	458	W. M. Gentry for Cris R. Gentry Vinita c/o Wilson & Davis Attys Vinita	Felix Witt

Notice Sent	Action	Remarks
3/25/05	Allottee is a minor Answer filed April 3, 1905 in which he states part of land is in contest Set for Claremore, I.T. April 21 1905 at $9^{\underline{30}}$ A.M. No appearance by either party	Certificates in file 3/25/05 Letter to Com relative to contest 3-30-05 Com advises that 20 acres are in contest

Cherokee Intruder Cases 1901 - 1909

Mar 19 '06	Case to be set for hearing
	Case set for hearing at Claremore on Aug 2nd No appearance
	Sent to Eldon Lowe for investigation

Date Received	No.	Allottee	Intruder
3/23/05	459	Charles Waters Jr. Remy I.T.	R B Sagley and T. H. Pington Long I.T.

Notice Sent	Action	Remarks
3/25/05	Return of service March 30, 1905	Certificates in file 3/25/05
	Answer filed April 1, 1905	Letter to Com relt. to contest
	Case to be set for hearing	3/30/05 Com reports contest
	Case set for hearing at Muskogee on July 27-05	on portion of Cand.
	Meh July 21 no appearance	
March 19 '06	Referred to Eldon Lowe for investigation	
April 4	Eldon Lowe reports that contest is pending Case dismissed and certificates returned	
April 26	Report of Eldon Lowe filed	
		Dismissed

Date Received	No.	Allottee	Intruder
3/22/05	460	Mrs. M. B. Martin for minors Porum	Iscar[sic] Hayes and W. L. Fortenberry Porum

Notice Sent	Action	Remarks
3/25/05	Return of service May 20, 1905	Certificates in file-3/25/05
		Letter to Com relative to contest
		3/30/05 Com reports
	4/4/05 Upon written application of Plaintiff case was dismissed	no contest
5/3/05	Upon appearance of plaintiff who that she insists never signed application for dismissal case was reset for Muskogee IT May 24 1905	Dismissed
5/24/05	Case called. Plaintiff appeared in person and by Gidney & Martin Attys	23626, 33632 33629 returned to Plaintiff 5/24/05
	An examination of plaintiff developed that no guardian had been	

175

Cherokee Intruder Cases 1901 - 1909

	appointed and the mother proves a non-citizen. She was advised that guardian should be appointed who could bring complaint, and case	Dismissed

Date Received	No.	Allottee	Intruder
3/20/05	461	James Martin for Susan J and David E and Geo W. Martin Cherokee City, Ark	A. J. Sobgreen Kinnison
Notice Sent		**Action**	**Remarks**
3/25/05		Return of service March 30 1905 Answer filed April 4, 1905 Set for Claremore, I.T. April 21, 1905 at $10^{\underline{00}}$ A.M.	Certificates in file 3/25/05 Letter to Com relative to contest 3/30/05 Com reports
	4/21/05	Case called. All parties appeared in person. It seems that ~~defendant~~ contention was as to ~~(Illegible)~~ *(Illegible)* of fence, pasturing the lands and defendant was instructed that he must make improvements as agreed and not graze lands and strictly conform to contract to which plaintiff assented, and certificates were returned to plaintiff and lease returned to defendant and case was	no contest Certs 999, 878, 1003, 880, 881, 1002 Dismissed

Date Received	No.	Allottee	Intruder
3/25/05	462	Louisa Anderson Ft Gibson IT.	Ella Yates Ft Gibson, I.T.
Notice Sent		**Action**	**Remarks**
3/25/05		Return of service March 29, 1905	Certificates files 3/25/05 Letter to Com relative to contest
		Case to be set for hearing Case set for hearing at Muskogee on July 27 - 05	3/30/05 Com reports no contests
	7/27/05	Case called and judgements rendered in favor of plaintiff, defendant to remove her fence by Aug the 6$^{\underline{th}}$ All parties present and defendant agrees to remove her fence, no evidence taken	

Cherokee Intruder Cases 1901 - 1909

Certificates ret'd to Allottee in person

Date Received	No.	Allottee	Intruder
3/24/05	463	Mary Manus for Bert Hampton Tahlequah, I.T.	vs Doctor Upton & family Welling I.T.
Notice Sent		**Action**	**Remarks**
3/27/05		Return of service April 6 1905	Cert filed 34044 3/27/05 Com requested to advise as to contest 4/3/05 Com reports no contest
		Case to be set for hearing Case set for hearing at Muskogee on July 27 - 05	
	7/27/05	Case called, all parties being present and it appears that all the lands held by the defendant is in contests Certificates ret'd and Case	Dismissed

Date Received	No.	Allottee	Intruder
3/25/05	464	Fannie Price for Georgia Bell Muskogee, I.T.	vs R. A. Evans Muskogee, I.T.
Notice Sent		**Action**	**Remarks**
3/27/05		Return of service April 5 1905	Certs filed 34782 24393 3/27/05 Com requested to advise as to contest 4/3/05 Com reports all in contest
		4/6/05 Defendant appears and states all land is in contest. Plaintiff advised that Com reports all lands are in contest and therefore case is	Dismissed

Date Received	No.	Allottee	Intruder
3/7/05	465	John Crittenden Collinsville, I.T.	vs Jane Phillips et al
	June 22	Case called at Claremore both parties present and Dfdts claim no right to possession through the Plaintiff Their only claim being that Dfdt is a claimant for citizenship as a Freedman	Seymour Riddle Atty Judge Standfield Vinita, I.T. Atty for defndt

Cherokee Intruder Cases 1901 - 1909

July 2	Com^r asked to report as to citizenship of Nancy J Phillips and Nancy J Campbell	
July 10 1906	See report of Com^r in #780	
" 10 "	Com^r reports application of Dfdt for enrollment as Cherokee Freedman is now pending Therefore case is dismissed	
		Dismissed

Notice Sent	Action	Remarks
3/17/05	Return of service April 1 1905	3/23/05 Com advises that certificates have been issued and no contest is pending
	Set for Claremore, I.T. April 21, 1905 at 10^{30} A.M.	
	4/21/05 Case called. Fact of defendant having made application as a~~n~~ Cherokee Freedman having been filed case under Departmental instructions March 7/05 case was held open	
May 9 1906	In compliance with instructions received from the Dept under date of April 19 1906, Com^r is requested to furnish this office with status of Allotment of Ptf and of citizenship of Dfdt in this case	
June 18 "	Case set for hearing at Claremore IT June 22/06	
June 22	Atty for Ptf states that a motion to review the citizenship of Dfdt has been filed with Comr	

Date Received	No.	Allottee		Intruder
3/2/05	466	Hettie Whitemire[sic] for Mamie Weiner I.T.	vs	Frank Brandon

Notice Sent	Action	Remarks
3/27/05	All letters mailed to plaintiff have been ret'd . uncalled for	3/23/05 Com advises that certificates have been issued and no contest is pending
	Set for hearing at Claremore, I.T. April 21, 1905 at 1^{00} P.M.	
	No appearance by either party Case to be set for hearing	
Mch 19 '06	Referred to Eldon Lowe for investigation	
April	Eldon Lowe reports that Hettie Whitmire is *(Illegible)* Gdn of Mamie Whitmire states he advised that a Legal Gdn should be appointed before the Agent can take Action(?)	

Cherokee Intruder Cases 1901 - 1909

Date Received	No.	Allottee	Intruder
3/6/05	467	Daniel D Miller for Nannie G Miller Zena I.T.	vs John Black et al

Notice Sent	Action	Remarks
3/27/05		3/23/05 Com advises that certificates have been issued
	Set for Claremore, I.T. April 21 1905 at 2^{00} P.M.	and no contest pending
4/27/05	Letter from plaintiff dated April 17, 1905 states that case has been settled and Allottee is in possession, thereupon case was	Dismissed

Date Received	No.	Allottee	Intruder
3/11/05	468	Phil Glass vs Santown[sic], I.T.	Rose Green Santown[sic] I.T.

Notice Sent	Action	Remarks
3/27/05		3/23/05 Com advises that certificates have been issued and no contest is pending
	7/10/05 Plaintiff requested to serve motion and make return to this office at once Return of service July 14 - 05 Case to be set for hearing	
Jan 22 - 06	Case dismissed by agent of pltf	Dismissed

Date Received	No.	Allottee	Intruder
3/9/05	469	Ahpahmala Drum vs Copan I.T.	John Cheeter Carrey Ks

Notice Sent	Action	Remarks
3/27/05	Return of service Mch 31, 1905	3/23/05 Com advises that certificates have been issued and no contest is pending
	Set for Claremore, I.T. April 21 1905 at 3^{00} P.M.	
	4/21/05 Case called. All parties appeared in person It appears from an examination that plaintiff claims that payments had not been paid, but defendant produced receipts for money and goods to the amount of $105^{00} in advance, on rents of 1905, and also receipts for all time prior to 1905, and had otherwise complied with contract to all which plaintiff assented and case was	Dismissed

Cherokee Intruder Cases 1901 - 1909

Date Received	No.	Allottee	Intruder
3/8/05	470	W^m McEwin for vs Lizzie McEwin Ramona, I.T.	Robt Botkins Ramona, I.T.
Notice Sent		**Action**	**Remarks**
3/27/05		Return of service March 31, 1905 Answer filed April 7, 1905	Certs N° 18866 14456
		Set for Claremore, I.T. April 21, 1905 4^{00} P.M. No appearance by either party	3-23-05 Com advises that certificates have been issued and no contest pending
7/7/05		Case dismissed. See letter of plaintiff in file Certificates returned to Allottee 7/7/05	Dismissed

Date Received	No.	Allottee	Intruder
3/27/05	471	Charles Lavin vs Bartlesville I.T.	Isaac Eads Bartlesville I.T.
Notice Sent		**Action**	**Remarks**
		Dismissed. See report of Com of Mch 24 1905	

Date Received	No.	Allottee	Intruder
3/27/05	472	Lewis Keener for son vs Daniel Keener Halbert I.T.	Hardy Stevenson Halbert I.T.
Notice Sent		**Action**	**Remarks**
4/6/05		Return of service April 22, 1905	3/9/05 Com requested to advise as to contest
		4/28/05 Defendant appeared but made no answer except he had nothing but verbal contract for one year and no complaint was made until after his crops were up	3/24/05 Com reports certificates as well and no contests
	6/27/05	Plaintiff requested to advise the present status of case	
	Mch 19 '06	Referred to Eldon Lowe for investigation	

Cherokee Intruder Cases 1901 - 1909

April 18	Report of Eldon Lowe filed and case dismissed upon request of Plaintiff
	Dismissed

Date Received	No.	Allottee		Intruder
3/1/05	473	Lydia Waters	vs	William Stiles
		Uniontown Ark		Uniontown Ark
Notice Sent		**Action**		**Remarks**
4/6/05				Certs filed 23770, 33827
				3/10/05 Com requested to advise as to contest
				3/24/05 Com advises that certificates issued and no contest
		5/17/05 Upon written application of plaintiff case was dismissed and certs returned to Lydia Waters, Uniontown Ark.		See No 490

Date Received	No.	Allottee		Intruder
3/28/05	474	Mrs Amanda Haynes	vs	Geo Tennor et al
		1213 S Maple St		Elliott I.T.
		Coffeyville, I.T.		
Notice Sent		**Action**		**Remarks**
4/5/05		Return of service April 8, 1905		Certs filed 5817, 8010
		Set for Claremore, I.T. April 22, 1905 no hour		4/6/05 Com requested to advise as to contest
		4/22/05 Case called. It was claimed by defendants that contest had been filed by them and plaintiff admitted that 18 acres was in contest. Plaintiff to be notified as to contest.		4/19/04 Com reports contest
		Case set for hearing at Claremore on Aug 2nd - 05		S 18.74 acres of Lot 6 Sec 6, T 28, N 16 certificates
Aug 2nd - 05		Case dismissed as to John E Bonner as there is a contest on land Case dismissed on act of land is in contest see telegram from Com^r in file		ret^d Aug 2nd 05 Dismissed Dismissed

181

Cherokee Intruder Cases 1901 - 1909

Date Received	No.	Allottee	Intruder
3/17/05	475	Carrie A Conley vs Childers I.T.	Robert Martin Jr Childers I.T.
Notice Sent		**Action**	**Remarks**
4/5/05			3/27/05 Com reports certs issued and no contest
		Set for Claremore, I.T. April 22, 1905 no hour	
4/17/05		Upon written application of Allottee case was	Dismissed

Date Received	No.	Allottee	Intruder
3/17/05	476	Daniel Young for vs Jessie Young-Taylor Rex I.T. c/o Theodore Potts Atty Wagoner I.T.	Harrie Sisson
	5/17/05	Instructions issued to Capt John C West to place Allottee in possession and report Action to this office. Captain West's report in file *(This line is completely illegible)* Defendant has given possession of all but the 10 acres that are in contest 3/19/06 Case Dismissed By order W.W.B.	Certificate returned to Dan Young Oct 19 - 05
Notice Sent		**Action**	**Remarks**
4/6/05		Return of service April 10, 1905	Cert filed #27080 3/20/05 Com requested to advise as to contest 3/27/05 Com reports that certificates will be *(Illegible)* as soon as possible and no contest on lands 5/10/05 Com reports No contest
	4/27/05	Instructions issued to Theodore Stidham to place Allottee in possession and make report of Action to this office	
	5/2/05	Capt West reports that he visited allotment to place Allottee in possession but found that she was in Oklahoma, on May 3/05 defendant and the husband of Jessie Young Taylor appeared and claims that he is a citizen by blood and owner of improvements and that he is now on his way to Tahlequah to institute contest for lands in question. Complaint was irregular and case restored and set for hearing at Muskogee, I.T. May 24$^{\underline{th}}$ 1905 at 2$^{\underline{00}}$ P.M.	

Cherokee Intruder Cases 1901 - 1909

Date Received	No.	Allottee	Intruder
3/16/05	477	Robert McPherson for vs Jennie & Jaemia McPherson Ochelata I.T. P.O. in Tahlequah, I.T. Judgement[sic] rendered in favor of pltf	John Jacob Ramona, I.T.
Mch 19th '06		Referred to Eldon Lowe for investigation	
April 18		Report of Eldon Lowe filed and case dismissed upon request of Plaintiff Certificates returned	Dismissed

Notice Sent	Action	Remarks
4/5/05	Return of service April 10 1905 Copy of contract filed 3/16/05 Set for Claremore IT April 22, 1905 no hour	3/27/05 Com reports certificates issued and no contest
4/22/05	Case called all parties present. Testimony taken showing that original contract was between plaintiff and original owner of lands and for two years, but later plaintiff was made grdn of the children and new contract was made by Clevenger Atty under power of attorney. Aug 26-05 Plaintiff requested to forward his letter of gdn to this office	Letter of gdn.
Nov 18 - 05	Dfdt notified to vacate within 20 days or he will be removed	filed Sept 5 - 05 Certificates filed Nov 15 - 05

Date Received	No.	Allottee	Intruder
3/18/05	478	Ida J Fitzsimmons Wann I.T.	vs E. O. Fitzsimmons Wann I.T.

Notice Sent	Action	Remarks
4/5/05	Sept 6 - 05t John M Bacon for investigation SenSet for Claremore, I.T. April 22, 1905 no hour No appearance by either party	3/27/05 Com reports certificates issued and no contest
7/14/05	Plaintiff requested to make return of service Case to be set for hearing	
1/3/06	No service and no reply	1/3 -06
Feb 1 - 06	Report of Backenstoce filed today	Dismissed for want of service

Cherokee Intruder Cases 1901 - 1909

Date Received	No.	Allottee	Intruder
12/30/04	479	John W Vickery vs Ft Gibson, I.T.	Geo Turley Ft Gibson, I.T.

Notice Sent	Action	Remarks
4/6/05	Return of service April 10 1905 4/13/05 Grant Foreman Atty for defendant appeared this day and advised that he had no notice of Action of Com in dismissing contest - case held 4/17/05 Grant Foreman Atty for Juliette Smith appeared and advise that she had filed contest	Cert filed #28502 4/6/05 Com requested to advise as to contest Judgment of Com showing that contest was dismissed Mch 20 1905 4/28/05 Com reports land in question is now involved in contest 5/24/05 Cert returned to plaintiff in person Dismissed

Date Received	No.	Allottee	Intruder
3/29/05	480	Famous Smith vs Webbers Falls I.T.	R. F. Ross Webbers Falls I.T.

Notice Sent	Action	Remarks
4/6/05	Return of service April 11, 1905 Answer filed Apr 19, 1905 4/27/05 Letter from plaintiff dated 4/18/05 stating that case had been settled, whereupon same was	Cert filed 16929, 22948 4/6/05 Com requested to advise as to contest 4/19/05 Com reports no contest Dismissed

Date Received	No.	Allottee	Intruder
3/27/05	481	Bernice N Wade vs Ft Gibson, I.T.	Tom Green Ft Gibson, I.T. WH Jones Falls City I.T. BE Parish Muskogee I T

Notice Sent	Action	Remarks
4/6/05	7/10/05 Plaintiff requested to make return of service Case to be set for hearing	Certs filed 12925 4/6/05 Com requested to advise as to contest

Cherokee Intruder Cases 1901 - 1909

Mch 19<u>th</u> -06 Referred to Eldon Lowe for investigation	4/20/05 Com reports no contest
April 12 Report of Eldon Lowe filed and case dismissed upon request of Plaintiff. Certificates returned	Dismissed

Date Received	No.	Allottee	Intruder
3/28/05	482	WW Ross Jr Jennie F Ross Fannie V Ross Tahlequah, I.T. Certificates ret'd to pltf Jan 20 - 06	vs I. W. Robins Whitmire, I.T.

Notice Sent	Action	Remarks
4/6/05	Return of service April 11, 1905 Answer filed April 19, 1905 Claiming he is not in possession of land belonging to Allottee and Allottee advised it would be necessary to have lines definitely located	Certs filed 21289, 11503, 18321 4/6/05 Com requested to advise as to contest 4/19/05 Com reports no contest
	Case set for hearing at Muskogee on June 23/05 at 200 P.M.	
6/23/05	Plaintiff appeared no appearance by defendant plaintiff evidence taken	
	6/24/05 Communication received from defendant asking to be heard 6/27/05 Defendant requested to appear and give evidence in the *(Illegible)*	
	7/10/05 Dismissed plaintiff states he has possession of his land See same in file	Dismissed

Date Received	No.	Allottee	Intruder
3/28/05	483	George Blevins for son vs Burrell Blevins Grove, I.T.	William Smith Hallow or Kennison I.T. Sept 11<u>th</u> 05 Case dismissed by request of pltf by report of Henderson in file
		7/12/05 Plaintiff advised that instructions had been retd to policeman Henderson to	

Cherokee Intruder Cases 1901 - 1909

Notice Sent	Action	Remarks
	place him in possession of the lands of his son	Dismissed
	7/12/05 Sent to policeman Henderson with instructions to place the Allottee in possession and report to this office	Certificates returned Sept 6 - 05
	7/14/05 Defendants Attys states that one Mary D. Walker is going to file a contest on lands of plaintiff	
Notice Sent	**Action**	**Remarks**
4/5/05	Return of service April 8, 1905	Certs filed 7971-9747
	7/12/05 Ans filed 7/12/05	
	Letters of guardianship filed Mch 28, 1905	5/6/05 Com requested to advise as to contest
	Set for Claremore, I.T. April 22, 1905 no hour	
	4/22/05 Case called. All parties present, when it appear that there is no contention except to possession of ten acres, that defendant holds no other lands embraced in suit, but his claim is by contrast with his sister for lands immediately south of allotment of plaintiff and ten acres located on said allotment. Held subject to report of Com which if it shows no contest plaintiff is to have possession which is agreed to.	
	Defendant notified to vacate at once, or he will be removed.	4/20/05 Com reports no contest
	6/26/05 Plaintiff asked to advise if he has possession of his land	6/20/06 Com reports no contest

Date Received	No.	Allottee		Intruder
3/28/05	484	Charles L Keys for *(Illegible)* Keys	vs	Wilson Gamble and Bill Walker
Notice Sent		**Action**		**Remarks**
4/6/05				Certs filed 19131 26422
		7/10/05 Plaintiff requested to make return of service and also advised that if Allottee is a minor that a guardian must be appointed before Action can be taken by this office		4/6/05 Com requested to advise as to contest 4/20/05 Com reports no contest
	Jan 22 - 06	Return of service 7/20/04		
	Mch 2/06	Sent to E.C. Backenstoce for		

Cherokee Intruder Cases 1901 - 1909

               investigation
               Referred to John Viets for
               investigation
April 10 Report of John Viets filed and certificates returned
               Case dismissed upon the request of Plaintiff
                                                               Dismissed

Date Received	No.	Allottee	Intruder
3/23/05	485	Stealer Swimmer vs Tahlequah, I.T.	James Greene Tahlequah, I.T.
Notice Sent		**Action**	**Remarks**
4/6/05		Return of service April 11, 1905 To be [sic] Case to be set for hearing Case set for hearing at Muskogee on July 26/05 7/26/05 No appearance by either party Case dismissed see letter in file	3/29/05 Com reports certs ~~not~~ issued and no contest

Date Received	No.	Allottee	Intruder
3/30/05	486	Charles M Buck vs Bushyhead, I.T.	Flora Klass Chelsea, I.T.
Notice Sent		**Action**	**Remarks**
4/5/05		Ans filed 7/3/05 Set for Claremore, I.T. April 22 1905 no hour 4/13/05 Upon written application of Allottee dated April 10, 1905 Certificates N° 24822 & 35445 were returned and case 4/11/05 Allottee states that he now has possession of his land and case	Certs filed 24822, 35445 4/6/05 Com requested to advise as to contest Dismissed 4/20/05 Com reports no contest

Date Received	No.	Allottee	Intruder
3/28/05	487	Joe Batt vs Stilwell, I.T.	U. L. Cowart Stilwell, I.T. M.F. Wilkerson Nowata, I.T.

Cherokee Intruder Cases 1901 - 1909

Notice Sent	Action	Remarks
4/6/05	Return of service April 10, 1905	Certs issued 4935, 5999
		4/6/05 Com requested to
	Case to be set for hearing in the near future	advise as to contest
		4/20/05 Com reports
	Case set for hearing at Muskogee on July 22 - 05	no contest
	Certificates returned to plaintiff Aug 3$\underline{rd}$ - 05	
	Case set for hearing at Muskogee on Sept 8 - 05	
	Jan 22 - 06 Sent to EC Backenstoce for investigation	
	Feb 1 - 06 Report of Backenstoce filed today states that defdts do not claim possession of pltfs land and pltf notified to take possession and case	Dismissed

Date Received	No.	Allottee		Intruder
3/31/05	488	Sopha Jones for daughter Ola Jones Wimer, I.T.	vs	Katie Thornton Vanford Hudson I.T.

Notice Sent	Action	Remarks
4/5/05	Return of service April 10, 1905	Cert filed 33533
	Answer of Katie Thornton filed April 14 1905	4/6/05 Com requstd[sic] to advise as to contest
	Set for Claremore I.T April 22 1905, no hour	
	6/22/05 Case called. It appears that defendant is a applicant for enrollment as Cherokee freedman and case was held under Departmental instruction of March 7 1905. Certificate returned and Case was	Dismissed
		4/20/05 Com reports no contest

Date Received	No.	Allottee		Intruder
4/3/05	489	Lenora M Auken, nee Taylor Oolagah, I.T.	vs	Sarah D McKrosky Oolagah I.T

Cherokee Intruder Cases 1901 - 1909

Notice Sent	Action	Remarks
4/10/05	Return of service April 12, 1905	Certificate filed 8583
		4/10/05 Com requested to
	Set for Claremore, I.T. April 22, 1905, no hour	advise as to contest
	4/22/05 Case called. It was found that complaint and certificate do not cover ground asked for in complaint. Certificate was returned and case	
		Dismissed
		4/27/05 Com reports no contest

Date Received	No.	Allottee		Intruder
4/5/05	490	Lydia Waters Uniontown I.T.	vs	William Stiles

Notice Sent	Action	Remarks
4/10/05		Certs filed 23770, 33837
		4/10/05 Com requested to
	It appears from examination of papers and complaint it seems the claim and complaint is identical with Cherokee 473 and this case was withdrawn and dismissed and certificates filed with N⁰ 473.	advise as to contest

Date Received	No.	Allottee		Intruder
3/23/05	491	George Washington for Bertha Washington c/o F.M. Frye Salisaw[sic] I.T.	vs	Dick Baker

Notice Sent	Action	Remarks
4/10/05		4/3/05 Com advises that certificates have been issued
	Case to be set for hearing	and no contest
	1/3 - 06 No *(Illegible)*	1/3 - 06 Dismissed

Cherokee Intruder Cases 1901 - 1909

Date Received	No.	Allottee	Intruder
4/3/05	492	Arva Ridge vs c/o P.E. Sadler Spavinaw I.T. or J. B. West Spavinaw I.T. Apr 13 -1907 Robt R. Bennett reports dfndt claims a motion pending for see eff[sic] filed	Nicey Vann Chaffee I.T. Defendant is applicant for enrollment as a Cher freedman - (... remainder illegible)
Notice Sent		**Action**	**Remarks**
4/10/05		Return of Service April 13, 1905 Answer filed April 18, 1905 Set for Claremore, I.T. April 22, 1905 no hour Refer to N° 114	Cert filed N⁰ 15843 4/10/05 Com requested to advise as to contest 4/17/05 Com reports no contest
5/4/05		Plaintiff appeared in person and was advised as to instructions of Dept Mch 7, 1905, and certificate returned in person.	
May 9, 1906		In compliance with instructions from the Dept. under date of April 19th, 1906 Com^r is requested to furnish this office with status of allotment of Ptf and of citizenship of Dfdt in this case	
June 18 "		Com^r reports motion for review pending Case dismissed	

Date Received	No.	Allottee	Intruder
3/23/05	493	Mrs Myrtle Thompson vs nee Jordan c/o R.E. Thompson Centralia, I.T.	Hyram Jenkins Centralia, I.T.
Notice Sent		**Action**	**Remarks**
4/10/05			4/3/05 Com reports certs have been issued and No contest
		Case set for Claremore, I.T. April 22, 1905 - no hour	
4/17/05		Upon receipt of notice from Allottee that defendant had vacated and she was in peacable[sic] possession ~~and~~ case was	<u>Dismissed</u>

190

Cherokee Intruder Cases 1901 - 1909

Date Received	No.	Allottee	Intruder
4/8/05	494	John C. Bratcher Gdn James T and Nettie Bratcher c/o E. B. Lawson, Atty Nowata, I.T.	Frank and Cynthia Gourd
Notice Sent		**Action**	**Remarks**
Apr 14 1905		Return of Service 4/18/05	Certs #25198 & #25199 filed.
		Case to be set for hearing	4/21/05 Com advises
7/26 - 05		Dismissed on personal application of Pltfs Atty and certificates (... *remainder illegible)*	no contest Dismissed

Date Received	No.	Allottee	Intruder
4/7/05	495	Isaac Batt for Eva E. and Mary E Batt c/o J. L. Springston Vian, I.T.	M. F. Wilkerson and W<u>m</u> Cowart Stilwell, I.T.
Notice Sent		**Action**	**Remarks**
April 14, 1905		Return of Service 4/26/05	
			Certs Nos 7850, 9608, 7849,
		Answer filed May 15, 1905	& 9607 filed
		Case to be set for hearing	4/21/05 Com advises
		Case set for hearing at Muskogee on July 27 - 05	no contest
		No appearance by either party Letter rec'd on July 31 - 05 stating that plaintiffs folks were sick and that he was unable to appear at the hearing	
Jan 22 - 06		Sent to E.C. Backenstoce for investigation	
Feb 1 - 06		Report of Backenstoce filed today states that defdts agree to *(illegible - vacate?)* and pltf so notified and certs ret'd to pltf and case	Dismissed

Cherokee Intruder Cases 1901 - 1909

Date Received	No.	Allottee	Intruder
4/11/05	496	Mrs Martha Pendergraft Needmore I.T. P.O. Change it to Empire City, Kans	Pete Dennis Zena I.T.
Mch 19th '06		Referred to Eldon Lowe for investigation	
May 25 ' 06		Certificates returned to Plaintiff and she is requested to advise this office if she is now in possession	
June 4		Plaintiff advises she has not received possession	
June 9		Instruction issued to Capt John C West, to induce Defendant to vacate <u>not</u> to remove him by force as it is understood that he is a Katooyah[sic]	
June 18 1906		Case dismissed as Capt West reports that he has made satisfactory settlement between the parties	
Notice Sent		**Action**	**Remarks**
4/14/05		Return of Service 20 of April '05	Certs #323 & 272 filed 4/27/05 Com report
		Case to be set for hearing	no contest
		Case set for hearing at Claremore on Aug 2nd - 05	
Aug 2nd 05		Case called, plaintiff appeared no appearance by defendant plaintiff's evidence taken judgement[sic] for plaintiff	
		ready for John	Aug 30 1905
Aug 19 - 05		Instructions issued to policeman Henderson to place the plaintiff in possession Report of policeman Henderson filed Aug 30 - 05	Report of Henderson filed

Date Received	No.	Allottee	Intruder
Ap 11-05	497	William H. Landers Porum, I.T.	Thos Brooks Webbers Falls I.T.
Notice Sent		**Action**	**Remarks**
Ap 14-05		Return of service Ap 19/05	Cert #31068 filed 4/26/05 Com advises
		4/27/05 Plaintiff advises case dismissed	no contest
		Cert #31068 ret'd 6/7/05	Dismissed

Cherokee Intruder Cases 1901 - 1909

Date Received	No.	Allottee	Intruder
Ap 10/05	498	Thomas Lowe, Gdn of Arthur, Ethel and Fannie Johnson Dawson I.T.	W. P. Standle, Dawson I.T. S R Lewis Atty Tulsa IT

April 4th Defendant directed to surrender possession to Ptf Lowe at once otherwise an order will issue to U.S. Indian Police to remove him
April 14 Instructions issued to Capt John C West to place Allottee in possession
April 11 Eldon Lowe reports recommending that the Allottee be placed in possession   4/16 S R Lewis notified of the Action taken.
April 17th Case dismissed upon request of Plaintiff and certificates returned
April 19th Report of Capt West filed

Notice Sent	Action	Remarks
Ap 14 '05	Return of Service Ap 19/05 Answer filed Apr 20/05	Certs #23780 & 33849, 23779 & 33848 filed
5/20/05	Letters of guardianship filed Matter being held for an opinion from Dept as to validity of a lease made by natural guardian Lease filed 6/17/05	Ap 26, 05 Com advises no contest
6/19/05	Communication from Master in Chancery Northern Dist that matter is to be investigated relative to dismissal of Guardian Lowe	
Mch 19th '06	Referred to Eldon Lowe for investigation	
~~Mch~~ Apr 4	A W Etchens Master in Chancery states his Docket shows no protest pending to revoke letters of Gdnship from Thos Lowe	

Date Received	No.	Allottee	Intruder
Ap 11-05	499	Bird Hare for himself and Jennie Hare, nee Littlejohn Hulbert I.T.	Charley Burns Melvin I.T.

Notice Sent	Action	Remarks
Apr 14 05	Return of service Apr 19, 1905 Answer filed Apr 24, 1905 Case to be set for hearing	Certs #15215, 13919, 12059 & 18025 filed 4/26/05 Com advises no contest
5/30/05	Certificates returned upon written request to Allottee at Hulbert I.T. Case set for hearing at Muskogee on July 28 - 05	
7/28/05	Case dismissed See mem in file Defendant appeared no appearance	

Cherokee Intruder Cases 1901 - 1909

by plaintiff
See letter to plaintiff dated Aug 1st

Date Received	No.	Allottee	Intruder
Apr 17-05	500	Alice May Lemaster Fairland, I.T.	Harry Kiefer and Thos Carden Fairland, I.T.
Notice Sent		**Action**	**Remarks**
May 1-05		Return of service May 6, 05 Answer filed 5/9/05 Case to be set for hearing Case set for hearing at Claremore on Aug 2nd - 05 No appearance by either party	Certs #37888 3226 filed 5/1/05 Com requested to advise as to contest May 6 1905-Commission reports no contest
Sept 6 - 05		Sent to John M Bacon for investigation	
Oct 2 - 05		Case dismissed by request of pltf See report of Bacon in file Certificates returned to plaintiff Oct 17-05	Dismissed

Date Received	No.	Allottee	Intruder
April 15-05	501	Sarah Calwood Spavinaw, I.T.	Mr. Soldier Saline I.T.
Notice Sent		**Action**	**Remarks**
May 1 '05			Cert #8981 filed 5/1/05 Com requested as to contest
		Case to be set for hearing Case set for hearing at Claremore on Aug 2nd - 05	5/6/05 Commission reports no contest
7/28/05		Case dismissed by request of plaintiff	Dismissed

Date Received	No.	Allottee	Intruder
Apr 15-05	502	J. B. Walker for Nannie E Walker Chloeta I.T.	James F Fields and Dick Van[sic]

Cherokee Intruder Cases 1901 - 1909

Notice Sent	Action	Remarks
May 1-05	Return of Service 5/5/05	Certs Nos 4561 & 3849 filed.
		5/1/05 Com requests as to
	Case to be set for hearing	contest
	Case set for hearing at Claremore on Aug 2nd - 05 No appearance	May 5, 1905 Commission reports no contest
	See letter from plaintiff filed July 24-05	Certificates returned to pltf Oct 11-05
Sept 9 - 05	Sent to John M Bacon for investigation	
Oct 9 - 05	Case dismissed by request of pltf See report of Bacon in file	Dismissed

Date Received	No.	Allottee	Intruder
Apr 24 '05	503	Lenora W Auten, nee Taylor Oolagah, I.T.	Samuel D McKrosky et al
		3/5 Dft says it is impossible to comply with order	
		3/8 Dft directed to surrender possession at once otherwise police will be sent to move her	
	April 7	Defendant reports she has vacated	
			Dismissed
	June 26	Homestead Cert 6289 returned	

Notice Sent	Action	Remarks
May 1-'05	Return of service May 3, '05	Cert #6289 filed
	Answer filed 5/9/05	5/1/05 Com requested as to
	Case to be set for hearing	contest
	Case set for hearing at Claremore on Aug 2nd - 05 No appearance	5/6/05 Commission reports NW/^{4} of NW/^{4} of SW^4 is in contest
	Letter from plaintiff filed July 26 - 05	
Sept 9 - 05	Sent to John M Bacon for investigation	
Feb 1 - 06	Report of Backenstoce filed today states that defdt does not claim ~~any~~ possession of pltf land and that pltf occupys[sic] a portion of land claimed by defdt and case	Dismissed

Cherokee Intruder Cases 1901 - 1909

Feb 8 - 06	and cert's ret'd Cert's ret'd to pltf in person 2/14 a letter from Dft. filed 2/29 Dft agreed to vacate by 3/15 '06 same satisfactory to Ptf

Date Received	No.	Allottee	Intruder
Apr 22-05	504	Clinton Cochran Chelsea, I.T.	Ben F Biel Chelsea IT
Notice Sent		**Action**	**Remarks**
May 1-05		Return of service May 10, 05 Answer filed May 13, 1905 Answer filed May 27, 1905	Cert $5381 filed 5/1/05 Com requested as to contest
	6/22/05	Dismissed by request of plaintiff Certificates returned 6/23/05	May 6, 05 Commission reports no contest

Date Received	No.	Allottee	Intruder
Mch 29-05	505	Hannah E. Jackson nee Davis Briartown, I.T.	Chas J. McClure Briartown I.T.
	Oct 8, 1906 Apr 5, 1907 present	A. T. Ingram of Porum ITy reports & encloses contract Husband of plntf appeared & contract delivered to him in person	
Notice Sent		**Action**	**Remarks**
May 1-05		Return of service May 5, 1905	Apr 17/05 Com reports certs issued to Hannah Davis & no contest
		Case to be set for hearing Case set for hearing at Muskogee on July 28 - 05	Contract exhibited
	7/28/05	Case called all parties being present and case See mem in file	Dismissed
	Sept 25, 1906	In compliance with verbal request of plntf notice to dfndt to surrender & vacate land for which he had no contract. Dfndt notified that if he did not surrender land for which he had no contract, an order would issue to remove him.	
	Oct 3, 1906	Mr. McClure appeared and stated that he is not dfndt, also exhibited contracts properly signed etc., and made plats showing that he nor Thresher are in possession of lands in question.	
	Oct 5, 1906	Pltf advised of above & requested to have land surveyed & report	

Cherokee Intruder Cases 1901 - 1909

Date Received	No.	Allottee	Intruder
Apr 4-05	506	John W. Dawson Afton I.T.	S. G. Victor Afton I.T.

Notice Sent	Action	Remarks
May 1-05	Return of service May 13, 1905 Answer filed May 18, 1905 Case to be set for hearing Case set for hearing at Claremore on Aug 2nd - 05	Ap 17-05 Com advises certs issued & no contest Original contract filed Aug 2nd - 05
Aug 2nd - 05	Case called, both parties being present or represented by Atty evidence taken plaintiff was not present but was represented by Atty Defendant was present in person	Feb 5 - 06 Report of Backenstoce filed today
Aug 2nd - 05	Latter[sic] plaintiff appeared and asked that case be	Dismissed

Date Received	No.	Allottee	Intruder
Apr 24-05	507	Edward Walkingstick Baron, I.T.	F. A. Parker Coffeyville, Kans.

Notice Sent	Action	Remarks
May 1-05	Return of service May 5/05	Certs #24540, 17922 24539 filed
	Rental contract filed by plaintiff Ap 24-'05	5/5/05 Com requested as to contest May 6, 05 Com reports
	Case to be set for hearing Case set for hearing at Claremore on Aug 2nd - 05 No appearance by either party	no contest
Sept 9 - 05	Sent to John M Bacon for investigation	
Jan 22 - 06	Case dismissed upon report of E. C. Backenstoce and certs ret'd to pltf	Dismissed

Date Received	No.	Allottee	Intruder
Apr 19-05	508	Mrs Charlotte Backbone Tahlequah, I.T.	Clem Hayden Choteau I.T.

Cherokee Intruder Cases 1901 - 1909

Notice Sent	Action	Remarks
May 1, 05	Return of service 6/23/05 Case to be set for hearing Case set for hearing at Muskogee on July 28 - 05	Certs Nos. 10234 & 12631 filed 5/2/05 Com advised as to contest
Jan 22 - 06	Sent to E C Backenstoce for investigation	5/9/05 Commission advises no contest
	Mch 21 '06 Referred to John Viets for investigation April 10 1906 Report of John Viets filed. Certificates returned and case dismissed upon request of plaintiff.	Dismissed

Date Received	No.	Allottee	Intruder
Apr 24-05	509	Rebecca Johnson for Joseph F & James Z Johnson Tahlequah, I.T.	B. S. Minor Centralia, I.T.

Notice Sent	Action	Remarks
5/2/05	Return of service May 6, 1905 Answer filed May 18, 1905 Certs returned 6/2/05 Case to be set for hearing	Certs #6318, 8622, 6321 & 8625 5/2/05 Com requested as to contest
7/27/05	Case set for hearing at Muskogee on July 28 - 05	5/9/05 Commission reports <u>no</u> contest
7/28/05	Case called all parties were present case dismissed as there is no guardian appointed	Dismissed

Date Received	No.	Allottee	Intruder
Apr 19-05	510	Jennie Morris, for Frank Nichols c/o W.D. Humphrey, Atty Nowata, I.T.	Charles Nichols Wimer, I.T.

Notice Sent	Action	Remarks
5/2/05	Return of service 6/9/05 Case to be set for hearing Case set for hearing at Claremore on Aug 3<u>rd</u> - 05 Defendant appeared no appearance by plaintiff	Apr 17 1905 Com advises certificates issued & no contest This is a minor case

Cherokee Intruder Cases 1901 - 1909

Aug 3rd - 05   Sent to John M. Bacon for investigation
Sept 9 - 05   Case dismissed by request of pltf
Oct 28 - 05   See report of Bacon in file

Date Received	No.	Allottee	Intruder
Apr 1-05	511	Jennie Morris c/o W.D. Humphrey, Atty Nowata, I.T.	B. D. Vansickle Wimer, I.T.
Notice Sent		**Action**	**Remarks**
May 2, '05		Return of service May 4, 1905 Answer filed May 12, 1905 Case to be set for hearing Case set for hearing at Claremore on Aug 3 - 05	April 17/05 Com advises certificates issued & no contest
Aug 3rd - 05		Defendant appeared no appearance by plaintiff	
Sept 9 - 05		Sent to John M. Bacon for investigation	Dismissed
Oct 8 - 05		Case dismissed by request of pltf	

Date Received	No.	Allottee	Intruder
Apr 24-05	512	Mary Welch Tahlequah, I.T.	Harey[sic] Martin <s>Tom Brown</s> Pensecola I.T.
Notice Sent		**Action**	**Remarks**
5/1/05		Return of service 7/3/05 Defendant an applicant for enrollment as Cherokee Freedman Certificates returned to Allottee 7/26/05	Certs Nos 23538 & 33458 filed 5/2/05 Com requested as to contest 5/9/05 Com reports no contest
May 9 1906		In compliance with instructions from the Department this office has requested the Com^r to furnish status of Citizenship of Dfdt and status of Allotment of Ptf in this case	
June 12 1906		Com^r reports no motion for review pending in citizenship case of Dfdt	
8/8 "		Case dismissed by order WWB	

Cherokee Intruder Cases 1901 - 1909

Date Received	No.	Allottee	Intruder
Mch 31-05	513	Lydia Bruere Broken Arrow, I.T.	Louie Bruere Catoosa, I.T.
	Feb 8 - 06	Instructions issued to policeman Musgrove to place pltf in possession	
	April 5	Policeman Musgrove has resigned and order was issued to Capt. West to place Ptf in possession	
	April 13	Capt John C West reports that he has removed the Intruder and placed the Allottee in possession - case dismissed	*Dismissed*
	May 1	Plaintiff states Defendant has again taken possession, was advised that instructions has again been issued to Capt West to place her in possession	
	May 22	Instruction reissued to Capt West 5/24 Capt West reports that land has been leased satisfactory to Ptf. Case is therefore dismissed.	

Notice Sent		Action	Remarks
5/1/05		Return of Service 5/8/05 Answer filed 5/8/05	Apr 17-05 Com reports Certs issued & no contest
			6/12 Lease contract returned to Geo A. Ward
		Case to be set for hearing	
		Case set for hearing at Muskogee on July 28 - 05	
	7/28/05	Letter rec'd from Allottee stating she is sick and unable to appear see same in file	
	7/28/05	Defendant appeared and he was given until the 1st of Jan. 1906 to get off to which he agrees and case See letter to plaintiff in file	Dismissed
Plntf states her husband is on her land & asks that he be removed. Jany 30 1907 Plntf advised that this office will take one action as she has leased same to parties who leased it to husband.	Jan 24 -06	Defdt directed to vacate at once or he will be removed. 2/24 Order given to Policeman Musgrove of Claremore to remove Dfts	

Date Received	No.	Allottee	Intruder
Apr 21-05	514	Ellis Chuculate c/o E. M. Fargo Atty Sallisaw I.T.	A.J. Farmer

Cherokee Intruder Cases 1901 - 1909

Notice Sent	Action	Remarks
5/1/05	Return of service 5/5/05	April 17/05 Com reports
	Answer filed May 16, 1905	certificates issued &
	Case to be set for hearing	No contest
	Case set for hearing at Muskogee on July 28 - 05	
Jan 22 - 06	Sent to EC Backenstoce for investigation	2/14 1906 Dismissed
Feb 14<u>th</u> 06	Case dismissed in accordance with agreement of parties	
	2/14 Ptf notified of dismissal.	

Date Received	No.	Allottee	Intruder
Apr 19-05	515	Thos P. Smith Muskogee, I.T.	John T Drew Ft Gibson, I.T. Wolfenberger [sic]

Notice Sent	Action	Remarks
April 28/05		Improvements on town lots in Ft Gibson, I.T.
	5/15/05 Set for hearing at Muskogee, I.T. 5/19/05 at 2 P.M.	
	5/16/05 Br direction of ~~the Special~~ Inspector J. Geo Wright instructions were issued to Capt John C West to place plaintiff in possession of the improvements on the lot in controversy removing defendant from said improvement	
	5/20/05 Report of Capt John C. West filed. Order executed May 18, 1905	Dismissed

Date Received	No.	Allottee	Intruder
April 25-05	516	Tams Bixby Muskogee, I.T.	Bishop & family

Notice Sent	Action	Remarks
April 28/05	~~Return of service May 17, 1905~~	Improvements on town lots in Ft Gibson, I.T.
	5/18/05 By direction of ~~Special~~ Inspector J. George Wright, instructions were	

Cherokee Intruder Cases 1901 - 1909

issued to Capt John C West to place plaintiff in possession of the improvement on the lot in controversy removing from said improvements all objectionable persons 5/20/05 Report of Capt John C West filed Order executed May 18, 1905 Report of Capt West filed Order executed May 31/05	Dismissed

Date Received	No.	Allottee	Intruder
April 27-05	517	Nannie L. Dudley for self & Richard E and W^m E Dudley Stilwell, I.T.	Thomas J Johnson Nowata

Notice Sent	Action	Remarks
5/5/05	Return of service May 22, 1905 Ans filed 6/22/05	Certs Nos 11687, 14729, 6094, 5012, 5013, & 6095
6/23/05	Plaintiff notified that a guardian must be appointed before Action can be taken by this office Case set for hearing at Claremore on Aug 3 - 05	filed-5/5/06 Com requested as to contest. 5/9/05 Com advises no contest
Aug 3rd 05	Telegram rec'd from plaintiff stating that she was sick and could not appear case continued	
Aug 5th 05	Case dismissed by request of plaintiff Certificates ret'd to plaintiff Aug 17 - 05	Dismissed

Date Received	No.	Allottee	Intruder
May 4-05	518	Richard B. Parks Chelsea, I.T. S.F. Parks Atty for plaintiff Chelsea, I.T. April 6th Report of Eldon Lowe filed and case dismissed upon request of Plaintiff	Agnes Williams & Sons Chelsea, I.T. Dismissed

Cherokee Intruder Cases 1901 - 1909

Notice Sent	Action	Remarks
5/5/05		Cert No 27860
		5/5/05 Com requested as to contest
	Answer filed May 13, 1905	
	Case to be set for hearing	5/9/05 Com report
	Case set for hearing at Claremore on Aug 3 - 05	no contest
	Letter from plaintiff filed July 26 - 05	Certificate ret'd
Aug 3rd-05	Case called all parties being present evidence taken. See evidence ~~judgement[sic] for plaintiff~~	Aug 3rd - 05 in person
Mch 19 ' 06	Aug 19 '05 Ptf requested to advise this office if he has obtained possession	
	Sent to Eldon Lowe for investigation	

Date Received	No.	Allottee	Intruder
May 3-05	519	Pompey and Louisa Thompson Braggs, I.T.	B. A. Mayhew

Notice Sent	Action	Remarks
5/5/05	Return of service 5/10/05	Certs Nos. 13478 and 13479 filed
	Answer filed April 25, 1905	
	Cert No 13478 returned to Allottee 6/5/05	5/5/05 Com requested as to contest
	Case set for hearing 6/20/05	5/9/05 Com report
6/20/05	Case heard all parties in interest being present. Defendant's Atty given 3 days in which to file a brief	no contest
	Certificates ret'd to Allottee in person	Aug 7 - 05
Aug 7th-05	Plaintiff appeared in person and stated that defendant was not in possession of the land described in this complaint and case	was <u>Dismissed</u>

Cherokee Intruder Cases 1901 - 1909

Date Received	No.	Allottee	Intruder
May 1-05	520	Ibbie Berry Afton, I.T.	Sam H Rule Afton I.T.
Aug 29-05		Plaintiff requested to advise this office if he has possession	
Sept 15 - 05		Instructions issued to policeman Henderson to place the plaintiff in possession	
Sept 21 - 05		Allottee has possession and case is <u>Dismissed</u> See report of Henderson in file Certificates returned to plaintiff Sept 22 - 05	<u>Dismissed</u>

Notice Sent	Action	Remarks
5/5/05	Return of service May 11, 1904 Answers filed May 13, 1905 See # 522 Case to be set for hearing Case set for hearing at Claremore on Aug 3rd-05 Aug 3rd-05 Case called plaintiff appeared no appearance by defendant plaintiff evidence taken See evidence Aug 3rd-05 Com asked if contest is pending Aug 26-05 Atty for defendant states that his client will vacate at once See letter in #522	Cert No 10945 filed 5/5/05 Com requested as to contest 5/9/05 Com report no contest Com reports no contest 5/31/05 Aug 12-05 Com reports no contest

Date Received	No.	Allottee	Intruder
May 1-05	521	Mrs Blanchie Collins c/o G. A. Collins Roland I.T. Case set for hearing at Muskogee Certificates returned to platf Oct 21 - 05	Mrs James Taylor Roland I.T. Defendant is a Cherokee freedman *(Illegible)* for citizenship

Cherokee Intruder Cases 1901 - 1909

Notice Sent	Action	Remarks
5/5/05	Return of service 5/8/05 Answer filed May 12, 1905 Case to be set for hearing	Cert No 23449 filed 5/5/05 Com requested as to contest
7/22/05	Dft files affidavit that she is a Cherokee Freedwoman Claimant to Citizenship & asks that case be continued - without date -	5/9/05 Commission reports NW^4 of SW^4 of NE^4 less 1 acre reserved for Church Sec 19, Tp 11 N, R 27 E and also claimed by defendant
May 9 - 1906	In compliance with instructions from the Dept under date of 4/19 1906 Com^r is requested to furnish this office with status of Allotment of Ptf and of citizenship of Dfdt in this case	
June 20 1906	Case dismissed as citizenship case of Dfdt is pending before Com^r	Dismissed

Date Received	No.	Allottee	Intruder
5/1/05	522	Francis M Crowell for Erda V Crowell Afton I.T. James S. Davenport Atty for plaintiff	Samuel H. Rule Afton I.T.
Aug 29 - 05		Plaintiff requested to advise this office if he has possession of his land	
Sept 9 - 05		Instructions issued to policeman Henderson to place the plaintiff in possession	
Sept 21 - 05		Allottee has possession and case is dismissed. See report of policeman Henderson in file	Dismissed and certificates returned

Notice Sent	Action	Remarks
5/6/05	Return of service 5/9/05 Answer filed May 13 1905 and put in jacket #520 Case to be set for hearing Case set for hearing at Claremore on Aug 3 - 05	Certs No. 9446 & 7717 filed 5/6/05 Com requested as to contest 5/12/05 Com report No contest
Aug 3rd - 05	Case called, plaintiff appeared no appearance by defendant plaintiff's evidence taken	Com reports no portion of land in contest 5/31/05

Cherokee Intruder Cases 1901 - 1909

	See evidence	
Aug 3rd - 05	Com asked if contest is pending	
Aug 26 - 05	Atty for defendant states that his client will vacate at once See letter in file	Aug 12 - 05 Com reports no contest

Date Received	No.	Allottee	Intruder
April 29-05	523	Sarah E. Porter, nee Coody Hereford, I.T.	Muskogee Development Co Checotah I.T.

Notice Sent	Action	Remarks
5-2-05	Return of service 5/6/05	Certs #1359 & 1170 filed 5/3/05 Commission requested as to contest
	Case to be set for hearing	
	Case set for hearing at Muskogee on July 28 - 05	
7/28/05	Plaintiff appeared today and was informed that the defendant appeared some time ago and stated that they did not claim any possession, plaintiff was then told that he could go and take possession and certificates were ret'd and	Case Dismissed

Date Received	No.	Allottee	Intruder
Apr 26-05	524	Joseph E. Smith by his wife, Hattie Smith Claremore, I.T.	A. J. Blackburn and J. L. Atchison Tulsa, I.T.
	7/31/05	Sent to policeman Sunday with instructions to place the Allottee in possession	
	Jan 8 -- 06	Case dismissed as pltf states that she has possession of her land and certs ret'd to her	J. M. Pixley Atty for Dfdt Dismissed

Notice Sent	Action	Remarks
May 2-05	Return of service May 17-1905 Answer filed May 24, 1905 Set for hearing at Muskogee, I.T. June 2 1905 11 00 A.M.	Certs Nos 29114 & 20867 filed 5/3/05 Com requested as to contest
6/2/05	Case heard all parties in interest being present, evidence taken and it	5/18/05 Com reports no contest

Cherokee Intruder Cases 1901 - 1909

	was decided that Allottee was entitled to possession J.W. Pixley was Atty for Defendant Plaintiff is to let this office know when she has made a settlement or when she has possession	
6/22/05	Defendant notified to vacate at once or make a settlement with the Allottee	

Date Received	No.	Allottee	Intruder
5/1/05	525	Rose Anne Crossland Foreman, I.T.	M. G. Gist J.G. McCombs Atty for defendant Sallisaw I.T.
Notice Sent		**Action**	**Remarks**
5/11/05		Return of service May 13, 1905 Answer filed May 16, 1905 Set for hearing at Muskogee, I.T. May 26, 1905 $3^{\underline{30}}$ P.M 5/20/05 Case called, all parties present. Testimony taken. Attorney for defense allowed leave to file contract 6/12/05 Instructions sent to Policeman Adair to place Allottee in possession See mem. in file 6/19/05 Allottee placed in possession by Policeman Adair and case is Certificates returned to Allottee 6/21/05	Certs Nos. 41980 & 28883 filed 5/11/05 Com requested to advise as to contest 5/18/05 Com reports no contest Dismissed

Date Received	No.	Allottee	Intruder
4/27/05	526	Lydia Lovett for Lucy Highland Braggs, I.T.	Samuel Fulton Braggs, I.T.

Cherokee Intruder Cases 1901 - 1909

Notice Sent	Action	Remarks
5/11/05	Case to be set for hearing Case set for hearing at Muskogee on July 29 - 05 Case dismissed by request of plaintiff filed July 27 - 05	4/26/05 Commission reports certs issued & no contest

Date Received	No.	Allottee	Intruder
5/2/05	527	Samuel H. Benge, Jr Ft Gibson, I.T.	J. M. Raley Ft Gibson, I.T.

Notice Sent	Action	Remarks
5/11/05	Return of service May 16, 1905	Cert #34165 filed 5/11/05 Commission requested to advise as to contest
	5/23/05 Both plaintiff and defendant appeared in person and a statement was made as to controversy, and memorandum was made as to agreement and filed herein, certificates returned to plaintiff in person	5/18/05 Com reports no contest Dismissed

Date Received	No.	Allottee	Intruder
5/3/05	528	Sam Still Christie, I.T.	Ernest Hubbard Christie

Notice Sent	Action	Remarks
5/10/05	Return of service May 26, 1905 Ans filed 6/2/05 Set for hearing at Muskogee, I.T. on 6/19/05 6/19/05 Defendant appeared, plaintiff did not Defendant agreed to have land surveyed and if any part of it is found to be in contest he will surrender same at once Dismissed by request of	4/28/05 Commission reports land in complaint is not in contest no certs issued All but ten acres of land is in <u>contest</u> plaintiff 6/19/05

Cherokee Intruder Cases 1901 - 1909

Date Received	No.	Allottee	Intruder
5/9/05	529	Mrs Johnnie A Brown Collinsville, I.T.	William S. Edmonds Collinsville, I.T.
		W. H. Jennings Atty for plaintiff	
Oct 13 1906		Atty High[sic] Jennings advises that plntf is not in possession	
" 16 1906		Instructions issued J. L. Walker U.S.I.P. at Dewey I.Ty.	
Oct 29 1906		Policeman Jno L Walker reports that he placed Allottee in possession	
Oct 31 1906		Case dismissed.	

Notice Sent	Action	Remarks
5/11/05	Return of service May 15, 1905 Ans filed 5/26/05 Case to be set for hearing Case to be set for hearing Certificate ret'd to Allottee July 25 - 05	Certs #7217 filed 5/11/05 Commission requested as to contest 5/18/05 Com reports no contest
	Case set for hearing at Claremore on Aug 2 - 05	
Aug 2nd-05	Case called, all parties being present plaintiff was also represented by Atty - evidence taken See evidence	Contract dated July 9 - 1903 introduced made by J.B. Brown made to W.S. Edwards[sic]
Aug 2nd - 05	Certificates ret'd in person	Reinstated
(Mch 19 '06	Case dismissed by order W W Bennett)	
April 5	Judgment rendered in favor of Ptf and Both parties so notified Deft given 15 days to vacate	

Date Received	No.	Allottee	Intruder
5/9/05	530	Taylor Buck, Guardian of William Buck Spavinaw I.T.	Jim Elliott Adair, I.T.

Notice Sent	Action	Remarks
5/11/05	Sept 9-05 Sent to John M Bacon for investigation	Cert #3556 filed 5/11/05 Commission requested as to contest 5/18/05 Com reports no contest
	Case to be set for hearing Case set for hearing at Claremore on Aug 3 - 05	
Dec 2-05	No appearance by either party Report of Bacon filed today states that	

Cherokee Intruder Cases 1901 - 1909

> defdt agrees to vacate upon notice from
> this office and pltf so notified
> Mch 19 '06 Sent to Eldon Lowe for investigation
> April 10th Report of Eldon Lowe filed in which he states that
> Dft will surrender possession at anytime that Plaintiff may request,
> certificates returned and Case dismissed

Date Received	No.	Allottee	Intruder
5/9/05	531	Daniel R. DeVaughn, Sallisaw, I.T. Defendants are applicants for enrollment as Cherokee Freedmen	Geo. & Thomas Bell and Lee Lemley
Notice Sent		**Action**	**Remarks**
5/11/05		Return of service May 24, 1905
Answer filed May 27, 1905
Set for hearing at Muskogee, I.T. June 15, 1905 2^{00} P.M.
Dismissed See mem in file
Certs returned 6/3/05 as requested Cert 41838 still in file	Certs Nos 41838, 28715 & 41839 filed
5/11/05 Commission requested as to contest
5/18/05 Com reports no contest
	6/30/05	Case reinstated as to Geo and Thomas Bell	
	6/30/05	Case set for hearing at Muskogee on July 11 - 05 at 1^{30} P.M.
Certificate returned to Allottee 7/11/05	
	May 9 1906	In compliance with instructions from the Department under date of April 19th 1906 Com^r is requested to furnish this office with status of Allotment of Ptf and of Citizenship of Defendant in this case	
	June 12 "	Com^r reports motion to review the Citizenship of Thomas Bell is pending but no motion is pending as to Citizenship of Geo Bell. Case Dismissed	

Date Received	No.	Allottee	Intruder
5/5/05	532	W. T. Brady, Guardian of Ruth T Brady Tulsa, I.T.	Nora B. Burgess
Notice Sent		**Action**	**Remarks**
5/11/05		Return of service March 19, 1905
Certs returned to Allottee 6/1/05
Dismissed by request of plaintiff	Cert #5620 filed
5/11/05 Commission requested as to contest

Cherokee Intruder Cases 1901 - 1909

				5/18/05 Com reports no contest Dismissed

Date Received	No.	Allottee		Intruder
5/5/05	533	Bert Buckmaster, Gd'n of Mary and Birdie Buckmaster, c/o Butts & Bliss, Atty Muskogee, I.T.		Tom Holman Tulsa
Notice Sent		**Action**		**Remarks**
5/11/05		Letters of Guardianship filed 5/20/05 Case dismissed by attorney for plaintiff. Certs returned to Butts & Bliss with Letters of guardianship also		Certs No 4969, 4200 & 4968 ~~filed~~ & 4199 filed 5/11/05 Commission requested as to contest Dismissed 5/18/05 Com reports no contest

Date Received	No.	Allottee		Intruder
5/11/05	534	Susan Waltrip Welling, I.T.	vs	Louis McClemore et al Welling I.T.
Notice Sent		**Action**		**Remarks**
5/15/05		Return of service May 26-05 Case to be set for hearing Case set for hearing at Muskogee on Jul 29 - 05 July 29 - 05 No appearance by either party Case set for hearing at Muskogee on Aug 18th - 05 Aug 18 - 05 Case called: plaintiff appeared no appearance by the defendant Plaintiff evidence taken and it appears that the defendant is not liveing[sic] on her land and case was		Cert filed N° 31199 5/15/05 Report of Com requested 5/20/05 Report of Com No Contest Dismissed

Cherokee Intruder Cases 1901 - 1909

Date Received	No.	Allottee	Intruder
5/2/05	535	Mary Mayo vs Vian, I.T.	Frank Vann and Sam Warne Ft Gibson, I.T.
Notice Sent		**Action**	**Remarks**
5/16/05		Return of service May 22, 1905	Cert filed 21811 Report 5/05 of Com requested 5/20/05 Com reports that
May 9 1906		In compliance with instructions from the Dept under date of 4/19/06 Com^r is requested to furnish this office with status of Allotment Ptf and of Citizenship of Dfdt in this case June 12 Com^r reports that a motion for review is pending	NE^4 of SE^4 of NE^4 S7, T 11N R 22E is in contest Dismissed

Date Received	No.	Allottee	Intruder
4/25/05	536	Caroline Scallole vs Catoosa I.T.	Bill Whitman H. Jennings Atty for defendant
Notice Sent		**Action**	**Remarks**
5/16/05		Return of service May 17, 1905 Answer filed May 19, 1905 Case to be set for hearing Case set for hearing at Claremore on Aug 3rd - 05 Aug 3rd - 05 Case called, all parties being present plaintiff told that the kinship must be determined before Action could be taken and subsequently case was Defendant is not occupying the lands of the plaintiff, but of her dec'd sister Alcy Johnson	No Certs filed 5/10/05 Com reports no contest Dismissed another party has been appointed administrator

Date Received	No.	Allottee	Intruder
5/12/05	537	Felix Nelems[sic] grd of vs Madeline Matthews Chelsea, I.T.	C.W. Bogard Chelsea, I.T.

Cherokee Intruder Cases 1901 - 1909

Notice Sent	Action	Remarks
5/15/04		Certs filed 2917, 3446
	Letters of guardianship filed 5/12/05	5/16/05 Com requested to report as to contest
	Case to be set for hearing	5/20/05 Com report filed
	Case set for hearing at Claremore on Aug 3 - 05	no contest
	Aug 3rd 05 Case called, all parties being present evidence taken, plaintiff states that the defendant can make his crop and remove his house but must move off of the land defendant to have 30 days to move his home from the lands of plaintiff to which he agrees and case was	Dismissed
	Aug 3rd-05 Certificates returned in person	

Date Received	No.	Allottee		Intruder
5/12/05	538	Ruth B Evans grdn for Henry Evans ofc Fee & Querry Attys Tulsa, I.T.	vs	John W. Turley
		Oct 23 1906 In answer to inquiry of 10/19/06 plntf advised that there are no certificates here. Were returned 6/19/05		

Notice Sent	Action	Remarks
5/16/05	Ans filed 5/31/05	Certf filed #10932, 8870
	Letters of guardianship filed 5/12/05	5/16/05 Report of Com requested
	Return of service 6/8/05	
	Set for hearing 6/19/05 at 10^{00} A.M.	5/20/05 Com reports no contest
	6/19/05 Decided that Allottee is intitled to possession	
	Plaintiff is to notify this office when he has possession	
	Defendant confesses judgementr[sic]	
	Case dismissed by request of plaintiffs Atty and certificates and letters of gdn returned	Dismissed

Cherokee Intruder Cases 1901 - 1909

Date Received	No.	Allottee		Intruder
5/15/05	539	Zachary T. Woodard Centralia, I.T.	vs	Seafus Minor & Otis Odell Centralia, I.T.
Notice Sent		**Action**		**Remarks**
5/17/05		Return of service May 20, 1905 Ans filed 6/1/05 Case to be set for hearing		Certs filed 10354, 8427 5/17/05 Report of Com requested
7/27/05		Case set for hearing at Claremore on Aug 3 - 05 No appearance by either party		5/24/05 Com reports no contest
Sept 9 - 05		Sent to John M Bacon for investigation		
Oct 17 - 05		Case dismissed by request of pltf. See report of Bacon in file Certificates returned to pltf Oct. 19-05		Dismissed

Date Received	No.	Allottee		Intruder
5/15/05	540	Gibson W. Alberty Christie, I.T.	vs	Allan Long Centralia, I.T.
Notice Sent		**Action**		**Remarks**
5/17/05				Certs filed 3380, 3973 5/17/05 Com asked to report
		Contract filed 5/15/05		on contest 5/24/05 Report of Com
		Case to be set for hearing Case set for hearing at Claremore on Aug 3 - 05 No appearance by either party		No contest
Sept 9 - 05		Sent to John M Bacon for investigation		
Nov 11 - 05		Case dismissed by report of Bacon and request of pltf and certificates returned to pltf.		

Date Received	No.	Allottee		Intruder
5/24/05	541	A. H. Craig for Warren R Craig Braggs, I.T.	vs	Saml Roach Braggs, I.T.

Cherokee Intruder Cases 1901 - 1909

Notice Sent	Action	Remarks
5/20/05	Return of service May 25, 1905	Certs filed 23692
	Certificates returned to Allottee 6/22/05	5/20/05 Report of Com requested
6/19/05	Allottee stated that he has possession of his land and case is dismissed	Com reports portion of land in contest
		Dismissed

Date Received	No.	Allottee		Intruder
4/24/05	542	David C. Davis Hulbert I.T.	vs	Bob King et al Hulbert I.T.

Notice Sent	Action	Remarks
5/20/05	Return of service 6/12/05	Certs filed 6039, 4967
	Case to be set for hearing	5/20/05 Report of Com requested
	Case set for hearing at Muskogee on July 29 - 05	Com reports no portion of land in contest
July 29 - 05	Defendant appeared and his evidence was taken no appearance by plaintiff	Rental contract filed 7/1/05 by defendant
	Case set for hearing at Muskogee on Aug 20 - 05	Certs ret'd in person to plaintiff Aug 22 - 05
Aug 20 - 05	Case called, plaintiff appeared no appearance by defendant, plaintiff states that he signed contract subsequent to allotting his land and case was	Dismissed

Date Received	No.	Allottee		Intruder
5/6/05	543	Nannie Chair nee Greece Welling I.T.	vs	Thos Mathis Welling I.T.

Notice Sent	Action	Remarks
5/24/05	Return of service 6/3/05	No certs filed
	Ans filed 6/7/05	5/18/05 Com reports
	Lease filed 6/7/05	no contest
	Set for hearing at Muskogee 6/19/05 @ 2^{00} P.M.	Certs issued Oct 23 - 05 Sent to Capt
6/19/05	Case heard: all parties in interest being present decided that Allottee is	West to place the pltf in possession

Cherokee Intruder Cases 1901 - 1909

intitled to possession Defendant notified to vacate at once 7/17/05 Sent to policeman Smith with instructions to place the Allottee in possession. Again sent to Smith Sept 5-05 Sept 20 - 05 Allottee placed in possession on Sept 16th 05 by report of policeman Smith. See same in file.	Nov 1-05 Report of Capt West filed today. See mem in file Dismissed

Date Received	No.	Allottee	Intruder
5/3/05	544	George Smith for Daniel vs c/o A. W. *(Illegible)* Atty Tahlequah, I.T.	A.G. Borens Peggs I.T.
Notice Sent		**Action**	**Remarks**
5/24/05		 Case to be set for hearing Case set for hearing at Muskogee on July 29 - 05 7/29 no appearance Mch 19 '06 Sent to Eldon Lowe for investigation April 18 Report of Eldon Lowe filed and case dismissed upon request of Plaintiff	No certs filed 5/24/05 Com reports certs issued no contest Dismissed

Date Received	No.	Allottee	Intruder
5/3/05	545	Mary Brown by vs Henry F Brown Ketchum, I.T.	Deyer Dining
Notice Sent		**Action**	**Remarks**
5/24/05		Return of service July 27-05 Ans filed Aug 4th-05 Case to be set for hearing Case set for hearing at Claremore on Aug 3-05	No certs filed 5/18/05 Com reports certs issued and no contest

Cherokee Intruder Cases 1901 - 1909

Aug 3rd-05	Plaintiff appeared and stated that her son was a minor consequently the case was	Dismissed

Date Received	No.	Allottee		Intruder
4/26/05	546	Emeline Green	vs	William Hae
		Collinsville, I.T.		

Notice Sent	Action	Remarks
5/24/05		No certs in file
		5/18/05 Com reports certs
	Case to be set for hearing	issued and no contest
	Case set for hearing at	
	Claremore on Aug 4th-05	
	No appearance by either party	
Sept 9-05	Sent to John M Bacon for	
Sept 18-05	investigation	
	Case dismissed by request of plaintiff	Dismissed
	See report of Bacon in file	

Date Received	No.	Allottee		Intruder
5/14/05	547	H. A. Landers grdn of	vs	Robt R Jackson
		Bertha & Wm H. Landers		McLane, I.T.
		Porum, I.T.		

Notice Sent	Action	Remarks
5/24/05	Case filed 6/6/05	Certs filed 20096, 20095
		31067
	Case to be set for hearing	5/24/05 Com requested to
6/10/05	Plaintiff states that he served notice and made return same has not been rec'd	advise as to contest Com reports no portion of land in contest
	Case set for hearing at Muskogee on July 29-05	Aug 26-05 Case Dismissed by personal request of
7/29/05	Plaintiff appeared and advised that defendant had not rec'd notice case to be reset	plaintiff and certificates returned
	Case set for hearing at Muskogee pm Aug 26-05	
June 5 '07	Contract returned to H. A. Landers in person	

217

Cherokee Intruder Cases 1901 - 1909

Date Received	No.	Allottee	Intruder
(No date given.)	548	*Ameritta Washington* vs o/c[sic] *Osborn & Osborn Coffeyville, I.T.* 3/8 '06 Instruction issued to Capt Alf McKay to place ptf in possession Nov 16 McCay[sic] reports that Ptf is in possession Case dismissed and ptf so notified.	*Wm Washington Coffeyville, Ks*

Notice Sent	Action	Remarks
5/29/05	Return of service 6/6/05	No certs filed
	Ans filed 6/7/05	5/18/05 Com reports certs
	Case to be set for hearing	issued and no contest
	Case set for hearing at Claremore on Aug 4th - 05	
Aug 4th 05	Case called, defendant states that all he wants is pay for improvements defendant is notified to remove off of the land within ten days to which he agrees, plaintiff to notify this office when he *(Illegible)*	
Aug 22 - 05	Instructions sent to policeman Edmonds to place the plaintiff in possession and make report to this office.	

Date Received	No.	Allottee	Intruder
5/24/05	548[sic]	Laura Wilson mother of vs Rory Sequouah[sic] Wilson o/c John A Vaughn Atty Ft Smith, Ark	Geo Wallen et al Muldrow, I.T.

Notice Sent	Action	Remarks
5/27/05	Return of service 6/30/05	Certs filed 23622 33628
	Ans filed 6/28/05	5/27/05 Com requested to
6/28/05	Case dismissed as Allottee is a minor and no Guar is appointed	advise as to contest
	Certificates returned to Allottee 6/28/05	Com reports portion of land in contest
		Dismissed

Cherokee Intruder Cases 1901 - 1909

Date Received	No.	Allottee	Intruder
5/7/05	549	Luna M McDaniel Tahlequah, I.T.	vs Burrell Taylor or Daniels Muskogee, I.T.
	June 6 1906	Com^r reports all land described in this case is involved in contest therefore case is dismissed	
			Dismissed
Notice Sent		**Action**	**Remarks**
5/27/05		Ans filed 6/2/05 Plaintiff notified that under a new ruling of the defendant that no motion could be taken to remove the defendant See ruling of department 6/9 1905 Ptf so advised Return of service 6/12/05	Certs filed 42050 28927 5/27/05 Com requested to report as to contest Com reports no portion of land in contest Nov 7 Certificates returned
	May 9 1906	In compliance with instructions from the Dept under date of April 19th 1906 Com^r is requested to furnish this office with status of Allotment of Ptf and status of citizenship of Dfdt in this case	

Date Received	No.	Allottee	Intruder
6/1/05	550	Rachael Silversmith Dodge, Ind. Ter.	Frank Gains Fairland, I.T.
Notice Sent		**Action**	**Remarks**
6/12/05		Return of service 6/22/05 Case to be set for hearing	Com reports no portion of land in contest and certs issued
		Case Dismissed See 561	

Date Received	No.	Allottee	Intruder
6/5/05	551	Nancy B. Fogle, nee Fields So West City, Mo	Charles Coppers Welch, I.T. Frank Gains Fairland, I.T.
Notice Sent		**Action**	**Remarks**
6/12/05		Return of service 6/23/05 Return of service 7/1/05 Case to be set for hearing Case set for hearing on Aug 4th-05 at Claremore	Certs in file 6/19/05 Com reports no portion of land in contest

Cherokee Intruder Cases 1901 - 1909

Aug 4th-05	Case called, defendant states that he has a verbal agreement with the plaintiff. Plaintiff was represented by her husband, evidence taken Defendant to remain on the land and house to be built by the 1st of Dec	Certificate ret'd to the plaintiff in person
	Case	Dismissed

Date Received	No.	Allottee	Intruder
6/1/05	552	Mary J Sherman Vinita, Ind. Ter.	Bert Hughes and tenants Vinita, I.T.
Notice Sent		**Action**	**Remarks**
6/12/05		Return of service 6/16/05	Cert in file 6/19/05 Com reports no
		Case to be set for hearing Case set for hearing at Claremore on Aug 4th-05 No appearance by either party	portion of land in contest
Sept 9-05		Sent to John M Bacon for investigation	
Oct 2-05		Case dismissed by request of pltf See report of Bacon in file Certificates ~~in file~~ returned to plaintiff Oct 17-05	Dismissed

Date Received	No.	Allottee	Intruder
6/6/05	553	George Martin Chelsea, I.T. Judge Stanfield Atty for plaintiff Vinita, I.T. Plaintiff is a Cherokee Freedman	Chriss[sic] Klause J.G. Brown Atty for defendant Chelsea, I.T.
Notice Sent		**Action**	**Remarks**
6/12/05		Return of service 7/10/05 Ans filed 7/11/05 Case to be set for hearing	Cert in file 6/19/05 Com reports no portion of land in contest
7/13/05		Receipt of ans. Ack. Cases set for hearing at Claremore on Aug 4th 05	
Aug 4-05		Case dismissed by request of plaintiff's Atty and certificates ret'd in person	Dismissed

Cherokee Intruder Cases 1901 - 1909

Date Received	No.	Allottee	Intruder
6/6/05	554	Joshua Martin Chelsea, I.T. Judge Stanfield Atty for Plaintiff Vinita, I.T. Plaintiff is a Cherokee Freedman	Flora Klaus Chelsea J.G. Brown Atty for defendant Chelsea, I.T.
Notice Sent		**Action**	**Remarks**
6/12/05		Return of Service 6/28/05 Case to be set for hearing Case set for hearing at Claremore on Aug 4th - 05	Cert in file 6/19/05 Com reports no portion of land in contest
	Aug 4th-05	Case called, all parties being present or represented by Atty, evidence taken Case Dismissed by request of plaintiffs Atty Aug 4-05 certificates ret'd in person	Defendant's Atty introduced contest made on April the 4th and filed Dismissed

Date Received	No.	Allottee	Intruder
6/10/05	555	Watt Mouse Eucha I.T.	Turquanna
Notice Sent		**Action**	**Remarks**
6/12/05		Return of service 6/23/05 Ans filed Aug 17-05 Case to be set for hearing Case set for hearing at Claremore on Aug 4th-05	Cert in file 6/14/05 Com reports no portion of land in contest Jan 9 -06 Certificates ret'd to pltf today
	Aug 4th-05	Case called, plaintiff appeared no appearance by defendant, to be given to Capt West to go and investigate	
	June 8 06	Capt John C West Instructed to try to effect a settlement between the parties	
	June 18 "	Capt West reports that he has placed Ptf in possession Case is therefore dismissed	Dismissed

Cherokee Intruder Cases 1901 - 1909

Date Received	No.	Allottee	Intruder
6/6/05	556	Rosa Spubuck, nee Chisholm Turley I.T.	Wm Turley Turley
Notice Sent		**Action**	**Remarks**
6/12/05		Return of service 6/14/05 Ans filed 6/21/05 Case set for hearing at Muskogee on June 20th - 05 at 10^{30}	Com reports no portion of land in contest and Certs issued
	6/29/05	Case continued until July 10-05 by stipulation of both parties	Original contract filed 7/10/05
	7/10/05	Case called, defendant appeared, plaintiff did not, defendants evidence taken	
	7/19/05	Plaintiff notified to appear at once so that his evidence may be taken and the case settled up	Copy of contract filed July 29-05
	7/27/05	Plaintiff wants case set at Claremore See letter in file Case set for hearing at Claremore on Aug 4th-05	
	Aug 4th-05	Case Dismissed See #568	See contract in #563

Date Received	No.	Allottee	Intruder
6/9/05	557	George P. Samuels Gann I.T.	Nathan Everett Gann I.T.
Notice Sent		**Action**	**Remarks**
6/12/05		Return of service 6/17/05	Certs in file 6/19/05 Com reports no portion of land in contest
		Case to be set for hearing Case set for hearing at Muskogee on July 29-05 Letter filed by plaintiff 7/18/05	
	Aug 14-05	Instructions issued to policeman Adair to investigate this matter and plaintiff so notified and certificates returned to him	
	8/21/14	Report of policeman Adair in file Aug 22-05 Instructions sent to policeman Adair to place the plaintiff in possession	Aug 28-05 Allottee placed in possession by policeman Adair and case Dismissed

222

Cherokee Intruder Cases 1901 - 1909

Date Received	No.	Allottee	Intruder
6/7/05	558	Rachel Lutes Wagoner I.T	James Cleland and A. G. Thomas Sleeper I.T.
Notice Sent		**Action**	**Remarks**
6/12/05		Return of service 6/26/05 Case to be set for hearing	Certs in file 6/19/05 Com reports no portion of land in contest
7/14/05		Case dismissed as it appears that the defendant is not occupying the plaintiffs land only landing a ferry boat on the public highway Certificates returned to Allottee 7/14/05	

Date Received	No.	Allottee	Intruder
6/10/05	559	Martin Ross by J.L. Springston Vian, I.T.	J. W. Harris Vian, I.T.
	Aug 28-05	This matter was adjusted by W.W. Bennett on Aug the 24th The certificates returned to plaintiff in person and case he having visited the allotment in person	Dismissed
	Sept 11-05	Instructions issued to Capt West to place the plaintiff in possession	
	Sept 15-05	Allotee placed in possession by Capt. West See report in file	Dismissed
Notice Sent		**Action**	**Remarks**
6/4/05		Return of service 6/26/05	Certs in file
6/26/05		Defendant Harris appeared at this office in person today and stated that he would vacate the lands belonging to Martin Ross, at once. Plaintiff to notify this office when defendant vacates	6/19/05 Com reports no portion of land is in contest
7/10/05		Defendant notified to vacate the lands of Martin Ross at once	7/27/05 Com reports contest on land
7/14/05		Dft makes answer claiming land is in contest before Com^r	

Cherokee Intruder Cases 1901 - 1909

	See letter from Defendant filed Aug 3rd 05
7/3/06	Pltf advised to file new complaint (see carbon in file)

Date Received	No.	Allottee	Intruder
6/22/05	560	Freeman Fields Southwest City Mo.	Chas Houshe Bluejacket I.T. and Gaines Bros Fairland, I.T.
Notice Sent		**Action**	**Remarks**
6/30/05		Return of service 7/11/05	Com reports no portion of land in contest and certificates issued
		Case to be set for hearing	
		Case set for hearing at Claremore on Aug 4th-05	Certificates filed 7/11/05
Aug 4th-05		Case called, judgements[sic] for plaintiff defendant to remain on the land until Jan 1st 06 and gather his crop and Case was Certificates retrd to plaintiff in person	Defendant introduced contract made before filing Dismissed

Date Received	No.	Allottee	Intruder
6/22/05	561	Miss Rachel Silversmith Dodge I.T.	Frank Gains and John Coppers
Notice Sent		**Action**	**Remarks**
6/30/05			Certificates in file
		Case to be set for hearing	7/10/05 Com reports that no
		Case set for hearing at Claremore on Aug 4th-05	portion of land is in contest
Aug 4th-05		Case called and case was See file	Dismissed Certificate retrd to plaintiff Aug 4th-05 in person

Cherokee Intruder Cases 1901 - 1909

Date Received	No.	Allottee	Intruder
6/22/05	562	Obidiah[sic] Tiblow Skiatook Ind. Ter. Cherokee Freedman	Milton Fenwick for Lula Phillips Skiatook Ind Ter Wade B Stanfield Atty for defendant Vinita Ind Ter
July 10 1906		Com^r reports that application of Lula Phillips for citizenship as a Cherokee Freedwoman is now pending Therefore case is dismissed	
Jany ~~26~~ 18, 1906		Plntf asks status of case	Dismissed
Jany 26 1906		Plntf advised	

Notice Sent	Action	Remarks
6/30/05	Return of service 7/8/05 Ans filed July 14-05 Case to be set for hearing Case set for hearing at Claremore on Aug 4th-05 No appearance by either party Certs ret'^{d} to pltf Feb 9 -06	Certificate in file 7/14/05 Com reports that no portion of the land is in contest
May 9 1906	In compliance with instructions from the Dept under date of April 19th 1906 Com^r is requested to furnish this office with status of allotment of Plaintiff of Citizenship of Defendant in this case	
June 18 "	Case set for hearing at Claremore, I.T. June 22/06	
June 22 "	Plaintiff appeared no appearance by Dfdt. This office to ask Com^r to report as citizenship of Lula Phillips	
July 2~~3~~	Com^r requested to report as to citizenship of Lula Phillips	

Date Received	No.	Allottee	Intruder
6/22/05	563	Nancy Chisholm Turley Ind. Ter.	William Turley Turley I.T.

Notice Sent	Action	Remarks
6/30/05	Return of service July 15-05 Ans filed July 19-05 Case to be set for hearing Case set for hearing at Claremore on Aug 4th-05	Certificates in file 7/10/05 Com reports that no portion of land is in contest Original contract exhibited Aug 4th-05
Aug 4th-05	Case called, all parties being present and defendant represented by Atty also evidence taken and case was	<u>Dismissed</u>

225

Cherokee Intruder Cases 1901 - 1909

Aug 4th-05	See evidence Certificates ret'd in person

Date Received	No.	Allottee	Intruder
6/13/05	564	Dennis Smith Coffeyville, Kans	Lewis F. Claussen Wimer Ind Ter
Notice Sent		**Action**	**Remarks**
6/30/05		Return of service 7/5/05 Case to be set for hearing Chattel mortgage filed by defendant July 12-05 Case set for hearing at Claremore on Aug 4th-05	Certificates in file 7/10/05 Com reports that no portion of land is in contest
Aug 4th-05		Case called, all parties being present, evidence taken judgement[sic] for plaintiff Defendant given 15 days to vacate plaintiff to notify the office when same is done	
Aug 23-05		Case dismissed as plaintiff states that he has possession of his land and certificates returned See letter in file	Dismissed

Date Received	No.	Allottee	Intruder
6/20/05	565	Lizzie E. Thomas Roland Ind. Ter.	Henry Shackleford Pawpaw Ind Ter
Notice Sent		**Action**	**Remarks**
6/30/05		Return of service 7/5/05 Ans filed 7/10/05 Case to be set for hearing and plaintiff so notified James S. Davenport is the real defendant	Certificates in file 7/10/05 Com reports that all of land is in contest
7/13/05		Case dismissed and certificates returned to Allottee	

Date Received	No.	Allottee	Intruder
6/28/05	566	John Anna England Vinita, Ind. Ter.	R. L. England Afton I.T.

Cherokee Intruder Cases 1901 - 1909

Notice Sent	Action	Remarks
6/30/05	Return of service 7/11/05 Ans. filed July 17-05 Case to be set for hearing Case set for hearing at Claremore on Aug 4th-05 No appearance by either party	Certificates in file 7/10/05 Com reports no portion of land in contest
Sept 9-05	Sent to John M. Bacon for investigation	
Oct 2-05	Case dismissed by request of pltf See report of Bacon in file certificates returned to pltf Oct 17-05	Dismissed

Date Received	No.	Allottee	Intruder
7/3/05	567	Thos P. Hickey, Gdn of Richard, John, Mary L. and William Hickey Wagoner Ind. Ter. Restraining order filed Aug 4th-05	C. L. Harkins Nowata, I.T.

Notice Sent	Action	Remarks
7/5/05	Return of service 7/14/05 Ans filed July 14-05 Case to be set for hearing Case set for hearing at Muskogee on July 27-05	Certificates and Letters of Guardianship in file 7/11/05 Com reports no portion of land in contest
7/27/05	Defendant Harkins telephones and states that he rec'd no notice of hearing but will be here Sat. morning at 9⁰⁰ A.M.	3/9 1906 Letters of Gdnship and Certificates returned
7/29/05	Case called all parties being present evidence taken and judgement[sic] rendered in favor of plaintiff	

Cherokee Intruder Cases 1901 - 1909

Date Received	No.	Allottee	Intruder
June 27-05	568	Nannie R. Durham Tahlequah, I.T.	G. H. Hobbs Pryor Creek I.T. and F. M. Rucker Claremore, I.T. Judge Jennings Atty for defendants
Notice Sent		**Action**	**Remarks**
Aug 5th-05		Return of service Aug 10th-05 Ans filed Sept 1st-05 Case to be set for hearing Set for hearing at Muskogee on Sept 7-05 at 2^{00} P.M. Set for hearing at Muskogee on Jan 4-06	Certificates and map in file Com reports no contest Aug 11th-05 See case #569
	Jan 4-06	Pltf appeared in person, Bennett called up Judge Jennings Atty for defdts and he stated that they did not claim the possession of Mrs. Durham's land and that she could take possession and she was so advised and certificates were retrd to her in person and case	Dismissed

Date Received	No.	Allottee	Intruder
June 27-05	569	William H Durham Gdn of Fred A and Henry C Durham Tahlequah Ind Ter Certificates and Letters of Gdn. retrd to pltf Oct 11-05	G. H. Hobbs Pryor Creek I.T. and F. M. Rucker Claremore, I.T. Judge Jennings Atty for defendants

        Mch 20 Ptf states that restraining order was "dissolved" Mch 8th by US Court at Claremore
Mch 28 Chas M Davidson Clerk of US Court N Dist requested to furnish this office with information as to what Action has been taken in this case
April 5 M.W. Clift Deputy Clerk of US Court ^ Claremore IT advises that injunction has been disolved[sic]
April 6 Instructions issued to Capt John C West to place Gaurdian[sic] in possession
5/5 Wm H. Durham requested to notify this office when he will be at

Cherokee Intruder Cases 1901 - 1909

Choteau to receive possession
May 10 Advises that as soon as possible he will make necessary arrangements to take possession of the allotments of his minor children
June 8 Capt John C. West reports that he has placed the Gdn in possession Case is therefore dismissed

Notice Sent	Action	Remarks
		Dismissed
Aug 5th-05	Return of service Aug 10th-05	Certificates and Letters of
(Illegible) 16-05	Judge Jennings and defendants appeared today and stated that they would file ans. Ans filed Sept 1st-05 Set for hearing at Muskogee on Sept 7-05 at 1^{30} P.M.	Gdn in file Com reports no contest Aug 11-05
Sept 7-05	Case called all parties being present evidence taken. See same in file.	Restraining order filed Sept 28-05 See mem in file
Sept 19-05	Judgement[sic] rendered in favor of plaintiff and defendant ordered to vacate within ten days or he will be removed; plaintiff requested to notify this office if same is done	

Date Received	No.	Allottee	Intruder
June 30th-05	570	Daniel E. Moore Verdigris I.T.	W. M. Fry Claremore
Notice Sent		**Action**	**Remarks**
Aug 5th-05		Return of service Aug 17-05 Certificates returned to plaintiff Aug 19-05 Ans filed Aug 21-05	Certificates in file Com reports no contest Aug 11-05 Certificates retrd to plaintiff
Sept 7-05		Defendants appeared no appearance by the plaintiff Case to be reset See letter from plaintiff in file	Aug 19-05
Sept 9-05		Sent to John M. Bacon for investigation	
Sept 25-05		Case dismissed by request of plaintiff. See report of John M Bacon filed today	Dismissed

Cherokee Intruder Cases 1901 - 1909

Date Received	No.	Allottee	Intruder
July 6-05	571	Daisy Hanks Webbers Falls I.T.	John Mceachin[sic] Sallisaw I.T. Shoenfelt and Tisdell Attys for defendant Muskogee, I.T.

Notice Sent	Action	Remarks
Aug 5th-05	Return of service Aug 11th-05 Ans filed by Shoenfelt and Tisdel[sic] Attys for defendant Aug 25-05 Set for hearing at Muskogee on Sept 11-05 at *(No time given)*	Certificate in file Com reports no contest Aug 11-05
Sept 11-05	Case heard; evidence taken all parties being present Certificates returned to pltf Oct 11-05	
Aug 15 1906	As new contract has been made between parties, This case is by W.W.B. Dismissed	

Date Received	No.	Allottee	Intruder
July 6th-05	572	Mack Quinton Brushy I.T. Merchison of Tahlequah Atty for plaintiff	Joseph Reinhart Nowata, I.T. W.A. Chan Nowata, I.T. Atty for defendant
Feb 6 -- 06		Certificates retrd to pltf in person today	
Mch 15, 1905		Mack Quinton appeared in office & states contest was ∧ filed against his allottment[sic] before Com^r & he is unable to control or collect rents from his allotment	
Mch 15, 1907		A letter given him, reciting proceedings in this case	

Notice Sent	Action	Remarks
Aug 7th-05	Return of service Aug 21-05 Ans filed Aug 28-05 Set for hearing at Muskogee I.T. Sept 14-05 at 2^{00} P.M.	Certificates in file Aug 12-05 Com reports no contest
Sept 14-05	Case called; plaintiff appeared in person and by Atty; no appearance by defendant, plaintiff's evidence	Oct 3-05 Instructions transferred to Frank West

Cherokee Intruder Cases 1901 - 1909

Sept 20-05 Defendant's Atty appeared today and stated that he would submit evidence on Sept 30 05 Sept 30 05 Plaintiff apeared[sic] but no apearance[sic] by Defendant as for agreement Default Judgment taken and instructions issued to Edmonds today	Allottee placed in possession by policeman West Oct 5-05 See report in file

Date Received	No.	Allottee	Intruder
June 30-05	573	Martha Bussey Claremore, I.T.	Geo W Tolbert Claremore
Notice Sent		**Action**	**Remarks**
Aug 7th-05		Return of service	Certificates in file Aug 12-05 Com reports
Sept 9-05		Sent to John M Bacon for investigation	no contest
Sept 25-05		Case dismissed by request of plaintiff and certificates returned to her. See report of Bacon filed today	Dismissed

Date Received	No.	Allottee	Intruder
July 10th-05	574	Claud L. Washburn Jr Eucha I.T.	John Thompson So West City, Mo
	Mch 28, 1907	Plntf again asks possession	
	~~Apr 9, 1907~~ ~~Letter Killed~~	~~Plntf advised that if he will go with policeman~~ ~~to accept possession, policeman will be sent~~	
Notice Sent		**Action**	**Remarks**
Aug 7th-05		Return of service Aug 31-05	Certificate in file Aug 12-05 Com reports
Sept 9-05		Sent to John M Bacon for investigation	no contest
Nov 18-05		Report of Bacon filed today recommends that pltf be placed in possession 1/12/06 Instructions sent Elijah Henderson U.S.I.P. to place ptf in possession 2/26 Instructions renewed	

Cherokee Intruder Cases 1901 - 1909

June 8/06 Instructions issued to Capt West to place the Allottee in possession
Aug 14 1906 Capt Jno C, West report in file
Aug 21 1906 Andrew J Alberty US Ind Policeman at Stilwell, I.T. instructed to try to persuade Thompson, dfdt, to remove his fence and explain matter to dfdt. Try to settle without out[sic] any violence as dft is full blood of Night Hawk faction.
Nov 9 1906 Policeman Alberty requested to report
Nov 17 1906 Policeman Alberty reports placed plntf in possession.
11/28 Dismissed.

Date Received	No.	Allottee	Intruder
June 26-05	575	Webster Chisholm Turley Ind. Ter.	William Turley Turley I.T.
Notice Sent		**Action**	**Remarks**
Aug 4th-05 Sept 6-05 Sept 18-05		Return of service Sent to John M Bacon for investigation Case dismissed by request of plaintiff See report of Bacon in file	June 24-05 Com reports no contest and certificates issued Dismissed

Date Received	No.	Allottee	Intruder
June 26-05	576	Caleb Gonzalas Braggs, I.T.	D. E. Bryson Campbell I.T.
Notice Sent		**Action**	**Remarks**
Aug 7th-05 Aug 28-05 Sept 9-05		Return of service Aug 23-05 Letter rec'd from defendant stateing[sic] that he had made a settlement with plaintiff Case dismissed by request of plaintiff and certificates returned	Certificates in file Aug. 12-04^{05} Com reports no contest Dismissed

Date Received	No.	Allottee	Intruder
July 24-05	577	Ludie G. Rowland nee Shoemake Webbers Falls, I.T.	Hughie Shoemake Webbers Falls I.T.

Cherokee Intruder Cases 1901 - 1909

Notice Sent	Action	Remarks
Aug 8th-05	Return of service Aug 19-05	Certificates in file
Dec 13-05	Letter rec'd from pltf stateing[sic] that dfdt had agreed to give her possession and she was requested to advise this office when she had	Aug 15-05 Com reports no contest
Feb 1 -06	possession	
	Case dismissed by request of pltf	Dismissed
April 11th 1906	Certificates returned to Plaintiff	

Date Received	No.	Allottee	Intruder
July 21-05	578	Lucy Rogers nee Harris Talala I.T.	L. J. Suarr Oologah I.T.

Notice Sent	Action	Remarks
Aug 8th-05	Return of service Aug 15-05	Certificates in file
Sept 6-05	Sent to John M Bacon for investigation Certificates ret'd to pltf Dec 29-05 Set for hearing at Vinita, I.T. on Jan 16 -06	Aug 15-05 Com reports no contest
Jan 10 -06	Defdt appeared today and stated that he did not hold possession of pltfs land and pltf so advised	
Jan 15 -06	Case dismissed by request of pltf	Dismissed

Date Received	No.	Allottee	Intruder
July 20th-05	579	Margaret E Holland Grove Ind. Ter.	Samuel Frazier Vinita, I.T.

Notice Sent	Action	Remarks
Aug 8th-05	Return of service Aug 14-05	Certificates in file
Sept 6-05	Sent to John M Bacon for investigation	Aug 15-05 Com reports no contest
Nov 18-05	Report of Bacon filed today states that defdt does not claim possession and pltf is notified *Dismissed*	3/9/1906 Certificates returned

Cherokee Intruder Cases 1901 - 1909

Date Received	No.	Allottee	Intruder
July 27-05	580	Delilah Falling Collinsville Ind Ter	Wesley Blackburn Collinsville Shoenfelt and Tisdell Attys for defendant Muskogee, I.T.
Notice Sent		**Action**	**Remarks**
Aug 8th-05		Return of service Aug 14-05 Ans filed Aug 12-05 Ans filed by defendants Attys Aug 25-05 Set for hearing at Muskogee Sept 12-05 at $2^{\underline{00}}$ P.M.	Certificates in file Aug 15-05 Com reports no contest Nov 24 05 Case dismissed as pltf
Sept 6-05		Sent to John M Bacon for investigation	stated that she has possession and
Sept 12-05		Case called all parties being present evidence taken	certs retrd to her
Sept 20-05		Judgement[sic] rendered in favor of plaintiff and defendant notified to vacate within ten days or he will be removed plaintiff to notify this office when same is done	Dismissed
Mch 19 '06		Referred to Eldon Lowe for investigation	
Mch 23		Case dismissed see report of Eldon Lowe and request of Ptf in file	Dismissed

Date Received	No.	Allottee	Intruder
July 22-05	581	Mollie E. Tygar Gdn of Rebecca Tygar heir of William Tygar dec'd c/o Geo Co. McCulloch Atty Vinita Ind Ter	William Mantooth Big Cabin Ind Ter
Notice Sent		**Action**	**Remarks**
Aug 8th-05		Return of service	Certificates and Letters of Gdn in file
Sept 7-05		Sent to John M Bacon for investigation	Aug 15-05 Com reports no contest
Oct 2-05		Case dismissed by request of pltf See report of Bacon in file Certificates returned to plaintiff Oct 12 -05	Dismissed

Cherokee Intruder Cases 1901 - 1909

Date Received	No.	Allottee	Intruder
July 24-05	582	Lucy J. Hitchcock Welling Ind. Ter.	Timothy B Hitchcock Afton Ind Ter
Notice Sent		**Action**	**Remarks**
Aug 8th-05		Return of service Aug 14-05 Ans filed Aug 15-05	Certificates in file Aug. 15-05 Com reports
Nov 10-05		Case dismissed by request of pltf and certificates returned to her	no contest Dismissed

Date Received	No.	Allottee	Intruder
Aug 18th-05	583	Mertie P Arrowood Owasso Ind. Ter.	George Blackwell Owasso I.T.
Notice Sent		**Action**	**Remarks**
Aug 11th-05		Sept 8-05 Sent to John M. Bacon for investigation	Certificates in file Aug 16-05 Com reports
		Sept 25-05 Case dismissed by request of plaintiff and certificates returned to her. See report of Bacon filed today	no contest Dismissed

Date Received	No.	Allottee	Intruder
Aug 1st-05	584	Henry Ratlingourd Claremore, I.T. Judge Jennings Atty Claremore, I.T.	R. F. Murphy Claremore, I.T. J. M. LaHay Atty for defdt. Claremore, I.T.

Mch 28 Case called at Claremore All parties present and evidence taken.
Dft. given additional time to introduce more evidence
Mch 30th More evidence taken
April 13 Judgment rendered in favor of Plaintiff both parties so notified and a copy of judgment sent to each of them Defendant requested to vacate within fifteen days from date of Judgment
June 8 Plaintiff requested to advise this office if he is now in possession of his allotment
June 10 Atty for Plaintiff states Allottee is in possession of his allotment
                                                                   Case Dismissed

Notice Sent	Action	Remarks
Aug 11th-05	Return of service Aug 19-05 Ans filed Aug 23 -04[sic]	Certificates in file Aug 16-05 Com reports
Nov 13-05	Sent to John M Bacon for investigation Set for hearing at Vinita, I.T.	no contest 3/28 Allotment certif No. 8240 Homestead cert No. 6006 filed

Cherokee Intruder Cases 1901 - 1909

	on Jan 16 -06	~~exibited~~[sic] by Ptf
Jan 16 -06	Case called, defdt appeared, no appearance by pltf, defdts evidence taken	at Claremore IT
Jan 21 -06	Report of Backenstoce filed today See report in file	
	2/10 1906 *(Illegible)*	2/10 '06 Dismissed
	Mch 17, Case reopened	
	Set for hearing at Claremore Mch 27 '06	
Mch 27 06	Case continued by agreement until 3/28 '06	

Date Received	No.	Allottee	Intruder
Aug 9-05	585	Fannie Ellis c/o S. R. Lewis, Agent Tulsa, I.T.	Cleon Berry Sperry I.T.
Notice Sent		**Action**	**Remarks**
Aug 11th-05		Return of service Aug 15-05 Ans filed Aug 16-05 Set for hearing at Muskogee on Sept 20-05 at 1:30 P.M.	Certificates in file Aug 16-05 Com reports no contest
Sept 18-05		Sent to John M Bacon for investigation	Dismissed
Sept 18-05		Case dismissed by request of plaintiff See report of Bacon in file Certificates returned Sept 19-05	Sept 20-05 copy of Lease filed today
Sept 20-05		" dated June 3-04 Defendant appeared, no appearance by plaintiff	

Date Received	No.	Allottee	Intruder
Aug 11-05	586	Fannie Brewer Rex, Ind Ter	Cross Hereford, and G. D. Sleeper Wagoner I.T.
Notice Sent		**Action**	**Remarks**
Aug 16-05		Return of service Aug 21-05	Certificates in file Aug 26-05 Com reports no contest
Sept 8-05		Sent to John M Bacon for investigation	
Sept 22-05		Instructions issued to policeman Odun Lynn Collins to place the plaintiff in possession	See report of Collins in file

Cherokee Intruder Cases 1901 - 1909

Oct 13-05 Allottee placed in possession by policeman Collins ^Sept 23 -05 and case was Oct 17-05 Case dismissed by request of pltf See report of Bacon in file Certificates returned to pltf Oct 19-05	Dismissed Oct 20-05 Com reports that no portion of land of pltf has been cancelled and is in contest

Date Received	No.	Allottee	Intruder
Aug 10-05	587	Polly Knight Christie, I.T.	Charles Smith and Mr. Cooper Lenapah I.T. Dfdt is a Cherokee Freedman and an application for citizenship
Notice Sent		**Action**	**Remarks**
Aug 16-05		Return of service Oct 13-05 Ans filed Oct 9-05	Certificates in file Aug 26-05 Com reports
Sept 9-05		Sent to John M Bacon for investigation Case held pending decision of dept. See report of Bacon in file	no contest
May 9 1906		In compliance with instructions from the Dept under date of April 19th 1906 Com^r is request[sic] to furnish this office with status of Allotment of Ptf and of citizenship of Defendant in this case	
June 12 1906		Case dismissed as Com^r reports that a motion to review case of Dfdt is pending Certificates returned	
			Dismissed

Date Received	No.	Allottee	Intruder
Aug 10-05	588	Chu-wa-na Chuwalooky Eucha I.T.	E.L. Foster and R. Lee Comer Independence, Kans
Notice Sent		**Action**	**Remarks**
Aug 16-05			Certificates and Rental contract in file
	Sept 9-05	Sent to John M Bacon for investigation	
	Jan 12 -06	Report of Backenstoce filed today	
	Jan 12 -06	Defdt Foster called today and states that he was not occupying the	

Cherokee Intruder Cases 1901 - 1909

land in land in[sic] pltfs complaint and case was dismissed and cert's ret'd to pltf.	Dismissed

Date Received	No.	Allottee	Intruder
Aug 11-05	589	Mary Cochran Tahlequah, I.T.	Joe Roundheart Nowata, I.T.
Notice Sent		**Action**	**Remarks**
Aug 16-05			Aug 11-05 Com reports no contest and
	Jan 22 -06	Sent to E C Backenstoce for investigation	certificates issued
	Feb 1 -06	Report of Backenstoce filed today See same in file	
	3/9	Case set for hearing at Claremore	
	Mch 27$\underline{th}$ 1906		
	Mch 27	Case called at Claremore neither Ptf nor Dft present	
	April 3$\underline{rd}$	Referred to John Viets for investigation	
	" 30	Report of John Viets filed and case dismissed upon request of Plaintiff	
		No Certificates returned to Plaintiff	
			Dismissed

Date Received	No.	Allottee	Intruder
Aug 11-05	590	Alexander Sanders Melvin I.T.	Lum Winn Watova I.T.
Notice Sent		**Action**	**Remarks**
Aug 16-05		Return of service Aug 22-05	Aug 11-05 Com reports no contest
	Sept 9-05	Sent to S A Mills for investigation	and certificates issued
	Jan 22 -06	Case dismissed upon report of E.C. Backenstoce	Dismissed

Date Received	No.	Allottee	Intruder
Aug 12-05	591	Jennie Greenfeather Ramona, I.T.	John Wilcox Ramona, I.T.
Notice Sent		**Action**	**Remarks**
Aug 16-05		Return of service Aug 25-05 Ans filed Aug 28-05	Certificates in file Aug 26-05 Com

Cherokee Intruder Cases 1901 - 1909

Sept 6-05	Sent to John M Bacon for investigation	reports no contest
Dec 7-05	Case dismissed and certificates ret'd to pltf by her request	
Dec 9-05	Report of Backenstoce filed today See same in file case	Dismissed

Date Received	No.	Allottee	Intruder
Aug 11-05	592	Maggie McDonald Tahlequah, I.T.	William A Madden Muskogee, I.T.
Notice Sent		**Action**	**Remarks**
Aug 16-05 Jan 22 -06		Return of service Aug 24-05 Sent to E C Backenstoce for investigation 2/12 Case dismissed upon recommendation of E. C. Backenstoce R A Evans Ptf to be given possession on or before 3/1 1906 Dismissed 2/9 Reports that Dft has not vacated; he was instructed to do so at once	Map in file Aug 11-05 Com reports no contest and certificates issued

Date Received	No.	Allottee	Intruder
Aug 11-05	593	Ben Sanders Tahlequah, I.T.	A.J. Harris Tahlequah, I.T.
Notice Sent		**Action**	**Remarks**
Aug 16-05		Return of service Aug 26-05 Ans filed Aug 30-05 stating that he does not hold possession of the lands for which pltf has made complaint and pltf is notified 2/24 Case is dismissed as land held by dft is in Contest	Com reports certificates issued and a portion of land in in contest Aug 11-05 Dismissed

239

Cherokee Intruder Cases 1901 - 1909

Date Received	No.	Allottee	Intruder
Aug 15-05	594	William H Fields Vinita, I.T.	Ben Gibson

Notice Sent	Action	Remarks
Aug 19-05	Return of service Sept 9-05 Ans filed Sept 11-05	Certificate in file Aug 26-05 Com reports
Sept 9-05	Sent to John M Bacon for investigation	no contest
Oct 9-05	Report of Bacon filed today states that defdt will vacate in ten days	
Oct 16-05	Instructions issued to policeman Henderson to investigate this matter and if he finds defendant removing improvements to dispossess him at once	
Nov 4-05	Policeman Henderson states that the pltf has possession and case is	Dismissed and certs retrd to pltf
May 26/06	Plaintiff requests possession of his allotments	

Date Received	No.	Allottee	Intruder
Aug 15-05	595	Mrs Dolly Pettit Edna Kans	Frank Parr Edna Kans

Notice Sent	Action	Remarks
Aug 19-05	9/5/05 Defendants appeared in person & advises that they are not occupying no lands except that in contest. plaintiff requested to advise if such is the fact 3/9 Case set for hearing at Claremore Mch 27th 1906	Certificates in file Aug 26-05 Com reports 40 acres in contest
Mch 27 1906	Case called at Claremore neither party appeared	
April 3rd	Referred to John Viets for investigation	Certificates returned
" 23	Report of John Viets filed and case dismissed upon request of Plaintiff	

Cherokee Intruder Cases 1901 - 1909

Date Received	No.	Allottee	Intruder
Aug 19-05	596	Josephine Ellis Ft Gibson, I.T.	Henery[sic] Emery Should be Emery Ritchie Ft Gibson, I.T.
Notice Sent		**Action**	**Remarks**
Aug 21-05		Ans filed Sept 6-05 Set for hearing at Muskogee on Sept 15-05 at $2^{\underline{00}}$ P.M. Return of service Sept 7-05 Sept 4th 05 Case called: all parties being present and it was agreed that unless the defendant filed contest by Sept 25-05 he was to vacate and leave improvements Mch 19 '06 Case dismissed by order of W.W.B.	Aug 19-05 Com reports no contest and certificates issued Oct 20-05 Com reports no contest *Dismissed*

Date Received	No.	Allottee	Intruder
Aug 4-05	597	Charles Choteau Lenapah I.T.	William Gunter Lenapah I.T.
Notice Sent		**Action**	**Remarks**
Aug 22-05 Sept 9-05 Sept 20-05 Oct 28-05 May 20 1907		Return of service Aug 26-05 Ans filed Aug 28-05 Sent to John M Bacon for investigation Ans and certified copy of order of court appointing a receiver filed today See same in #606 Report of Bacon filed states land is in contest and case pending report of Com Certificates of Allotment & homestead returned -	Certificates in file Sept 1st-05 Com reports portion of land in contest Contest pending on land held by Deft.

Date Received	No.	Allottee	Intruder
Aug 25-05	598	Sarah Crutchfield for herself and as gdn of Eli and Lewis Crutchfield Claremore, I.T.	George Morehead and Chas. McClure Tiawah I.T.

Cherokee Intruder Cases 1901 - 1909

Notice Sent	Action	Remarks
Aug 29-05	Return of service Sept 8-05 Ans filed Sept 7-05 by Chas. McClure. Ans filed by Geo Morehead Sept 6-05	Certificates and Letters of gdn in file Sept 6-05 Com reports contest on land
Sept 9-05	Sent to John M Bacon for investigation	
Sept 20-05	Ans and certified copy of order of court appointing a receiver filed today See same in case #666 Plaintiff so notified	
Sept 25-05	Case dismissed by request of pltff and certificates returned to plaintiff See report of Bacon filed today	Dismissed

Date Received	No.	Allottee	Intruder
Aug 29-05	599	Stan Suagee c/o Philip H. Cass Atty Coffeeville Kans	W. Fine

Notice Sent	Action	Remarks
Aug 31-05	New notices sent Sept 14-05 Return of service Sept 20-05	Certificates in file Oct 20-05 Com reports no contest
Sept 9-05	Sent to John M Bacon for investigation Ans filed Sept 23-05 Set for hearing at Vinita on Jan 16-06	
Jan 23-06	Case dismissed by request of pltf and certs retrd to him	Dismissed

Date Received	No.	Allottee	Intruder
Sept 2-05	600	Mrs Elizabeth Wolf c/o J. F. Mann Stilwell, Ind. Ter	W. A. Hensley Aztec, Ind. Ter. George Brady, *(Illegible)* I.T. J.F. Mason

Notice Sent	Action	Remarks
Sept 6-05		Certificates in file Oct 11-05 Com reports no contest.

Cherokee Intruder Cases 1901 - 1909

Sept 9-05 Sent to John M Bacon for investigation
3/9 Case set for hearing at Claremore
Mch 27 1906
Mch 27 '06 Case called at Claremore neither party present
April 3rd Refund to John Viets for investigation
              reports that Ptf
Mch 28 Atty for Ptf, ^ was sick and could not be present at hearing mentioned above
May 22 Report of John Veits[sic] filed and case dismissed as the restriction have been removed from the land in question and same has been conveyed by deed Therefore it is without they jurisdiction of this office Certificates returned to Plaintiff
                                                                                    Dismissed

Date Received	No.	Allottee	Intruder
Sept 2-05	601	Lula Gist Zena or Cove I.T.	Josh B Howard Cove I.T.
Notice Sent		**Action**	**Remarks**
Sept 6-05		Return of service Sept 14-05 Ans filed Sept 16-05	Certificates in file Oct 11-05 Com reports
Sept 9-05		Sent to John M Bacon for investigation	no contest
Oct 9-05		Certificates returned to pltf Oct 11-05	Dismissed
		Case dismissed by request of pltf	
Jan 5 -06		See report of Bacon in file, defdt agrees to vacate by Jan 1st 06 Instructions issued to policeman Henderson to place the pltf in possession	
Jan 19 -06		Policeman Henderson reports that defdt has vacated and case is	Dismissed

Date Received	No.	Allottee	Intruder
Sept 6-05	602	Eurrutler[sic] Shook Uniontown, Ark	Moke Hide, Dave Wilson and John Thompson Uniontown, Ark
Notice Sent		**Action**	**Remarks**
Sept 12-05		Return of service Sept 22-05 Ans filed Sept 28-05 Set for hearing at Muskogee on Oct 17-05 at 2$\underline{^{00}}$ PM	Sept 6-05 Com reports no contest

Cherokee Intruder Cases 1901 - 1909

Nov 9-05	Case dismissed by request of Pltf	Dismissed

Date Received	No.	Allottee	Intruder
Sept 6-05	603	Lucy Buzzard Afton I.T.	James Neighbors Afton, I.T.
Notice Sent		**Action**	**Remarks**
Sept 12-05		Return of service Sept 25-05 Ans filed by Jas M Scott on Aug 23-05	Sept 6-05 Com reports no contest and certificates issued
Oct 10-05		Case dismissed by request of plaintiff	Dismissed

Date Received	No.	Allottee	Intruder
Sept 5-05	604	Thomas W Keener Hulbert I.T.	Joe Bartles Dewey I.T.
Notice Sent		**Action**	**Remarks**
Sept 12-05		Return of service Oct 9-05 Ans filed Oct 11-05	
Nov 13-05		Sent to John M Bacon for investigation	
Jan 22 -06		Sent to EC Backenstoce for investigation	
Jan 22 -06		Case dismissed upon report of E.C. Backenstoce and cert's ret'^{d} to pltf.	Dismissed

Date Received	No.	Allottee	Intruder
Sept 6-05	605	Lucinda Tincup Pryor Creek I.T.	Rubin Delozier and Geo F Mitchell Adan, I.T.
Notice Sent		**Action**	**Remarks**
Sept 12-05			Certificates in file Oct 11-05 Com reports no contest
Oct 18-05		Case dismissed by request of pltf and certificates returned to her today	Dismissed

Cherokee Intruder Cases 1901 - 1909

Date Received	No.	Allottee	Intruder
Sept 8-05	606	Mary Willis nee Crutchfield c/o Davenport and Hall, Attys Claremore, I.T.	George Morehead Tiawah I.T. Ben Willis Claremore, I.T.
Notice Sent		**Action**	**Remarks**
Sept 12-05 Sept 20-05		Return of service Sept 18-05 Ans and certified copy of order of court appointing a receiver filed today. See same in file Plaintiff so notified *Dismissed*	Certificates in file Oct 11-05 Com reports no contests 3/9 1906 Certificates returned

Date Received	No.	Allottee	Intruder
Sept 9-05	607	Samuel A. Bigbey[sic] Dutch Mills, Ark.	Eugene Titsworth Coweta, I.T.
Notice Sent		**Action**	**Remarks**
Oct 3-05 Oct 3-05 Nov 25-05		Return of service Oct 11-05 Sent to John M Bacon for investigation Report of Bacon filed today	Certificates in file Oct 24-05 Com reports land in contest and case is <u>Dismissed</u>

Date Received	No.	Allottee	Intruder
Sept 9-05	608	Dora D. Morgan Lenapah, Ind. Ter.	Joseph M. Mayfield Nowata, I.T. Defendant claims that he is citizen and is going to file contest
Notice Sent		**Action**	**Remarks**
Oct 3-05 Oct 3-05 Oct 28-05		Return of service Oct 17-05 Sent to John M Bacon for investigation Ans filed Oct 17-05 Case dismissed by request of pltf See report of Bacon in file Certificates returned to pltf Oct 31-05	Certificates in file Oct 28-05 Com reports no contest <u>Dismissed</u>

Cherokee Intruder Cases 1901 - 1909

Date Received	No.	Allottee	Intruder
Sept 16-05	609	Nancy Brewer Rex, I.T.	Crow Hereford, Rex I.T. G. D. Sleeper Wagoner, I.T.
Notice Sent		**Action**	**Remarks**
Oct 3-05		Return of service Oct 11-05	Certificates in file
Oct 3-05		Sent to John M Bacon for investigation	Oct 28-05 Com reports no contest
Oct 17-05		Report of Bacon filed today recommending that pltf be placed in possession. See same in file	Certificates retrd to pltf's husband Jan 6 -06, who states that land in in contest
Jan 6 -06		Case dismissed as land is in contest	Dismissed

Date Received	No.	Allottee	Intruder
Sept 15-05	610	Nancy J Reese Proctor, I.T.	Geromeo[sic] Cook Proctor, I.T.
Notice Sent		**Action**	**Remarks**
Oct 9-05		Return of service Oct. 7-05	Certificates in file
Oct 3-05		Sent to John M Bacon for investigation	Oct 24-05 Com reports no contest
Oct 13-05		Case dismissed by request of pltf	Dismissed
Oct 13-05		Certificates returned to pltf	
Nov 11-05		Report of Bacon filed Nov 11-05 See same in file	

Date Received	No.	Allottee	Intruder
Sept 18-05	611	Amanda Brown, c/o E. B. Lawson, Atty at Law Nowata, I.T.	Robert Berry Lenapah I.T.
Notice Sent		**Action**	**Remarks**
Oct 3-05 Oct 3-05		Sent to John M Bacon for investigation	Certificates and contract in file
Oct 17-05		Ans filed Oct 11-05 See same in #619	Oct 28-05 Com reports no contest
Oct 19-05		Case dismissed by request of pltf See report of Bacon in file Certificates return to pltf	Dismissed

Cherokee Intruder Cases 1901 - 1909

Date Received	No.	Allottee	Intruder
Sept 18-05	612	Wat Sanders c/o W. L. Curtlss, Atty Sallisaw, I.T.	W. A. Poindexter Marble, I.T.
Notice Sent		**Action**	**Remarks**
Oct 3-05			Certificates in file
Oct 3-05		Sent to John M Bacon for investigation	Oct 18-05 Com reports no contest
Nov 4-05		Report of Bacon filed today states that pltf and defdt have made a compromise agreement in which the defdt agrees to vacate on Jan 1 -06 or make satisfactory arrangements with pltf and case was	Dismissed and certs retrd to pltf.

Date Received	No.	Allottee	Intruder
Sept 14-05	613	Paralee Reed Claremore, I.T.	William Horner Claremore, I.T.
Notice Sent		**Action**	**Remarks**
Oct 3-05		Return of service Oct 16-05	Certificates and contract in file
Oct 3-05		Sent to John M Bacon for investigation	Oct 28-05 Com reports no contest
Oct 17-05		Report of John M Bacon filed today recommending that defendant be allowed to remain in possession consequently the case was Certificates returned to pltf Oct 19-05 Ans filed Oct. 17-05	Dismissed

Date Received	No.	Allottee	Intruder
Sept 13-05	614	Lizzie E Gwinn Tahlequah, I.T.	Albert Kelley Nowata, I.T.
Notice Sent		**Action**	**Remarks**
Oct 3-05		Return of service Oct 9-05	Certificates in file
Oct 3-05		Sent to John M Bacon for investigation Ans filed Oct 24-05	Oct 26-05 Letter rec'd from Defdt in which he states that pltf can have possession Oct 28-05
Oct 28-05		Case dismissed by request of pltf	

Cherokee Intruder Cases 1901 - 1909

See report of Bacon in file Certificates returned to pltf Oct 31-05	Pltf requested to take possession and so notify this office Oct 28-05 Com reports no contest

Date Received	No.	Allottee	Intruder
Sept 12-05	615	Jesse Vann c/o Thos J. Watts. Atty. Muldrow, I.T.	W. A. Chase Nowata, I.T.
Notice Sent		**Action**	**Remarks**
Oct 4-05 Oct 4-05 Oct 28-05		Sent to John M Bacon for investigation Report of Bacon filed today states that defdt does not hold possession of land and case was	Certificates in file Oct 24-05 Com reports no contest Dismissed

Date Received	No.	Allottee	Intruder
Sept 20-05	616	Isaac L Chrisman gdn. of Allen Chrisman South West City, Mo	Henry Nichols South West City, Mo
Notice Sent		**Action**	**Remarks**
Oct 4-05 Oct 4-05 Nov 18-05		Return of service Oct 16-05 Sent to John M Bacon for investigation Ans filed Oct 16th 05 Report of Bacon filed today states that defdt agrees to vacate by Jan 1st 06 and pltf so notified 3/5 Case dismissed as Ptf advises that he is in possession of his land 3/5 Letter of dismissal referred to Restrictions Dept	Certificates and Letters of gdn in file Oct 24-05 Com reports no contest 3/5 Certificates and Letters of Gdn. ship returned to ptf. Dismissed

Date Received	No.	Allottee	Intruder
Sept 20-05	617	Enoley Morris Stilwell, I.T.	James Scacewater[sic] Stilwell, I.T.

Cherokee Intruder Cases 1901 - 1909

Notice Sent	Action	Remarks
Oct 4-05	Return of service Oct 13-05	Certificates in file
Oct 4-05	Sent to John M Bacon for investigation	Oct 24-05 Com reports no contest
Nov 11-05	Ans filed Oct 16-05 Case dismissed by request of pltf and certificates returned to pltf See report of Bacon in file	

Date Received	No.	Allottee	Intruder
Sept 20-05	618	Johnson Lowery Muskogee, I.T.	Tuxy Reese Muskogee

Notice Sent	Action	Remarks
Oct 4-05	Return of service Oct 9-05	Certificates in file
~~Oct 4-05~~	~~Sent to John M.~~	Oct 24-05 Com reports no contest
Oct 22-05	Defendant appeared today Set for hearing at Muskogee on Oct 30[sic]-05 at 1$^{\underline{00}}$ P.M.	
Oct 31-05	Case called all parties being present evidence taken and it was agreed that defdt hold land until Mch 21st 1906 when he was to turn over the land with all improvements and was not to cut any more timber. See evidence	Case <u>dismissed</u> and certificates retrd to pltf in person
	April 3$^{\underline{rd}}$ Ptf states that Defendant has not complied with the agreement mentioned above. Instructions were issued to Capt West to remove Defendant and place Allottee in possession April 4$^{\underline{th}}$ Capt West reports that agreement has been made between the parties and Dft will vacte[sic] ~~in th~~ in two weeks	Case dismissed

Date Received	No.	Allottee	Intruder
Sept 26-05	619	Annie Lucas, c/o Eugene Lawson, Atty. Nowata, I.T.	Robert Berry

Notice Sent	Action	Remarks
Oct 4-05	Return of service Oct 10-05 Ans filed Oct 4-05	Certificates in file Oct 24-05 Com reports
Oct 4-05	Sent to John M Bacon for	no contest

Cherokee Intruder Cases 1901 - 1909

Oct 17-05	investigation Case dismissed as report of Bacon filed today states that defendant has surrendered lease and agrees to vacate within ten days. See report in file. Certificate returned to pltf Oct 19-05	Dismissed

Date Received	No.	Allottee	Intruder
Sept 29-05	620	Mrs Nannie West nee McLain Ft Gibson, I.T. Defdt claims citizenship as a Cherokee Freedman	Oma Campbell Ft Gibson
Sept 4 1906		Nannie West encloses Allotment certificates & demands possession of her land stating that there is no contest on her land.	
Sept 7 1906		Allottment[sic] certificates & *(Illegible)* complaint form mailed to pltf with request that she make new complaint	

Notice Sent	Action	Remarks
Oct 4-05	Return of service Oct 9-05	Certificates in file
Oct 4-05	Sent to John M Bacon for investigation	Oct 24-05 Com reports no contest
Dec 2-05	Report of Bacon filed today states that defdt is a Cherokee Freedman claimant for citizenship	
	3/22 '06 Ptf advised status of case	
May 10	In compliance with instructions from Dept. under date of April 19th 1906 Com^r is requested to furnish this office with status of allotment of Plf. and status of citizenship of Dfdt. in this case	
June 18 1906	Com^r reports motion to reconsider case of Dfdt pending therefore case is dismissed	
		Dismissed
Aug 15 1906	Pltf advised per request that no Action can be taken as motion to reconsider citizenship case of Oma Campbell pending before Comr	

250

Cherokee Intruder Cases 1901 - 1909

Date Received	No.	Allottee	Intruder
Sept 26-05	621	Aimy[sic] and Sunday Hogtoater for J. L. Springston Vian, I.T.	William Moss Vian, I.T.
June 10 -07		Sunday Hogtoater writes Sec'y Interior in re lease contract made with William Moss	
July 8 -07		S.H. c/o Atty advised of Action of this office in above case and as to jurisdiction over cases made after allotment	
Jan 8/08		Referred to Backenstoce	
Oct 3 08		Report made to Com^r & pltfs advised	

Notice Sent	Action	Remarks
Oct 4-05	Return of service Oct 16-05	Certificates and contracts in file
Oct 4-05	Sent to John M Bacon for investigation Ans filed Oct 18-05 Set for hearing at Muskogee on Oct 27-05	Oct 24-05 Com reports no contest
Nov 8-05	Pltf notified that this office will not take Action to remove defdt from land See carbon in file Ans. filed Nov 17-05 ~~Dismissed~~	Plat of pltfs land filed by J.L. Springston Dec 20-05 3/9 '06 Certificates returned

Date Received	No.	Allottee	Intruder
Sept 28-05	622	John Henry Ross #625 South 5th Street Muskogee, Ind. Ter.	French, Joe or Joe Jones

Notice Sent	Action	Remarks
Oct 4-05	Return of service Oct 10-05	Certificates in file
Oct 4-05	Sent to John M Bacon for investigation	Oct 24-05 Com reports land is in contest

Date Received	No.	Allottee	Intruder
Oct 5-05	623	Thomas A. Chandler Vinita, Ind. Ter.	Watt Ridenour Bartlesville I.T.

Notice Sent	Action	Remarks
Oct 10-05		Certificates in file
Oct 10-05	Sent to John M Bacon for	Nov 1-05 Com reports

Cherokee Intruder Cases 1901 - 1909

Dec 9-05	investigation Report of E.C. Backenstoce filed today states that defdt had vacated the land in question, consequently the pltf was notified to take possession and the case was	no contest Dismissed

Date Received	No.	Allottee	Intruder
Oct 5-05	624	Sarah Guinn nee Roach, Chetopa, Kansas c/o Cox and Coursey, Attys Tahlequah, Ind. Ter.	C. E. Holderman Tahlequah
Sept 10 - 1906		Lease contract of dfdt delivered to dfdt, C.E. Holderman, in person	

Notice Sent	Action	Remarks
Oct 10-05	Return of service Nov 2-05	Certificates in file
Oct 10-05	Sent to John M Bacon for investigation Ans filed Nov 10-05 Lease contract Set for hearing at Muskogee on Nov 21-05 at 10$^{\underline{00}}$ A.M.	Nov 1-05 Com reports no contest
Nov 21-05	parties can not get here before 1$^{\underline{00}}$ P.M.	
Jan 15 -06	All parties appeared & evidence of both plaintiff & defendant taken Judgement[sic] rendered in favor of defdt and case and certs retrd to pltf	Dismissed
Feb 5 -06	Report of Backenstoce filed today	

Date Received	No.	Allottee	Intruder
Oct 5-05	625	John Comingdeer gdn of George Roach, Jr. c/o Cox and Coursey, Attys Tahlequah, I.T.	M. Holderman Chetopa Kans and C.E. Holderman Tahlequah, I.T.

Notice Sent	Action	Remarks
Oct 10-05	Return of service Nov 2-05	Certificates and Letters of gdn in file
Oct 10-05	Sent to John M Bacon for investigation	Nov 1-05 Com reports no contest
Nov 10-05	Defdt Holderman appeared today and exhibited a contract which was	

Cherokee Intruder Cases 1901 - 1909

Feb 5 -06	executed by pltf a gdn of Allottee and made with the approval of the court and case was and certificates returned to pltf. Report of Backenstoce filed today	Dismissed

Date Received	No.	Allottee	Intruder
Oct 2-05	626	Harry Smith Warner, I.T.	John Johnson Porum, I.T. Fanny Starr Porum, I.T.
Notice Sent		**Action**	**Remarks**
Oct 23-05		Return of service ~~Oct~~ Nov 1-05	Certificates in file
Oct 23-05		Sent to John M Bacon for investigation	Nov 2-05 Com reports no contest
Nov 25-05		Report of Bacon filed today states that defdt agrees to vacate by Jan 1 - 06 and pltf is notified	
Mch 19th '06		Referred to Eldon Lowe for investigation	
May 31		Eldon Lowe reports that satisfactory settlement has been made and case is therefore dismissed Certificates returned to Plaintiff	Dismissed

Date Received	No.	Allottee	Intruder
Oct 19-05	627	Savanna Morris Tahlequah, I.T.	Dayton Leuskove Tahlequah, I.T. John Decker and Tom Hudson Owasso I.T.
Notice Sent		**Action**	**Remarks**
Oct 23-05		Return of service Oct 27-05	Certificates in file
Oct 28-05		Sent to John M Bacon for investigation	Nov 2-05 Com reports no contest
Jan 22-05		Return of service Nov 20-05 Case dismissed upon report of E.C. Backenstoce and certs ret[rd] to pltf.	Dismissed

Cherokee Intruder Cases 1901 - 1909

Date Received	No.	Allottee	Intruder
Oct 14-05	628	Nancy Phillips Texanna, I.T.	Ben F. LaFayette and Brothers, Checotah I.T.
Notice Sent		**Action**	**Remarks**
Oct 23-05		Return of service Nov 8-05	Certificates in file
Oct 28-05		Sent to John M Bacon for investigation	Nov 2-05 Com reports no contest
Nov 28-05		Case dismissed by request of pltf and certs retrd to her See report of Bacon in file	Dismissed

Date Received	No.	Allottee	Intruder
Oct 11-05	629	Albert Ross Evansville Ark	W. D. Hogan
Notice Sent		**Action**	**Remarks**
Oct 23-05			Certificates in file
Oct 28-05		Sent to John M. Bacon for investigation	Nov 2-05 Com reports no contest
Nov 11-05		Case dismissed as requested of pltf and certificates returned to pltf. See report of Bacon in file	Dismissed

Date Received	No.	Allottee	Intruder
Oct 20-05	630	Jim T. Hall gdn. of Mary, Cincia and J. Thomas Hall Jr Tahlequah, I.T. J.W. Swarts Chelsea, I.T. Atty for Complainant	Jack Walker Ft Gibson Bill Dyer Chelsea, I.T. Soper, Hacklebury and Owen, Atty for defdts Muskogee, I.T.
April 10		Ptf states Defendants are still in possession	
April 14 06		Instructions issued to Richard F. West US I Policeman to place plaintiff in possession	
April 20		Policeman Richard F West reports that he has placed the Allottee in possession	
		Certificates returned to Plaintiff and case dismissed	
June 2		Plaintiffs' Atty advises that Plf is not in possession	Dismissed
		June 11/06 Attys for Ptfs advises that the Gdn. is not in possession	

Cherokee Intruder Cases 1901 - 1909

	June 14 Instructions issued to Capt. John C West to place the Gaurdian[sic] in possession of the allotments of the minors June 26 R.E. Williams Policeman to whom Capt John C West referred the order above mentioned Reports that on June 14 1906 he placed the Ptf in possession Case is therefore dismissed	
		Dismissed
Notice Sent	**Action**	**Remarks**
Oct 24-05	Return of service Nov 6-05 Ans filed Nov. 11-05	Certificates in file Nov. 2-05 Com reports
Oct 28-05	Sent to John M Bacon for investigation	no contest Letters of gdn. on file in the
	Jan 2/6 Ptffs Atty notified and copies of defts answer sent him Set for hearing at Vinita, I.T. on Jan 16 -06	Oil Lease dept. Defdts Attys state that application has been made to the U.S. Court for the
Jan 16 -06	Pltf appeared in person no appearance by defdt	appointment of a receiver
Jan 17 -06	Pltf again appeared no appearance by defdt, pltfs evidence taken 3/8 Judgement[sic] rendered in favor of Ptf, both parties so notified and a copy of the judgment sent to each of them. The Dft given 15 days in which to vacate	

Date Received	No.	Allottee	Intruder
Oct 20-05	631	Susan Cook #1506 Olive St St Louis, Mo	George W Miller Tulsa, I.T.
Notice Sent		**Action**	**Remarks**
Oct 23-05		Return of service Oct 29-05	Oct 20-05 Com reports no
Oct 23-05		Sent to John M Bacon for investigation	contest and certificates issued
Nov 25-05		*(This line completely illegible)* Case dismissed as the defdt claims in a written statement that he is not holding possession of pltfs land See report of Bacon in file	 Dismissed

Cherokee Intruder Cases 1901 - 1909

Date Received	No.	Allottee	Intruder
Oct 20-05	632	George B Downing Westville I.T.	G. S. Victor Afton, I.T.
Notice Sent		**Action**	**Remarks**
Oct 23-05 Oct 23-05 Nov 11-05		Return of service Oct 31-05 Sent to John M Bacon for investigation Ans filed Nov 6-05 with a request from defdt that case be set about Dec. 15-05 as he is in Washington and unable to appear at this time Case dismissed by request of pltf and certificates returned to pltf. See report of Bacon in file.	Oct 20-05 Com reports no contest and certificates issued Dismissed

Date Received	No.	Allottee	Intruder
Oct 20-05	633	Mary L. Duncan Baron, I.T.	George C. Crittenden Greenbriar I.T.
Notice Sent		**Action**	**Remarks**
Oct 23-05 Oct 23-05		Return of service Nov 20-05 Sent to John M Bacon for investigation Report of Bacon filed today states that defdt claims possession and pltf so notified 3/8$_{06}$ No reply case dismissed. *Dismissed*	Oct 20-05 Com reports no contest and certificates issued

Date Received	No.	Allottee	Intruder
Oct 20-05	634	Effie C Bowers Vinita, I.T. W.P. Thompson, Atty for pltf Vinita, I.T.	Marcus L Brittler Winnwood I.T.
Notice Sent		**Action**	**Remarks**
Oct 23-05 Oct 23-05 Jan 16 -06		Sent to John M Bacon for investigation Set for hearing at Vinita, I.T. on Case dismissed by request of pltfs Atty	Oct 20 05 Com reports no contest Dismissed

256

Cherokee Intruder Cases 1901 - 1909

Date Received	No.	Allottee	Intruder
Oct 20-05	635	Mrs Lola Hubbard #623 S 16th St. Ft Smith, Ark	Herman J Vann Porum, I.T.

Notice Sent	Action	Remarks
Oct 24-05	Return of service Nov 1st 05	Oct 20-05 Com reports no contest and certificates issued
Oct 24-05	Sent to John M Bacon for investigation	
	Ans filed Nov 13-05	
Nov 25-05	Report of Bacon filed today states that defdt agrees to give possession to pltf at any time upon her request and pltf so notified	Dismissed

Date Received	No.	Allottee	Intruder
Oct 20 -06	636	Richard Holcomb for self and gdn of Mary Holcomb c/o R. J. Scott, Atty for pltf Sallisaw I T	Thomas J Avant Vian, I.T. Jess W Watts Atty for defdt Sallisaw I.T.

Notice Sent	Action	Remarks
Oct 25-05		Certificates and Letters of gdn in file
Oct 25-05	Sent to John M Bacon for investigation	Nov 2-05 Com reports no contest
Nov 4-05	Ans filed Nov 4-05	Dec 7-05 Com reports control reinstated and under advisement
	Bacon report filed today	
	Set for hearing at Muskogee on Nov 20-05 at 10:00 A.M.	
Nov 23-05	Continued until Nov 23rd 05	
	Case called evidence taken	
May 9 1906	Letters of Gdnship. Certificates and rental contract returned to Ptf in person	
June 6/06	Case dismissed as contract is pending By W.W.B.	Dismissed

Date Received	No.	Allottee	Intruder
Oct 23-05	637	Nancy Logan Gans, I.T.	Lawson Logan and Robert *(Illegible)* Gans, I.T.

Cherokee Intruder Cases 1901 - 1909

Notice Sent	Action	Remarks
Oct 26-05	Ans filed Nov 1-05	Certificates in file
Oct 26-05	Sent to John M Bacon for investigation	Nov 2-05 Com reports no contest
	Set for hearing at Muskogee on Nov 20-05 at 1$\underline{^{30}}$ P.M.	
Nov 4-05	Bacon report filed today	
	Return of service Nov 7-05	
	Case continued until the 23$\underline{^{rd}}$ of Nov	
	Complaint only described to surplus land. Not having jurisdiction (freedman) was dismissed & ctf^s retrd to Allottee in person	

Date Received	No.	Allottee	Intruder
Oct 24-05	638	Amanda Wood Zena I.T.	Samuel Hiner Cove I.T.

Notice Sent	Action	Remarks
Oct 26-05	Return of service Oct 31-05	Certificates in file
Oct 26-05	Sent to John M Bacon for investigation	Nov 2-05 Com reports no contest
	Ans filed Nov 3-05	Nov 25-05 Com reports no contest
Nov 11-05	Defdt notified this office that has filed a contest See report of Bacon in file	Nov 29-05 Com reports no contest
	Set for hearing at Vinita, I.T. on Jan 16-06	
Jan 10 -06	Case dismissed by request of pltf and certificates retrd to pltf.	Dismissed

Date Received	No.	Allottee	Intruder
Oct 20-05	639	Richard F Boudinot Braggs, I.T.	Margaret Falling Braggs, I.T.

Notice Sent	Action	Remarks
Nov 2-05	Return of service Nov 13-05	Certificates in file
Nov 2-05	Sent to John M Bacon for investigation	Nov 10-05 Com reports no contest
	Set for hearing at Muskogee on Dec 23-05	Settled by order of plaintiff
Dec 28-05	Rec^d Ctf No 35311 in person Richard F Boudinot	Dec 5-05
June 11 1906	Com^r reports no contest pending	

Cherokee Intruder Cases 1901 - 1909

Date Received	No.	Allottee	Intruder
Oct 26-05	640	Joe Hiner gdn. for Mary B and Joseph Hines, c/o S. G. Mayes, Atty, Bartlesville I.T.	John Morrison

Notice Sent	Action	Remarks
Nov 2-05	Return of service Nov 2-05	Oct 26-05 Com reports no contest and certificates issued
Nov 2-05	Sent to John M Bacon for investigation	
	Ans filed Nov 21-05	
	Set for hearing at Muskogee on Jan 5 -06	
Dec 3-05	Case dismissed by request of pltfs Atty and letters of gdn ret^{d} to him in person	Dismissed
Jan 22 -06	Report of Backenstoce filed today	

Date Received	No.	Allottee	Intruder
Oct 26-05	641	Jennie Morris Stilwell I.T	F. M. Anderson Bartlesville I.T. Frank Price
May 21		Report of John Viets filed and case dismissed as Mr Viets states that Defendant has surrendered possession *(Illegible)* the report was enclosed the rental contract executed by Jennie Morris to Frank Price	
			Dismissed

Notice Sent	Action	Remarks
(Date illegible)		Oct 26-05 Com reports no contest and certificates issued.
Nov 2 -05	Sent to John M Bacon for investigation	
Nov 13-05	Notice ret^{d} to this office by pltf as she unable finan[sic] to serve same	
Nov 16-05	Notice sent to defdt today with a request that he act same	
	Set for hearing at Muskogee on Feb 2 -06	
	3/9 Case set for hearing at Claremore Mch 27 1906	
Mch 27 '06	Case called at Clearemore[sic] neither party present	
April 3$\underline{rd}$	Referred to John Viets for investigation	

Cherokee Intruder Cases 1901 - 1909

Date Received	No.	Allottee	Intruder
Oct 26-05	642	Melvina S. Draper, nee Gustin, now Moore, Hulbert I.T.	Cinna Force Wagoner, I.T.

Notice Sent	Action	Remarks
Nov 2-05	Return of service Nov 13-05	Oct 26-05 Com reports no contest and certificates returned
Nov 2-05	Sent to John M Bacon for investigation	
	Ans filed Nov 10-05	
	Set for hearing at Muskogee on Nov 21-05 at $1^{\underline{00}}$ P.M.	
	Nov 21 No appearance	
June 8 1906	Referred to S A Mills [John Viets] for investigation	
Nov 14 1906	Case set for hearing at Muskogee, I.T. Nov 27, 1906	
Nov 27 1906	Case called No appearance	
Jan 22, 1907	Referred to Robt R. Bennett for investigation	
Feby 25 1907	Robt R Bennett enclosed request for dismissal	
Mch 2 1907	Case <u>dismissed</u>	

Date Received	No.	Allottee	Intruder
Oct 25-05	643	Willie Ellis Turley I.T.	Cleon Berry Sherry I.T.

Notice Sent	Action	Remarks
Nov 2-05	Return of service Nov 8-05	Oct 26-05 Com reports no contest and certificates issued
Nov 2-05	Sent to John M Bacon for investigation	
	Ans filed Nov 19-05	Receipts filed by dept Nov 19-05
	Dec 30/5[sic] Dismissed on report of Backenstoce	<u>Dismissed</u>

Date Received	No.	Allottee	Intruder
Oct 26-05	644	Willie Helen Davis Briartown I.T.	W.P. Ringo Nowata, I.T.

Notice Sent	Action	Remarks
Nov 2-05	Return of service Jan 2-06	Oct 26-05 Com reports no contest and certificates issued
Nov 2-05	Sent to John M Bacon for investigation	
Jan 22-06	Case dismissed upon report of E.C. Backenstoce	<u>Dismissed</u>

Cherokee Intruder Cases 1901 - 1909

Date Received	No.	Allottee	Intruder
Nov 17-05	645	Malderine E. Vincent Foyil, I.T.	Alfred Foyil, O.C. Johnson and Brockway Foyil, I.T.
Notice Sent		**Action**	**Remarks**
Nov 17-05		Return of service Nov 23-05	Certificates in file
Nov 17-05		Sent to S.A. Mills for investigation	Nov 27-05 Com reports no contest and certificates issued
Nov 22-05		Report of Bacon filed today recommending that pltf be placed in possession at once also a statement by defdt that if the land was surveyed by a competent surveyor and they are shown to be trespassing on said land that they will vacate at once and pltf so notified	Affidavit filed by pltf Dec 18-05 Dec 14-05 Com reports land is in contest and case is dismissed

Date Received	No.	Allottee	Intruder
Nov 2-05	646	Izora Sunday Foreman I.T.	C.P. and F.A. St Clair and tenants Muskogee, I.T.
Notice Sent		**Action**	**Remarks**
Nov 29-05		Return of service Dec 5-05	Nov 2-05 Com reports no contest and cert's issued. See report in file
Dec 5-05		Answer filed by W R. Terrell Set for hearing at Muskogee I.Ter. Jan 26-06 Answer filed by C.P. St. Clair also rental contract Jan 4-06	Lease contract in file
Jan 26-06		Case called; all parties being present evidence taken 3/6 Judgment rendered in favor of Dft. copy sent to each party *Dismissed*	*Lease contract returned 3/6 to ptf.*

Date Received	No.	Allottee	Intruder
Nov 3-05	647	Lucy Ellis Turley I.T.	George Berry Spurry I.T.
Notice Sent		**Action**	**Remarks**
Nov 29-05		Return of service Dec 27-05	Nov 3-05 Com reports no contest and certificates

Cherokee Intruder Cases 1901 - 1909

	12/22/05 Answer filed Set for hearing at Vinita Ind Ter on Jan 16-06	issued
Jan 16-06	Case called, defdt appeared no appearance by pltf, defdts evidence taken	
	Jan 19-06 Case dismissed by request of pltf	Dismissed

Date Received	No.	Allottee	Intruder
Nov 3-05	648	Jonathan R. Payne Claremore, I.T.	George James and Mr Anltfield[sic] Claremore, I.T.
Notice Sent		**Action**	**Remarks**
Nov 29-05			Nov 13-05 Com reports no contest and certificates issued
		Set for hearing at Vinita, I.T. at on Jan 16-06	
Jan 22-06		Sent to E.C. Backenstoce for investigation	
Feb 1-06		Report of Backenstoce filed today states that pltf notified him that defdts pave have vacated and case	Dismissed

Date Received	No.	Allottee	Intruder
Nov 16-05	649	Jane Krigbaum Ramona, I.T.	T. M. Anderson Tahlequah, I.T.
Notice Sent		**Action**	**Remarks**
Nov 29-05		Return of service Dec 8-05 Set for hearing at Vinita, I.T. on Jan 17-06	Nov 10-05 Com reports no contest and certificates issued
Jan 22-06		Sent to E.C. Backenstoce for investigation	
		Jan/23 Dismissed upon request of ptf	Dismissed

Date Received	No.	Allottee	Intruder
Nov 10-05	650	Robert M Terral for himself and Emma Terral Vian, I.T. c/o J. L. Springston, Atty	J. M. Walters

Cherokee Intruder Cases 1901 - 1909

Notice Sent	Action	Remarks
Nov 29-05		Nov 10-05 Com reports no contest and certificates issued
	Jan 22-06 Sent to E C Backenstoce for investigation	
	2/12 Case dismissed upon recommendation of E.C. Backenstoce	
	2/14 Ptf notified of dismissal 2/12 Dismissed	

Date Received	No.	Allottee	Intruder
Nov 8-05	651	M. L. H. C. Bozarth Chelsea, I.T.	Bramble Bozarth Chelsea, I.T.

Notice Sent	Action	Remarks
Nov 29-05		Nov 30-05 Com reports no contest and certificates issued
	Set for hearing at Vinita, I.T. on Jan 17-05	
	Jan 22 -06 Sent to E C Backenstoce for investigation	
	~~Feby 21 1907~~ 2/23 Case dismissed as Mr. Backenstoce reports Ptf is in possession Dismissed	

Date Received	No.	Allottee	Intruder
Nov 7-05	652	Mary Martin Chaffee, I.T.	Pat J Lawless Daws[sic], I.T. Riddle of Vinita, Ind. Ter. Atty for defdt.

Notice Sent	Action	Remarks
Nov 29-05	Return of service Dec 26-05	Certificates in file
	Set for hearing at Vinita, I.T. on Jan 17-06	Dec 7-05 Com reports no contest
	Ans filed Jan 2-06	2/10 1906 Rental contract returned to Dft and certificates returned to Ptf.
	Jan 17-06 Case called and continued until Jan 18-06	
	Jan 18 -06 Case called all parties being present evidence taken	
	2/10 Judgement[sic] rendered in favor of Defendant Dismissed	

Cherokee Intruder Cases 1901 - 1909

Date Received	No.	Allottee	Intruder
Nov 3-05	653	Return J. Lowery Briartown, I.T.	Finas Sykes Briartown, I.T.
Notice Sent		**Action**	**Remarks**
Nov 29-05		Return of service Dec 7-05	Certificates in file
Jan 22 -06		Sent to E C Backenstoce for investigation	Dec 6-06 Com reports no contest
Mch 21		Referred to S John Veits[sic] for investigation	
April 13		Report of John Viets filed and case dismissed upon request of Plaintiff Certificates returned	
			Dismissed

Date Received	No.	Allottee	Intruder
Nov 6-05	654	Jackson Cookinghead Stilwell, I.T.	George Horn Briartown I.T.
Notice Sent		**Action**	**Remarks**
Dec 1-05		Return of service Dec 16-05 Ans filed Dec 16-05 Set for hearing at Muskogee on Feb 2-06 2/12 Case dismissed upon request of Ptf Dismissed	Certificates in file Dec 6-05 Com reports no contest 2/16 Certificates returned
Sept 8 1906		Pltf writes from Stilwell I Ty & asks that his certificate of allotment be returned to him	
Sept 12 1906		Pltf advised that as per former request certificate was sent to him c/o Comstock Bros., Uniontown, Arkansas.	

Date Received	No.	Allottee	Intruder
(Date illegible)	655	Daisy Hensley #103 N. Main St Muskogee, I.T. Cass M Bradley, Atty for pltf Muskogee, Ind Ter	John A Beaver P.W. Marsh Muskogee, I.T. and Edna, Kansas Eck E Brooks Musk Atty for Defts

Cherokee Intruder Cases 1901 - 1909

Notice Sent	Action	Remarks
Dec 4-05	Return of service Dec 5-05 Dec 12/5[sic] Ans filed by Deft Set for hearing at Muskogee on Jan 4-06 at 2$\underline{^{00}}$ P.M.	Certificates and contract in file Dec 6-05 Com reports no contest
Jan 4-06	Case called, all parties being present, evidence taken Continued until the 13$\underline{^{th}}$ of Jan 06	
Jan 13 -06	Case called all parties present, evidence taken and judgement[sic] rendered in favor of defdt and case and cert's ret'^{d}.	Dismissed
April 9$\underline{^{th}}$	Certificates and rental contract returned to Cass M Bradley in person	

Date Received	No.	Allottee	Intruder
Nov 11-05	656	Robert A Young Afton I.T. John J Hubbard Atty for pltf Afton Ind Ter Pltf is in Colorado	John M Fuser Afton I.T. ~~Defdt is in Colorado~~

Notice Sent	Action	Remarks
Dec 1-05	Return of service Dec 7-05 Answer filed Dec 11-05 Set for hearing at Vinita, I.T. on Jan 17-06	Certificates in file Dec 6-05 Com reports no contest Affidavit filed by defdt's Atty Jan 17-06
Jan 17-06	Defdt's Atty filed an amended ans today	Contract and Cert filed by defdt's Atty Jan 17-06
Jan 17-06	Case called, defdt appeared in person and by Atty, pltf appeared by Atty only, evidence taken 2/10 1906 Judgment rendered in favor of Defendant *Dismissed*	2/10 Rental Contract returned to Dft Certificates returned to Ptf

Cherokee Intruder Cases 1901 - 1909

Date Received	No.	Allottee	Intruder
Oct 31-05	657	Joel L Baugh Choteau I.T. James S Davenport Atty for pltf Vinita Ind Ter	Joanna Cook Defdts claim citizenship as a Cherokee Freedman J.P. Bledsoe, Atty for defdts Choteau, I.T.
	Jan 12 1906	Com^r reports motion for review Case pending Dismissed and certificates returned	Dismissed

Notice Sent	Action	Remarks
Dec 1-05	Return of service Dec 5-05	Certificates in file Dec 6-05 Comm. reports no contest
	Set for hearing at Vinita, I.T. on Jan 17 -06	
	Jan 17-06 Case called, all parties being present evidence taken and both sides being represented by Attys also. "See evidence"	
	Feb 1-06 Com reports motion to reopen contest filed by Joanna Cook	
	May 10 In compliance with instructions from the Dept. under date of April 101191 1906, Com^r is requested to report as to the status of Allotment of Plf and of citizenship of Defdt in this case	

Date Received	No.	Allottee	Intruder
Nov 14 -05	658	Ernest L. Stephens Lometa I.T.	W^m, Fred M.V. Davis Lometa I.T.

Notice Sent	Action	Remarks
Dec 1-05	Return of service Dec. 5-05	Certificates in file
Dec 26-05	Instructions issued to Capt. West to place the pltf in possession 3/8 Capt West reports verbally that Ptf is in possession Dismissed	Dec 6-05 Comm reports no contest 3/9 Certificates returned

Date Received	No.	Allottee	Intruder
Nov 11-05	659	William Edward Warner, I.T.	W.E. Wilkinson Warner, I.T.

Cherokee Intruder Cases 1901 - 1909

Notice Sent	Action	Remarks
Dec 1-05	Return of service Dec 5-05	Certificates in file
Dec 18-05	Case dismissed by request of pltf and certificates ret'd to him	Dec 6-05 Comm. reports no contest
		Dismissed

Date Received	No.	Allottee	Intruder
Nov 17-05	660	James D. Griffin, gdn of Lewis, John, James Jr, Nannie and Addie Griffin ~~Copan I.T.~~ Fawn, Ind Ter	Jackson C Davis Copan I.T. Butte and Bliss, Attys for defdt Muskogee, Ind. Ter.

Pltf appeared at this office stated agreement not complied with by deft
June 5 1907 Deft requested to advise in re his compliance with cont
Deft advises he will meet all requirements of contract by fall
June 14 07 Plff advised of deft's statement

Notice Sent	Action	Remarks
Dec 1-05	Return of service Dec 14-05 Ans filed Dec 28-05 Set for hearing at Vinita, I.T. on Jan 17-06 No appearance by either party Case is to be heard at Muskogee Set for hearing at Muskogee on Feb 2nd 06	Certificates in file Dec 6-05 Comm reports no contest 2/8 Certificates returned to Ptf
Feb 2-06	Case called, all parties being present, evidence taken 3/8 '06 Judgment rendered in favor of Dft. and a copy of the judgment was sent to each party. Case dismissed and both parties so notified	Dismissed

Date Received	No.	Allottee	Intruder
Nov 5-05	661	Charles Craft Warner, I.T.	Bush Fields, Warner, I.T.

Notice Sent	Action	Remarks
Dec 1-05	Return of service not dated	Nov 8-05 Com. reports no

Cherokee Intruder Cases 1901 - 1909

		contest and certificates issued Dismissed upon application of plaintiff of Dec 05

Date Received	No.	Allottee	Intruder
Nov 17-05	662	Frank T. H. Higgins gdn of Claude E. Dowell Wann, I.T. L Box 1	Isaac and John Hurtz, R.F.D. #1 Coffeyville, Kan.

Notice Sent	Action	Remarks
Dec 1-05	Return of service Dec-7-05	Certificates and Letter of gdn in file
Dec 8-05	Answer filed	
	Set for hearing at Vinita, I.T. on Jan 17-06	Dec 6-05 Comm reports no contest
Jan 17-06	Pltf appeared in person, no appearance by defdt, pltf evidence taken	
Jan 31-06	Case dismissed by request of pltf and cert's and letter of gdn ret'd	Dismissed

Date Received	No.	Allottee	Intruder
Nov 18-05	663	Minnie Brown, nee Foreman Coffeyville, Kans	Kirk Radcliff and Wesley Morris Elliott I.T.
	Feby 19, 1907	Robt R Bennett reports dfndt not in possession	
	Feby 23, 1907	Plntf requested to go in to possession & report	
	June 15 07	Plff again requested relative to possession	
	Jan 8 -08	Case dismissed by order of W.W.B.	

Notice Sent	Action	Remarks
Dec 2-05	Return of service Dec 18-05	Certificates in file
Jan 17-06	Case dismissed as to defdt Morris by personal request of pltf.	Dec 7-05 Comm reports no contest
Jan 17-06	Case called, pltf appeared, no appearance by defdt, pltf's evidence taken	Jan 12-06 Com reports portion of land in contest and had been awarded to defdt Morris
Jan 17 -06	Certificates ret'd to pltf in person	
June 8/06	Plaintiff requested to advise this office if *(Illegible)* has been satisfactorly[sic] settled	Pltf is to have lines located by a competant[sic] surveyor See evidence
Jany 22 1907	Referred to Robt. R. Bennett for investigation.	

Cherokee Intruder Cases 1901 - 1909

Date Received	No.	Allottee	Intruder
Nov 18-05	664	Mary Chisolm nee Johnson Melvin, I.T.	Wash. Reaves Melvin, I.T.

Notice Sent	Action	Remarks
Dec 2-05 Jan 22 -06	Sent to E C Backenstoce for investigation 2/14 Case dismissed upon recommendation of E.C. Backenstoce 2/14 Ptf notified of dismissal *Dismissed*	Certificates in file Com. Reports no contest on lands Dec 7-05

Date Received	No.	Allottee	Intruder
Nov 22-05	665	Minnie Copple Catoosa I.T.	Jeff M Gravitt, George and Wm Cole

Notice Sent	Action	Remarks
Dec 2-05 Dec 26-05	Return of service Dec 5-05 Case dismissed by request of pltf and cert's ret'd	Certificates in file Dec 7-05 Com reports no contest Dismissed

Date Received	No.	Allottee	Intruder
Nov 23-05	666	Beatric[sic] McConnell nee Vann Choteau, I.T.	Lewis Greathouse Choteau, I.T.

Notice Sent	Action	Remarks
Dec 2-05	Return of service Dec 9-05 Ans filed by defdt Dec 20-05 in which he states that he will vacate by Jan 1st 06 2/2/ Case dismissed as ptf states she is in possession of land *Dismissed*	Nov 23-05 Com reports no contest and certificates issued

Cherokee Intruder Cases 1901 - 1909

Date Received	No.	Allottee	Intruder
Nov 24-05	667	Maggie Williams nee Hannon Nowata, I.T.	Manly C Lybarger Nowata, I.T.
Notice Sent		**Action**	**Remarks**
Dec 2-05		Return of service Dec 7-05	Certificates in file
Dec 7-05		Answer filed by J.A. Tillotson Set for hearing at Vinita, I.T. on Jan 18-06	Dec 7-05 Com reports no contest
Jan 6-06		Defdt's Atty states that his client has vacated and pltf now has possession Pltf requested to advise this office if same has been done so that case can be dismissed	
Jan 13-06		Pltf's father appeared today and stated that defdt had vacated and case was dismissed and cert's retrd to him in person	Dismissed

Date Received	No.	Allottee	Intruder
Nov 23-05	668	Charlotte Temple Taylor, c/o Mr. C. A. Storke, Atty Santa Barbara, Cal.	Hugh Watson Vera, I.T.
Notice Sent		**Action**	**Remarks**
Dec 2-05			Certificates and case in file
		Ans and copy of contract filed Dec 30-05	Dec 7-05 Com reports no contest
		Set for hearing at Vinita, I.T. on Jan 18-06	Contracts retrd to defdt. Jan 18-06
	Jan 18-06	Case called, defdt appeared in person no appearance by pltf, defdt's evidence taken	Contract filed Jan 22 -06 Feb 8-06 Contracts retrd to pltf
		Defdt to file affidavit. 2/10 1906 Judgement[sic] rendered in favor of the Defendant	2/10 Certificate returned Dismissed

Date Received	No.	Allottee	Intruder
Nov 25-05	669	Lillie Smith c/o E. L. Crawford, Pryor Creek, I.T.	John Combs Bartlesville, I.T.

270

Cherokee Intruder Cases 1901 - 1909

Notice Sent	Action	Remarks
Dec 2-05		Nov 25-05 Com reports no contest and certificates issued
	Set for hearing at Vinita, I.T. on Jan 18-05	
Jan 22 -06	Sent to E C Backenstoce for investigation	
Feb 5 -06	Case dismissed upon report of E.C. Backenstoce	Dismissed

Date Received	No.	Allottee	Intruder
Nov 25-05	670	Laura Townsend Welling, I.T.	John Abercrombie Collinsville, I.T.

Notice Sent	Action	Remarks
Dec 2-05	Return of service Dec 8-05	Nov 25-05 Com reports no contest and certificates issued
Jan 22-06	Sent to E C Backenstoce for investigation	
Mch 21 '06	Referred to John Viets for investigation	
April 10 190[sic]	John Viets reports that contract is being complied with, as far as it is the wish of the Plaintiff. Plaintiff so advised and case dismissed	Dismissed

Date Received	No.	Allottee	Intruder
Nov 25-05	671	Susie Smith c/o E, L. Crawford Pryor Creek, I.T.	John Combs Bartlesville, I.T.

Notice Sent	Action	Remarks
Dec 2-05		Nov 25-05 Com reports no contest and certificates issued
Jan 22 -06	Sent to E C Backenstoce for investigation	
	Set for hearing at Vinita, I.T. on Jan 18-06	
	2/14 -06 Dismissed upon recommendation of E. C. Backenstoce	2/14 Dismissed
	2/14 Ptf notified of dismissal	

Cherokee Intruder Cases 1901 - 1909

Date Received	No.	Allottee	Intruder
Nov 25-05	672	Charley Smith c/o E. L. Crawford, Pryor Creek, I.T.	John Combs Bartlesville, I.T.
Notice Sent		**Action**	**Remarks**
Dec 2-05		Set for hearing at Vinita, I.T. on Jan 18-06	Nov 25-05 Com reports no contest and certificates issued
	Jan 22 06	Sent to E C Backenstoce for investigation 2/14 Case dismissed upon recommendation of E.C. Backenstoce	2/14 Dismissed

Date Received	No.	Allottee	Intruder
Nov 27-05	673	Timothy Petit Warner, I.T.	John Hampton
Notice Sent		**Action**	**Remarks**
Dec 2-05		Return of service Dec 6-05	Certificates in file
	Jan 13-06	Certificates retrd to pltf in person	Dec 7-05 Comm reports no contest
	Jan 13-06	Case dismissed by personal request of pltf.	Dismissed

Date Received	No.	Allottee	Intruder
Dec 1-05	674	Soney Smith c/o Henny C. Walker Tulsa, I.T.	E. D. Wertsel, Tulsa, I.T. Martin and Rice, Attys for deft Tulsa, Ind. Ter.
Notice Sent		**Action**	**Remarks**
Dec 4-05		Return of service Dec 9-05 Ans filed Dec 27-05 See same in #676 Set for hearing at Vinita, I.T. on Jan 18-06	Dec 1-05 Com reports no contest and certificates issued
	Jan 18-06	Case called, all parties being present evidence taken and judgement[sic] rendered in favor of defdt and case See evidence	Dismissed
	Feb 5-06	Lease contract retrd to defdt today	

Cherokee Intruder Cases 1901 - 1909

Date Received	No.	Allottee	Intruder
Dec 5-06	675	Pearl J. Perdue, Eucha, Ind Ter	Marion Henegar, Eucha, I.T.
Notice Sent		**Action**	**Remarks**
Dec 12-05		Return of service Dec 19-05	Dec 5-05 Com reports no contest and cert's issued
		Set for hearing at Vinita, I.T. on Jan 18-06	
		No appearance by either party	
		3/9 Case set for [sic] at Claremore on 3/28 1906	
Mch 29 1906		Case called at Claremore, neither party appeared	
April 3rd		Referred to John Viets for investigation	
May 31/06		John Viets reports that Plaintiff is in possession case dismissed	
			Dismissed

Date Received	No.	Allottee	Intruder
Dec 5-05	676	Soney Smith gdn. of David Smith, Tulsa, I.T.	E. D. Wertsel Tulsa, I.T.
Notice Sent		**Action**	**Remarks**
Dec 12-05			Dec 5-05 Com reports no contest and certificates issued
		Ans filed Dec 27-05	
		Set for hearing at Vinita I.T. on Jan 18-06	Letters of gdn in file
Jan 18-06		Case called, all parties being present, evidence taken and judgement[sic] rendered in favor of defdt and case dismissed	
Feb 5-06		See evidence	
		Lease contract ret'd to defdt today.	

Date Received	No.	Allottee	Intruder
Dec 5-05	677	Annie Cochran by Dave L. Guyette, gdn, c/o J. D. Cox, Atty, Tahlequah, I.T.	R F. King and Ceaf Parker, Hulbert, I.T.
		Cases 677 and 679 are combined and same evidence to govern in both cases	
July 4 -1906		Case dismissed upon personal request of Atty for Ptf. Certificates and letters of Gdnship returned to Ptf's Atty and case dismissed.	
			Dismissed

Cherokee Intruder Cases 1901 - 1909

Notice Sent	Action	Remarks
Dec 12-05	Return of service Dec 30-05 Ans filed Dec 29-05 See same in #679 Set for hearing at Muskogee on Jan 24-06	Letters of gdn in file Dec 5-05 Com reports no contest and certificates issued
	Jan 25 -06 Case called, pltf was represented by Atty. no appearance by defdt, pltf's Atty made a statement under oath See same in file 2/9 Aff filed by Ptf 3/6 Judgment rendered in favor of Ptf and both parties so notified. Dft given 15 days to vacate June 8 Ptf requested to advise this office if he is now in possession.	Consolidated with case #679 Certificates filed Jan 25 -06

Date Received	No.	Allottee	Intruder
Dec 5-05	678	Eliza Cochran, c/o J.D. Cox Atty Tahlequah, I.T.	R. F. King and Ceaf Parker Hulbert, I.T.

Notice Sent	Action	Remarks
Dec 12-05	Return of service Dec 20-05 Ans filed Dec 29-05 See same in #679 Set for hearing at Muskogee on Jan 24-06	Dec 5-05 Com reports no contest and certificates issued
	Jan 25 -06 Case called, pltf appeared in person and by Atty., no appearance by defdt pltf's evidence taken Mch 13 Atty for Ptf. called and stated he would advise this office of settlement was made April 5th J.D. Cox Atty for Plaintiff appeared at this office and stated that settlement had been made and upon his request case was dismissed	Dismissed

Date Received	No.	Allottee	Intruder
Dec 5-05	679	Dave L Guyette gdn of Louis and Dollie Cochran, c/o J.D. Cox, Atty Tahlequah, I.T.	R. F. King and Ceaf Parker Hulbert, I.T.

Cherokee Intruder Cases 1901 - 1909

Notice Sent	Action	Remarks
Dec 12-05	Return of service Dec 20-05	Letter of gdn in file
	Ans filed Dec 29-05	Dec 5-05 Com reports no
	Set for hearing at Muskogee on	contest and certificates
	Jan 24-06	issued
Jan 25 -06	Case called See case #677	Consolidated with case #677
	2/9 Aff. filed by Ptf	Certificates filed Jan 25 -06
	3/6 Judgement[sic] rendered in favor	
	of Ptf. and Both parties notified	
	Dft given 15 days to vacate	
June 8	Ptf requests to report as to wheather[sic] or not he has been given possession	
July 14 1906	Case dismissed upon personal request of Atty for Ptf and Letters of Gdnship returned to him.	
		Dismissed

Date Received	No.	Allottee	Intruder
Dec 5-05	680	Milly Frye, c/o Geo E. McCulloch, Atty Vinita, I.T.	W. C. Boyd Ketchum Preston S. Davis Atty for defdt Vinita, I.T.

Notice Sent	Action	Remarks
Dec 12-05	Return of service Dec 20-05	Certificates in file
	Dec 26/05 Ans filed by Deft and copy	Dec 18-05 Com reports no
	of rental contract, expiring Jan 1/5[sic]	contest
	Set for hearing at Vinita, I.T. on	Consolidated with #681 and
	Jan 19-06	evidence in this case to
Jan 19-06	Case called, all parties present	govern in #681
	evidence taken	See stenographer's mem.
Feb 9-06	Judgement[sic] rendered in favor of	
	defdt and contract retrd to him and case	Dismissed
	Cert's retrd to pltf Feb. 9-06	

Date Received	No.	Allottee	Intruder
Dec 5-05	681	Andy Frye, c/o Geo E. McCulloch, Atty Vinita, I.T.	W. C. Boyd Preston S. Davis Atty for defdt Vinita, I.T.

Notice Sent	Action	Remarks
Dec 12-05	Return of service Dec 20-05	Certificates in file
	Dec 26/5 Ans. filed by deft (See Case	Dec. 15-05 Com reports no

Cherokee Intruder Cases 1901 - 1909

Jan 19-06	680) and copy of rental contract Set for hearing at Vinita I.T. on Jan 19-06 Case called, evidence taken, all parties present See case #680 Contract filed Jan 19-06 by defdt.	contest Consolidated with #680 Evidence taken in case #680 is to govern in this case.

Date Received	No.	Allottee	Intruder
Dec 2-05	682	Jack Downing Foyil, I.T.	J. W. Stewart et al

Notice Sent	Action	Remarks
Dec 12-05	Return of service Dec 18-05	Certificates in file
Dec 22-05	Case dismissed by request of pltf and cert's ret'd.	Dec 18-05 Com reports no contest

Date Received	No.	Allottee	Intruder
Dec 6-05	683	Nancy Taylor Woodley, I.T.	A. J. Pitchford et al Edgar Smith, Vinita I.T. Atty for Deft
	April 11th '06	Judgment rendered in favor of Dft both parties so advised and a copy of the judgment sent to each of them, certificate returned and case dismissed	
			Dismissed

Notice Sent	Action	Remarks
Dec 12-05	Return of service Dec 22-05	Certificates in file
	Dec 26/05 Ans filed by Deft's Attorney	Dec 18-05 Com reports
	3/9 Case set for hearing at	no contest
	Claremore I.T. on 3/28 1906	Exibit[sic] A

Mch 28th Case called at Claremore Ptf present and her evidence taken
Original contract exhibited by Dft' Atty Exibit[sic] "B" "Order of Court".
Defendant's evidence taken Exibit "C" a contract made, but did not
become effective. Case held open until Mch 31 st.
The 3 papers mentioned above as "Exibits" "A" "B" and "C" are filed
3/31 Evidence of U.B. Taylor and A M Archer taken at Vinita I.T.
Contract mention above as Ex. "C" was delivered in person to W.B.
Taylor

Cherokee Intruder Cases 1901 - 1909

Date Received	No.	Allottee	Intruder
Dec 8-05	684	Emma Riley, Santown[sic], I.T.	F. R. Reed, et al

Notice Sent	Action	Remarks
Dec 12-05	Return of service Dec 28-05 Ans and Case filed Dec 28-05 Set for hearing at Muskogee on Jan 22-06	Dec 8-05 Com reports no contest and certificates issued Jan 25 -06 Contracts filed by defdt.
Jan 23-06	Case called, defdt appeared and his evidence was taken, no appearance by ptf	
~~Dec~~ Jan 25-06	Pltf appeared today and her evidence was taken 3/6 Judgement[sic] rendered in favor of Dft. Ptf. notified of same and case dismissed Dft. & Ptf. sent copy of Judgement	Dismissed

Date Received	No.	Allottee	Intruder
Dec 7-05	685	Sam O. Fields, Kansas, I.T.	Canary Oil Co Bartlesville, I.T.

Notice Sent	Action	Remarks
Dec 12-05	Return of service Jan 11-06 Ans filed Jan 8-06 Set for hearing at Vinita, I.T. on Jan 18-06	Certificates in file Dec 18-05 Com reports no contest
Jan 22-06	Sent to E.C. Backenstoce for investigation	
Feb 1-06	Case dismissed upon report of Backenstoce and cert's ret'd.	Dismissed

Date Received	No.	Allottee	Intruder
Dec 11-05	686	Eliza J Hughes Johnston, Kansas, I.T.	C. B. Hughes Vinita, I.T. Wade S. Stanfield Atty. for defdt Vinita, I.T.
May 14	John Viets reports that a new lease has been executed by Ptf to Dfdt. and that matter amicably adjusted		
May 16	Ptf requested to notify this office if above statement is correct.		

277

Cherokee Intruder Cases 1901 - 1909

Notice Sent	Action	Remarks
Dec 14-05	Return of service Jan 4-05	Dec 11-05 Com reports no contest and certificates issued
	Set for hearing at Vinita, I.T. on Jan 19-06	
Jan 19-06	Case called, all parties being present, evidence taken pltf's evidence was taken, but defdt's was not as his Atty was not present and had all of his papers, defdt's evidence is to be taken at some future date	
	3/9 Case set for hearing at Claremore on 3/28 1906	
Mch 28	Case called at Claremore neither party appeared	
April 3ʳᵈ	Referred to John Viets for investigation	
" "	Defendant states settlement has been made	

Date Received	No.	Allottee	Intruder
Dec 15-05	687	M. M. Wright, gdn of Emma, Manuel K and Joe B Wright c/o S.F. Parks Atty, Vinita, I.T.	Clark Gibson and Yates Ragland Vinita I.T.
		Mch 15 Elijah Henderson reports and enclosed request of Ptf to have case dismissed	

Notice Sent	Action	Remarks
Dec 14-05	Return of service Dec 26-05	Certificates and Letters of gdn in file
	Set for hearing at Vinita, I.T. Jan 19-06	Dec 23-05 Com reports no contest
Jan 19-06	Case called, all parties present and defdt given 30 days to vacate and remove his buildings, to which he agreed [Error]	3/17 Certificates returned
Jan 19-06	Case called, all parties being present evidence taken	
Feb 8-06	Judgement[sic] rendered in favor of pltf and defdt given 15 days in which to vacate	
	2/28 Orders given Policeman Elijah Henderson to place Ptf in possession	

Cherokee Intruder Cases 1901 - 1909

Date Received	No.	Allottee	Intruder
Dec 13-05	688	Ailsy Ridge, Eucha, I.T.	Dan Price et al
Aug 8th 1906			
Oct 20 1906		Plntf writes that dfndt will not move out of house	
" 20 1906		Dfndt given ten days in which to remove effects & surrender possession	
Jany 19 1907		Case dismissed Certificates returned	
Feb 14 -08		Defdt ordered to remove his improvements and vacate pltf's land & pltf so notified	

Notice Sent	Action	Remarks
Dec 16-05	Return of service Dec 26-05	Certificates in file
	Dec 26/5 Ans filed by deft Fox[sic]	Dec 23-05 Com reports
	Set for hearing at Vinita I.T. on Jan 19-06	no contest
Jan 19-06	Case called, all parties present and defdt given 30 days in which to vacate and remove his buildings to which he agrees	
	See stenographer notes	
Mch 19 '06	Referred to Eldon Lowe for investigation	
May 14 '06	Answer filed by Dr G. H. Bremer for Dan Price	
June 7/'06	Case dismissed upon request of Plaintiff and certificates returned Error	
June 14	Defendant reports that he will vacate	
June 15	Plaintiff requested to take possession	
		Dismissed

Date Received	No.	Allottee	Intruder
Dec 15-05	689	Mrs Ella Paul Warner, I.T.	Dr. J. W. Henson Checotah, I.T. Ben D Crow, Atty. for defdt Checotah, I.T.

Notice Sent	Action	Remarks
Dec 20-05	Return of service Dec 30-05	Certificates in file
	Ans filed Dec 30-05	Dec. 30-05 Com reports
	Set for hearing at Muskogee, I.T. on Jan 27-06	no contest
Jan 27-06	Case called all parties present evidence taken	
	3/7 '06 Judgement[sic] rendered in	

Cherokee Intruder Cases 1901 - 1909

April 6	favor of Ptf and Dft given 15 days to vacate Both parties notified Ptf states she is in possession certificates returned and case dismissed
	Dismissed

Date Received	No.	Allottee	Intruder
Dec 15-05	690	Geo M Gunter Redland, I.T.	Charles S Perry
Notice Sent	**Action**		**Remarks**
Dec 20-05	Return of service Dec 28-05 Ans filed Jan 2nd -06		Certificates in file Dec 30-05 Com reports land is in contest and ~~Action withheld~~ and case Dismissed and certificates ret'd to pltf.

Date Received	No.	Allottee	Intruder
Dec 28-05	691	Lucinda Leader for Joe Leader Texanna, I.T.	Sam Bumgarner Checotah, I.T.
Notice Sent	**Action**		**Remarks**
Jan 3-06 Jan 22-06 April 25	Return of service Jan 17-06 Sent to E C Backenstoce for investigation 3/21 Referred to John Veits[sic] for investigation Report of John Viets filed. Case dismissed and certificates returned to Plaintiff		Certificates in file Jan 11-06 Com reports no contest Dismissed

Date Received	No.	Allottee	Intruder
Dec 21-05	692	Rosa L. Dallas, for herself and Lena G. Dallas, Fred R. Goodtraveler, and Cora M. Byron, Ramona, I.T.	J.J. Pearce and Doss Pearce

Cherokee Intruder Cases 1901 - 1909

Notice Sent	Action	Remarks
Jan 3-06		Certificates in file
		Jan 11-06 Com reports
	Set for hearing at Vinita, I.T. on Jan 19-06	no contest
	Jan 4-06 Letter rec'd from pltf stateing[sic] that defdts have agreed to vacate and he was requested to notify this office when same was done	2/21 Certificates returned
Jan 13-06	Case dismissed by request of pltf	Dismissed
	2/21 Rosa L Dallas Ack. receipt of certificates	

Date Received	No.	Allottee	Intruder
Dec 15-05	693	John Johnson for self and Arlie, Redbird, Peggie and Lucy Johnson, Hulbert, I.T.	Jim Davis, Sam Butler and Cliff Butler, Hulbert, I.T.

Notice Sent	Action	Remarks
Jan 3-06	Return of service Jan 22-06	Certificates in file
Jan 22 -06	Sent to E C Backenstoce for investigation	Jan 11-06 Com reports no contest
Feb 5 -06	Defdts appeared today and agree to vacate and they are to notify this office of the date they will vacate	2/27 Certificates returned
Feb 7 -06	Defdts state that they will vacate on or before Feb 22 -06	
	2/14 Dismissed upon recommendation of E.C.-1906 Backenstoce 2/14-1906 Dismissed	3/12 Receipt of certificates Ack. by A W Swett
	2/14 Ptf notified of dismissal	

Date Received	No.	Allottee	Intruder
Dec 21-05	694	Clem Cole Pryor Creek, I.T.	A. J. Centers, Chappell, I.T.

Cherokee Intruder Cases 1901 - 1909

Notice Sent	Action	Remarks
Jan 3-06		Certificates in file
		Jan 4-06 Com reports
	Set for hearing at Vinita I.T. on	no contest
	Jan 19-06 No appearance	
Jan 22 -06	Sent to E C Backenstoce for investigation	
	2/9 Case set for hearing at Claremore	
Mch 28th	3/28 1906	
	3/20 Answer filed by Dft.	
	Case called at Claremore neither party appeared	
	April 3 Referred to John Viets for investigation	
	" 23 Report of John Viets filed and case dismissed upon request of Plaintiff	
	Certificates returned to Plaintiff	Dismissed

Date Received	No.	Allottee	Intruder
Dec 21-05	695	J.L. Balch, gdn of Mattie Louvern and Roxie L Miller c/o Glass and Weaver. Attys Nowata, I.T.	P.J. Lawless Dawes, I.T. Seymour Riddle, Atty for defdt. Vinita, I.T.

April 11th 1906 Defendant requested to make satisfactory arrangements with the legal Gdn, or the order will issue to U.S.I.P. to remove him.
April 14 Judgment rendered in favor of Ptf and Defendant given fifteen days in which to vacate. Both parties notified of the decision and a copy of the judgment sent to each of them. April 20 Seymour Riddle states that case is pending in the U.S. Court.
June 8/06 Seymour Riddle and A M Etchens requested to furnish this office with the status of this case as it is pending in U.S. Court
June 13['06] A.M. Etchens states there is a case pending before him, also states he will notify this office as to the Action taken
June 15/7 A.M. Etchens requested to advise relative to his Action in this case
June 20/7 A.M. Etchens advises order issued to deft to turn allotments over to J.L. Balch
June 24/7 Pltf requested to advise in re possession
Oct 21/07 Pltf requested to advise if in possession
Oct 31/07 Glass & Weaver reports that Balch is no longer Gdn. & they do not know whether poss has been had or not
Nov 5, 1907 A.M. Etchens reports Com. Vinita requested to advise if land was

282

Cherokee Intruder Cases 1901 - 1909

	turned over to Mr Lawless in accordance with Ref of Judge Gill (see carbon) Jan 8/08 Case Dismissed by order of Mr. Bennett.	
Notice Sent	**Action**	**Remarks**
*(Date covered)*3-06		Letters of gdn in file Dec 21-05 Com reports no contest and certificates issued
	Set for hearing at Vinita I.T. on Jan 19-06	
*(Date covered)*19 -06	Defdt appeared no appearance by pltf 3/5 Proof of service returned bearing date 2/22 1906 3/9 Case set for hearing at Claremore 3/28 1906	
(Month covered) 28 *(Month covered)* 10	Ptf. J.L. Balch appeared and his evidence taken. Defendant did not appear Defendant states he is in possession by virtue of a *(word covered)* executed by the mother of the minors to him	

Date Received	No.	Allottee	Intruder
Dec 30-05	696	Daniel Grass, Daggers Dist. 5, I.T.	So Weston Oil, Gas and Coal Co., and J. J. Snarr
Notice Sent		**Action**	**Remarks**
Jan 3-06		Return of service Jan 15-06	Dec 30-05 Com reports no contest and certificates issued
		Set for hearing at Vinita, I.T. on Jan 19-06	
Jan 22 -06		Sent to E C Backenstoce for investigation	
Feb 1 -06		Report of Backenstoce filed today and case dismissed upon said report and contract ret'd	Dismissed

Date Received	No.	Allottee	Intruder
Jan 4-06	697	William Hern, father of Hellen Hern Westville, Ind. Ter.	Tom Denny Pryor Creek, I.T.
Notice Sent		**Action**	**Remarks**
Jan 10-06		Return of service Jan 22-06 Ans filed Jan 19-06	Certificates in file Jan 16-06 Com reports no contest
	Jan 22-06	Sent to E C Backenstoce for investigation	

Cherokee Intruder Cases 1901 - 1909

2/27 Case dismissed as as[sic] contract was made by natural Gdn No Legal Gdn appoint.   certificates returned

Dismissed

Aug 31 1906 Dfdt called at office & in compliance with his verbal request was advised as to status of case.

Date Received	No.	Allottee	Intruder
Jan 3-06	698	James Shaw Copan, I.T. A. H. Norwood, Atty Dewey, I.T.	John Hendershot Copan, I.T.

Notice Sent	Action	Remarks
Jan 10-06	Return of service Jan 17-06	Certificates in file
Jan 22 -06	Sent to EC Backenstoce for investigation	Jan 16-06 Com reports no contest
	3/9 Case set for hearing at Claremore Mch[sic] 28 1906	
April 28	Case called at Claremore neither party appeared	
June 8	Case reset for hearing at Claremore I.T. June 19/06	
" 18	Case dismissed upon personal request of Plaintiff Certificate returned in person	Dismissed

Date Received	No.	Allottee	Intruder
Jan 10-06	699	Phoeby Dudley, Stilwell, Ind. Ter.	H. C. Hurst Welch, Ind. Ter.

Notice Sent	Action	Remarks
Jan 15-06	Return of service Jan 31-06	Certificates in file
Feb 2 -06	Sent to EC Backenstoce for investigation	Jan 19-06 Com reports no contest
	2/19 Dismissed upon recommendation of EC Backenstoce	
	Apr 9 1907 F F Dudley for plntf asks return of certificates	
	Apr 9 1907 Certificates Nos. 17793 2699 returned Stilwell, I.Ty.	

Cherokee Intruder Cases 1901 - 1909

Date Received	No.	Allottee	Intruder
Jan 13-06	700	Anna Reed Vian, Ind. Ter.	J.R. Brannan Webbers Falls, I.T.

Notice Sent	Action	Remarks
Jan 19-06		Certificates in file
Feb 2 -06	Sent to E C Backenstoce for investigation	Jan 26-06 Com reports no contest
	2/12 Proof of service returned	
	2/20 Dft states he has filed contest	
	2/20 Com reports contest pending	2/27 Certificates returned
	2/27 Case dismissed as land in question is involved in contest	*Dismissed*
April 20	Letter from Ptf filed	

Date Received	No.	Allottee	Intruder
Jan 13-06	701	J. W. Rider for C. Augustus, *(Illegible)*, Austin W. and Thos. Needles Rider c/o E M Fryer, Atty, Sallisaw, I.T.	John Rose Osborn and Sullivan Atty for defdt Coffeeville, Kansas Allottee claims as Cherokee Freedman
		Defendant is claimant for citizenship as Cherokee Freedman	

Notice Sent	Action	Remarks
Jan 19-06	Return of service Feb 2-06	Certificates in file
Feb 2 -06	Sent to E C Backenstoce for investigation	Jan 26 -06 Com reports no contest
	Ans filed Feb 5 -06	
May 10 1906	In compliance with instructions from the Dept under date of April 19th 1906 Com^r is requested to furnish this office with status of allotment and Ptf and status of citizenship of Dfdt. in this case.	
June 12 1906	Com^r reports motion for review pending Case dismissed and certificates returned	Dismissed

Rec'd	No.	Allottee	Intruder
Jan 16-06	702	Mary Ellen Eli, for Goldie Eli Coodys Bluff, I.T.	Clarence Lord Ruby, I.T.

285

Cherokee Intruder Cases 1901 - 1909

Notice Sent	Action	Remarks
Jan 20-06		Jan 16-06 Com reports no contest and certificates issued
	Feb 2 -06 Sent to E C Backenstoce for investigation	
	3/9 Set for hearing at Claremore	
	Mch 28 1906	
	3/20 Case dismissed upon request of Ptf report of John Viets filed	
	Mch 30 Defendant advises that has surrendered possession to Plaintiff	
		Dismissed

Rec'd	No.	Allottee	Intruder
Jan 16-06	703	Beulah Ralston nee Monroe, Afton, I.T.	P.J. Rose, Echo, I.T.

Notice Sent	Action	Remarks
Jan 20-06	Return of service Jan 30-06	Jan 16-06 Com. reports no contest and certificates issued
	Feb 2 -06 Sent to E C Backenstoce for investigation	
	Ans. filed Feb 1-06	
	2/26 Backenstoce reports agreement entered into between Ptf and Dft *(illegible)* whereby Ptf will hold land until Mach 1st 1906	

Dismissed

Rec'd	No.	Allottee	Intruder
Jan 16-06	704	Ada Thurman for Elizabeth Thurman, Foyil, I.T.	D.H. Dowling, Foyil, I.T.

Notice Sent	Action	Remarks
Jan 20-06	Return of service Feb 5-06	Jan 16-06 Com reports no contest and certificates issued
	Feb 2 -06 Sent to E C Backenstoce for investigation	
	Feb 5 -06 Defdt appeared today	
	2/19 Articles of agreement filed by Ptf	
	2/23 said articles returned to Ptf	
	2/19 E C Backenstoce reports Dft is in possession without legal authority	
	2/27 Dft notified to vacate at once	
	3/6 Dft states he has has[sic] surrendered possession 3/10 Ptf requested to notify this office if same is true	

Cherokee Intruder Cases 1901 - 1909

April 7	Ptf advises that she is in possession and therefore case is dismissed

Rec'd	No.	Allottee	Intruder
Jan 16-06	705	William F. Cave for James L. Cave Lenapah, I.T.	W. H. Buffington Lenapah, I.T.
	June 12	Com^r reports that Dfdt has been denied citizenship	
	June 16	Case set for hearing at Claremore June 22/06	
	June 22	Case called at Claremore Both parties appeared motion filed for a continuance filed by Dfdts. Dfdts state that a motion for review of citizenship has been filed with Com^r Dfdts waived all right to possession save that of his citizenship	
	July 2	Com^r requested to report	
	July 17 1906	Com^r reports a motion for rehearing pending in the case of Wm H. Buffington Therefore this case is dismissed	Dismissed

Freedman claimant

Notice Sent	Action	Remarks
(Dates on this side covered by a piece of paper)	Return of service Jan 15-06 Ans filed Jan 22-06 Sent to EC Backenstoce for investigation 3/10 Case set for hearing at Claremore Mch 29th 1906	Jan 16-06 Com reports no contest and certificates issued
29	Case called at Claremore all parties present and it was found that the Dft is a *(word covered)* man and a Claimant for citizenship in Cherokee Nation. Claims he made the place *(this part covered)* is in possession	
(Month covered) 10 1906	In compliance with instructions from the Department, under date of April 19th 1906 Com^r is requested to report as to the status of allotment of Ptf and of citizenship of Dfdt	

287

Rec'd	No.	Allottee	Intruder
Jan 16-06	706	Mrs. H.R. McGury Cimarron, Colo. c/o D and R. G. Hotel	W. A. Robbins Tulsa, I.T.
	May 10	Certificates returned to Plaintiff and Case dismissed as Ptf states she is in possession	Dismissed

Notice Sent	Action	Remarks
Jan 20-06	Return of service Jan 21-06 Ans filed Jan 31-06	Jan 16-06 Com reports no contest and certificates issued 3/29 [sic]
Feb 12 -06	Sent to EC Backenstoce for investigation 3/10 Case set for hearing at Claremore Mch 29th 1906	2/29 Copy of contract filed certificates filed #5881 A 8077
Mch 23 '06	Ptf requested that her ^husband be allowed to represent her at Claremore 3/29 '06 which request was granted	
Mch 29th 06	Case called at Claremore both parties appeared and their evidence was taken (by J.E.B.)	
Mch 30	Dft asks to be informed as to date of filing of Plaintiff and was referred to Comr	
April 10 '06	Judgment rendered in favor of Ptf; both parties so notified and a copy of the Judgment sent to each of them. Defendant notified to vacate within 10 days.	

Rec'd	No.	Allottee	Intruder
Jan 13-06	707	Flora Smith Johnson Skiatook, Ind. Ter. Joe M Lahay, Atty Claremore, I.T. Freedman	E. B. Weitzel, Tulsa, I.T. Martin and Rice Attys Tulsa, I.T.
(Note: continuation from the end of this case)	May 26	if he wishes do so otherwise Judgment will be rendered on evidence already taken Judgment rendered in favor of Defendant both parties so notified and a copy of the Judgment sent to each of them.	
	June 22	Certificates returned to Ptf and contract to Defendant and case dismissed Letter from Dept. filed	Dismissed

Notice Sent	Action	Remarks
Jan 26-06	Return of service Feb. 2-06	Jan 24-06 Com reports no contest 3/29 Letter exibtd "B" Ptf Introducing E B Weitzell

Cherokee Intruder Cases 1901 - 1909

Feb 2nd -06	Sent to E C Backenstoce for investigation	$^{3/29}$ Dft Ex "A" a lease contract
	2/8 Answer filed	3/1 Lease contract filed
	2/2 Proof of service returned	$^{3/29}$ Letter from agent Ex "A"
	3/10 Case set for hearing at Claremore Mch 29th 1906	$^{3/29}$ Homestead certificate No 33871 - Allotment cert No 54551
Mch 29th 10 am	Case called at Claremore. All parties present evidence taken. Case continued by consent of both parties until 3/30th '06 3/29 Original Leasee[sic] appeared in afternoon and his evidence taken.	
April 13	Atty for Ptf was granted additional time to introduce evidence for Ptf in rebuttal to the evidence of the Original Leasee[sic] (J.E.B. Stenographer) Ptf's Atty requested to submit further evidence at once	

(Note: continued at the beginning of this case)

Rec'd	No.	Allottee		Intruder
Oct 24-05	708	Sarah E Murray for Annie Murray Wagoner I.T.		George W Cleland Sr Wagoner, I.T.
Notice Sent		**Action**		**Remarks**
Jan 27 -06		Sent to E C Backenstoce for investigation 2/12 Sent to E C Backenstoce for investigation 2/14 Proof of service returned 2/28 Dismissed upon recommendation of E C Backenstoce *Dismissed*		Oct 24-06 Com reports no contest and certificates issued

Rec'd	No.	Allottee	Intruder
Jan 22-06	709	Benjamin F Fields *(Location illegible)*	H. W. Hicks Blue Jacket, I.T.
Notice Sent		**Action**	**Remarks**
Feb 10-06		Feb 10-06 Sent to E C Backenstoce for investigation 2/17 Proof of service returned 2/17 Backenstoce states that Dft is not in possession and claims right to land *Dismissed*	Jan 29-06 Com reports no contest and cert's issued

Cherokee Intruder Cases 1901 - 1909

Rec'd	No.	Allottee	Intruder
Feb 1-06	710	Victoria Jordan, c/o S. F. Parks, Atty Vinita, Ind. Ter.	Alvie Desman Adair, I.T.
Notice Sent		**Action**	**Remarks**
Feb 10-06 06	Feb 10- April 10	Sent to E C Backenstoce for investigation 2/19 Backenstoce reports Dft agrees to vacate by 3/1'06 which is satifactory[sic] to Ptf 3/20 Referred to Eldon Lowe for investigation Report of Eldon Lowe filed and case dismissed upon request of Plaintiff	Feb 1-06 Com reports no contest and cert's issued Dismissed

Rec'd	Allottee	Intruder
Jan 24 '06	711 Mrs Narcissus Scarobough[sic] Santown[sic] I.T.	Charley Rodgers Vian I.T.
Notice Sent	**Action**	**Remarks**
2/12 April 2nd Aug 21 1907	Sent to EC Backenstoce for investigation 2/26 Proof of service returned 3/21 Referred to John Veits for investigation John Viets reports and from his report it appears that the Dft is a "Night Hawk" or "Kaytooyah" and has lived upon the land for 15 years. Ptf says she will file another and surrender the land in controversy in this case to the Dft if Com^r will allow her to do so. Com^r asked to advise this office if same can be done. As no report Ca~~se dismissed~~	Jan 31'06 Com reports no contests pending

Rec'd	Allottee	Intruder
Jan 15	712 Mrs. Lettia Foreman Moody I.T.	Samuel B Passel Moody I.T.
Notice Sent	**Action**	**Remarks**
2/12 Notice Sent 2/12'06	Sent to E C Backenstoce for investigation	Jan 26th '06 Com reports no contest pending

Cherokee Intruder Cases 1901 - 1909

2/12 Proof of Service returned, and answer filed by Dft.
3/8 Case dismissed upon recommendation of E.C. Backenstoce   *Dismissed*

		Allottee	Intruder
Jan 18 '06		713 Jennie Snyder	O. F. Campbell
		Westville I.T.	Coffeyville Kans
		Action	Remarks
2/12 Notice Sent 2/12 '06		Referred to EC Backenstoce for investigation	Jan 26 '06 Com reports no contest pending
		2/24 Proof of Service returned	
		3/10 Case set for hearing at Claremore Mch 29th 1906	
		3/17 Case dismissed upon request of Plaintiff ~~and case Dismissed~~	
		3/22 Report of John Veits[sic] filed	*Dismissed*

		Allottee	Intruder
Jan 21 '06		714 Ina M. Tossaway	Mary E. Jones
		Owasso I.T.	Owasso I.T.
		Action	Remarks
2/12 Notice Sent 2/12 '06		Sent to EC Backenstoce for investigation	Jan 31 1906 Com reports no contest pending
	2/21	Case dismissed upon request of Ptf.	*Dismissed*

Rec'd	No.	Allottee	Intruder
Jan 27	715	Miss Mary Welch	Harvey Martin
		c/o E M Frye, Atty	Adair, I.T.
		Sallisaw, I.T.	
	Dec 4 1906	Com^r asked to report as to citizenship of Harvey Martin	
	Mch 12 1907	Com^r asked c/o citizenship of Harvey	
Notice Sent		Action	Remarks
2/12'06			2/27'06
	2/12	Sent to E.C. Backenstoce for investigation	Filed allotment certificate No 33458

291

Cherokee Intruder Cases 1901 - 1909

3/3 Case dismissed as Dft is an applicant for citizenship. See report of E C Backenstoce in file *Dismissed*	Homestead certificate No 23538 2/17 Com reports no contest pending 3/3 Certificates returned

Rec'd	No.	Allottee	Intruder
Jan 26	716	J.W. Rider for Thomas Needles Rider c/o E.M. Frye Atty Sallisaw, I.T.	Noley Couch Nowata, I.T.

Notice Sent	Action	Remarks
2/12'06	2/17 Sent to E.C. Backenstoce for investigation	Jan 26 1906 Certificate of Allotment
	3/10 Case set for hearing at Claremore Mch 27th 1906	No 18564 Homestead Certificate No 14267
	Mch 20th John Viets reports that Dft waives all right to possession and all authority to rent or lease the land in controversy and that as far as he is concerned the Plaintiff may, at any time assume possession of the land allotted to him. Therefore case is dismissed and certificates returned	2/17 Com reports no contest pending
		Dismissed
Aug 1st 1906	Letter to Watts and Curtis Attys Sallisaw I.T.	

Rec'd	Allottee	Intruder
Jan 20th	717 Rebecca Vann Santown[sic] I.T.	Geo Bean and Wm Rofe Sallisaw I.T.

Notice Sent	Action	Remarks
2/13'06	2/13 Sent to E C Backenstoce for investigation	Filed certificate of Allotment No 3696
	2/17 Returns proof of notice	and Certificate of
	2/23 Answer filed	Homestead No 8975
	2/28 Dft instructed to vacate at once	2/16 Com reports
Mch 19th 06	Referred to Eldon Lowe for investigation	no contest pending
April 6	Report of John Viets filed Case dismissed upon request of Ptf. and certificates returned	
April 23	Report of Eldon Lowe filed	
		Dismissed

Cherokee Intruder Cases 1901 - 1909

Rec'd	Allottee	Intruder
Jan 31st	718 Caleb Thorne Tahlequah I.T	Rowe, Stacey and J.A. Blasing Tahlequah I.T.

Notice Sent	Action	Remarks
2/13'06	2/13 Sent to E.C. Backenstoce for investigation 3/1 Proof of Service returned 3/2 Given to U.S.I.P. Thos Roach for investigation 3/8 Case dismissed upon recommendation of EC Backenstoce Both parties notified *Dismissed*	1/31 Certificate of allotment No 48460 2/16 Com reports no contest pending 2/8 Certificate returned

Rec'd	Allottee	Intruder
Feb 1'06	719 Mrs Sarah Dolen Fair Pryor Creek, I.T. J.L. Batlenfield Atty	Stward[sic], Riley and Nancy Pryor Creek, I.T.

(Note: continuation from the end of this case) Pryor Creek, I.T.
    Mch 26 Ptf nor her Atty were not[sic] present
    April 12 Allottee requested to forward her allotment certificates to this office Certificates refiled by Ptf.
    May 7 Instructions issued to Capt John C West to place Allottee in possession
    May 7 Certificates returned to Ptf
    " 22 Capt West reports that he has placed the Allottee in possession
    Case dismissed

Notice Sent	Action	Remarks
2/14 1906 2/24[sic]	2/14 Sent to EC Backenstoce for investigation 2/23 Receipt of Proof of service Ack. 2/23 Case dismissed as land in question is involved in contest 3/12 Reinstated as all land is not in contest 3/13 Case set for hearing at Claremore Mch 27 1906	2/1 Allotment certificate No 1759 filed 2/17 Com reports portion of land in contest

Cherokee Intruder Cases 1901 - 1909

Mch 26 '06	Nancy Stewart Dft ʌ appeared and acknowledged that she had no contract from the Allottee, but that she is a Cherokee Indian by blood and the land is hers, she is not enrolled and was *(Illegible)* to vacate. See Memo in file
	(Note: continued at the beginning of this case)

Rec'd	Allottee	Intruder
Dec 22	720 Phoena[sic] Manley Sleeper I.T.	Allen Lancaster Sleeper I.T.
Notice Sent	**Action**	**Remarks**
2/14'06	2/14 Sent to E.C. Backenstoce for investigation 2/24 Proof of Service returned 3/12 Case dismissed upon recommendation of John Viets and request of Ptf *Dismissed*	2/2 06 Com reports no contest pending

Rec'd		
Feb 5th 06	721 James L. Murphy for Lizzie Murphy Marble I.T.	R.T. Kellum
Notice Sent		
2/14'06	2/14 Sent to A[sic] C Backenstoce for investigation 2/23 Proof of Service returned 3/6 Ptf notified this office that Dfts had vacated therefore case is dismissed 3/22 J.L. Murphy Ack. receipt of Letters of Gdnship. *Dismissed*	2/5 1906 Allotment certificate no 40214 2/14 Letters of Gdnship filed by Ptf 2/17 Com reports no contest pending 3/6 Certificates returned 2/15 Letters of Gdnship returned

Rec'd		
Feb 9 '06	722 Wm L Hensley, Gdn John F and Ethel L Lee Muskogee I.T. Rose and Bradley Attys Muskogee	P W Marsh Edna Kans Eck. E. Brook Atty Muskogee J.A. Reaves, Muskogee Made party Dft.

Cherokee Intruder Cases 1901 - 1909

Notice Sent		
2/14 '06	2/14 Sent to E C Backenstoce for investigation
2/28 Proof of Service returned
3/6 J A Reaves appeared at this office and asked to be made party Dft, which was granted
3/14 Answer filed
3/15 Case set for hearing at Muskogee 4/2 '06 2:00 PM
4/2 Again continued by agreement until April 9th '06	
	April 9th Atty Bradley appeared for Ptf and requested that case be dismissed as a settlement had been made. Certificates and letters of Gdnship were returned to him in person.
Dismissed	

Rec'd	Allottee	Intruder
Feb 3 '06	723 Rosa Blackwell Brown
Nowata IT	Wm Jacobs and Wife and Arthur Jacobs
	April 5th Instructions issued to Capt West to remove alledged[sic] Intruders and place Allottee in possession	
	April 7th Capt West reports that he has removed objectionable parties and placed the Allottee in possession. Case dismisses and certificates returned.	
		Dismissed

Notice Sent	Action	Remarks
2/14'06	2/14 Sent to E C Backenstoce for investigation
2/23 Proof of Service returned
2/26 Backenstoce recommends that Ptf be placed in possession
3/2 Instructions sent to U.S.I.P. Clement R Musgrave to place Ptf in possession
3/20 C.R. Musgrave request to report what Action he has taken in re. instructions issued 3/2 '06
3/19 Sterling P. Parks filed a letter in which he states he should be allowed to move his improvements	2/17 1906
Com reports no contest pending
2/10 '06 filed Homestead certificates Nos 9811 and 36038
	April 5th Policeman Musgrave has resigned and this order has not been executed	

Cherokee Intruder Cases 1901 - 1909

Rec'd	Allottee	Intruder
Jan 20 '06	724 Thomas Martin Santown[sic] I.T.	Jerry Albert
Notice Sent	**Action**	**Remarks**
2/15 '06	2/12 Sent to E C Backenstoce for investigation 3/5 Proof of Service returned bearing date of 2/24 1906 3/21 Referred to John Viets for investigation April 6 JohnViets reports that amiciable[sic] settlement has been made. Case dismissed and certificates returned to Ptf.	2/13 '06 filed Plat and ~~Allotment~~ Homestead No 19937 2/20 Com reports no contest pending and certificates issued Dismissed

Rec'd	Allottee	Intruder
Feb 13 '06	725 W^m H White Fairland I.T.	Scott Nance Fairland I.T.
Notice Sent	**Action**	**Remarks**
2/15 '06	2/15 Sent to E C Backenstoce for investigation 2/20 Proof of Service returned 2/21 Dft filed answer stating he had instituted contest against Ptf 2/27 Com. reports land involved in contest 2/27 Case dismissed Jany 23 1907 Plntf asks status of case Jany 26 1907 Plntf requested to file new case	2/13 06 Certificates of allotment No 45898 2/27 Certificates returned Dismissed

Rec'd	Allottee	Intruder
Feb 13 '06	726 Wm H. Inlow and Nancy Inlow Grove I.T.	Holland, Alfred C and Chas Norwood
Notice Sent	**Action**	**Remarks**
2/15 '06	2/15 Sent to EC Backenstoce for investigation 2/20 Com reports contest pending 2/17 Answer filed by Dft 2/19 Proof of service returned 2/27 Case dismissed as land in question is in contest	2/13 Plot of land in question and allotment certificates Nos 58644, 58649 and Homestead certificates Nos 35692 and 35693 2/2 Certificates returned

Cherokee Intruder Cases 1901 - 1909

Dismissed 2/20 Com reports contest pending

Rec'd	Allottee	Intruder
Feb 15 '06	727 E.A. Jackson Gen. of Leona E and Otto R Jackson c/o Harry O. Bland Atty Afton I.T.	Phillip Donohoo Afton I.T. R.B. Lewis Needmore I.T.
April 3rd and June 7th	Case set for hearing at Claremore	
" "	I.T. for June 20 1906	
June 12	Atty for Ptf states that Gdn. is now in possession of the allotments of the minors case is therefore dismissed All parties notified that it will not be necessary for them to appear at Claremore on June 20/'06	
June 15	Certificates returned to Plaintiff	
" 20	Atty for Ptf appeared at Ardmore and states that Dft refuses to give possession	
June 30	Defendant directed to vacate within 10 days otherwise an order will issue to remove him	
July 17 1906	Ptf requested to advise this office if he is now in possession	

Notice Sent	Action	Remarks
(Month covered) 9 '06 2/19	Sent to EC Backenstoce for investigation	2/16 06 the following were filed
	Proof of Service returned 3rd of March	2 lease contracts Letters of Gdnship
	3/10 Set for hearing at Claremore Mch 29th 1906	2 Allotment certfs. Nos 7206 and 7205 and
	3/12 Report of John Viets filed Dft agrees to vacate in 10 days	Homestead cert Nos 6927 and 6926
	3/27 Atty for Ptf requested to notify this office as to whether or not agreement affected by Viets has been complied with	2/24 Com reports no contest pending
(Month covered) 29	Telegram from Dft rec'd at Claremore states he is unable to attend on account of sickness 3/29 Case called [sic] Claremore neither party present	

Rec'd	Allottee	Intruder
Jan 16 1906	728 Johnson Groves Texanna I.T.	Lawrence, Milo E Checotah IT
	July 6, 1906 Status of case furnished Johnson Groves	P.C. West Atty Muskogee

Cherokee Intruder Cases 1901 - 1909

Notice Sent	Action	Remarks
2/20 06	2/20 Sent to EC Backenstoce for investigation 3/6 Proof of Service returned hearing date of 3/3 1906 3/12 Answer filed 3/15 Case set for hearing at Muskogee Mch 24th 2:00 P.M. Mch 24 Case continued by agreement until April 2nd 10: A.M. April 2nd Case called at Muskogee all parties present evidence taken (E.B. stenographer) April 16th Submitted to J. Geo. Wright U.S. Indian Insp. for Ind. Ter. recommending that proceedings be initiated in the U.S. Court for the cancellation of a lease executed by Grove Johnson to Milo E Lawrence	Filed 2/17 '06 Homestead certificate No 18561 and Allotment Cert No 25568 Rental contract in Duplicate and agreement between Johnson Groves and Milo E Lawrence 2/24 Com reports no contest pending Dismissed

Rec'd	Allottee	Intruder
Feb 19 '06	729 Sallie Benge Fort Gibson I.T.	Betsy Talley and Andrew Talley

Notice Sent	Action	Remarks
2/21 '06	2/21 Sent to E C Backenstoce for investigation 2/28 Proof of Service returned 3/8 Case dismissed upon recommendation of E C Backenstoce Mch 30th Plaintiff appeared and stated that Dfts has[sic] not surrendered possession to her as agreed April 5 Instructions issued to Capt West to place Ptf in possession April 10 Capt John C. West reports that he has placed the Allottee in possession and removed all objectionable persons Case dismissed	Filed 2/19 '06 Allotment certificate No 34167 2/27 Com reports no contest pending Certificate returned Dismissed

Rec'd	Allottee	Intruder
Feb 19 1906	730 Nellie Young c/o Geo P. Fogle Atty Vinita I.T.	Frank Davis Vinita I.T.

Cherokee Intruder Cases 1901 - 1909

Notice Sent	Action	Remarks
2/24 1906	2/24 Sent to EC Backenstoce for investigation 3/10 Case set for hearing at Claremore Mch 29th 1906	2/9 Lease filed
Mch 29th	Case called at Claremore I.T. neither party appeared 3/28 Case dismissed by request of Ptf. Report of John Viets filed. Dismissed	

Rec'd	Allottee	Intruder
Feb 9 [1906]	731 Annie Sexton for Leo Johnson ~~Coffeyville~~ Kans Caney, Kans	Woster Wiley Caney Kans

Notice Sent	Action	Remarks
2/24 1906	2/24 Referred to EC Backenstoce for investigation 3/8 Case set for hearing at Claremore Mch 30 1906 3/22 Report of John Viets filed and case dismissed upon request of Ptf	2/9 Plat file
		Dismissed
April 9th	Notices returned unclaimed	

Rec'd	Allottee	Intruder
March 1st 1906	732 Charlotte T. Taylor Atty in fact for John S. Stubbs Muskogee I.T.	Claude M. Young Copan I.T.

Notice Sent	Action	Remarks
3/1	3/1 Referred to E.C. Backenstoce for investigation 3/10 Case set for hearing at Claremore Mch 30th 1906 Mch 19 Case dismissed upon request of Ptf 2/20 Report of Viets filed	
		Dismissed

Rec'd	Allottee	Intruder
Feb 13	733 Emma Ann Parkhill By A G Parkhill Hillside I.T.	Robert Frakes Oologah I.T.

Cherokee Intruder Cases 1901 - 1909

Notice Sent	Action	Remarks
3/16 1906	3/6 Sent to EC Backenstoce for investigation 3/10 Case set for hearing at Claremore Mch 30th 1906 3/15 Proof of service returned dated 3/13 '06 3/19 Answer filed	2/20 Com reports no contest pending
Mch 30th	W. N. Hall Atty for Ptf appeared and requested that case be dismissed as agreement had been made between Ptf and Dft	
3/26	Ptf requests that case be dismissed	
		Dismissed

Rec'd	Allottee	Intruder
Feb 5 1906	734 Okla Tadpole Pryor Creek I.T.	Samuel Wheeler Claremore I.T. A.C. Brewster Atty for Dft. Pryor Creek I.T.
April 25	Atty for Dfdts advises that Settlement has been made	
May 3	Atty for Dfdts advised that Plaintiff will have to notify this office of the settlement before case can be dismissed	
June 8	Plaintiff requested to advise this office if she is now in possession	
		Dismissed
Jany 26 1907	Certificates of Allottment[sic] returned as per request of plntf Nos 6279 -8672	

Notice Sent	Action	Remarks
3/6 1906	3/6 Sent to EC Backenstoce for investigation 3/10 Case set for hearing at Claremore Mch 30th 1906 3/13 Proof of service returned dated Mch 9th 1906	2/17 Com reports no contest pending 3/20 Homestead Cert No 6279 and Allotment Certificate No 8572 in file
Mch 30th	Case called at Claremore all parties present. Dft introduced a rental contract which is designated as Ex, "A". A second rental contract was introduced by Dfts and is designated as Ex "B" Evidence of both Ptf and Dft's taken. (E.B. stenographer)	
April 16th	Judgment rendered in favor of the Plaintiff both parties so notified and a copy of the judgment sent to each of them. Defendant 10 days from date of Judgment to vacate.	

Cherokee Intruder Cases 1901 - 1909

Rec'd	Allottee	Intruder
Feb 8th 1906	735 William C. Ragsdale	W.W. Wheeler
	Muldrow I.T.	Sallisaw I.T.
	~~Jan 26 1907~~ ~~As per request of plntf 1/22/06 Allottment[sic]~~ ~~certificates #~~	
	Jany 26 1907 Certificates of Allottment[sic] returned as per request of plntf Nos 6279 -8672	

Notice Sent	Action	Remarks
3/6 1906	3/6 Referred to E.C. Backenstoce for investigation	2/17 Com reports no contest pending
	Mch 21 Proof of service returned dated 3/10 '06	
Mch 28	Report of John Viets filed and Ptf notified to take possession, should Dft refuse to give him possession he is requested to notify this office	
April 26	Case dismissed as the Plaintiff states that he is in possession	
		Dismissed

Rec'd	Allottee	Intruder
Feb 1th[sic] 1906	736 Tom Kirk Gdn. of	J. F. Whitney
	Albert and Ezekiel P. Kirk	Dawson I.T.
	Tahlequah I.T.	

Notice Sent	Action	Remarks
3/6 1906	3/6 Referred to E.C. Backenstoce for investigation	2/21 Letters of Gdnship filed
	3/10 Case set for hearing at Claremore Mch 30th 1906	2/17 Com reports no contest pending
	Mch 20th Proof of service returned dated Mch 19th	
	Mch 30 Case called at Claremore neither party present	
	April 3rd Referred to John Viets for investigation	
	" 23 Report of John Viets filed and case dismissed as[sic] as Mr Viets reports that E.D. Allenwood is now in possession under a lease contract executed by Ptf as Legal Gdn.	
		Dismissed

Rec'd	Allottee	Intruder
Jan 30 1906	737 Jenny Holt	Richard Anderson
	Vian I.T.	Vian I.T.

Cherokee Intruder Cases 1901 - 1909

Notice Sent	Action	Remarks
3/6 1906	3/6 Referred to E.C. Backenstoce for investigation	2/26 Com reports no contest pending
	April 6ᵗʰ John Viets' report filed and case dismissed upon an[sic] request of Plaintiff. Certificates returned	
		Dismissed

Rec'd	Allottee	Intruder
Feb 15 1906	738 Sue Williams	Clark M Drummon
	Claremore I.T.	Claremore I.T.
	A.F. Moore	W.F. Seaver Atty for Dft
(Note: continuation from the end of this case)	Claremore I.T.	Claremore I.T.
	Both parties notified of the decision and a copy of the judgment sent to each of them	
	June 8 Pltf requested to advise this office is she is now in possession of her allotment	
	June 13 Case dismissed as Plaintiff advises that Defendant has surrendered possession	

Notice Sent	Action	Remarks
3/6 1906	Referred to E.C. Backenstoce for investigation	2/24 Com reports no contest pending
	3/10 Case set for hearing at Claremore Mch 30ᵗʰ 1906	2/30 ~~Defendant~~ Plaintiff Williams filed letter from Com showing date of filing
	3/12'06 Proof of Service returned hearing date of Mch 10ᵗʰ 1906	
	3/20 Answer filed 3/20 Additional answer filed by defendant's Atty	
Mch 30	Case called at Claremore all parties present evidence taken by (E,B, Stenographer) Ex "A" A Summons signed by Ptf and her husband which was served upon Dft. Ptf admitted that case had been mitiated[sic] in the U.S. Court at Claremore	
April 14	Judgment rendered in favor for Plaintiff and Dft given fifteen has from date of Judgment in which to vacate	

Rec'd	Allottee	Intruder
Feb 21 1906	739 Mrs Jennie Scott	John Hess
	Chance I.T.	Chance I.T.

Cherokee Intruder Cases 1901 - 1909

Notice Sent	Action	Remarks
3/6 1906	3/6 Referred to EC Backenstoce for investigation 3/10 Case set for hearing at Claremore Mch 30th 1906 3/25 Case dismissed as Ptf states compromise has been made between herself and Dft. 3/20 Answer filed.	2/21 Homestead certificate No 21571 filed 3/10 Com reports no contest pending Dismissed

Rec'd	Allottee	Intruder
March 7 1906	740 Lennie B Jones, for Golie *(or Galie)* Hereford Warner I.T.	Sorrel Baker and family

Notice Sent	Action	Remarks
3/9 06	3/9 Sent to John M Bacon for investigation	3/7 Certificate of Allotment No 50979 filed
April 16	Report of John Viets filed and case dismissed upon request of Plaintiff. Certificate returned	3/15 Com reports no contest pending Dismissed

Rec'd	Allottee	Intruder
Mch 8th	741 Samuel W. Hudson Nat Gdn for Nancy Hudson Chelsea I.T. Archibald Bonor Atty Chelsea I.T.	Lem Parris Chelsea I.T.
8/29 -07	Pltf to be further advised as soon as Com report is rec'd	
8/29 -07	Com. asked for report	
Sept 7 07	Plaintiff advised no further Action in this case will be taken until appraised value had been paid for improvements	
Sept 3 '07	Com^r reports improvements appraised to Isabella J Paris.	

Notice Sent	Sent to / Action	Remarks
3/13 '06	3/13 John Veits[sic] for investigation 3/19 Set for hearing at Claremore Mch 30th 1906 3/20 Proof of service returned dated Mch 16th 1906 3/19 Answer filed	3/8 Homestead cert No 36327 and Allotment Certf. No 60185 3/20 Com reports no contest pending

Cherokee Intruder Cases 1901 - 1909

Mch 30th Case called at Claremore I.T. Ptfs appeared and their evidence was taken
Mch 27 (by EB Steno)
Dft advises that he has instuted[sic] contest. Com[r] requested to report on same
April 9th Com[r] report contest pending.
Certificates returned and case dismissed
                     Dismissed

	Allottee	Intruder
Verbal complaint Jan 29 06	742 Rebecca Nugin Hulbert I.T.	Mrs A.C. Archer and Tenants Tulsa Geo W Mowbray Tulsa I.T.
	May 28 Submitted to J.G. Wright U.S. Indian Insp recommending that proceedings initiated in the US Court for the cancellation of the contract purporting to have been executed by the Ptf. Such proceedings to be brought under act of Mch 3 1905	
		Dismissed
Notice Sent	**Action taken**	**Remarks**
3/26	Jan 29th Referred to E.C. Backenstoce for investigations 2/9 E.C. Backenstoce report filed Mch 16th 1906 Case set for hearing at Claremore 3/27th '06	3/23 Com reports no contest pending 3/26 Copy of contract filed by Geo W Mowbray

Mch 26 Case called at Claremore, Geo W. Mowbray represented the Dft and his evidence was taken. John M. Ingram, second witness for Dft heard. Ptf did not appear (Evidence taken by EB)
April 10 Plaintiff requested to appear at this office on April 21 1906 that her evidence may be taken. Dft advised that she may be present if she so desires.
April 21st Case called at Muskogee I.T. Both parties present and evidence taken

	Allottee	Intruder
Feb 27 1906	743 Chas J. Lynch c/o J. C. Starr Atty Vinita I.T.	Arthur Bridgmon Sam Adams and JJ Spencer Vinita I.T.

Cherokee Intruder Cases 1901 - 1909

Notice Sent	Action taken	Remarks
3/24'06	3/24 Referred to Eldon Lowe for investigation. 3/13 Com^r reports no contest pending	
April 28	Report of Eldon Lowe filed and case dismissed upon request of Plaintiff	
Oct 1 1906	Letter from plntf to Secy Interior, asking to be placed in possession.	
Oct 4 1906	Pltf advised as to former Action in this case & asked to explain former Actions.	Dismissed

Rec'd	Allottee	Intruder
Feb 24	744 Moses Downing for Chas W. Downing, a minor Shakespeare I.T. Watts and Carter Attys Sallisaw I.T.	Leonard and Fannie Gately Shakespeare I.T.

Notice Sent	Action	Remarks
3/20/06	3/24 Referred to Eldon Lowe for investigation	

Defendants filed answer in which they state[sic]
April 17 Defendants filed answer in which they state that they are not holding any of the land described in this case. The land they are holding is in contest
April 19 Plaintiff advised of the statement of the Defendants and were requested to have the land surveyed by a competent Surveyor
April 26 Report of Eldon Lowe filed and case dismissed upon request of Plaintiff

                                                          Dismissed

Rec'd	Allottee	Intruder
Mch 19 1906	745 Webster Wickett Zena I.T.	vs Thomas Hall Grove I.T. E.B. Hardy Zena I.T.
Aug 21 1906	Case called at Vanita[sic] I.Ty. Pltf appeared and his testimony taken Certificate #55997 ret. in person. Pltf instructed to have land surveyed and if dfts are ~~tresp~~ occupying land to report to this office	

Cherokee Intruder Cases 1901 - 1909

Sept 26 1906 Pltf instructed to have land surveyed in order to ascertain if
Save in Intruders are in possession of any portion of it.
746

Jany 22 1907 Referred to Robt R. Bennett for investigation
Mch 23 1907 Robt R. Bennett encloses request for dismissal
Mch 26 1907 Case <u>dismissed</u>

Notice Sent	Action	Remarks
3/24 06	3/24 Referred to Eldon Lowe for investigation	3/19 Allotment Certificate No 55997
	Mch 30th Com^r reports no contest pending and certificates issued	
	April 4 Proof of service returned dated Mch 31st 1906	
	" " Answer filed by EB Hardy and Tom Hall	
	" 28 Eldon Lowe reports that Dfdts claim they are not in possession of any of the land allotted to Webster Wickett and that if they are they will surrender same to Allottee as soon as same is determined by a competent surveyor	
	May 2 Ptf advised to have his allotment surveyed	
	Aug 8 1906 Case set for hearing at Vanita[sic] I.Ty. Aug 22 -1906 All parties notified.	

Index

ABBOT, Rosie R 38
ABBOTT, S M 38
ABERCROMBIE, John 271
ADAIR
   George 148
   Pearl 148
   Policeman 136,207,222
   Tandy W 83,84,136
   Yula 148
ADAMS
   Frank 53
   Mary 102
   R C 70
   Sam 304
   Wm H 103
ALBERT, Jerry 296
ALBERTY
   Andrew J 232
   Gibson W 214
   Lula L 32
   Spencer L 32
ALLEN
   Isom M 58
   Marcellus 58
   Osceola 1
   Paden 148
   Robert 58
   W R 93
ALSTON, Sarah C 36
ANDERSON
   F M 259
   Louisa 176
   Richard 301
   T M 262
ANLTFIELD, Mr 262
APPLEGATE
   C R 74
   George 74
ARCHER
   A M 276
   Mrs A C 304
ARMSTRONG, Mrs S E 40
ARNOLD, Victoria 38
ARROWOOD, Mertie P 235
ARTER, J H 33,43
ASH
   W G 50

Willis G 108
ATCHISON, J L 206
AUKEN, Lenora M 188
AUTEN, Lenora W 195
AVANT, Thomas J 257
AXTON, Betsey 67
BACKBONE, Mrs Charlotte 197
BACKENSTOCE 164,183,195,197,
236,237,239,251,259
   E C 186,188,191,197,198,201,
238,244,252,253,260,262,263,264,269
,271,272,277,280,281,282,283,284,
285,286,287,288,289,290,291,292,293
,294,295,296,297,298,299,300,301,
302,303,304
BACON 250
   John C 248
   John M 139,156,159,160,162,164,
166,183,194,195,197,199,209,214,217
,220,227,229,231,232,233,234,235,
236,237,239,240,241,242,243,244,245
,246,247,248,249,250,251,252,253,
254,255,256,257,258,259,260,303
BAILEY
   D 152
   Ella 145
BAKER
   Dick 189
   Eliza 108,109
   Etta M 108
   Freddie E 108
   M T 108
   Malissa E 150
   Mary A 150
   Myrtle E 150
   Sorrel 303
BALCH, J L 282,283
BALDRIDGE
   Delila E 148
   George W 148
   Jno 47
BALLARD
   Carrie 126
   William 126
BANKHEAD
   Eunice A 4
   John H 30

Index

John T 30
BARBEE, Policeman................... 76
BARKER, J L 12
BARKS
   Grace 5
   John E 5
   Victoria.. 5
   Willie E 5
BARNES
   J T 52
   Robert... 143
BART 27
BARTLES 102
   Joe 244
BATE, Dr S R 98
BATLENFIELD, J L 293
BATT
   Eva E 191
   Isaac... 191
   Joe 187
   Mary E... 191
BAUGH, Joel L 266
BEAMER
   Debbie N 170
   Johnson... 170
BEAN
   Geo 292
   Louisa.. 58
   Murphy.. 58
   Nancy J 141
   Phenia... 86
BEANS, Dennis................................ 170
BEAR, Harrison 13
BEARDEN, Robert 57
BEARS, Harrison 43
BEAVER, John A.............................. 264
BELL
   Charles.. 117
   Ed 107
   Geo 210
   George 83
   Georgia.. 177
   J P 1
   Mattie J 86
   Thomas 210
   Thos 172
BENGE

Miss Georgia 171
   Sallie.. 298
   Samuel H, Jr 208
BENNETT.................................101,228
   Mr..168,283
   Robt R 190,260,268,306
   W W 209,223
BERLEY, Jim.................................... 110
BERRY
   Cleon 236,260
   George 261
   Ibbie... 204
   Robert.......................................246,249
   Roxie D 81
BIBLES
   Jessie... 119
   Louis.. 119
   Margaret 9
BICE
   Benj F 23
   Lela... 23
BIEL, Ben F 196
BIGBEY, Samuel A 245
BIGFEATHER
   Ben 133
   George 133
   Lydia.. 133
BISHOP.. 201
BITTICK, Thomas 149
BIXBY, Tams...............................115,201
BLACK, John 179
BLACKBIRD, Jennie........................ 110
BLACKBURN
   A J 206
   Wesley 234
BLACKBURN & HUTCHINSON..... 103
BLACKWELL
   George 235
   Rosa.. 70
BLAND, Harry O 297
BLASING, J A 293
BLAYBURN, Mary 4
BLEDSOE, J P 266
BLEVINS
   Burrell.. 185
   Emmette 71
   George 27,185

Index

Joseph 27	Barnet 15
BLUE, Col 76,98,163	Fannie 236
BLUE & BULGER 97,98	Nancy 246
BOGARD, C W 212	BREWSTER, A C 300
BOHANAN, John 92	BRIDGMON, Arthur 304
BOLAND, Ross 43	BRIGGS, John 152
BOLDEN, A P 85	BRIGHT
BONEY, Dan 75	George 69
BONNER, John E 181	Wm J 69
BONOR, Archibald 303	BRITTLER, Marcus L 256
BORENS	BROCKWAY 261
A G 216	BROOK, Eck E 294
R J 133	BROOKS
BOTKINS, Robt 180	Eck E 264
BOUDINOT	Thos 192
Harriet G 149	BROUGHT
Mary C 148	C G 7
R F 149	Cynthia 7
Richard F 258	BROWN
BOWERS, Effie C 256	Amanda 246
BOX, Will 152	Andrew A 69
BOYD	Anna L 154
J M 22	Birt M 116
James F 22	David I 3
R J 108	Dee 72
W C 275	George 50
BOZARTH	Henry B 216
Bramble 263	J B 209
M L H C 263	J G 220,221
BRADFORD, James 138	James B 69
BRADLEY	Lilly M 69
Atty 295	Mary 120,216
Cass M 264,265	Minnie 268
BRADY	Mrs Johnnie A 209
George 242	Myrtle 69
Ruth T 210	Robert H 154
W T 210	Rosa Blackwell 295
BRANDON, Frank 178	Thos S 35
BRANER, Ettie 31	Tom 199
BRANNAN, J R 285	William 120
BRATCHER	William H 116
James T 191	Wm M 69
John C 191	BROWNING, J K 44
Nettie 191	BROWNSON, Julia 46
BREEDLOVE, W W 63,174	BRUE, Benj F 23
BREMER, Dr G H 279	BRUERE
BREWER	Louie 200

Index

Lydia 200
BRYAN, Benj 64
BRYANT
  Ella 54
  Sherman 100
BRYSON, D E 232
BUCK
  Charles M 187
  Taylor 209
  William 209
BUCKMASTER
  Bert 211
  Birdie 211
  Mary 211
BUFFALO, Lincoln 106
BUFFINGTON
  Alexander C 142
  Georgia L 142
  Mary 29
  W H 287
  Wm H 287
BUFORD
  Jennie 73
  Johnson 73
  Walter 73
BUMGARNER, Sam 280
BURGESS
  Elizabeth 4
  Flora E 9
  J B 4
  James O 30
  Jesse B 161
  Joseph D 9
  Mary J 30
  Nora B 210
  Wm A 30
BURKHART, Harley 30
BURNS, Charley 193
BURR 138
  Alexander 137
  Calvin 137
  Geo W 137
BURRIS, Monroe 1
BURTON
  Dr Summer 82
  Rufus 40
BUSHYHEAD, Geo W 50
BUSKUK, Wm 3
BUSSEY, Martha 231
BUSTER
  Charles 13
  Wm 13
BUTLER
  Cliff 281
  John G 57
  Mary U E 57
  R E 114
  Sam 281
BUTTE & BLISS 267
BUTTER, T J 100
BUTTS, D W 38
BUTTS & BLISS 211
BUZZARD, Lucy 244
BYRD
  Anna L 58
  Edward 70
  Jane 70
BYRON, Cora M 280
CALDWELL
  Benjamin 11
  Jno C 11
  Jno J 11
  Joella 11
  John J 11
  Mary 113
CALWELL
  Mary 55
  Nancy 55
CALWOOD, Sarah 194
CAMPBELL
  Nancy J 178
  O F 291
  Oma 250
  Zelena 49
CANARY OIL CO 277
CAPTAIN, Betsey 67
CARDEN, Thos 194
CAREY, David L 71
CARPENTER
  Alice 32
  Wm 48
CARROLL, J 11
CARSON, Jason 29
CARTER, Mr 52

Index

CASE, George W 119
CASS
  Iddo G 32
  Philip H 242
CATCHER
  Minnie 57
  Rinty 57
CAULEY
  Mary T 121
  Walter 81
CAVE
  James L 287
  William F 287
CENTERS, A J 281
CHAIR, Nannie 215
CHAMBERLAIN 54,71,73,76,78,103
  Arthur F 33,67,118,154
  A F 19,25,65,81,89,90,102,105, 106,112,118,137
  Policeman 1,2,9,11,12,20,23,28, 29,33,43,44,50,53,59,114
CHAN, W A 230
CHANDLER
  Fannie E 86
  Josie 155
  Thomas A 251
CHASE, W A 248
CHEATER, Sarah 137
CHEETER, John 179
CHILDERS, Thos B 24
CHISHOLM
  Nancy 225
  Rosa 222
  Webster 232
CHISM, S L 19
CHISOLM, Mary 269
CHOATE
  Bill 54
  Mary 152
CHOTEAU, Charles 241
CHRISMAN
  Allen 248
  Isaac L 248
CHRISMON, Mrs Ida 49
CHUCULATE, Ellis 200
CHUWALOOKY
  Beaver 78

Chu-wa-na 237
David 20
CINCIA, Mary 254
CLAPP
  Alex 52
  Francis 52
  James 52
CLARK, Charles 64
CLAUSSEN, Lewis F 226
CLAYTON & BRAINERD 153
CLELAND
  George W, Sr 289
  James 223
CLIFT, M W 228
CLINE
  Ezekial 64
  William B 64
CLYDE, Rev Lee 75
COATES, Susie D 10
COCHRAN
  Annie 273
  Clinton 196
  Dollie 274
  Eliza 274
  John 166
  Louis 274
  Mary 238
  Rufus 47
COLBERT
  James 68,161
  Jas 161
COLE
  Clem 281
  George 269
  Wm 269
COLEMAN, Charley 3
COLLIER
  Mack 60
  Silas 21
COLLINS
  G A 204
  Mrs Blanchie 204
  Odun Lynn 236
  Policeman 237
COMBS, John 270,271,272
COMER
  Mary E 28

Index

R Lee 28,237
Wm J 28
COMINGDEER, John 252
COMSTOCK BROS. 264
COMSTOCK, Mr 83
CONAND
   John N 88
   Thos J 88
   Thos W 88
CONLEY, Carrie A 182
CONNER, F M 174
COODY
   Joseph 126
   Sarah E 206
COOK
   Geromeo 246
   Joanna 266
   Susan 255
COOKINGHEAD, Jackson 264
COOPER
   James 49
   Mr 237
   Wm A 53
COPPERS
   Charles 219
   John 224
COPPLE, Minnie 269
CORDRY, Andy 54
CORKRUM, Sarah 77
CORNSILK
   Jennie 31
   Johnson 31
CORSILK, Johnson 31
COUCH
   Noley 292
   R H 113
COUNCIL, Andy 35
COUTS, Jane 90
COWAN, Felix G 162
COWARD, Thomas J 88
COWART
   U L 187
   Wm 191
COWELS
   J C 3
   Lucian B 3
COX
   Dovie 113
   J D 273,274
   John N 113
COX & COURSEY 252
CRAFT, Charles 267
CRAIG 56
   Annie L 152
   A H 214
   Warren R 214
CRAIN, Emeline 154
CRAVENS, W M 135
CRAWFORD, E L 270,271,272
CRITTENDEN
   George C 256
   John 177
   William 106
CROCKET, John 32
CROCKETT, John 7
CROSSLAND, Rose Anne 207
CROW, Ben D 279
CROWELL
   Erda V 205
   F M 34
   Francis M 205
CRUTCHFIELD
   Eli 241
   Lewis 241
   Mary 62,245
   Sarah 62,241
CUMMINGS
   James 126
   Maggie E 122
CUNNINGHAM, Frank 157,159,160
CURTIS & WATTS 83
CURTISS, W L 247
DALLAS
   Lena G 280
   Rosa L 280,281
DANENBERG, Jno C 163
DANIELS, Burrell 219
DANNENBERG
   Daniel E 163
   J C 163
DANNENGBERG, D E 164
DARTSON, Joe 110
DAUGHERTY, T J 46
DAVENOIRT, J S 59

Index

DAVENPORT
  J S 135
  James 7
  James S 205,226,266
  Jas S 135
DAVENPORT & HALL 245
DAVID
  Geo 77
  Hannah 196
  King 150
  Nellie 11,14
  Stephen 14
DAVIDSON, George 149
DAVIS
  Alexander D 154
  Alley 74
  Chancey 59,60
  David C 215
  Frank 298
  Fred M V 266
  Hannah E 196
  J W 156
  Jackson C 267
  James 74
  Jim 281
  Laura 74
  Lucy 150
  Napoleon 59
  Preston S 275
  Sarah 77
  Stand W 107
  Thomas 59
  Trixie 20
  Willie Helen 260
  Wm 59,266
DAWNS, A F 154
DAWSON
  Iola M 167
  John Hubert 5
  John W 197
  William R 5
DECKER, John 253
DEERINWATER
  Charles 172
  John 172
  Richard 18
DEGRAFFENREID, R P 84

DELOZIER, Rubin 244
DEMORSE, Wheeler 89
DENNIS, Pete 192
DENNY, Tom 283
DESMAN, Alvie 290
DEVANEY, Jane 27
DEVAUGHN, Daniel R 210
DINING, Deyer 216
DIXON
  Francis M 29
  George W 29
DOBSON
  Harry Lee 24
  Leonidas 24
DOHERTY, Wm H 53
DOLAN, Sarah 17
DOMING
  Elizabeth 17
  Houston 17
DONOHOO, Phillip 297
DOUGLAS, John G 23
DOWELL, Claude E 268
DOWLING, D H 286
DOWNING
  Charles W 117
  Chas E 305
  Chas W 117
  Elizabeth 139
  George B 256
  Houston 139
  Jack 276
  Mack 79
  Moses 305
  Ned 102
  Ruthie 129
  Sallie 96
  Sarah 156
DRAKE, Norman T 89
DRAPER, Melvina S 260
DREW, John T 201
DROWNINGBEAR, Wm 8
DRUM, Ahpahmala 179
DRUMMON, Clark M 302
DU BOIS, Nancy J 158
DUBBLEHEAD
  Bird 85
  Filey E 85

Index

DUDLEY
  F F 284
  Nannie L 202
  Phoeby 284
  Richard E 202
  Wm E 202
DUNCAN
  Benjamin F 125
  Elizabeth 124,125
  Harry A 125
  J A 19
  J C 125
  Jewell 125
  Jewell C 124
  Joel C 125
  Johnson 139
  Martha 150
  Mary L 256
  Robert C 125
  William 90
DUNKEN, Elizabeth 124
DURHAM
  Fred A 228
  Henry C 228
  Nannie H 39
  Nannie R 228
  William H 44,228
  Wincie M 44
  Wm H 39,228
DYE
  N E 131
  W E 101,117
DYER, Bill 254
EADES, Isaac 11
EADS, Isaac 14,180
EARP, Joseph 166
EATON
  Ada G 71
  Geo W 39,44
ECHOLS
  J W 118
  Mr 93
EDMONDS 231
  Bessie 73
  Beulah A 73
  Emma B 73
  Hazel D 73

  Policeman 5,7,8,218
  Sam 104
  Saml 104,119
  Samuel F 73
  William S 209
EDWARD, William 266
EDWARDS
  W C P 26
  W S 209
EIFFERT
  Henry 52
  Sue 36
ELDRIDGE
  Tailor 47
  Taylor 57
ELI
  Goldie 285
  Mary Ellen 285
ELLER, Dave 31
ELLIOTT
  Anna 121
  Annie 121,122
  Jim 209
  Pennie K 121
  Pennie R 121
  William 121
  William Harlan 121
ELLIS
  Blair 156
  Fannie 236
  J W 156
  James 3
  Josephine 241
  Lucy 261
  Mary M 10
  Richard 156
  Willie 260
EMERY, Henery 241
ENGLAND
  John Anna 226
  R L 226
ERWING
  J N 66
  A W 65
ESTES, Sarah 146
ETCHENS
  A M 282

Index

A W 193
ETHRIDGE, Jeff 86
EVANS
  Annie 161
  Henry 213
  Jeff 68
  Marion 21
  Mattie 21
  Mrs Annie 161
  R A 177
  Rube 20
  Ruth B 39,213
  William 18
EVERETT, Nathan 222
EWERS
  Charles 115
  George 115
  George, Jr 115
EWNING, I W 84
FADDEN, Jacob M 53
FAIR
  Mrs Sarah Dolen 293
  Sarah 17
FALLING
  Delilah 234
  Margaret 258
FALTER, John 142
FANCHER, C L 131
FARGO, E M 200
FARLEY, R W 8
FARLOW, John 95
FARMER, A J 200
FAULK, Joseph 58,65
FAULKNER, Alexander 18
FEE & QUERRY 213
FENWICK, Milton 225
FETCHER
  John R 71
  Nora 71
FIELDS
  Benjamin F 289
  Bertha G 160
  Bush 267
  Clyde 160
  Freeman 224
  Geo 17
  Geo W 139

  James F 194
  James M 160
  Joseph A 1
  Laura 82
  Moses O 82
  Nancy B 219
  Sam O 277
  W G 92
  Walter G 1,92
  William H 240
FINE, W 242
FITE, D R 48
FITZSIMMONS
  E O 183
  Ida J 183
FLIPPIN, Curtis 104
FLOOD
  Thomas 72
  W R 72
FLOURNEY 139
  Oscar 138
FLUORNEY, J Edgar 138
FLYING
  Jessie J 6
  John 6
  Linda A 6
  Rebecca 6
FOGE, John 58
FOGLE
  Geo P 298
  Nancy B 219
FORCE, Cinna 260
FOREMAN
  Alia 20
  Alice 8
  Clara 34
  Effer E 69
  Frank 8
  Grant 184
  John 168
  Johnson 8
  Mary E 69
  Mary F 8,20
  Minnie 268
  Mrs Lettie 290
  Nettie E 69
  Switch 69

Index

Wm H 37
Wm Henry 8,19,20
FORTENBERRY
  T P 61
  W L 175
  Wm 147
FORTUNE, A J 104
FOSTER
  E L 237
  J W 43
  Joseph 7
FOULKS, Walter 6
FOX
  Eliza 66
  Jennie 143
  Lucinda 65
  Pasy 84
  Susie 65,66
FOYIL, Alfred 261
FRAKES, Robert 299
FRANKS, C H 61
FRAZIER
  Daniel 65
  Samuel 233
FREDRICK, Bill 52
FREEMAN, Daniel 62
FRENCH
  Joe 251
  John H 35
FRISCO R.R. CO 138
FRY, W M 229
FRYE
  Andy 275
  E M 291,292
  F M 189
  Milly 275
FRYER, E M 285
FULLER, James S 91
FULSOM, Levi 104
FULTON, Samuel 207
FUSER, John M 265
GABERILE, George N ... 73
GABLE, L G 8,20
GAINES BROS 224
GAINS, Frank 219,224
GAMBLE, Wilson 186
GARNER, E B 15

GARRETT, George 24
GARTUER, Charles 150
GATELY
  Fannie 305
  Leonard 305
GATES, Lucy 150
GATLY, Lenord 117
GAY, H A 88
GENTRY
  Cris R 174
  W M 174
GEORGE & JULIAN ... 117,131
GIBSON
  Ben 240
  Clark 278
  M A 38
GIDNEY & MARTIN 175
GILL, Judge 283
GILLESPIE, William M .. 73
GILLSTRAP, John 61
GILSTRAP, John 74
GIST
  Lula 243
  M G 207
  Montgomery 166
GLADNEY, Lizzie B ... 155
GLASS
  Phil 179
  Tom 121
GLASS & WEAVER 67
GLASS & WEAVER 282
GLAZE, Dr Geo 74
GOATLY, F M 35,45
GODDARD, Oscar 155
GONZALAS, Caleb 232
GOODAL, Lila 8
GOODMAN, Edward T .. 81
GOODTRAVELER, Fred R .. 280
GORE, Henry B 13
GORHAM
  Clarence 105
  Wm 105
GOSS, Jack 33
GOTT, A M 67
GOURD
  Cynthia 191
  Eliza R 38

Index

Frank ... 191
Mariah R ... 37
Sarah R ... 37
Thomas R ... 37
GRAHAM
   J N ... 5
   James M ... 104
GRASS, Daniel ... 283
GRAVITT, Jeff M ... 269
GRAY
   Ann Eliza ... 68
   J C ... 141
   Laura E ... 104
GRAYSON, Samuel ... 140
GREATHOUSE, Lewis ... 269
GREECE
   Nannie ... 215
   Wattie ... 53
GREEN
   Emeline ... 217
   Mary J ... 149
   Rose ... 179
   Silas ... 4
   Tom ... 184
GREENE, James ... 187
GREENFEATHER
   Jennie ... 238
   Laura ... 40
GREGG, J W ... 6
GRIFFIN
   Addie ... 267
   James D ... 267
   James, Jr ... 267
   Jennetta ... 75
   John ... 267
   Lewis ... 267
   Nannie ... 267
GRIGGS, John W ... 137
GROVES, Johnson ... 297,298
GUINN, Sarah ... 252
GUNTER
   Geo M ... 280
   William ... 241
GUSTIN, Melvina S ... 260
GUTHRIE, Loren P ... 137
GUYETTE, Dave L ... 60,131,132,273,274
GWINN, Lizzie E ... 247

HADLEY, W W ... 137
HAE, William ... 217
HAIRSTON, J T ... 39
HALL
   Georgiana Jennie ... 126
   J Thomas, Jr ... 254
   Jim T ... 254
   Josephine ... 126
   Josephne ... 126
   Julia ... 67
   Thomas ... 305
   Tom ... 306
   W N ... 300
   Will ... 138
   Wm H ... 66
HAMILTON
   Annie ... 16
   Green ... 50
   Nannie ... 16
   Roswell ... 16
   Squirrel ... 16
HAMPTON
   Bert ... 177
   Floratta M ... 111
   John ... 272
   Qwilliam C ... 111
   Ritchie L ... 111
   William C ... 111
HANBY, John ... 16
HANCOCK, W Q ... 80
HANKS, Daisy ... 230
HARDIN, O C ... 40,105
HARDRICK, Dick ... 127
HARDY, E B ... 305,306
HARE
   Bird ... 193
   Jennie ... 193
HARGROVE
   J S ... 1
   Nancy ... 1
   Policeman ... 170
HARKINS, C L ... 173,227
HARPER, Elsie ... 33
HARRINGTON
   Elizabeth ... 163
   L H ... 163
HARRIS

Index

A J 239
J W 223
Lucy 233
Willie 101
HARRISON, Henry 4
HARRON, Joe 84
HARWOOD, J H 51
HASKINS, J L 18
HATCHER, John 30
HATFIELD, W H 87
HATHCOAT, Josie A 142
HAWKINS
   Rube 22
   S W 100
   Sam 54,100
   Walter H 54
HAYDEN, Clem 197
HAYES
   Iscar 175
   L 94
   Oscar 65
HAYMON, Jake 64
HAYNES, Mrs Amanda 181
HAYS, J W 24
HEAPAE, Lenora 40
HEATH, Emma E 99
HEISTAND
   Abraham 108
   Adam 108
HELL, John 302
HENDERSHOT, John 284
HENDERSON 137
   Elijah 58,231,278
   Lizzie 162
   Policeman 117,118,170,185,
   186,192,204,205,240,243
   Ursey A 162
HENDRICKS
   George 81
   Jessie L 43
   Susan 103
   Thomas J 96
HENEGAR, Marion 273
HENLEY, H A 13
HENSLEY
   Daisy 264
   W A 242

Wm L 294
HENSON, Dr J W 279
HEREFORD
   Cross 236
   Crow 246
   Dennis B 94
   Galie 303
   Golie 303
HERN
   Hellen 283
   William 283
HICKEY
   John 173,227
   Mary L 227
   Mary Lou 173
   Nellie M 173
   Rachael 173
   Rachel 173
   Rachel C E 173
   Richard 173,227
   Thomas 173
   Thos P 227
   William 173,227
HICKS
   H W 289
   Millard D 63
HIDE, Moke 243
HIGGINS
   Frank 268
   Lillie O 5
   Nettie M 5
   Robt J 5
HIGHLAND
   Lucy 207
   Nellie 25
   Wm 25
HIGHTOWER, Cora L 152
HILDEBRAND, Joe 119
HILDERBRAND
   Kate 18
   Maggie 18
HILL 163
   Dick 94
   F I 73
   Henry S 162
   Maggie S 74
   S C 78

Index

HILLS, H A 162
HINDS, Ida L 78
HINDSELMAN, W F 131
HINER
   Joe 259
   Joseph 259
   Mary B 259
   Samuel 258
HITCHCOCK
   Lucy J 235
   Timothy B 235
HOBBS
   G H 228
   W N 160
HOCKETT
   Fred 36
   Wm 36
HODGES, Arthur 70
HODSON, W B 168
HOGAN, W D 254
HOGTOATER
   Aimy 251
   Sunday 251
HOLCOMB
   Mary 257
   Richard 257
HOLDERMAN
   C E 41,42,77,79,252
   M 252
HOLLAND
   Alfred 296
   Chas B 18
   John W 26
   Maggie 26
   Margaret E 233
   Millie 18
   Noah, Jr 18
   Noh S 18
   Robert 26
   Virgil C 114
HOLMAN, Tom 211
HOLT, Jenny 301
HORN, George 264
HORNER, William 247
HORNETT
   Charley 89
   Daniel 89,90

   Jennie 89
   Lucinda 89
   Sarah 89
HOSKINS, Ned 151
HOTEL
   D 288
   R G 288
HOUDESHELL
   Grace 12
   Jas T 12
   Mary 12
   W L 12
HOUGH, Wm H 96
HOUSEBUG
   Bettie 26
   John 26
   Johnson 26
   Robert Hermie 26
HOUSHE, Chas 224
HOWARD
   Geo Samuel 85
   I J 85
   John W 19,37
   Josh B 243
   Russell R 7
HOWELL
   Horne 82
   Mrs Elizabeth 3
   Tom 82
HOYT
   W R 9,10,12,13,14
   Wm R 10,13,23,24
HUBBAD, Ernest 208
HUBBARD
   John J 265
   Mrs Lola 257
HUCKLEBERRY 167
HUDSON
   Nancy 303
   Samuel W 303
   Tom 253
HUGHES
   Bert 220
   C B 277
HUMATUBBY, Delphia 52
HUMPHREY
   Altha 166

Index

W D 198,199
  William L 152
HUNT
  Jim 116
  W T 87
HUNTER
  Bill 85
  Mary 85
HURST
  H C 284
  J R 2
HURTZ
  Isaac 268
  John 268
HUTCHINSON 82
  R B 21
HYATT, Martha L 63
INGRAM
  John M 304
  A T 196
INLOW
  Nancy 296
  Wm H 296
IRONS, Andy 101
ISBELL, Morris F 23
JACKSON
  E A 297
  Hannah E 196
  Leona E 297
  Lula 116
  Mary 116
  O 54
  Otto R 297
  Robt R 217
JACOB, John 183
JACOBS
  Arthur 295
  Wm 295
JAMES
  Charles 101
  Charles H 101
  George 262
  Joseph 7
  Lizzie 101
JARBO, Ben 56
JENKINS, Hyram 190
JENNINGS

H 212
High 209
Judge 228,229,235
W H 209
JESTER, H A 39
JINKINSES, Hill 151
JOHNS, Willy 114
JOHNSON
  Alcy 212
  Ann 59
  Arlie 281
  Arthur 7,193
  Blake 59
  Ethel 193
  Fannie 7,193
  Flora Smith 288
  Frank 20
  Grove 298
  Hallie 7
  Isreal 7
  James Z 198
  Jesse 19
  John 49,113,253,281
  Joseph F 198
  Joseph T 36
  Leo 299
  Leonidas R 83
  Lucy 281
  M A 19
  Mary 269
  O C 261
  Peggie 141,281
  Rebecca 198
  Redbird 281
  Thomas J 202
JOHNSTON
  Edmond F 144
  Eliza J Hughes 277
  Mrs E E 144
JONES
  Archie D 138
  Jack 93
  Joe 251
  Lennie B 303
  Mary E 291
  Mary F 21
  Ola 188

Index

Sopha 188
W H 184
JORDAN
  Myrtle 190
  T J 118
  Victoria 290
JORDEN, Marcus L 9
JOURNEYCAKE
  Buster B 165
  I N 165
KALLAM, Lee 88
KANE BROS 74
KEEFER
  Nora A 81
  Nora E 81
KEENER
  Daniel 180
  Lewis 180
  Thomas W 244
KELLEY
  Albert 247
  Fred L 111
KELLUM, R T 294
KELLY, Lige 36
KENYON, D C 56
KERR 59
  Henry 58
  Laura 40
  O W 40
KETCHER
  Ellis 147
  George 171
  Richard 168
KETTLE, John 107
KEYS
  Charles L 186
  G A L 120
  John A 87
  Riley 70
  Riley V 70
  Stuart 87
  V M 3
  Victoria M 3
  W R W C 120
KIEFER, Harry 194
KING
  Bob 215
  David 150
  Lucian 21
  Lusian 39
  R F 273,274
KIRK
  Albert 301
  Ezekiel P 301
  P D 67
  Tom 301
KIRKLAND, Wm 135
KLASS, Flora 187
KLAUS, Flora 221
KLAUSE, Chriss 220
KNIGHT, Polly 237
KORNEGAY, W H 111
KORNEGAY & TURNER 78
KOZER, Geo 10
KRIGBAUM, Jane 262
LACKEY, A O 29
LAFAYETTE, Ben F 254
LAHAY
  J M 235
  Joe M 288
LAHAY & SHAW 170
LAMB 110
  V 87
LANCASTER, Allen 294
LANDERS
  Bertha 217
  H A 217
  William H 192
  Wm H 217
LANDRUM, John 5
LANGLEY, J Howard 168
LARENY, Jessie 4
LAREY, Nellie 69
LASSITER, W H 2
LAUGHLIN, George W 151
LAVIN, Charles 180
LAWHEAD
  Albert 154
  Celia 154
LAWLESS
  Mr 283
  P J 282
  Pat J 263
LAWRANCE, Mr 6

Index

LAWRENCE
  F C 1
  Milo E 297,298
LAWSON
  E B 191,246
  Eugene 249
LEACH
  Jemima 153
  John A 153
  Peggie 153
LEADER
  Joe 280
  Lucinda 280
LEE
  (Illegible) 145
  Amelia A 125
  Amelia Alice 124
  Ethel L 294
  John F 294
  Rau 124
  Raw 90
LEERSKOV
  Andrea 52
  D W 52
  Mary N 52
  Melina N 52
LEMASTER
  Alice May 194
  Edward 10
  John Adair 19
  Joseph 19
LEMLEY, Lee 210
LENANT, H 38
LESLEY, W A 55
LEUSKOVE, Dayton 253
LEWIS
  Alex S 94
  Olie 7
  R B 297
  S R 31,193,236
LIPE, Mary 146
LITTEN
  Naomi A 88
  Theo L 88
LITTLE
  Aggie 167
  N E 122

LITTLEJOHN, Jennie 193
LOCUST, Maggie 48
LOFER, P L 78
LOFTAY, Joe M 165
LOGAN
  John 132
  Lawson 257
  Nancy 257
LONCHBAUGH, O E 77
LONG, Allan 214
LORD
  Clarence 285
  A W 46
LOUVERN, Mattie 282
LOVETT, Lydia 207
LOWE
  Eldon 91,110,117,139,141,145,
  149,150,156,157,158,159,162,171,175
  ,178,180,181,183,185,192,193,202,
  203,210,216,234,253,279,290,292,305
  ,306
  Frank 97
  John 157
  Thomas 193
  Thos 7,193
LOWERY
  Ben F 6
  Johnson 249
  Mary 56
  Return J 264
  W L 43
LUCAS, Annie 249
LUCKER, F M 25
LUKE, Mary J 93
LUTES, Rachel 223
LYBARGER, Manly C 270
LYLY, R Lee 142
LYMAN, Lewis W 59
LYNCH
  Chas J 304
  Cicero L, Jr 109
  Joseph 29
  Mrs Maria 109
  William 67
MADDEN, William A 239
MAGES, Geo 91,92
MANLEY, Phoena 294

Index

MANN, J F 242
MANSFIELD, G W 142
MANTOOTH, William 234
MANUEL, Sallie 47,57
MANUS
   Joseph L 87
   Mary 177
MARKS
   L W 139
   Lemuel A 30
MARLIN, John 28
MARRS
   D M 27
   David M, Jr 27
   James 104
MARSH, P W 264,294
MARTIN
   Arvey 291
   David E 176
   Frank 159
   Geo W 176
   George 220
   Harey 199
   Harve 122,123
   Jack 17
   James 176
   Jerome 157
   John 159,160
   Joshua 221
   Mary 263
   Mrs M B 175
   R B 8
   Robert 30
   Robert, Jr 182
   Susan 159
   Susan J 176
   Thomas 296
MARTIN & RICE 272,288
MARTION, Jennie 109
MASON, J F 242
MATHIS, Thos 215
MATSON, Cal 140
MATTHEWS
   Madeline 212
   Thos B 127
MAY, Tam 32
MAYES
   C Y 80
   S G 259
MAYFIELD
   Joseph M 245
   Wattie L 93
MAYHEW, B A 203
MAYHUE, Charley 34
MAYNARD, Geo 58
MAYO, Mary 212
M^{C}ADOO
   Dr F 36
   J T 36
   Margurate E 36
M^{C}ANNERM, Henry 97
M^{C}CAFFREE
   F O 58
   Georgia C 65
M^{C}CAULEY, Mary 121
M^{C}CLAIN
   Gus 18
   Susan 103
M^{C}CLARNEY, Nan 46
M^{C}CLELLAN
   C M 69
   J F 69
M^{C}CLLOCH, Geo E 90
M^{C}CLURE
   Chas 241,242
   Chas J 196
   Henry 47
M^{C}COMBS, J G 136,166,207
M^{C}CONNELL, Beatric 269
M^{C}COY
   Grover 89
   James 164
   Jeff D 89
   Laura 89
M^{C}CULLOCH
   Geo Co 234
   Geo E 56,89,275
   James 62
M^{C}CULLOUGH
   Bessie 57
   W S 133
M^{C}CULLUGH
   Lillian M 7
   Netton M 7

Index

W P 7
Wm M 7
M^CDANIEL
   Joseph T 35
   Kate E 35
   Luna M 219
   W L 14
M^CDONALD
   Maggie 239
   Robert 106
M^CDOUGAL, John 57
M^CEACHIN, John 230
M^CEWIN
   Lizzie 180
   Wm 180
M^CFARLAND, Mary L 3
M^CGARTY, Thos 57
M^CGAW, C V 57
M^CGEHEE, Joseph Fox 10
M^CGHEE
   Albert V 75
   Belle 8
   Bertie O 8
   Bluford 75
   Buena Vista 8
   Clavattie 75
   John Ross 14
   Nellie J 75
   Rosa M 75
   S B 8
M^CGURY, Mrs H R 288
M^CHALE, Jack 58
M^CINTOSH
   Monnie 105,116,122
   Policeman 109
M^CKAY, Capt Alf 218
M^CKINLEY, Bud 50
M^CKROSKY
   Samuel D 195
   Sarah D 188
M^CLAIN, Nannie 250
M^CLAUGHLIN, George 104
M^CLEMORE, Louis 211
M^CNEER, Annie 46
M^CNEILL, James 14
M^CPHERSON
   Jaemia 183

Jennie 183
Robert 183
M^CTUSH
   Mrs 90
   Niles 90
MEASELS, Jefferson 1
MEASLES
   Algia 18
   Thos B 18
MEFFORD, George 97
MEYERS, Andrew 102
MILES
   Annie E 134
   Bud 111
   Eliza 134
   Jessie E 134
   Willis E 134
MILLER
   Charles 2,157
   Daniel D 179
   Frank 138
   George W 255
   Henry 157
   Ida 77,157
   Jackson 2
   James J 2
   James T 17
   June 133
   Louis 2
   Malissa 138
   Mary 77
   Nannie 15
   Nannie G 179
   Ray 15
   Roxie L 282
   Rufus 77
   Wm H 56
MILLIGAN, B 89
MILLS 34,38,42
   Eliza 89
   Jack 60
   S A 24,33,35,37,39,40,41,42,
   43,44,45,46,47,48,49,238,261
   Thomas 149
   Thos 136
   William 60
MINOR

Index

B S 198
   Seafus 214
MITCHELL, Gco F 244
MIZER, Sarah 8
MONROE, Beulah 286
MONYER, John 87
MOOLE, Francis M 29
MOORE
   Daniel E 229
   A F 302
   Lee P 109
   Mary J 30
   Melvina S 260
   Mr 155
   Nelson 45
MOOREHEAD, George 62
MOREHEAD, George 241,245
MORGAN
   A A 75
   Amanda P 39
   Cynthia 163
   Dora D 245
   Jno 163,164
   John 163,164
   Mr 99
MORITZKY, W F 1
MORRIS
   Enoley 248
   Jennie 198,199,259
   Saranna 253
   V E 79
   Wesley 268
MORRISON 174
   Delila L 1,173
   John 259
   Robt F 173
MORTON, A D 106
MOSES, Sequoyah 98
MOSS, William 251
MOUNTS, J H 143
MOUSE, Watt 221
MOWBRAY, Geo W 304
MOYERS, John W 87
MULKEY
   Jack Rose 118
   Lewis R 93
   Wiley 23

MULLEN, Jean 24
MURPHY
   J L 294
   James L 294
   Lizzie 294
   R F 235
   R L 32
MURRAY
   Annie 289
   Sarah E 289
MUSGRAVE
   C R 295
   Clement R 295
   J J 87
MUSGROVE, Policeman 200
MUSKOGEE DEVELOPMENT CO 206
NANCE, Scott 296
NAPPER, Aaron 10
NASH
   F H 120
   Hilda 120
NAVE, Henry D 64
NEIGHBORS, James 244
NELEMS, Felix 212
NELMS, Arch E 44
NELSON
   Cora F 145
   Jennie 145
   Lola M 145
   Wm N 145
NEMISE, Frederick 64
NEWMAN, Sallie F 86
NEWPORT, Jake 43
NEWTON
   (Illegible) C 54
   Eldrigde 54
NICHOLS
   Charles 198
   Frank 198
   Henry 248
   J M 120
NICHOLSON
   Gilbert W 107
   Henry 20
NORFORK, Harve 9
NORWOOD
   Chas 296

Index

A H 284
W H 22
NOUSHEE, Charles 82
NUGIN, Rebecca 304
ODELL, Otis 214
OKERSON, Albert 173
OLSON
   Andrew B 106
   Ole 106
ON-THE-HILL, John 154
ORE, Wm St 148
ORR, J W 167
OSAGE, Nancy J 158
OSBORN
   Mr 155
   Mrs Elizabeth 111
   R C 128,130
OSBORN & OSBORN 218
OSBORN & SULLIVAN 285
OSBORNE
   Roy 142
   Wm 59
OWEN, Thos H 94
OWEN & BAILEY 133
PALMER, John 173
PANN, Richard 95
PARISH, B E 184
PARKENSON, Joe 38
PARKER
   Ceaf 273,274
   F A 197
   Harry 141
   L A 34
PARKHILL
   Emma An 299
   A G 299
PARKS
   L W 140
   Richard B 202
   S F 202,278,290
   Sterling P 295
PARR, Frank 240
PARRIS
   Laura 43
   Lem 303
PARTAIN
   John 63

Lydia 75
Wm T 105
PARTIN
   Everett T 105
   W T 105
PASSEL, Samuel B 290
PATTERSON
   A E 167
   Mary 118
PAUL, Mrs Ella 279
PAYNE
   Edith B 15,60
   James M 15,60
   Jonathan R 262
   Laura E 48,135
   Lena 60
   Lena E 15
   Maggie D 15,60
   Mary E 15
   William B 60
   Wm B 15
PAYTON, John 22
PEARCE 280
   Doss 280
   J J 280
PENDERGRAFT, Mrs Martha 192
PERDUE, Pearl J 273
PERRIMAN, E C 28
PERRY
   Amanda 109
   Charles S 280
   J B 72
   Jesse J 166
   Samuel 109,133
PETERS, Cynthia 127
PETIT, Timothy 272
PETTET, Beula 54
PETTIT, Mrs Dolly 240
PFANNKUCHE, Agnes O 151
PHARISS, John B 14
PHEASANT, Thos Marcus 46
PHILLIPS
   Ewell 107
   Frank 107
   Jane 177
   Lula 225
   Nancy 254

Index

Nancy J 178
Spencer D 107
Ula Maud 107
William 47
PHILPOT, Alex 52
PICKARD, W A 149
PILGRAN, John 4
PINMGTON, T H 175
PITCHFORD, A J 276
PITTS, Frances F 51
PIXLEY
   J M 206
   J W 207
POINDEXTER, W A 247
POLECAT
   Isaac 72
   Wattie 72
POOLE
   C W 48
   Carlisle 48
   Walton C 48
POPE
   Georgia K 55
   Georgie K 55
   Madalyn 55
   S 55
PORTER, Sarah E 206
PRICE
   Dan 279
   Fannie 177
   Frank 259
   J R 140
   James 19
   Mary B 19
   Nancy B 10
PROVENCE, Maggie E 122
QUALLS, Wm A 17
QUERRY, A L 40
QUINTON
   Joseph 144
   Mack 144,230
RADCLIFF, Kirk 268
RAGLAND, Yates 278
RAGSDALE
   John 54
   Sarah 28
   William C 301

RAINCROW
   Lacie 48
   Sallie 48
RALEY
   Geo W 6
   J M 208
   Jos M 6
   Martha 6
   Oliver W 6
   Oscar C 6
RALSTON, Beulah 286
RATCLIFF
   E N 26
   Eliza 68
   Ella 68
RATLIFF
   Eliza 161
   Ella 161
RATLINGOURD, Henry 235
RATTLER
   Lillie 61
   Rider 61
REAVES
   J A 294,295
   Wash 269
RECTOR, Alex 106
REED
   Anna 285
   F R 277
   J W 48
   Paralee 247
REEDER, Julius 82,83
REESE
   Nancy J 246
   Tuxy 249
REEVES, A D 30
REINHART, Joseph 230
REMSON, Alice M 53
RENFROW, Mrs Emma 162
REYNOLDS, Babe N 53
RHODES
   Lillie A 61
   Margaret E A 15
RICE, Nora E 81
RICHARDS
   Beatrice 111
   Carrollton M 111

Index

Earl 111
Joe R 111
Lelia R 111,112
RICHARDSON, John 5
RIDDLE 263
  Chas W 24
  Seymour 177,282
RIDENOUR, Watt 251
RIDER
  Austin W 285
  C Augustus 285
  Henry 82,127
  J W 285,292
  Luvinia 127
  O L 135
  Thomas Needles 292
  Thos Needles 285
RIDGE
  Ailsy 279
  Arva 190
RILEY
  Edward E 24
  Emma 277
  James P 24
RINGALE, Mack 91
RINGO
  A R 148
  W P 260
RITCHIE, Emery 241
ROACH
  George, Jr 252
  Policeman 49
  Saml 214
  Sarah 252
  Thos 293
  Tom 115
ROARK, Wm 3
ROBBINS, W A 288
ROBERST, Clem W 55
ROBERTS
  Amy 66
  C C 66
  Edna 66
  Margaret E A 2
  Sam 60
ROBIN
  Eli 115

  Mrs Ollie 115
ROBINS, I W 185
ROBINSON
  Charles 45
  Elizabeth M 35
  Fannie E 44
  A G 44,45
RODGERS, Charley 290
ROFE, Wm 292
ROGER, Ben 114
ROGERS
  Anderson 46
  Beulah E 135
  Chas B 87
  Clem 170
  Geo W 2
  H L 135,136
  J R 7
  John L 25
  Lucy 233
  Rob 170
ROLLINGS, Joseph 43
ROOKS, Rob 17
ROSE
  Jennie 4
  John 285
  Mose 126
  P J 286
ROSE & BRADLEY 294
ROSS
  Albert 254
  Alex 105
  Altie E 40
  David 41,42
  Fannie V 185
  Jennie F 185
  John Henry 251
  Lewis W 140
  Malissa 50
  Martin 223
  Mrs Jacob 41
  R F 184
  W W, Jr 185
  Walter 119
ROUNDHEART, Joe 238
ROUSEY
  Paul E 13

W E 13	SELLERS
ROWE	James D 44
Perry 36	Jim 51
Stacey 293	SELLORS, J D 39
ROWLAND, Ludie G...................... 232	SEXTON
ROWSEY, Mrs...................................... 13	Annie 299
RUCKER, F M 228	Thomas D 73
RULE	SHACKLEFORD, Henry 226
Sam H 204	SHAFFER, Geo 146
Samuel H 205	SHAMBLIN, James 132
RUMSEY, P L 43	SHANAHAN
RUSSELL	I P 30
James 157	P 25
Kate 28	SHANKLING
SADLE, P E 190	Mary 2
SAGLEY, R B 175	Richard 2
SAMUELS, George P 222	SHARP, Margaret E Wilkie 117
SANDERS	SHAW
Alexander 238	Bessie B 3
Ben 239	James 284
Jack 27	Wallace 26
Joe 53	SHAWNEE
Luis Elias 114	Charles J 112
Pegeon 53	Chas 3
Peggie 129	William 112
Robert 136	SHELTON
Robert S 149	Claude S 1
Wat 247	Johnnie B 1
SAUNDERS, Sam R 51	Mary J 1
SCACEWATER, James 248	SHERMAN, Mary J 220
SCALLOLE, Caroline 212	SHEWMAKER, Boney 78
SCAROBOUGH, Mrs Narcissus 290	SHOEMAKE
SCOTT	Hughie 232
Jas M 244	Ludie G 232
John 82	SHOEMAKER, John 118
Joseph P 117	SHOENFELT & TISDEL 230
Mr 109	SHOENFELT & TISDELL 230,234
Mrs 109	SHOOK, Eurrutler 243
Mrs Georgia 36,102	SHOWMAKER
Mrs Jennie 302	David W 29
Polly 151	Dora Ann 29
R J 257	Franklin C 29
SCOVILLE 20	Wm J 29
SEABOLT, Victoria 99	SHUHAM, Mike 32
SEAVER, W F 302	SIDELL, W M 134
SECONDINE, Katie 131	SILK
SELLARS, James D 144	Anderson 91,125

Index

Annie 125
SILVERSMITH
  Miss Rachel 224
  Rachael 219
SIMPSON
  John 71
  Walter 71
  Walter D 86
SIMS, W B 13
SISSON, Harrie 182
SIXKILLER, Johnson 171
SLAUGHTER, Bud 59
SLEEPER, G D 236,246
SLOAN, Lizzie H 2
SMART, L J 156
SMILEY, R M 158
SMITH
  Ada G 71
  Amanda A 62
  Betsey 31
  C C 129,130
  Call cay al 63
  Callcayah 174
  Charles 237
  Charley 272
  Daniel 133,216
  Datus Smith 62
  David 273
  Dennis 226
  Edgar 276
  Emma 145
  Eugene Cook 31
  Famous 184
  Frank 128,129
  G G 133
  George 31,133,216
  Harry 253
  Hattie 103,206
  Henry 35,44,45
  Isaac 63,174
  Jesse 43
  Joe 145
  Joseph E 206
  Juliette 184
  A L 15
  Lamech 43
  Lawrence 35,44,45

  Lillie 270
  Maria 109
  Mary E 62
  Pearl 128
  Policeman 77,216
  Rachel 62
  Soney 272,273
  Susie 271
  Thos 172
  Thos P 201
  Walter 62,63,174
  William 185
SNARR
  J J 283
  L J 170
SNODEN
  Kitt 91
  Luella 91
SNYDER, Jennie 291
SO WESTON OIL, GAS & COAL CO 283
SOBGREEN, A J 176
SOLDIER
  Julia 34
  Mr 194
  Peter 34
  Whitaker 34
SOPER, P L 138,139
SOPER, HACKLEBERRY & OWEN 254
SOUSLEY, John 25
SOUTHER, Minnie V 39
SPARKS, Sidney 9
SPEER, John E 152
SPENCER, J J 304
SPLITNOSE, Tom 147
SPRINGER, Jno 9
SPRINGSTON, J L 191,223,251,262
SPUBUCK, Rosa 222
SPYBUCK
  Annie 46
  Henny 46
ST CLAIR
  C P 261
  F A 261
ST ORE, Wm 148
STANDFIELD, Judge 177
STANDLE, W P 193
STANFIELD

Index

Judge 220,221
   Wade B 225
   Wade S 277
STAR, Henry 166
STARKWEATHER & VIVERS 14
STARR
   Fanny 253
   J C 97,168,304
   John 164
   Lucinda 164
   Mr 122
   Samuel S 84
STARR & PATTEN 163
STARR & PATTERSON 122
STARR & PATTON 76,97
STEAD, Harry 110
STEDHAM 20
   Policeman 61
STEEN, Dick 23
STEERS, Wm 8
STEPHENS, Ernest L 266
STEVENS, William 12
STEVENSON, Hardy 180
STEWARD, Nancy 294
STEWART
   J W 276
   James A S 134
   John W 134
   Margaret 134
   Nancy 17
STIDHAM 79
   Theo E 37,120,136
   Theodore 37,136,182
   Theodore E 99,120
   Thos E 59
STILES, William 181,189
STILL, Sam 208
STINSON, Lena M 16
STOGSDILL, Benjamin 137
STOKES
   Gretta E 110
   Mrs Georgia A 110
STONEBARGER, Tom 4
STORKE, Mr C A 270
STORREY, Ed 134
STOUT, Martha 59
STOVER

   Lizzie 140
   Mrs 140
STREAM, J W 88
STREITTER, James 158
STUBBS, John S 299
STURDIVANT, Elizabeth 72
STWARD
   Nancy 293
   Riley 293
SUAGEE
   Bessie May 12
   Dennis 12
   Margaret A 12
   Ray L 12
   Stan 242
   Stan, Jr 12
   Thomas 12
SUARR, L J 233
SULLIVAN
   Ella 6
   Florence 6
   Jefferson D 6
   Wm J 6
SULT, Iola M 167
SUMMERS, Mary 5
SUNDAY
   Izora 261
   James 49
   Policeman 7,59,144,206
   Thomas 49
   W M 7
   Wm M 59,108
SWAN
   Rheben 133
   Rheuben 109
SWARTS, J W 254
SWETT, A W 281
SWIFT
   Geo S 161
   Geo W 6
SWIMMER, Stealer 187
SYKES, Finas 264
TADPOLE
   Annie 83
   Eli 83
   Elmer 162
   Emma 83

Index

Grover 162	James H 96
Lilian 83	Jesse 90
Okla 83	Jim 153
Olka 300	John 231,243
Rufus 162	Louisa 203
Wm H 83	Lucinda 92,124
TALBORT, H W 95	Mrs Myrtle 190
TALLEY	Ollie 33
Andrew 298	Policeman 54,55
Betsy 298	Pompey 203
TATUM	R E 190
Anderson 131	Rev Gilbert 48
Genie 131	Sam 153
James 122	W P 256
TAYLOR	Wm 23
Albert A 167	Wm B 28
Burrell 219	THORNE
C H 14	Caleb 293
Charlotte T 299	Jacob H 76
Charlotte Temple 270	W P 76
David 32	Walter 76
G A M 14	THORNTON, Katie 188
George A M 14	THRESHER 196
Jessie Young 182	THURMAN
Lenora M 188	Ada 286
Lenora W 195	Elizabeth 286
Mrs James 204	TIBLOW, Obidiah 225
Nancy 276	TIEOSKIE, Elizabeth 130
U B 276	TILLOTSON
W B 276	J A 117,119,270
TENNOR, Geo 181	S A 168
TERRAL	TIMMS, Mattie 167
Emma 262	TIMPSON, John 61
Robert M 262	TIMSON
TERRELL, W R 261	John 74
THOMAS	Maude 74
A G 79,223	TINCUP, Lucinda 244
Grace 21	TINDELS, Sarah 28
Hannah 21	TITSWORTH, Eugene 245
Henry 21	TIVIS, James 7
Lizzie E 226	TODD
Mrs Annie 15	John 30
Wm 131	Rachel 172
THOMAS & FOREMAN 108	William 171
THOMPSON 232	Wm 172
Blue 10	TOLBERT, Geo W 231
Henry 92,124	TOSSAWAY, Ina M 291

Index

TOWNSEND, Laura 271
TRAMMELL, Tennessee 63
TRINDLE, J W 48
TRITTHART, Chas 40
TROTT, William L 3
TRUEMAN, John 69
TUCKER
   Cynthia 100,114
   Geo 144
   John 139
TURK, Ann 165
TURLEY
   Geo 184
   John W 213
   William 225,232
   Wm 222
TURNER
   Brit 150
   C W 84
TURNHAM, Dr 99
TURQUANNA 221
TYGAR
   Mollie E 234
   Rebecca 234
   William 234
TYNER
   Daniek 72
   Daniel 34
   Della 72
   John H 90
   Sarah 72,104
TYSON
   Andrew 56
   Lillie B 56
UPTON, Doctor 177
VAN, Dick 194
VANDERGRIFF, Alice M 53
VANFLETT, Chas 31
VANFORD, Katie Thornton 188
VANN
   Ada 82
   Ann 165
   Beatric 269
   D W 3
   David W 2
   Ed 6
   Florence 88

   Frank 212
   George West 29
   Herman J 257
   James 146
   James W 88
   Jerry 55
   Jesse 248
   John 96
   Nannie Ruth 82
   Nicey 190
   Nicy 33
   Rebecca 292
   Reed 12
   Skillie 51
VANSICKLE
   B D 199
   Mrs Susan 102
VAUGHN, John A 218
VEITS, John 243,264,280,290,303
VICKERY
   J N 132
   John 102
   John W 102,184
VICTOR
   G S 256
   S G 157,197
   Samuel G 71
VIETS, John 168,187,198,238,240,
243,259,264,271,273,278,280,282,286,
290,292,294,296,297,299,301,302,303
VINCENT, Malderine E 261
VINEYARD, Joshua 112
WADE
   Bernice N 184
   James M 36
WALDRON, S W 16
WALKER
   Alexander 86
   Bill 186
   Dan 5
   Daniel 39
   Emily 49
   Henny C 272
   J B 194
   J L 209
   J R 168
   Jack 254

Index

Jim 94
Jno L 209
Martha L 63
Mary D 186
Nannie E 194
Policeman 165
Policeman J L 165
R M 9
Tom 120
Walter H 6
Wesley 6
WALKINGSTICK
   Calvin 141
   Edward 197
   Melinda D 50
WALLEN, Geo 218
WALROND, Z T 152
WALTERS
   Annie 26
   Charles 26
   J M 262
   Jimie 26
   Wm 26
WALTRIP, Susan 211
WARD
   Emanuel 76
   Geo A 200
   George M 113
   John F 25
   Thomas 80
WARE
   Dan 120
   Dora 158
   Zenora 158
WARNE, Sam 212
WARREN, John F 147
WARSEAT
   Ella 119
   Levi 119
   Lucy 119
WASHBURN, Claud L, Jr 231
WASHINGTON
   Ameritta 218
   Bertha 189
   George 189
WATERS
   Charles, Jr 175
   George W, Jr 166
   Lydia 181,189
WATKINS, John 16,153
WATSON
   Bessie 20
   Drucilla 20
   Hugh 270
   Jessie 20
   Luy 20
   Nannie 15
   Nathaniel 20
WATTS
   Jess W 257
   Thos J 143,248
   Thos T 172
WATTS & CARTER 305
WATTS & CURTIS 292
WAUGERTY
   Ed 53
   Mary 53
WEAR, Joe 19
WEAVER
   George W 132
   Herman 107
   Nannie 132
   Thomas 113
   Wm Floyd 132
WEITZEL, E B 288
WELCH
   Mary 199
   Miss Mary 291
   Mrs Cinthy A 95
   Victoria 98,99
WELCOME
   Amanda 143
   Lenard 143
WERTSEL, E D 272,273
WEST
   Bert 22
   Cap. 36
   Capt 59,171,172,182,215,216, 223,249,266,295
   Capt Jno C 232
   Capt John C .... 21,136,154,170, 173,182,192,193,200,201,202,221,228 ,229,255,293,298
   Frank 230

Index

J B 190
James 141
James B 33
John C 36
John D 22
Mrs Nannie 250
Nate 162
P C 297
Policeman 231
Richard F 254
WETZEL, Geo H 48
WHEELER
  Samuel 83,300
  W W 301
WHITE
  Emma 139
  Peter 139
  Thomas J 114
  W C 135
  Wm H 296
WHITEMIRE
  Hettie 178
  Mamie 178
WHITFIELD
  Benjamin 132
  Luke 132
WHITM., Sim 53
WHITMAN, Bill 212
WHITMIRE
  Edward 98
  George 5
  Hettie 178
  Mamie 178
  Zeke 97,98
WHITNEY, J F 301
WICKETT
  Sarah 42
  Webster 305,306
WILCOX, John 238
WILEY
  Milo J 12
  R Lee 102,113,142
  Woster 299
WILKERSON
  A G 45
  James 10
  M F 187,191

WILKINS
  John 115
  Mrs Pair 115
WILKINSON, W E 266
WILLEY, Addie 12
WILLIAMS
  Agnes 202
  Ann 165
  Charles 16
  David 42
  Elizabeth 80
  Maggie 270
  R E 255
  Sam 66
  Sue 302
  Wiley 93,170
  Wyley 170
WILLIS
  Ben 245
  E B 113
  Leander 45
  Mary 245
  Nathaniel D 94
WILSON
  D A 154
  Dave 243
  Dorcas 166
  I W 28
  James D 89
  Laura 82,218
  Letitia M 89
  Rory Sequouah 218
WILSON & DAVIS 27,174
WINN, Lum 238
WITT
  F N 11
  Felix 174
WOFFORD
  Jeneva 128
  Taylor 127
WOLF
  Joseph 130
  Mrs Elizabeth 242
WOLFE
  Joe 128,129,130
  Joseph 130
WONEN, Samuel 15

Index

WOOD
- Amanda ... 258
- Marion F ... 78
- Marion Y ... 77
- T A ... 68

WOODALL
- Robert L ... 103
- Robt ... 96

WOODARD, Zachary T ... 214
WOODEN, John ... 77
WOODWARD, Jno S ... 11
WOOLEY, James ... 31

WRIGHT
- Emma ... 278
- J G ... 304
- J Geo ... 201,298
- J George ... 201
- Joe B ... 278
- M M ... 278
- Manuel K ... 278
- Melinda D ... 50
- Tillman ... 50

WYLEY
- Lee L ... 35
- R Lee ... 79,84,87

WYLY
- Policeman ... 87
- R Lee ... 35
- William B ... 34

YADAN, Daisy D ... 134
YADEN, Daisy ... 134
YARGIN, John ... 93

YATE
- Bell ... 81
- Curt ... 81

YATES, Ella ... 176

YORK
- Jim ... 39,44
- Mrs ... 44

YOUNG
- Amanda ... 51
- B H ... 80
- Charlie ... 31
- Claude M ... 299
- Dan ... 182
- Daniel ... 182
- Frank L ... 104
- John R ... 69
- Nellie ... 298
- Robert A ... 265

ZINN
- Melvin J ... 92
- R W ... 92

www.ingramcontent.com/pod-product-compliance
Lightning Source LLC
Chambersburg PA
CBHW020240030426
42336CB00010B/558